Queer Postcolonial Narratives and the Ethics of Witnessing

Queer Postcolonial Narratives and the Ethics of Witnessing

Donna McCormack

BLOOMSBURY
NEW YORK • LONDON • NEW DELHI • SYDNEY

Bloomsbury Academic
An imprint of Bloomsbury Publishing Inc

1385 Broadway
New York
NY 10018
USA

50 Bedford Square
London
WC1B 3DP
UK

www.bloomsbury.com

Bloomsbury is a registered trade mark of Bloomsbury Publishing Plc

First published 2014

ISBN: HB: 978-1-4411-1100-5
ePDF: 978-1-4411-6310-3
ePUB: 978-1-4411-1378-8

Library of Congress Cataloging-in-Publication Data
McCormack, Donna.
Queer Postcolonial Narratives and the Ethics of Witnessing / Donna McCormack.
pages cm
Includes bibliographical references and index.
ISBN 978-1-4411-1100-5 (hardback) – ISBN 978-1-4411-6310-3 (epdf) – ISBN 978-1-4411-1378-8 (epub) 1. Power (Social sciences) in literature. 2. Witnesses in literature. 3. Postcolonialism in literature. 4. Violence in literature. 5. Queer theory. 6. Testimony (Theory of knowledge) I. Title.
PN56.P57M33 2014
809'.93355–dc23
2013031043

Typeset by Newgen Knowledge Works (P) Ltd., Chennai, India
Printed and bound by CPI Group (UK) Ltd, Croydon, CR0 4YY

Contents

Acknowledgements

The writing of this book has been a long and sometimes difficult process. Trying to understand how violence may be lessened in our daily lives is both a reality for and subject of concern to many of the colleagues and friends with whom I have the great pleasure to share my life. The initial research for the project was made possible with financial support from a University of Leeds Research Scholarship. Many friends and colleagues in the School of English at the University of Leeds read very early drafts of the chapters in this book. I am grateful for their thoughtful input and friendship. The Helsinki Collegium for Advanced Studies unconditionally supported me during the completion of this work, and made it possible for me to work peacefully in an idyllic workspace. An environment where there is continual support for thinking about and exploring ideas, and writing on multiple, sometimes disparate, subjects is rare. I am grateful to all those who supported my time in Helsinki in immeasurable ways, especially Sami Pihlström and Maria Soukkio. Haaris Naqvi has remained supportive of this project even when it continued to be delayed. He is an ideal editor: thoughtful, considerate and understanding. I really appreciate his patience, and I am thankful to all at Bloomsbury Academic for making this book possible.

Margrit Shildrick has read the whole of this book and provided insightful, generous and thought-provoking feedback. She continues to make an exceptional intellectual contribution to my own thinking, and remains a supportive and caring friend. I am glad we met when we did, and I look forward to many more transplant conversations over wine. Denise DeCaires Narain inspired and challenged me to think about the relationship between queer bodies and colonial violence. She has been a supportive colleague and an ideal gin and tonic friend. I cannot thank her enough for being amazing, and for forcing (and encouraging) me to question and have confidence in my own ideas. Sam Durrant has lived with this project for a very long time. Not only did Sam offer intellectual conversations and critical input, but he also listened to much of my life when the personal could not stay out of my work. His attentive listening allowed us to share more about our lives than I ever expected. I am grateful that Sam recognized the need for a shared process where we had to talk as much about our bodies as about the words that had to be written. His unwavering support has ensured this project continued and I thank him for that. Jim House is a dear friend, who guided me through a very early learning process and who remained steadfast in his belief that I could complete such a large piece of work. His knowledge of Francophone fiction and histories has informed and strengthened the analyses throughout this book (particularly the work on Tahar Ben Jelloun). I am grateful that he gave up his time to read my work and offer thoughtfully nuanced feedback. I look forward to many more dinners where we share our thoughts and lives. Damien Riggs gave extensive support throughout the writing of this project, and even managed to find the financial means to fly me to Australia to take time away when it was exactly what I needed. Not only has he read multiple pieces of my work, but he has also listened endlessly to my thoughts, engaged in what was probably infinite conversations on queer postcoloniality, and shared a love of tea and cake. I am happy to have a friend who enjoys my work and encourages me to both write more and take more breaks.

When I moved to Finland in 2010, I had not expected to find friends who would take me into their homes, share their lives with me, and be committed to surviving winters and enjoying summers together. Taavi Sundell has probably heard every word of this book. Despite our vehement disagreements on all subjects and our divergent epistemological interests, he is a unique and caring friend without whose support I would never have finished this project. His eternal pessimism and his faith only in cats made me laugh and gave me the energy to refine my arguments in thoughtful ways. His friendship is as good as a cup of tea. Mulki Al-Sharmani was a feminist ally from the start. Our afternoon teas together were a chance to explore everything. She has listened when things were great and not so good, and then listened some more. She has given so much of her self to me and I am grateful for this gift of friendship. The struggle for words has not prevented us from talking, and the distance has allowed us to seek out different ways of communicating. I thank you for your committed friendship, your affection and your endless responses. Kaisa Apell was the yogi I needed when I just wanted to hide away in the warm. She offered endless support in understanding the Finnish system of everything. Most of all, she offered her home and her friendship. That her door was always open meant that my time in Helsinki was exceptional. I am looking forward to sharing more tea and champagne in your new home. Antti Sadinmaa was open, sociable and suitably weird. I loved our endless conversations that moved so easily from Agamben to Dr Who. I am certain I would have finished so much more work if you had not been around, but I would not have missed that precious time. My multisensory experience of Helsinki was heightened by the dear friendship of Monique Truong. Smells and tastes seeped into our lives and into the body. I treasure those memories.

Many people outside of my immediate work place were welcoming and supportive. Tuija Pulkkinen opened the doors to the Department of Gender Studies, and shared many a social occasion. Being a part of gender studies was vital to my academic and social life in Helsinki. Leena-Maija Rossi, like Tuija, was a friendly face when all was new and uncertain. Her invitation into gender studies allowed me to teach a new course in my field and to present on my own research. She remained open to my ideas and she offered her own inspirational work on performativity when I needed it. Despite the distance, Leena-Maija has remained generous with her time and her input into this work is immeasurable. I am not only thankful for her intellectual contribution, but I am touched by her thoughtful generosity and her affectionate encouragement. Rita Paqvalén is an inspiring friend, who has taught me everything I know about Finland, especially all the bars and restaurants. Rita is one of the first friends I made in Finland and I cannot imagine my life without her. She is strong, caring and intelligent, and I loved our time together. My understanding of Helsinki is so deeply tied to Rita that I often long to return to the city, but perhaps what I search is our friendship. I am sure that you know that you are written into this book, especially into the Mootoo chapter. I hope I did justice to our conversations.

Although much of this book has been produced in isolation, I am indebted to those friends who read this work over and over again. Milena Marinkova has caressed the words with her eyes, and shared her critical thinking with me every step of the way. She has also engaged in many email and text conversations, and always been willing to talk. Her friendship over the years has oozed into my work and leaked into my life in so many wonderful ways. Alix Cunningham has never read any of my work and for that I love her deeply. Despite her own unbearable sadness, Alix remains a passionate friend who understands how class is embodied and who knows how to bring love to my doorstep over and over again. Karen McCormack gave financial support when it was most needed, and has offered much emotional love and many happy memories. Gary McCormack has kept me attentive to swimming and yoga, and ensured that I move away from my desk to places near and far. Amy McCormack is my dear friend, and champagne always tastes better with her.

There are so many stories to tell in this short space of thanking all those people who have supported me in immeasurable ways. There are also some stories that can never be told. I therefore dedicate my love, my self and my body to the two people who sustain my life in incomprehensible and disturbingly wonderful ways. To the one I lost in 1992, I offer this book in the memory of what I cannot quite know. To Ingrid Young, I give you this book that I know you have read far too many times. I have written these words while sharing my life with you. They could not have been written without you, and yet they go beyond our life and seek what may yet be lived and imagined. I look forward to queerer imaginings.

Introduction: Embodied Memories

> *Let's face it. We're undone by each other. And if we're not, we're missing something. [. . .] One does not always stay intact. One may want to, or manage to for a while, but despite one's best efforts, one is undone, in the face of the other, by the touch, by the scent, by the feel, by the prospect of the touch, by the memory of the feel.*[1]
>
> *Unlike the tank or the missile that is clearly visible, the weapon carried in the shape of the body is invisible. Thus concealed, it forms part of the body. It is so intimately part of the body that at the time of detonation it annihilates the body of its bearer, who carries with it the bodies of others when it does not reduce them to pieces. The body does not simply conceal a weapon. The body is transformed into a weapon, not in a metaphorical sense but in the truly ballistic sense.*[2]

By destroying the body in a political act that targets the occupying colonial authorities, suicide bombers attempt to realize the vision of an independent, postcolonial nation. Simultaneously revered as heroes of the fight for national independence and criticized for destroying the unity and purported peace of the existing nation, these ballistic actors make patently apparent that the body can communicate. Rather than working through institutionalized political channels or processes of verbal negotiation, suicide bombers use the flesh both to destroy self and other and to render visible and audible a politics that is failing to be seen or heard. The refusal to adhere to existing institutional protocols and laws is a call for a radical reworking or abolition of dominant structures of power.

Although it does not guarantee an attentive listener, violence towards self and other (especially in this case) calls for someone to listen and, thereby, demands a response. It is paradoxically a wilful act of power over those who labour to ensure that power remains within the existing state apparatus and of disempowerment as the self destroys itself to enable the continuation of a greater cause. In a pro-independence and nationalist

1 Judith Butler, *Precarious Life: The Powers of Mourning and Violence* (London and New York: Verso, 2004), pp. 23–4.

2 Achille Mbembe, 'Necropolitics', trans. by Libby Meintjes, *Public Culture* 15.1 (2003), 11–40 (p. 36).

logic, the splattered flesh is testament to continued national and personal oppression, the unity and strength of the fight against the oppressors, and how communal aims must supersede all personal needs. It both seeks to stop the violence to which many are subjected under the existing rule and to implement a separate or independent nation state that sets clear parameters around who belongs and the privileges of such attachments. Sutured to nationalism, such struggles, wars and violence often, in turn, result in the implementation of a regime based on a series of exclusions, which include precolonial ideals, heteronormative conjugality and procreation, and a purity of ethnic, biological and cultural origins. The dismembered dead are remembered and metaphorically (but not literally) sewn back together in a teleological narrative where martyrdom founds the history of the independent nation state. Flesh is woven into history as both the bloody deaths necessary to achieve the desired goals and the skin on which it has become possible to write these new foundational narratives.

The entanglement of flesh and national histories is the focus of this book. It asks: Why is the body used to communicate with and to demand responses from others? Why is language often not the principal form of communication or not even a possibility? What responses are possible to such embodied, sometimes destructive, cries? Increasingly queer postcolonial narratives give voice – although already words fail to grasp the literary form – to characters who have survived trauma by having them articulate their histories without sole recourse to linguistic forms or narrative structures. These histories are expressed through subtle bodily gestures, ex-centric sexual acts and a melange of sensory evocations. The listener, or the gathering of listeners, is responsible for translating these precarious, multivalent and ambiguous traces into words and into narrative. Much emphasis in trauma studies has been placed on survivor narratives and the need for survivors to *speak of* or *tell* their histories of trauma to an attentive listener.[3] However, *Queer Postcolonial Narratives* takes issue with how responsibility for avoiding the repetition of intimate and public and intimately public violence is placed on the survivors, as if by articulating their stories they might be able to both lessen the burden of history and stop similar events from reoccurring. I explore the role of listeners in bearing witness to unarticulated, unknown and unspeakable histories, examining how responsibility is a shared endeavour. Where trauma studies takes the listener to be a professional, knowledgeable enabler of testimony, this book focuses on friends, carers, lovers, strangers, family members who tentatively, inexpertly and

[3] When I discuss trauma studies as a (academic and therapeutic) discipline I am referring to a wide array of texts that do not neatly cohere and are critically nuanced in their analyses of trauma. It should be apparent from my own work that I am deeply indebted to this work. However, my critique is of the prominence of speech and the necessity of professional intervention, especially in Shoshana Felman and Dori Laub, *Testimony: Crises of Witnessing in Literature, Psychoanalysis and History* (New York and London: Routledge, 1992). This text is seminal to trauma studies and thus its emphasis on speech is worrying. I am also referring to similar and important work in the text: Cathy Caruth, *Unclaimed Experience: Trauma, Narrative and History* (Baltimore and London: Johns Hopkins University Press, 1996). The unquestionable centrality of speech in the therapeutic context and in dealing with trauma is also visible in texts that offer critical feminist insights into post-traumatic stress, including Laura S. Brown, *Cultural Competence in Trauma Therapy: Beyond the Flashback* (Washington, DC: American Psychological Association, 2009) and Jane Kilby, *Violence and the Cultural Politics of Trauma* (Edinburgh: Edinburgh University Press, 2007).

haphazardly take on the responsibility for listening to the unspoken.[4] I am interested in how histories are shared without professional intervention, how listening is an act of reciprocity (not an exchange but a transformation of all lives), and how such intimate moments transform realities.

The proximal sensations of carrying explosives on the skin – fear, excitement, sadness, elation, martyrdom, itchiness, irritation, weight – reflect the morphological changes of a body that is both human and technological innovation and destruction. The histories articulated through this interaction of flesh and machines are opaque, interpreted posthumously often without any words from the dead suicide bomber, and usually through the prism of media sensationalism and political rhetoric. An outright condemnation of the violence and/or an elation at the risks undertaken to gain political freedom are posited as the only viable dichotomous epistemological trajectories. Yet, what if we were to focus on the embodied address, asking why and how flesh has become the only viable means of communication, even when it destroys self and other? Do we have a responsibility to listen to what is articulated through these deadly splattered bodies? *Queer Postcolonial Narratives* takes seriously the role of the body and its ability and desire to communicate what has not been or cannot be articulated in words. It explores the creative and destructive ways in which those who have been subjected to colonial and familial violence resort to and actively engage the body to share the unspeakable. Although the suicide bomber highlights the contemporary political salience of how we need to listen to bodies and how we may need to learn creative ways to respond to such acts of violence, despair, desperation and hope, this heroic and demonized figure is not the concern of this book. Instead, I focus on intimate stories narrated *between* a gathering of listeners, stories that deal with pasts which are continually haunting the present. Although moments of intimate violence may be located in a specific time, known and lived as the past, there is no linear progression. In queer postcolonial histories events reoccur and are relived repeatedly throughout the generations. I therefore explore the importance of repetition to queer postcolonial narratives and relate such hauntings to contemporary theories of performativity in queer theory, postcolonial studies and trauma studies.

Performativity is a theory of power made prominent in postcolonial studies and queer theory largely, although not exclusively, through the works of Judith Butler (who is working with J. L. Austin's theories) and Homi Bhabha (who is indebted to Frantz Fanon for his exploration of mimicry). It is my contention that power (be it colonial, familial, national, state, intimate) is currently understood as a performative structure and technology that can be undermined because it is unstable. Because sedimentation of institutional practices takes place repetitively and repeatedly, then the conclusions drawn in much work in queer theory and postcolonial studies are that systems of

[4] This is how Laub describes the psychoanalytic listener:

> The listener, therefore, has to be at the same time a witness to the trauma witness and a witness to himself. It is only in this way, through his simultaneous awareness of the continuous flow of those inner hazards both in the trauma witness and in himself, that he can become the enabler of the testimony – the one who triggers its initiation, as well as the guardian of its process and of its momentum. (*Testimony*, p. 58)

condensed power can be undermined, reworked and reimagined.[5] Not only do I suggest that such simplifications halt the political work necessary to potentially imagine and bring about change, but I also offer ways of thinking through what has been eliminated from and left out of theorizations of performative power. Furthermore, trauma studies has also taken on theories of performativity to describe the repetitive structure of narratives and experiences of trauma: on the one hand, trauma studies insists that traumatic events are constantly, if unwittingly, relived and, on the other hand, that stories must be relived in the telling of an unacknowledged and undigested history if the memory is to become a 'real' event. Performativity points to the gap between the existing sense of reality and the newly emerging narratives that reconfigure what was imaginable and what is possible.[6] Transformation of the narrator/survivor occurs precisely because the world as previously experienced and constructed is reimagined and configured differently.

I concur that the institutionalization of systems that monitor and encourage individuals to be normative citizens is a repetitive, ongoing process always and only ever (appearing as) temporarily static. Normativity – or normalizing systems, practices and communal belonging – is so appealing and prominent (or dominant) because of the elastic commonalities it seems to create and keep in place. To challenge the plasticity of normativity and to resist the stabilization of further norms, I argue, is not as easy as suggesting that multiplicity reveals the inherent flaw of the original and therefore that the purported original has little power. Although multiple histories, embodiments, sexualities, morphologies and epidermal schemas do destabilize accounts that adhere to grand narratives and the Truth, I want to address the issue of whether multiplicity is sufficient to drive a political project concerned with the violence of colonialism and the

[5] I find Bhabha's theories of performativity problematic, and because of his use of dense language very little work has been done on interrogating his assumptions around power. This book is an attempt to investigate how we may interrogate and develop his understandings of performativity. In contrast, Butler has constantly sought to clarify her own analyses of performativity and therefore offers much to a reader interested in trying to understand possible interventions into normative structures. On the one hand, I want to critique Bhabha's simplification of the relationship between the body and power, and explore Butler's theorizations in relation to nationhood. On the other hand, my critique is an expression of a concern with how the work of these two theorists is taken up in cultural and literary studies. Their theories of performativity are assumed rather than critically analysed, and thus the ideas are reiterated as a given that is collectively agreed upon. I find such critical assumptions problematic, given that the challenge to power requires something more than us knowing that it is repetitive and thus subject to alterations. See, for example, Joel Baetz, 'Tales from the Canadian Crypt: Canadian Ghosts, the Cultural Uncanny and the Necessity of Haunting in Ann-Marie MacDonald's *Fall on Your Knees*', *Studies in Canadian Literature* 29.2 (2004), 62–83; Angela Brüning, 'The Corporeal and the Sensual in Two Novels by Shani Mootoo and Julia Alvarez', *The Society for Caribbean Studies Annual Conference Papers*, ed. by Sandra Courtman (2002), 1–19 <www.caribbeanstudies.org.uk/papers/2002/olv3p17.PDF> [accessed 22 March 2008]; Corey Frost, 'Intersections of Gender and Ethnic Performativity in Ann-Marie MacDonald's *Fall on Your Knees*', *Canadian Review of American Studies* 35.2 (2005), 195–213; Coral Ann Howells, *Contemporary Canadian Women's Fiction: Refiguring Identities* (New York: Palgrave Macmillan, 2003); and Jarrod Hayes, *Queer Nations: Marginal Sexualities in the Maghreb* (Chicago, IL and London: University of Chicago Press, 2000).

[6] For further discussion of the importance of repetition to traumatic memory and recovery, see: Kaja Silverman, *Male Subjectivities at the Margins* (London and New York: Routledge, 1992). For an excellent elaboration of Silverman's work, see: Karen Ann Caplan, *Trauma Culture: The Politics of Terror and Loss in Media and Literature* (New Brunswick, NJ: Rutgers University Press, 2005).

home. Therefore, *Queer Postcolonial Narratives* asks: What are the possible differences between performativity as a description of the workings of colonial and familial power and performativity as a disruption of the very structures that make life unbearable and unlivable for many; and, what is the role of testimony in both opening up the present to unimagined possibilities and realizing something in excess of normativity? In order to address these questions I turn to the fleshy body – to multisensory embodiment – and suggest that the intimate and collective process of embodied witnessing, where listeners take responsibility by attempting to translate into narrative form these unarticulated histories, is integral to the possibility of seeking out non-violent belonging, intimacy and friendship in the performative assemblage of power.

To this extent *Queer Postcolonial Narratives* is arguing that the selected literary texts bear witness to histories of intimate violence that leave traces often only in, on and through the body. Queer and postcolonial are brought together, on the one hand, to describe the creative form through which these histories are articulated and, on the other hand, in an attempt to trace the intricate ways in which the novels weave together desire, bodily morphology, and embodiments with colonial institutions, pedagogy, practices and violence. In many ways, the idea of *Queer Postcolonial Narratives* is to capture how technologies of colonial surveillance and control hone in on the most intimate experiences of embodied being. It is also to examine how livable lives are carved out for those subjected to familial and colonial violence through an attachment to both the family home and the nation state. The forms these histories and desires take are communal, uncertain, tentative, repetitive and indefinite. Indeed, queer postcolonial histories are an invitation to the reader – a demand and a responsibility placed on the reader – to respond and thus act upon the narrative.

This book focuses on three contemporary authors whose works explore queer postcoloniality in varying colonial and postcolonial contexts. Shani Mootoo's *Cereus Blooms at Night* portrays an elusive Caribbean context haunted by histories of Canadian missionaries and British colonialism. Tahar Ben Jelloun's *L'Enfant de sable* presents the period of transition from French colonial rule through to the founding of a post-independent Moroccan nation. And, Ann-Marie MacDonald's *Fall on Your Knees* conveys life on Cape Breton Island on the East Coast of Canada where British colonial ideals sexualize and racialize gendered familial and social relations. I analyse these novels next to each other because of their challenges to colonial violence through queer reconfigurations of familial and national belonging. Furthermore, historiography in the selected texts is an encounter with epistemic limits. They portray the absolute necessity of recounting histories of familial and national trauma, and yet the impossibility of completing such an undertaking. It is this ethical engagement with epistemology, especially with how histories can be heard, that is of central concern to queer postcolonial narratives. In other words, queer postcoloniality is less a mode of categorizing than an approach to the process of reading. It refers not only or simply to the presence of evidently 'gay' characters in novels that explore European colonization. It examines how reading itself is reconfigured in texts that call upon the reader to take responsibility for the stories being told and the livability of marginalized being. Finally, queer postcolonial texts reach to bodies to explore epistemologies that undo the colonial endeavour to gaze at, categorize, own, and catalogue things and people. The novels give space to how our senses inform our relations with others and our modes of producing knowledge.

Queer postcolonial narratives, or a note on methodology

Regarding what he describes as third-world literature, Frederic Jameson infamously stated that, 'the story of the private individual destiny is always an allegory of the embattled situation of the public third-world culture and society'.[7] From Jameson's initial problematic flourished the debate surrounding whether allegory was (or was not) the plight of the postcolonial writer. Aijaz Ahmad rebuffed his words stressing that writers from the Global North also represent characters allegorically, that there is not a shared aesthetic across 'third-world literatures', and that neither nationalism nor imperialism determines the political preoccupations of authors from the Global South.[8] Yet, even in these engaging discussions, very little attention has been given to the fact that the characters – the ones who embody the metaphors and the allegories – are often queer and *different*. There has been little mention in postcolonial studies of why non-normative embodiment or sexual desires are allegorically significant. Morphological diversity, queerness and disability are usually read for their allegorical potential in showing the illnesses and ailments of the developing nation. The physically disabled body reveals the *crippling* effects of colonialism and nationalism, and the diseased body shows how the body politic is rotting and corrupted by an unwanted, festering presence. Yet, the materiality of these bodies – that postcolonial authors often write extremely visceral representations – is ignored. As Clare Barker argues, 'It is this aspect of disability representation – the depiction of disabled characters as embodied agents, as national subjects as well as symbols – that is missing from current postcolonial scholarship, perhaps precisely because of their hyperlegibility in terms of national and cultural allegory'.[9] Although Barker does not explore the overlaps between disability and queer, it is apparent that, despite the centrality of the material flesh to both disabled and queer embodiments, genders and desires, the body is critically reduced to a metaphorical state that precludes queer and disabled identities, political subjectivities and existence within postcolonial spaces. In light of this gap in postcolonial studies, the chapters that follow actively engage with the viscerality of the represented body, as well as with the existing allegorical and metaphorical analyses. I want to explore the space given in postcolonial texts to the body in all its messiness, morphological uncertainty and queerness. I want to address what is missing when critics read only for allegory or metaphor, and to suggest that the flesh gives form to histories, modes of belonging and intimacies silenced in national narratives and allegorical readings. I also want to make

7 Frederic Jameson, 'Third-World Literature in the Era of Multinational Capitalism', *Social Text* 15 (1986), 66–88 (p. 69).

8 Aijaz Ahmad, 'Jameson's Rhetoric of Otherness and the "National Allegory"', *Social Text* 17 (1987), 3–25.

9 Clare Barker, *Postcolonial Fiction and Disability: Exceptional Children, Metaphor and Materiality* (Hampshire: Palgrave Macmillan, 2011), p. 3.

a rather obvious, and yet much-ignored, point that queer and disabled embodiments, desires, genders and subjectivities are integral to postcolonial contexts.

Often research produced in the field of postcolonialism is separate and distinct from work published in gender, sexuality and queer studies. For postcolonialists, the focus tends to be nation and diasporas, with assumed heterosexual and dyadic gender norms. For queer theorists, gender and sexuality tend to dominate and structural racial inequalities are often simplified or ignored. Yet my book is indebted to interdisciplinary work that creates intersectional analyses where race, gender, sexuality, class, migration and disability are considered for their complementary and antagonist relations and histories.[10] Although Sara Ahmed, Gayatri Gopinath, Siobhan Somerville, Jasbir Puar, Rey Chow, Lisa Lowe, José Esteban Muñoz, Aihwa Ong and Robert McRuer are challenging readers to think about how to analyse global intimacy, the mainstream political agenda remains rights-focused with an emphasis on static identities and productive progress. I agree with Gopinath, Ahmed and Puar, among others, that current transnational gay, lesbian and trans liberal politics often constructs '"Third World" sexualities as anterior, pre-modern, and in need of Western political development'.[11] On International Human Rights Day in December 2011, Hillary Clinton, the then secretary of state for the United States, declared that, '[It] should never be a crime to be gay'.[12] Referring to the United States' policy to bring sexual freedom to the world, especially to those countries deemed backward, uncivilized and radically conservative, Clinton's international aid rhetoric wipes from view the continued oppression of queers in the United States (and other Western countries) and does not acknowledge the bind between sexual freedom and imperialist endeavours. Elaborating on how nationalist sexual rhetoric protects sexual minorities while targeting 'developing' countries, Jasbir Puar states, 'This benevolence [afforded by liberal discourses of multicultural tolerance and diversity] toward sexual others is contingent upon ever-narrowing parameters of white racial privilege, consumption capabilities, gender and kinship normativity, and bodily integrity'.[13] Living without being subjected to homo- or transphobic violence is an important sociopolitical goal. However, these ends are pursued through increased violence against those individuals who and those countries that do not conform to imperialist liberal agendas, through increased surveillance of how bodies circulate through space, and through technologies that encourage and invite the capitalist consumption of identities and lifestyles. Not only is there a rise in the assumption

10 Disability often remains absent from these works, even when the author is explicitly dealing with disabled subjects. Robert McRuer and Anna Mollow make this critique explicit, when they ask: 'what is gained – and lost – by referring to "HIV-positive barebackers" and "drug addicts" as "queer subjects" rather than, say, "disabled subjects" – or "crip" or "queercrip" subjects?' (Robert McRuer and Anna Mollow, 'Introduction', in *Sex and Disability*, ed. by Robert McRuer and Anna Mollow (Durham, NC and London: Duke University Press, 2012), p. 26).

11 Gayatri Gopinath, *Impossible Desires: Queer Diasporas and South Asian Public Cultures* (Durham, NC and London: Duke University Press, 2005), p. 12.

12 Karen McVeigh, 'Obama Tells Officials to Use Overseas Aid to Promote Gay Rights', *The Guardian*, 6 December 2011 <www.guardian.co.uk/world/2011/dec/06/us-overseas-aid-human-rights?INTCMP=SRCH> [accessed 6 December 2011].

13 Jasbir Puar, *Terrorist Assemblages: Homonationalism in Queer Times* (London and Durham, NC: Duke University Press, 2007), p. xii.

that gayness and whiteness are natural bedfellows, but also that being of colour both forecloses any possibility of queer desires, kinships and embodiments and reveals an inherent homo- and transphobic attitude.[14] Thus, what it means to be queer, to embody queerness, and to express queer sexualities and genders is curtailed and policed in liberal, mainstream politics, where the aim is to obtain the same rights as heterosexuals for gay men, lesbians and sometimes trans. While the fight for gay marriage may afford state protection for some, this narrow political focus encourages the privatization of sex and public life, and disaggregates sexual politics from institutionalized race and class violence.

What I am calling queer postcolonial narratives, while not always or necessarily direct responses to these debates, offer entry points into exploring the continued political potency of queerness in colonial and postcolonial contexts. More specifically, I argue that queer postcolonial texts imagine worlds that challenge, collide with and chip away at the supposed permanent and traditional structures of heteronormative, racist colonial and neocolonial societies. They are concerned with how sexuality and gender are imbricated in the racialized colonization of bodies. They challenge the teleological structure of colonial, nationalist and gay liberal politics, which emphasizes the freedom of the individual who is liberated from either the 'backward' claws of a religiously conservative (increasingly Muslim) state or the confines of the heteronormative closet. Multiply imbibed in colonial promises of freedom, equality and progress, queer postcolonial texts both resist mimicking the prominent trope of the coming out story (even while characters may discover their queer sexualities and genders) and portray the violence of implementing a supposed plan of modernization through a white, heteronormative colonial regime. To this extent, queer postcolonial narratives are concerned with how bodily violence is deployed as racialized and sexualized labour necessary to achieve the public manifestation of civilized humanness. Aspirational dreams of climbing the social ladder, of becoming whiter, and of reproducing an idyllic heteronormative family and home are revealed to be foundational to the existing and ever-growing structural inequalities. Such dreams are built upon and necessitate racialized, sexualized and transnational slave and unequal labour systems. Haunted by histories of slavery, indentured labour and violent struggles for independence, many of the characters in these queer postcolonial novels search out less trodden paths and take perverse roads that lead simultaneously nowhere and to multiple lines of flight. As the texts resist linearity, they also seek out modes of living that are not repetitive of the very structures that are implicated in the originary violence. Indeed, by refusing to be productive and reproductive, the characters do not simply make individual and

[14] While my arguments are sympathetic with and build on Puar's nuanced analysis of the imbrications of race, sexuality and national belonging, I do not concur with Puar regarding the extent to which the analysis of race is separate from gender, sexuality and queer studies. She states, 'The history of Euro-American gay and lesbian studies and queer theory has produced a cleaving of queerness, always white, from race, always heterosexual and always homophobic' (*Terrorist Assemblages*, p. 78). To a certain extent, I agree with Puar's political and epistemological point that queer theory often fails to include race and ethnicity within its analyses. However, such sweeping statements too easily remove the strong and exciting work produced by feminists and queers of colour from the disciplines of queer, sexuality and gender studies.

personal choices, but also refute the institutional logic of racial, sexual, able-bodied and gendered violence. In Ahmed's words: '[People] deviate from the paths they are supposed to follow. Deviation leaves its own marks on the ground, which can help generate alternative lines, which cross the ground in unexpected ways. Such lines are indeed traces of desire'.[15] The characters diverge from the expected paths, re-emerge along the same – and sometimes different – roads, but always desire and create something a little queerer.

Queer theory is throwing into question the forward-thrusting narratives that frame, form and dominate our current living. With Judith Halberstam's recent text *The Queer Art of Failure*, we are witnessing a queer shift towards interrogating the contemporary emphasis on narratives of success and productivity. The three main chapters of *Queer Postcolonial Narratives* explore novels that have at their centre the figure of the child. These children are abused and/or mistreated by figures of authority, usually by the father. Yet, this is not the familiar child image with which we are presented in contemporary culture: the innocent victim who must be protected at all costs to ensure the survival of the future itself. Lee Edelman explores this obsessive reiteration of the imaginary Child and how it drives the cultural imaginary (and policy) with its focus on futurity. He describes 'reproductive futurism' as the 'absolute privilege of heteronormativity' in political discourse.[16] For Edelman, the Child is the assured way of constraining politics towards a future- and family-orientation. He suggests queer must resist such future-dominated structures that curtail sexual and gender desires and expressions, bodily morphologies, and modes of belonging, and must instead embrace its amoral, system-busting image. Similarly, Halberstam critiques what she terms 'reproductive temporality'.[17] In its place, she proposes 'queer time' and 'alternative temporalities', which according to her are where 'futures can be imagined according to logics that lie outside of those paradigmatic markers of life experience – namely, birth, marriage, reproduction, and death'.[18] Because queer lives are marked by medical histories, where non-normative sexualities and genders are considered (curable) diseases and where such bodies are understood as 'risky' (especially in terms of HIV and sexually transmitted infections and contamination of innocent – heterosexual – others), they already forge different temporal logics to heteronormative ones.[19] Similarly, although not examined by Halberstam, disabled temporalities are not necessarily heteronormative insofar as disability is often considered to preclude the possibility of sex and procreation (especially among the intellectually disabled). Illness

15 Sara Ahmed, *Queer Phenomenology: Orientations, Objects, Others* (Durham, NC and London: Duke University Press, 2006), p. 20.

16 Lee Edelman, *No Future: Queer Theory and the Death Drive* (Durham, NC and London: Duke University Press, 2004), p. 2.

17 Judith Halberstam, *In a Queer Time and Place: Transgender Bodies, Subcultural Lives* (New York and London: New York University Press, 2005), p. 4. Although Halberstam and Edelman are both critiquing future-orientated sociopolitical structures, their approach is very different. Indeed, Halberstam critiques Edelman's work on the child in *The Queer Art of Failure*.

18 Ibid., p. 2.

19 It is important to note that heterosexuality is not coextensive with heteronormativity. I agree with Lauren Berlant and Michael Warner's definition of heteronormativity in 'Sex in Public', *Critical Inquiry* 24.2 (1998), 547–66 (p. 548).

may not be a surprise, the effect of growing old, or an end of a long life for many of the disabled. Thus, time is not straightforwardly organized around such traditional moments of expectation and recognition.[20]

Trauma theorists also insist on a non-linear time where the traumatic event repeatedly haunts the present. For the trauma survivor, the lived moment is a simultaneous experience of reality as it unfolds and the so-called past reoccurring in a tangible and distressing sense. If as Cathy Caruth insists trauma 'is an experience that is not fully assimilated as it occurs',[21] then she is also right to suggest that the reality and truth of the traumatic event remain 'unknown in our very actions and our language'.[22] Because the traumas of national histories cannot be simply or easily assimilated at the time of their occurrence, history cannot be the recording of linear events as nations neatly progress from one (lesser modern) stage to the next (further modernized) stage. I would go further and suggest that precisely because traumatic events cannot be fully or easily assimilated in the experiential moment, then memory – the persistent act of remembering – cannot be reduced to linear, coherent narrative structures. Speaking on 'postcolonial time', Bhabha states that, it 'questions the teleological traditions of past and present, and the polarized historicist *sensibility* of the archaic and the modern'.[23] Furthermore, it 'reveals the strange temporality of disavowal implicit in the national memory'.[24] In this book, time is queer and postcolonial. The present is both haunted by a past of which there is no definitive memory or narrative, and forged through temporalities that cannot and will not stay attached to reproductive futurity. Indeed, I would argue that the selected novels explore whether and how erotic pleasure is possible after sexual trauma. Queer postcolonial time is concerned with how private spaces, such as the home, are haunted by public colonial technologies. It specifically refers to the processes through which racialized surveillance is sexualized in the home and violently imposed and yet cognitively forgotten or misremembered. It elucidates how sexual, able-bodied and gendered norms are implemented through the desire for an imagined colonial futurity of heteronormative nationalism, where the inability to achieve these ideals brings about traumatic, unacknowledged and unarticulated violence. Queer postcolonial time gives space to these hauntings without demanding that the trauma survivor translate such ghostly awakenings into words. Indeed, we – as readers – are called upon to be attentive to these embodied spectralities and to sense their embodied impact. The listeners must assume mutual responsibility for these sensory impressions and attempt to translate into words what has remained unarticulated, cognitively absent and perhaps unspeakable.

Queer postcoloniality is, thus, a methodological approach and sometimes a form of literary categorization. It is not a formula through which texts can be read or

[20] Of course, this point does not foreclose the possibility that either or both disabled and queer peoples will follow such life trajectories where important events are marked by birth, marriage, reproduction and death.

[21] Caruth, *Unclaimed Experience*, p. 5.

[22] Ibid., p. 4.

[23] Homi Bhabha, *The Location of Culture* (London: Routledge, [1994] 2000), p. 220.

[24] Ibid., p. 231.

pigeonholed, but it is the desire to open up texts to readings that do not assume a disaggregation of postcolonialism from queer or disabled morphologies, desires and sexualities. It keeps embodied histories to the forefront of analyses and gives space to the possibility that the flesh is an important epistemological tool.

How queer is deployed and the critical work we demand of the term is of increasing concern. We must address the exclusions produced by queer's attachments both to transgression and to moving beyond existing parameters of belonging. Queer scholarship institutes the idea that some *things* and *spaces* are more queer than others. It hierarchizes mobility over stillness; opaque being over transparent identities; and liberal politics over religious practices. However, similar to Gopinath's exploration of queer diasporas, I examine the multiple valences of queerness and argue that, queer cartographies articulate 'other forms of subjectivity, culture, affect, kinship, and community that may not be visible or audible within standard mappings of nation, diaspora, or globalization. What emerges within this alternative cartography are subjects, communities, and practices that bear little resemblance to the universalized "gay" identity imagined within a Eurocentric gay imaginary'.[25]

While queer is intimately tied to non-normative sexualities and genders – and this is often the dominant focus in queer analyses – I am also interested in the queer assemblages that are brought to life, resurrected, allowed to die, passively created, actively nurtured and hauntingly embodied in the lives of gay, straight, trans, heterosexual, lesbian and non-categorizable peoples, relationships and communities. Indeed, like Gopinath, I am interested in how queer takes multiple forms in the home, not only as an expression of non-normative sexuality and gender, but also as creative living, bonding and history-making. Migration is integral to all the characters' lives, as both the histories that instituted colonial regimes (and thus the violence they are undergoing) and the possibility of transforming the present by leaving the (domestic and/or national) home. Yet, leaving the familial space is not always desirable or possible, and staying attached to the familial home is sometimes the only or the desired option. Some of the characters build micro-queer lives, nurturing the home queerly; some flaunt their queer genders and illicit sexualities, provocatively disturbing others; and others are tentative in their intimacy, imagining non-violence through the self and the self's proximity to its environment and to language. Queer is not an abrogation of staticness, identities and boundaries; it is, in this book, the questioning of the technologies that normalize reproductive futurity and imperial hierarchies.

Similar to queer theory's valorization of mobility and fluidity, postcolonial scholarship has idealized the transgression of national borders as the visible manifestation of a non-adherence to exclusionary nationalist ideologies and practices. Yet, I have chosen a set of novels that delve into the difficulties of movement and the complexities of staying put. I am interested in how staying in the family home is an adherence to normative relational structures of belonging, a resistance to familial and colonial violence, and a radical reworking of the interrelations between embodiment and the environment. I

[25] Gopinath, p. 12.

therefore agree with Ahmed's critique of how queer and postcoloniality may disvalue staticness and traditional attachments:

> Indeed, the idealisation of movement depends upon a prior model of what counts as a queer life, which may exclude others, those who have attachments are not readable as queer, or indeed those who may lack the (cultural as well as economic) capital to support the 'risk' of maintaining antinormativity as a permanent orientation.[26]

And:

> [Home] becomes associated with stasis, boundaries, identity and fixity. Home is implicitly constructed as a purified space of belonging in which the subject is too comfortable to question the limits or borders of her or his experience, indeed, where the subject is so at ease that she or he does not think.[27]

Queer postcoloniality moves between the appeal of fitting in, the desire for non-violent spaces of belonging, and the pleasure in sexual, gender and morphological queerness. This intersection recalls the violence to which many are subjected because they are read as *different* from that which is considered normal. It is also an orientation towards non-violence within what may be perceived as ordinary domestic arrangements. Indeed, queer, here, gives recognition to heterosexuality as multiply diverse and not always or necessarily as reiterative of exclusionary norms.[28] Queer postcoloniality is imbricated in heterosexuality, not as its radical opposite or alternative, but as the fleshy and ideological line we all walk in wanting to feel the frisson of both queer desires and intimate familial connections. Queer postcoloniality does not entail rejecting or proving all norms are bad. Its political power is in its potential to question the violence produced through technologies of normativity. It needs to labour in articulating and exercising a politics that does not reproduce the exclusionary violence integral to state legislation, national familial blood bonds, and hetero- and homonormative rights-based rhetoric. Queer labours in this text to reinvigorate the materiality of postcolonial analysis by focusing on queer domesticity, genders, desires and embodiments. Similar to Lauren Berlant and Michael Warner's work on public sex, a queer analysis is the refusal to accept that state politics is a public concern whereas what goes on in the home is a private (read: non-political) matter. Like feminism's earliest cries, it takes the personal as political and does not prioritize the public over the private. Queer postcoloniality gives recognition to the ways in which spaces are produced through the disaggregation of the home from the nation and sexuality, race, gender and morphological normalcy from political/state concerns.

[26] Sara Ahmed, *The Cultural Politics of Emotion* (Edinburgh: Edinburgh University Press, 2004), p. 152.

[27] Sara Ahmed, *Strange Encounters: Embodied Others in Postcoloniality* (London: Routledge, 2000), p. 87.

[28] See my work on queer heterosexuality in Mootoo's recent novels: 'Illicit Intimacies, the *Rāmāyana* and Synaesthetic Remembering in Shani Mootoo's *Valmiki's Daughter*', in *Critical Perspectives on Indo-Caribbean Women's Literature*, ed. by Joy Mahabir and Mariam Pirbhai (New York: Routledge, 2012), pp. 203–28; and 'Multisensory Poetics and Politics in Shani Mootoo's *The Wild Woman in the Woods* and *Valmiki's Daughter*', *The Journal of West Indian Literature* 19.2 (2011), 9–33.

Performative listening

Contemporary theorizations of performativity grapple with the reiterative and repetitive structure of norms, institutions and regulatory power. Whether in the field of postcolonial studies, queer theory or trauma studies, performativity connotes the gaps and fissures that emerge when each repetition fails to be the same.[29] Performativity therefore reveals how there is no pervading original or authentic starting point, and how repetition cannot be traced back to a perfect or ideal model. Instead, the imaginary and constitutive norm is produced through reiterative (and unstable) practices. Butler, Bhabha, and Shoshana Felman and Dori Laub, I would argue, have brought performativity to the fore of much cultural analysis. The possibility of theorizing race and ethnicity, sexuality and gender, trauma, nation and narrative without discussing repetition and performativity has, problematically, become largely unimaginable where the potential for change exists precisely because there are multiple interstices between norms and everyday practices.[30]

The epistemological trajectory of performativity (from linguistics through gender studies, postcolonial studies and trauma studies) reveals how these interdisciplinary and innovative theorizations have become largely static, consolidated and simplified. Regardless of the (historical, embodied, national or traumatic) context, theories of performativity stand in for and assume the radical potential to undo existing institutional (and sometimes personal) violence. They offer the possibility of bringing into being new, less violent and less traumatic worlds. With very few exceptions (most notably Kelly Oliver),[31] the use of performativity (except where the aim of the work is to critique Butler) reiterates the transgressive nature of repetition and thus how change occurs by seizing this moment of difference, of queerness.[32] To repeat, mimic, copy, imitate and reiterate, as well as to be haunted by an event, memory, time or being, are currently assumed to be integral to undermining the forces of (all forms of) power. I do not wish to explore how repetition may not be central to the workings of power, although this seems to me to be a potentially important political project. Rather, I seek to examine how repetition is not always or necessarily transformative, and how for repetition to bring about a challenge to existing forms of violence we need more nuanced analyses of structures of power and intersubjective modes of being with others.

Butler's critical analysis and reformulation of Austin's work on (linguistic) performativity in *Gender Trouble*, *Bodies that Matter* and *Excitable Speech* have made

[29] In the chapters that follow I explore particular readings of the selected novels that focus on the performative structures of sexualities, narrative, genders, race and belonging. The work of these critics reveals the predominance of a theory of performativity that is banal, cohesive and at best self-satisfying. I am suggesting that much of this work in these three disciplines has emerged from the nuanced and thoughtful analyses of Judith Butler, Homi Bhabha, and Dori Laub and Shoshana Felman.

[30] I am, of course, referring to work within the fields of cultural and social analysis. Studies situated in political science, international relations, development and governmentality often take a very different approach to nation and state relations.

[31] Kelly Oliver, *Witnessing: Beyond Recognition* (Minneapolis, MN: University of Minnesota Press, 2001).

[32] There are notable exceptions to this largely uncritical work on Butler and Bhabha, particularly the special edition of the journal *Theory, Culture and Society*, ed. by Vikki Bell, 16:2 (1999), 1–239.

the most significant contribution to rethinking how (gender and sexual, but also racial) norms are simultaneously consolidated and destabilized through repetitive practices.[33] Initially Butler argued – and was criticized for suggesting – that gender is a series of stylized acts and not necessarily something physical. Readings of *Gender Trouble* were orientated towards an emphasis on how similar gender is to drag and how, because it was constructed, it could be donned or removed on a whim or as one might choose.[34] Although Butler attempted to show that the constructed nature of gender (and sex) is not equivalent to the individual subject being able to exercise agency as s/he feels or determines, she did assert that 'gender is an "act"' and that the 'hyperbolic exhibitions of "the natural" [. . .] reveal its fundamentally phantasmatic status'.[35] She also clarified, in a moment that bears striking similarity to the theories Bhabha would go on to develop in postcolonial studies (but not relate to Butler's original work), that 'the critical task is [. . .] to locate strategies of subversive repetition [so as] to affirm the local possibilities of intervention'.[36] Butler makes repetition the very site through which to destabilize and even eradicate norms.

As is apparent from Butler's subsequent publications and her preface to the second edition of *Gender Trouble*, much of her work has since sought to clarify her position on and understanding of theories of performativity.[37] Although Austin and Jacques Derrida haunted *Gender Trouble*, Butler reframes her take on performativity in both 'Critically Queer' and *Bodies that Matter* by explicitly engaging with Derrida's reading of Austin and John Searle.[38] Through citationality she draws out how agency is tied to the law and thus how agency is not an individual sovereign act but is instead a compulsive citation. In Jay Prosser's words, 'Like a law that requires citing to be effective, *Bodies That Matter* argues, sex comes into effect through our citing it, and, as with a law, through our compulsion to cite it'.[39] Butler describes how sex materializes through citations over which one cannot exercise control. The subject only emerges through this compulsory matrix of racialized and classed gender, sex and sexuality. This nexus of power is therefore not some *thing* that can be willed away, but the very means through which we become recognizable as subjects. Yet this process of materialization, the purported

33 Judith Butler, *Gender Trouble: Feminism and the Subversion of Identity* (New York: Routledge, [1990] 1999); *Bodies That Matter: On the Discursive Limits of 'Sex'* (New York and London: Routledge, 1993); and *Excitable Speech: A Politics of the Performative* (New York: Routledge, 1997).

34 For a vehement, but not theoretically rigorous, critique of Butler, see Martha Nussbaum, 'The Professor of Parody', *New Republic* 22 February 1999 <www.tnr.com/archive/0299/022299/nussbaum022299.html> [accessed 18 January 2011]. For more general criticisms of Butler's work on performativity and post-structuralism, see Selya Benhabib, 'Subjectivity, Historiography and Politics', in *Feminist Contentions: A Philosophical Exchange*, ed. by Selya Benhabib, Judith Butler, Drucilla Cornell and Nancy Fraser (New York: Routledge, 1995), pp. 107–26; and from the same collection two essays by Nancy Fraser, 'False Antitheses', pp. 59–74 and 'Pragmatism, Feminism and the Linguistic Turn', pp. 157–72. For an engaged critique of Butler, see Biddy Martin, 'Sexualities without Genders and Other Queer Utopias', *Diacritics* 24.2/3 (1994), 104–21.

35 Butler, *Gender Trouble*, p. 187. Evidently the use of inverted commas around the term 'act' should have alerted Butler's readers to the instability of the term.

36 Ibid., p. 201.

37 Ibid., pp. vii–xxviii.

38 Judith Butler, 'Critically Queer', *GLQ: A Journal of Lesbian and Gay Studies* 1.1 (1993), 17–32.

39 Jay Prosser, *Second Skins: The Body Narratives of Transsexuality* (New York: Columbia University Press, 1998), p. 28.

literalization of matter (specifically of sex), is not stable (despite appearances and sensations) and thus the institutional norms that produce this semblance of fixity can be undermined and potentially reworked. In Butler's words:

> Crucially, then, construction is neither a single act nor a causal process initiated by a subject and culminating in a set of fixed effects. [. . .] As a sedimented effect of a reiterative or ritual practice, sex acquires its naturalized effect, and, yet, it is also by virtue of this reiteration that gaps and fissures are opened up as the constitutive instabilities in such constructions, as that which escapes or exceeds the norm, as that which cannot be wholly defined or fixed by the repetitive labor of that norm. This instability is the *de*constituting possibility in the very process of repetition, the power that undoes the very effects by which 'sex' is stabilized, the possibility to put the consolidation of the norms of 'sex' into a potentially productive crisis.[40]

Haunting Butler's citationality and the reiteration of norms is the necessity of a group or groups of peoples to ensure, maintain and sediment the imagined and imaged fixity and certainty of sex and its ties to dyadic gendered behaviour. Although it may seem an obvious assumption to make that norms are stabilized only through a group or groups of peoples cohering around and through them, I would argue that this emphasis on (a non-cohesive, non-identitarian, non-dogmatic and non-congealed) community is one of the primary elements that is dropped from theories of performativity (and not necessarily fully explored in Butler's earlier works).

It should be apparent that, similar to Butler, I am not suggesting groups actively choose to adhere to norms (although this does happen) or that we are witnessing a subject acting wilfully (although this is possible), but that there are everyday and communal modes of being that temporarily maintain the purported fixity of norms.[41] Of course, terms such as heteronormativity and gender normativity are often used to stand in for the processes through which groups of individuals repeatedly and compulsively become recognizable through the law, how their bodies take effect through the law, and thus how they in turn cite (and embody) the law. Yet Butler's intertwining of the law and citationality suggests that when the law fails to be adequately consolidated, something falters, something crumbles and that in these moments there must be collective responses. Thus, as early as *Bodies that Matter* and more explicitly in *Gender Trouble*, Butler suggests that agency is required to instigate change. However, I want to argue more explicitly that the response required to such epistemological, embodied and shared tremblings must involve the exercise of collective agency: the repeated and active involvement of multiple persons over a period of time. Indeed, I want to tease out the connection between the gaps and fissures and the exertion of agency, which is largely absent in Butler's work. I therefore want to ask: who recognizes this gap, or how does this gap gain the recognition necessary to instigate change? If the individual is not

40 Prosser, *Second Skins*, p. 10.

41 To some extent, this process is passive in that there may be no sense in which individuals feel or act in ways that actively reinforce norms or hierarchies, but the term 'passive' could require a subject who makes a choice to act this way. This is why 'choice' creates a problematic paradigm through which to read contemporary social structures, because it suggests all acts are wilful and undertaken by sovereign subjects.

an omniscient being who exerts agency at will over such powerful structures as gender (and I agree with Butler that change and power are not simply about the exertion of the sovereign will), then how can this gap become a 'productive crisis', one which leads to a potential challenge to the law and even to possible change?[42] How does such a crisis become productive in the sense that Butler suggests (where something other than the expected can begin to materialize or be recognized as matter that exists)?

In *Bodies That Matter* Butler offers a possible starting point for addressing these questions, employing an argument that is redolent of Fanon's suggestion that racism takes effect through the historicity of the hierarchization of the epidermis.[43] Working through Derrida's reading of how the success of the performative is secured only through its being identifiable as a citation, Butler states:

> If a performative provisionally succeeds (and I will suggest that 'success' is always and only provisional), then it is not because an intention successfully governs the action of speech, but only because that action echoes prior actions, and *accumulates the force of authority through the repetition or citation of a prior, authoritative set of practices.* [. . .] In this sense, no term or statement can function performatively without the accumulating and dissimulating historicity of force.[44]

Norms are that towards which we may be forced, encouraged or enabled to orientate ourselves, without necessarily choosing to embody or adopt them. Their force and authority are endlessly gained over time, and, even when norms change, their power is in their purported timeless quality. Yet Butler does not give much attention to how the challenge to norms may also require a 'historicity of force', perhaps not a 'dissimulating' force, but collective orientations towards challenging norms and towards potentially imagining into being other modes of being with others. These temporary, shifting and ephemeral collectivities do not necessarily seek to reinstate new, wider or more inclusive norms – Butler makes clear in *Undoing Gender* and *Precarious Life* that the consolidation of new norms cannot be the goal of a queer, anti-imperialist politics.[45] Rather, these collectivities articulate and embody a varied and changing politics that is orientated around queer, disabled and anti-imperialist objects, desires and everyday practices. These gatherings may not be wilful, but rather may be randomly or more forcibly comprised of people who collide or meet through their inability or refusal to be normative or normal.

Butler's seemingly endless work on performativity intersects with and yet is divergent from Bhabha's more limited engagement with mimicry, repetition and performativity via Lacan, Fanon and Derrida. Although Bhabha has not acknowledged any indebtedness to Butler, he follows a similar psychoanalytic and Foucaultian

42 Butler, *Bodies That Matter*, pp. 226–7.

43 Franz Fanon, *Black Skin, White Masks*, trans. by Charles Lam Markmann, forewords by Ziauddin Sardar and Homi K. Bhabha (Sidmouth: Pluto Press, [1952] 1986), pp. 84–7.

44 Butler, *Bodies That Matter*, pp. 226–7.

45 See Judith Butler, *Undoing Gender* (New York and London: Routledge, 2004, pp. 17–39; and *Precarious Life*, pp. 19–49.

trajectory to her, albeit with very little reference to French feminism.[46] Where Butler focuses mainly on gender, sex and sexuality, Bhabha concentrates on time, nation, ethnicity and narration. Defining the potentiality of performativity, he states,

> Minority discourse acknowledges the status of national culture – and the people – as a contentious, performative space of the perplexity of the living in the midst of the pedagogical representations of the fullness of life. Now there is no reason to believe that such marks of difference cannot inscribe a 'history' of the people or become the gathering points of political solidarity. They will not, however, celebrate the monumentality of historicist memory, the sociological totality of society, or the homogeneity of cultural experience.[47]

Although Bhabha could be described as concurring with Butler on the idea that performative structures of institutionalized power are consistently revealed to be precarious through everyday practices, he is more insistent on a divide between what he terms as the performative and the pedagogical. Thus, the performative is the daily messy living that interrupts the neatness of the pedagogical, where the latter is understood as the ideology of normative national and colonial narratives. The performative, unlike the pedagogical, is 'the repetition that will not return as the same' and 'results in political and discursive strategies where adding *to* does not add up but serves to disturb the calculation of power and knowledge, producing other spaces of subaltern signification'.[48] The pedagogical is normative and normalizing, whereas the performative is the excess that never quite lets boundaries, narratives or historical accounts cohere. Such a distinction – between the pedagogical and performative – is not present in Butler's account, which describes power itself as performative. In other words, the very structures of institutional authority are performative, even when they congeal into violent norms, laws and practices. There is nothing inherently positive about performativity in Butler's work. Instead, the very form of power – as Foucault similarly argues – allows for its constant and repeated destabilization and undermining. I agree with Butler that performativity has no inherent moral value and yet, like Bhabha, Butler still tends towards performativity as a theory of radical potentiality, as always opening up the possibility of change. She does not account for why challenges can sometimes occur and other times not be imaginable. This is where I see Bhabha's coinage of the pedagogical as useful.

Despite Bhabha's simplified and problematic dichotomous approach to institutional power, what I find appealing about this split (between the performative and the pedagogical) is how it makes apparent that repetition does not guarantee change.[49]

[46] Bhabha does engage very briefly with Julia Kristeva, mainly to show how the performative intervenes in the pedagogical. See Bhabha, pp. 219–22.

[47] Ibid., p. 225.

[48] Ibid., pp. 232–3.

[49] Both Jenny Sharpe and Stéphane Robolin make insightful critiques of how Bhabha's theories are reductive of power relations. Robolin's analysis of the problems with Bhabha's formulation of the performative structure of power insists, 'gender is not an additive component to culture but rather a constitutive one' ('Gendering Hauntings: *The Joys of Motherhood*, Interpretive Acts and Postcolonial Theory', *Research in African Literatures* 35.3 (2004), 76–92 (p. 85)). Jenny Sharpe argues, 'For the colonial subject who can answer the colonizers back is the product of the same vast ideological machinery that silences the subaltern' ('Figures of Colonial Resistance', *Modern Fiction Studies* 35.1 (1989), 137–55 (p. 143)).

For Bhabha, the pedagogical is the constraining hold of colonial authority, which reconfirms the cohesiveness of a people and the coherence of national discourse. Yet, his aim in employing this term (the pedagogical) and making this division is to make patently apparent that those subjected to colonial rule (and therefore objectified in its moral and political economy) are also subjects who can subvert this unstable authority. He aims to transform Fanon's reworking of Lacan's mimicry from 'the familiar exercise of *dependent* colonial relations through narcissistic identification' to his own idea of the '*menace* of mimicry'.[50] The latter is defined as '*double* vision which in disclosing the ambivalence of colonial discourse also disrupts its authority'.[51] This is the potential of performativity, where a 'gap' or 'split' emerges in the grand narrative of History and in the linear time of the nation resulting in the disruption of coherent and sanitized images (and thereby creating the potential for minority signification).[52] Unlike Fanon, Bhabha is suggesting that even mimicry that endorses and idealizes the actions and practices of the colonizers still renders visible how the original, which seeks (identitarian) effect, is a fantasy.

However, I want to argue that the constraining effect of copying and repeating should not be abandoned simply because it may be politically desirable to show how agency can be exercised in the context of colonial occupation. Indeed, I want to suggest that the constraining hold of mimicry is the site through which we can begin to see how power functions to ensure that there is apparent replication and not difference. I agree with Fanon that analysing the continued hold and appeal of violent structures and relations helps us understand how they function and thus allows us to begin to potentially undermine them.[53] I do not agree with Bhabha that mimicry is always the possibility of a radical intervention into colonial authority (Bhabha very rarely considers gender or sexuality). Interdictions, norms and authorities do sometimes produce their desired effects and affects, and mimicry is sometimes the reproduction of the desire to embody the image of those who are in or who hold power. Indeed, knowledge that there is no original, or that, for example, gender is unstable, cannot be the goal (i.e. endpoint) of political analysis. The assumption that knowledge leads to transformation is itself a problematic ideal, reiterated not only by academics, but also by governments and their advisors. I suggest that the pedagogical structure of power – where we understand the pedagogical as a reiterative and unstable practice that succeeds in sedimenting norms – asserts its authority through, in and on the body. The appeal of norms is thus not only about conformity and the desire or pressure to be like everyone else, but also the embodied sense of belonging and the viscerality of recognition.

Postcolonial literary texts, for Bhabha, appear emblematic of the process through which the performative disrupts the coherence of the pedagogical. Their haunting,

[50] Bhabha, p. 126.

[51] Ibid.

[52] Ibid., p. 212. Bhabha employs many phrases to discuss time as not linear including 'strange temporality' (ibid., p. 225) and 'incommensurable temporalities' (ibid., p. 227), but generally they work synonymously.

[53] Fanon is optimistic in that he sees his analysis as having the potential to destroy the very structures that keep in place the hierarchization of the epidermis created through colonial relations that are then able to justify violence against supposed inferior black people.

non-linear narratives defy the linear form of national History and allow histories of colonial violence to seep through the cracks in these idealized national images. However, Bhabha's readings of literary texts are somewhat troubling to the extent that they reveal what I would describe as a normalizing impulse. Analysing Toni Morrison's novel *Beloved*, Bhabha comments, 'It is difficult to convey the rhythm and the improvisation of those chapters, but it is impossible not to see in them *the healing of history*, a community reclaimed in the making of a name'.[54] Contra this reading, where the emphasis is placed on the final coming together of disparate histories, I suggest that queer postcolonial narratives (including Morrison's *Beloved*) portray an incoherence and falling apart that is central to the lives of the characters as well as to the structure of the texts. The social, political, medical and epistemological demand for 'healing', I argue, restrains the possibility of other ways of living. For Sethe to experience the '*healing of history*', would she have to work, be a 'good' mother and not be too disorientated by the embodied memory of Beloved to continue with her daily life? The imperative to heal is itself an act of disavowal that renders invisible those who cannot get out of bed, those who cannot speak, and those whose bodies continue to disrupt the everyday demand to work, eat and reproduce certain values and embodied forms. In contradistinction, the disruptive narrative form, the unresolved endings, and the bodies that are locatable in existing taxonomies and yet fail to stay within those boundaries in queer postcolonial narratives are a manifestation of a refusal and inability to heal, and a desire not to be subjected to the violence of everyday normative existence.

To be unable or unwilling to heal, insofar as healing requires a reintegration into the very family, community, nation and other social structures that are responsible for the originary violence, is not equivalent to suggesting that queer postcolonial narratives propose an isolated, asocial and destructive existence.[55] Rather, the narratives make space for the disruptive process that is living with a body that has been subjected to violence, that cannot mourn, and that needs a world where it can live in what (from a normative perspective) may seem a perplexing and even self-destructive state. Imagining and creating spaces in which one can exist during and after familial and national violence is not simply to narrate one's history and continue living within the same sociopolitical structures that endorsed (or actively ignored) the initial violence. Instead, it is the desire to imagine and cultivate modes of being with others that are different, less violent and a little queerer. Furthermore, rather than pathologizing non-normative and even self-violent acts, I would argue that queer postcolonial narratives actively represent such responses to violence as creative events that open up the possibility (with no guarantees) of non-violent gatherings. Testifying to trauma need not only be defined as oral articulation or an adopting of the narrative form. I

[54] Bhabha, p. 25, emphasis added. Toni Morrison, *Beloved* (London: Vintage, 1997).

[55] Some critics argue that destructive behaviour and isolation from society demonstrate a lack of political potential and an unawareness on the part of cultural theorists of the damage of such ways of living. I certainly do not valorize self-harm, isolating practices or lack of support, but I do want to suggest that other modes of existence are possible (even if they may appear as harmful). I also see this definition of 'political' as founded on a traditional understanding of politics as public. See, for example, Lorna Burns, 'Politicising Paradise: Sites of Resistance in *Cereus Blooms at Night*', *Journal of West Indian Literature* 19.2 (2011), 52–67.

argue that bearing witness to trauma can take many creative forms, including cutting, burning and generally engaging the body in unexpected forms of communication.

The structure of testimony is performative insofar as the speech act bears witness to and makes possible the very process of narrative production, where such a creation has previously been unimaginable. Testimonies to trauma are performative in that they often compulsively, endlessly and repetitively bear witness to an event for which the narrative form cannot quite do justice. If we follow the logic of Felman, Laub and Caruth (which overlaps with Butler's description of citationality), the survivor is unconsciously compelled to repetitively relive the originary trauma.[56] For trauma theorists, testimony requires a psychoanalytic process and a professional listener. In other words, central to the process of witnessing (which is performative) is an *institutionalized* listening that enables and supports the work of memory. The speech act necessitates a witness. Testimony instantiates the possibility of address; it is 'the event of *creating an address* for the specificity of a historical experience which annihilated any possibility of address'.[57] This need for a 'listening community' is central not only to the performative structure of testimony, but also to the performative structure of power itself.[58] These listeners, I would argue, are what render change not only imaginable but also possible.

Before drawing out how the witness has always been central to the performative – even if largely ignored by Bhabha and by critics of Butler – I want to briefly draw a further parallel between trauma theory and performativity, particularly Bhabha's form of performativity. In trauma studies, bearing witness is the event that renders real that which has been derealized through the impossibility of oral articulation; entering into dialogue with an institutionalized other opens up the possibility of a previously unarticulated story coming forth through language. Silence, on the other hand, is figured as a destructive act, as an inability and/or refusal to 'deal' with the past. It prevents the survivor from living a productive or fulfilled (what one might call a 'normal') life. Like Bhabha's 'healing of history', Felman and Laub stress 'peace' as the goal of witnessing and thus instantiate an imperative to speak to realize this goal. In their words, 'None find peace in silence, even when it is their choice to remain silent'.[59] For me, the suggestion that the damage of trauma can only be lessened or brought to a halt through words and narrative reveals a normalizing impulse on behalf of professional practitioners, and trauma and postcolonial theorists. I want to ask: What impact does the emphasis on healing, peace and speaking have on those who survive trauma but who cannot heal, find peace or articulate their own experiences in words? Should we always place the responsibility for speaking about violence (whether

56 See Cathy Caruth, 'Traumatic Awakenings', in *Performativity and Performance*, ed. by Andrew Parker and Eve Kosofsky Sedgwick (New York and London: Routledge, 1995), pp. 89–108; and Felman and Laub, *Testimony*.

57 Felman and Laub, *Testimony*, p. 38.

58 Ibid., p. 41.

59 Ibid., p. 79.

intimate or public or both) on the survivor?[60] Indeed, what do peace and healing mean in the context of national and intimate trauma? Do you find 'peace' when you become able to narrate your story and/or when you socialize effectively, maybe having a long-term relationship, having children, sustaining a job and/or enjoying evenings with friends; or when you stop self-harming, cease to drink large quantities of alcohol, narrate coherent rather than incoherent stories and/or no longer feel the painful burden of life?[61] A questioning of what peace and the healing of history might mean is not intended to undermine the fundamental role narrating one's histories plays in many of our lives and the ways in which such acts contribute to rendering life bearable. The above questions point to the ways in which 'peace' and healing *may* be assessed and how this assessment is often situated in the sociopolitical norms that are responsible for the very harm lived as traumatic. For many, as Laub notes, peace, even through narrative, is not possible. He goes so far as to suggest that the narration of a trauma can be experienced as a reliving of the trauma itself and, thus, lead to the destruction of the self, namely through suicide.[62] Despite this possible devastation and/or destruction, Laub places great emphasis on the act of re-externalizing events, stating that the most 'productive' space for this to take place is within the psychoanalytic process.[63]

Rather than reiterating that speech – however traumatic – is integral to witnessing and that the performative speech act (eventually) brings individual or national healing or peace (if undertaken with a professional, supportive listener), I argue that witnessing – the event that reinstates the possibility of address, the very intersubjective relationality that makes ontology possible – can take multiple forms. Instead of binding the trauma survivor's act of witnessing to language and narrative, I suggest that embodied forms of witnessing are prevalent in many queer postcolonial narratives, and that these witnessing events open up new understandings of how people may live with traumatic experiences, pasts and awakenings. I do not wish to underestimate the importance and even centrality of narrative to witnessing. On the contrary, embodied witnessing is an act that is eventually translated into words by a gathering of listeners. Translation into the narrative form is one facet of the mutual and enduring sense of responsibility that these histories necessitate and demand. However, I do want to emphasize that the one subjected to violence is not obligated to speak and that responsibility for histories is placed less on the trauma survivor and more on those who survive, those who must ensure the stories are heard, and those who must try to stop such violence from reoccurring.

60 There is undoubtedly a need for survivors to talk and to narrate their version of events. There should also be attentive listeners available for these survivors who need and want to talk. My point is that the prominence of the 'talking cure' paradigm in postcolonial and trauma studies and in popular culture leads to an imperative and compulsion to talk. If one does not talk about one's trauma, then in our contemporary time, one is failing to deal with something that should be talked about. I disagree with Laub, silence can be a necessary form of effective (and even productive) survival.

61 One could quite easily suggest that to narrate an incoherent story is in contemporary, postcolonial literature quite normative. This is why an interrogation of transgression is so important, namely to unpack how form, subject matter and acts become a sustaining challenge to norms.

62 Felman and Laub, *Testimony*, p. 67.

63 Ibid., p. 69.

My reasons for questioning the current emphasis placed on speech are not only motivated by a desire to explore how trauma is experienced and expressed through the body, but also to examine how witnessing can be a non-institutionalized event. The strength of the psychoanalytic context is in trying to help individuals or groups of individuals (narrate a coherent story), but its weakness is in its lack of engagement with the social structures that encourage and enable and even sanction and commit violence. A shift towards therapeutic culture – a collective sentiment of the need to talk, hear and watch both our own and other people's distress, uneasiness and unhappiness – has brought with it a focus on individuals and their supposed problems.[64] More precisely, the appeal of consumable affects has strengthened with the growth of neoliberalism, where technologies of the state encourage individuals to self-govern in order to 'optimize' their selves, well-being and all aspects of a 'good' life.[65] The rise and consolidation of neoliberalism (even while neoliberalism continues to transform into ever newer forms of governmentality) has sedimented the sentiments and practices (i.e. the ideologies) of the individual as both the cause of and solution to her or his problems. Robert McRuer argues, 'neoliberalism is a highly flexible system that can incorporate a range of policies in the overall aim of increasing privatization, supporting markets, and demanding personal responsibility'.[66] Trauma and affect are privatized in both the experience of and dealing with their impact and effects. Individuals are encouraged and assisted in solving their personal (private and individual) problems, but discouraged from engaging with the very structures that may cause, enable or ignore the violence to which they have been – and continue to be – subjected.

I concur with Ann Cvetkovich that trauma theory and therapies are indicative of and instantiate 'a shift from movement politics toward therapeutic culture as the means to a transformation that has become personal rather than social'.[67] I also agree that, 'Witnessing is fraught with ambivalence rather than fulfilling the melodramatic fantasy that the trauma survivor will finally tell all and receive the solace of being heard by a willing and supportive listener'.[68] Because many queer, trans, people of colour, crips, morphologically different people, sex and gender deviants, and freaks have been routinely subjected to the rhetorical and literal violence of medical, national, familial

64 See, for example, Frank Furedi, *Therapy Culture: Cultivating Vulnerability in an Uncertain Age* (New York: Routledge, 2004); Dana Becker, *Myth of Empowerment: Women and the Therapeutic Culture in America* (New York: New York University Press, 2005); and Katie Wright, *The Rise of the Therapeutic Society: Psychological Knowledge and the Contradictions of Cultural Change* (Washington, DC: New Academia Publishing, 2011).

65 Aihwa Ong, *Neoliberalism as Exception: Mutations in Citizenship and Sovereignty* (Durham, NC and London: Duke University Press, 2006), p. 3.

66 Robert McRuer, 'Cripping Queer Politics, or the Dangers of Neoliberalism', guest ed. by Joseph N. DeFilippis, Lisa Duggan, Kenyon Farrow and Richard Kim, 'A New Queer Agenda', *The Scholar & Feminist Online* 10.1–10.2 (2011/2012) <www.sfonline.barnard.edu/a-new-queer-agenda/cripping-queer-politics-or-the-dangers-of-neoliberalism/2/> [accessed 27 September 2011].

67 Ann Cvetkovich, *An Archive of Feeling: Trauma, Sexuality and Lesbian Public Cultures* (Durham, NC and London: Duke University Press, 2003), p. 33. For feminist criticism of trauma studies, see, for example, Louise Armstrong, *Rocking the Cradle of Sexual Politics: What Happened When Women Said Incest* (Reading, MA: Addison-Wesley, 1994); Laura S. Brown, 'Feminist Therapy', in J. L. Lebow (ed.), *Twenty-First Century Psychotherapies* (Hoboken, NJ: John Wiley & Sons, 2008), pp. 277–306; and Brown, *Cultural Competence in Trauma Therapy.*

68 Cvetkovich, p. 22.

and religious institutions, many have felt the absolute necessity of seeking out other less violent and non-institutionalized forms of listening to and engaging with each other. Queer, disability and postcolonial histories show how people come together to assist, work with and ensure the survival of each other when state institutions fail these 'outsiders'. Cvetkovich, in contrast to Laub who tends to romanticize the psychoanalytic listener as 'the enabler of the testimony',[69] is 'concerned with trauma as a collective experience that generates collective responses'.[70] She, like Berlant, shows that queers have had (and continue) to be creative when trying to live a life rendered unlivable and unbearable by institutions of the state and of care. Witnessing in queer postcolonial narratives involves and requires communal responses and political mobilizations. Violence in the home, school, church and nation space is not solely a private, individual experience; it is communal, shared by many, and it continues not only because individuals are 'evil' anomalies, but also because the normative structures continue to promote idealized images of these institutions.[71] Indeed, violence in the home is often silenced because of the shame it brings both to the individual (who may be thought of as having instigated the 'attention') and to the family (who has 'failed' to live up to the ideal image of the familial unit).

Contra Felman and Laub, *Queer Postcolonial Narratives* does not propose an ideal listener who is an enabler of testimony, full of knowledge, in control and confident in his task. Listening is a much more tentative process and involves those who are uncertain of where this sharing may lead. It is intimate, life-changing and involves an unforeseeable visceral, psychic and epistemological impact. The transformation in self and other and other others is powerful, unprepared for and does not promise a brighter future. Instead, all those gathered listen, share, exchange, get things wrong, try again and importantly keep on listening, talking and seeking out innovative forms of communication. It is all a bit queer in that the paths taken may diverge from the norm, while being haunted by what others have previously done. In *Queer Postcolonial Narratives* witnessing is the intersubjective relationality through which the indefinite process of narrating unspoken or unknown histories begins.

Historicizing witnessing

The witness, more commonly, is a person who is present when an event occurs and who is then able to testify, under oath, to a court of law. This witness is legally bound, by the institution of law, to conform to the established conventions and thereby to speak the truth. This institution, married as it is to a notion of history as an overarching factual and accurate account of events, interprets the truth as that which can be proven by empirical facts and non-circumstantial evidence. Austin ties the performative to this

69 Felman and Laub, *Testimony*, p. 58.

70 Cvetkovich, p. 19.

71 Despite the evidence of violence within these structures (be that church or family), there is a continued valorization of normative family values (above all other configurations of communal existence).

legal, institutionalized form of witnessing. In *How to Do Things with Words* he defines the performative in the following terms:

> The name is derived, of course, from 'perform', the usual verb with the noun 'action': it indicates that the issuing of the utterance is the performing of an action – it is not normally thought of as just saying something.[72]

Austin distinguishes performative utterances from (constative) statements insofar as the latter can be true or false whereas the former are doing something and, thus, cannot be described as true or false but only as meeting all the conditions required. Therefore, performative utterances are 'happy' when all the conditions are met and 'unhappy' when 'infelicities' occur.[73]

Austin places great emphasis on conventional acts and the ways in which they are constrained by (institutional) procedures, and one of his main and oft-quoted examples is (the institution of) marriage. Simultaneously placing the emphasis on the words stated and the conditions under which the utterance takes place, he wavers between 'to say a few certain words is to marry' and 'to marry is, in some cases, simply to say a few words'.[74] On the subject of promising, he adds:

> It is obviously necessary that to have promised I must normally
>
> (A) have been heard by someone, perhaps the promisee;
>
> (B) have been understood by him as promising.
>
> If one or another of these conditions is not satisfied, doubts arise as to whether I have really promised, and it might be held that my act was only attempted or was void. Special precautions are taken in law to avoid this and other infelicities, e.g. in the serving of writs or summonses.[75]

Austin is highlighting an integral, but often forgotten or little discussed, part of the performative utterance: for it to be happy, the conditions, often institutional and thus iterative, have to be right. That is, what renders the promise 'happy' (successful) is the institutional witness, who can be defined as the representative of a legally and/or religiously binding system of regulations.

If we stay with marriage as the prototypical example of the performative utterance, there must be a legal and/or religious person who is present at the ceremony for the marriage to be binding; if the act of saying I take this man/woman to be my *lawfully* wedded husband/wife is to be happy then there must be an *institutional* witness. Therefore, one could suggest that the witness is always and already tied to and bound by a legal and/or religious matrix of conventions. The performative function of the act of marriage, the consolidation of the convention through repetition, re-enacts and reinforces marriage as the socially desirable and necessary way of being. In *Bodies that*

[72] J. L. Austin, *How to Do Things with Words* (London: Oxford University Press, 1962), pp. 6–7.

[73] For all the conditions necessary for a performative to be happy, see Austin, 'Lecture II', *How to Do Things with Words*, pp. 12–24.

[74] Ibid., p. 8.

[75] Ibid., p. 22.

Matter, Butler emphasizes the relationship between performativity and the institutional policing of bodily acts through religious and legal events:

> Performative acts are forms of authoritative speech: most performatives, for instance, are statements that, in the uttering, also perform a certain action and exercise a binding power. Implicated in a network of authorization and punishment, performatives tend to include legal sentences, baptisms, inaugurations, declarations of ownership, statements which not only perform an action, but confer a binding power on the action performed. If the power of discourse to produce that which it names is linked with the question of performativity, then the performative is one domain in which power acts *as* discourse.[76]

The performative is thus the regulation of bodies in communal spaces through authorizing, enabling, coercive and prohibitive practices.

While Austin focuses on the official witness's role in ensuring a happy performative (in the case of marriage the registrar or religious representative) and Butler stresses the cultural and political systems that attempt to ensure bodily and social conformity, Andrew Parker and Eve Kosofsky Sedgwick emphasize the friends and family who listen at the marriage ceremony in a somewhat passive role. They hone in on the function of those present who do not protest and who, in not speaking out, act as witnesses to the marriage:

> Any queer who's struggled to articulate to friends why we love them, but just *don't want to be at their wedding*, knows it from the inside, the dynamic of compulsory witness that the marriage ceremony invokes. Compulsory witness not just in the sense that you aren't allowed to absent yourself, but in the way that a much fuller meaning of 'witness' (a fuller one than Austin ever treats) gets activated in this prototypical performative. It is the constitution of a community of witness that makes the marriage; the silence of witness (we don't speak now, we forever hold our peace) that permits it; the bare negative, potent but undiscretionary speech act of our physical presence – maybe even *especially* the presence of those people whom the institution of marriage defines itself by excluding – that ratifies and recruits the legitimacy of its privilege.[77]

Parker and Sedgwick highlight a paradox that I would argue is central to the act of witnessing: the silent speech act of the witness. Their emphasis on the 'undiscretionary speech act of our presence' refers to the body's presence as serving (passively) to reiterate,

[76] Butler, *Bodies That Matter*, p. 225.

[77] Andrew Parker and Eve Kosofsky Sedgwick, 'Introduction: Performativity and Performance', in *Performativity and Performance*, ed. by Andrew Parker and Eve Kosofsky Sedgwick (New York and London: Routledge, 1995), pp. 1–18 (pp. 10–11). Parker and Sedgwick use the singular form of witness, despite the awkward phrasing. Although they do not comment on their rationale, I would suggest that the singular form stresses the uniform and collective role of the witness (i.e. they are one group that performs a single normative role). In terms of the context of marriage, it should be apparent that, although Parker and Sedgwick are referring to straight marriage, the same argument applies to gay marriage. In other words, the normative desire for institutional recognition, while sometimes absolutely necessary, should not reinforce further exclusionary practices or commit violence towards others.

to performatively sanction, the institution of marriage. One's very body can ratify an institutional practice through its presence, even as that institution negates one's own very existence. If the queer presence is 'potent', it is neutralized in a context where the legal and/or religious iterative processes remain all-pervasive and all-powerful.

Despite this neutralizing potential of institutional power, I want to suggest that Parker and Sedgwick add an invaluable queer dimension to theories of performativity: the body can speak. The 'undiscretionary speech act of our physical presence' suggests that bodies, in their very being, are already enacting a non-verbal form of communication. In the context of marriage, the queer body is the body that speaks but remains unheard – one definition of the 'undiscretionary speech act of our physical presence'. In other words, there is no witness to testify to the presence of someone or something different from that of the legal and/or religious call for heteronormative and homonormative relationships and forms of belonging. Nonetheless, I want to take Parker and Sedgwick's idea that the body can speak and queerly ask: Is it possible to speak, in silence, through the body and destabilize the very acts that negate one's existence? If the body speaks without recourse to language, to whom does it make its address?[78] And how can the institutional violence of non-listening be avoided so that the queer body can be heard?[79]

Although often absent from discussions of performativity, an idea of a gathering of peoples is central to the notion of witnessing in its performative legal and religious contexts. As Sedgwick and Parker state, 'It is the constitution of a community of witness that makes the marriage'.[80] It is the creation of a community that ratifies and recruits the legitimacy of the privilege of being a subject in the institutional sense. That communities ratify existing structures of power through their silent bodily speech acts and that bodies can defy institutional norms through their organic speech acts emphasize two key principles of performativity and witnessing I suggest are central to queer postcolonial narratives: one, the body is able to communicate (despite institutional silencing); and, two, that it is only at the point where a gathering comes into being that a process of (non-institutionalized) witnessing can begin to take place. In other words, the challenge to the violence of the national, religious family comes into being through the communal desire to listen to that silenced, visceral speech act. To listen to that which has been rendered silent through reiterative normalizing practices,

78 I am placing this emphasis on silent speech because I want to suggest that there is the potential for embodied speech acts. I am thus building on the epistemological trajectory of Austin and Butler, and do not want to lose the centrality of the speech act by referring solely to the body's capacity to convey information by using the term 'communication'.

79 Felman makes a similar point in *The Scandal of the Speaking Body*, where she draws out the way in which Austin's theorizing relies on the organic body to make the promise (in this case, to marry) and, at the same time, how that very body is the site which invariably breaks its own promise. The power of language to exercise control over the physical, through the legal and/or religious promise, is thrown into question as the body becomes the embodied means through which that very promise can easily be broken. Language can and does exert power over the body but its viscerality, for Felman, Butler, Sedgwick and Parker, is a potential disruption to the normalizing institutional demands. See Shoshana Felman, *The Scandal of the Speaking Body: Don Juan with J. L. Austin or Seduction in Two Languages*, trans. by Catherine Porter, foreword by Stanley Cavell and afterword by Judith Butler (Stanford, CA: Stanford University Press, 2003).

80 Parker and Sedgwick, 'Introduction', p. 10.

to the body that has no witness, I argue, is at the heart of queer postcolonial narratives. Furthermore, the focus on the body that does not speak through language points to the very ways in which power can be interrogated through an engagement with other modes of communication. I therefore propose a multisensory coming together as one possible way of listening to the body and, thus, of avoiding the reiteration of institutional silencing and violence. The body's supposed silence is revealed as a visceral desire to communicate through a body constrained and violated by others. This sensory engagement is then tentatively translated into fragmentary words through a process of witnessing where the listeners are literally touched into verbal expression.

An ethics of witnessing, or multisensory epistemologies

Bearing witness to trauma is an embodied event. Testimony is not only a speech act that renders a traumatic event 'real', it is also a sensorial expression of the unspeakable or the unarticulated. Flesh – the viscera comprising body and mind – stores memories. Indeed, memory is not simply a cognitive capacity, but also a visceral, affective, chemical, hormonal, electrical and sensorial activity. Oliver Sacks has shown that memory is a synaesthetic experience, that sensorial effectiveness is learned, and that the plasticity of the brain coheres around how we *feel* our bodies.[81] For Sacks, *feeling* the body – even body parts or senses that may be considered absent, such as in the experience of phantom limbs – is a synaesthetic, proprioceptive and neurological attempt to give coherence to the self.[82] Speaking on somato-sensory mapping – 'a body-image map in which the visible features of the body [each have] a corresponding site on the cortical surface' – Margrit Shildrick argues that the neural pathways through which the physical body is sensed and through which the self emerges are not static, and that neural plasticity implies that previous, existing and new morphologies may be remembered, relearned and reimagined.[83] One might go so far as to suggest that the body not only forms our sense of self, but also remembers what may be physically or cognitively absent. Shildrick's work, especially with heart transplant recipients, suggests the possibility of somatic memory, of memories that are stored in body parts.[84] Here, however, I am less interested in how memories may be passed on through the actual exchange of matter (e.g. in the form of organ transplantation), and much more concerned with how unspoken memories and silenced histories are communicated

81 For Sacks, the senses are learned through a synaesthetic coordination. However, this does not mean that someone born blind or deaf can learn to see or hear without professional intervention. He does suggest that when surgery allows people to begin to see or hear that they must learn how to use these senses, and that the capacity to use the visual and the auditory takes time and can often involve external support.

82 Sacks insists that the brain is adaptable and plastic and in so being is always trying to 'construct a coherent self and world' (Oliver Sacks, *An Anthropologist on Mars* (London: Picador, 1995), p. xv). Prosser builds on Sacks's argument to suggest that the *sense* of bodily structure constitutes the ego and thus that the ego is first and foremost bodily (Prosser, *Second Skins*, p. 79).

83 Margrit Shildrick, 'Corporeal Cuts: Surgery and the Psycho-social', *Body & Society* 14.1 (2008), 56–75 (p. 42).

84 Margrit Shildrick, 'Imagining the Heart: Incorporations, Intrusions and Identity', *Somatechnics* 2.2 (2012), 233–49.

through embodied narratives. It is my contention that the body and intimate objects that touch the body carry traces of histories, and that these embodied memories may be shared both via narrative and multisensory engagements. Indeed, the multisensory is not simply another form of communication that complements the spoken and written word; rather, it is central to how the sense of self comes into being, to our relations with others and to how we remember.

How is it possible to bear witness through the body, intimacy with others and intimate objects? How do we *recognize* histories through our bodies even before we begin the potentially overwhelming and impossible task of translating these stories into words? How is the ethical imperative to narrate histories of trauma connected to queer postcolonial narratives and multisensory entanglements? And, how is subject formation reconfigured through such multisensory reimaginings of intimacy and history? Aristotle and Plato affirm a clear hierarchy of the senses, with vision as the primary sense and touch relegated to an inferior, (too) intimate and primitive way of relating to others.[85] Hegel and Lacan consolidate the purported superiority of vision and its centrality to the formation of self, the relation between self and other (and thus how subjectivity is formed), and domination and violence as constitutive of subjectivity and relationality. Hegel posits a master–slave dialectic where recognition of self and of other requires vision – the noblest of the senses.[86] The master recognizes the slave solely as a passive object and this state of slave-*thingness* consolidates the master's status as an active subject: 'The lord puts himself into relation with both of these moments, to a *thing* as such, the object of desire, and to the consciousness for which thinghood is the essential characteristic'.[87] Hegelian recognition is a mechanism of control that denies the interdependence or relationality of *subjects* by seeking to dominate the one (the object) who is looked at. This process of objectification attempts to render the other static as an object of repulsion, desire, violence, labour and inferiority.

Lacan's account of the mirror stage further ratifies this association between vision, mastery and domination (of self and self over other).[88] Through scopic recognition the infant moves from a state of bodily dependence to a corporeally integrated self. This is a 'jubilant assumption of his specular image' that leads 'to the assumption of the armour of an alienating identity, which will mark with its rigid structure the subject's entire mental development'.[89] Distinct from the visualized object, the infant

85 Aristotle insists that touch, smell and taste are animalistic and therefore inferior to vision that gives humans a distance from the (dirty) ground. Descartes describes vision as the 'noblest' of senses. See, *Discourse on Method, Optics, Geometry and Meterology*, trans. by Paul J. Olscamp (Indianapolis: Bobbs-Merrill, [1637] 1965), p. 65.

86 For a discussion of the history of the consolidation of vision as the noblest of senses and subsequent critiques of this hierarchical positioning, see especially Martin Jay, *Downcast Eyes: The Denigration of Vision in Twentieth-Century French Thought* (Berkeley and Los Angeles, CA: University of California Press, 1994).

87 G. W. F. Hegel, *Phenomenology of Spirit*, trans. by A. V. Miller (Oxford: Clarendon Press, 1977), p. 115.

88 Prosser argues that Lacan's emphasis on bodily image, at the expense of the bodily ego, was a significant divergence from Freudian understandings of the ego. Prosser states, 'The body is not only not commensurable with its "mental" projection but responsible for producing this projection. The body is crucially and materially formative of the self' (Prosser, *Second Skins*, p. 65).

89 Jacques Lacan, *Ecrits: A Selection*, trans. by Alan Sheridan (London: Routledge, [1966] 1977), p. 2 and p. 5.

as subject gains recognition as 'a singular self in a singular body'.[90] Any previous (or continued) tactility, intimacy and/or interdependence (especially with primary carers) is rendered incidental to the formation of the child's subjectivity. As Luce Irigaray, Shildrick, Prosser and Oliver show, the logic of Lacan's mirror stage is dependent upon a discrete and whole body. Shildrick affirms that both Cartesian (the affirmation of a clear split between the mind and the body) and Lacanian models disavow 'existential vulnerability'.[91] Prosser suggests that the mirror can be 'an anguishing shattering of the felt already formed imaginary – that sensory body of the body "image"'.[92] Oliver is much more insistent that the Hegelian and Lacanian logic instigates 'a sense of lack, castration, or alienation, the sense of being cut off from the world or being alone' as central to recognition.[93] According to Lacanian thinking, optical subject formation instantiates distance and violence as integral to recognizing self and other-object. It reinforces a sense of detachment, where the other is *not* self. Here, others are a potential threat to the integrity of the self, and thus the self must protect its borders and keep its self intact. Furthermore, there is a normativizing impulse that necessitates both a coherence between the self-image and the felt body, and a complete separation of the contained and sealed body from the other's distinct body. The implications are that if there is a dissonance between the tactile and the scopic body image then the self will not only be shattered but also that the psychically prevalent image must prevail (and Prosser is writing against this paradigm, proposing that the tactile image take priority). Furthermore, there is no space for morphological diversity or for the mutually dependent ways in which we live our embodied lives. Lack of wholeness, unity or properness of the body is disavowed in the process of subject formation and the integrity of psychic self must triumph. Yet what is denied is not simply the fact that there are morphologically diverse bodies – which is clearly the case – but, and perhaps more importantly, that vulnerability of structure, matter and image forms the subject. Our bodies and our images of self and of other never quite cohere or congeal; there is always leakiness, (physical and psychic) openness, and change (which may be sensed within and through the body). Central to subject formation is an ontological and existential vulnerability.

Before discussing the vulnerability of bodily and communal borders, I want to briefly examine how Hegelian and Lacanian notions of recognition have been taken up in varying contemporary studies of colonial technologies of sex, race, ability, class and gender. In postcolonial, feminist and queer studies, vision is critiqued as one of the principal means through which sociopolitical structures consolidate ideologies and acts of violence and disempowerment. Colonial scopic technologies fix groups of people into distant and distinct objects, and specifically connect visible traits to purported backwardness. They create a spectacle of otherness. The process of racializing and sexualizing others demonizes difference as embodied by inferior others who must

90 Margrit Shildrick, *Embodying the Monster: Encounters with the Vulnerable Self* (London: Sage Publications, 2002), p. 105.
91 Ibid., p. 106.
92 Prosser, *Second Skins*, p. 100.
93 Oliver, p. 189.

be repudiated. Within a colonial vision, difference indicates inferiority, because it marks a deviation from the ascendency of white patriarchal heteronormativity. Anne McClintock rightly states that 'anatomy becomes an allegory of progress and history is reproduced as a technology of the visible'.[94] Ann Laura Stoler adds that the visual politics of bodies, especially genitalia, confirms that 'colonialism was that quintessential project in which desire was always about sex, that sex was always about racial power, and that both were contingent upon a particular representation of non-white women's bodies'.[95] I would add not only that optical technologies are deployed to racialize and sexualize women's bodies as objects (of desire), but also that the demonization of queers, crips and people of colour normalizes white, heteronormative familialism.[96]

The visual seeks mastery of both self and other. Vision promises – or is heralded as the promise of – complete and definitive knowledge, as if Truth can be revealed through technologies of the eye. Central to the colonial encounter is that knowledge of the other as an object of difference keeps the viewer – who is a knowing subject – intact and unaltered by the contact. Similar to many scholars working at the intersections of postcolonial and feminist criticism, Meyda Yeğenoğlu argues that 'knowledge and vision are part of an interlocking desire for modern, disciplinary colonial governing, for such a desire is also a part of the sadistic desire to physically master the object of gaze'.[97] The gaze, it is often concluded, is the masculine, colonial modality of domination and subjugation. I certainly agree that optical relations are tied to hierarchies of normative belonging, where the self is understood, perceived and experienced through a prejudicial and often exclusionary (and therefore reductive) image of others. However, I would argue that optical entanglements are not determined by this hierarchical relation of subject to object, as if vision were always and only about sexualization, domination, racialization, distance and violence. Furthermore, the priority given to the relation between vision and distance fails to recognize both the role of all the senses in subject formation and how vision can be an intimate modality of being with others. Similar to Shildrick, I would argue that the self does not emerge solely through the visual. I would also agree with Oliver that optics is not an empty space, a vacuum, which creates distance. Instead, 'vision is the result of pressures, vibrations, particles, and waves affecting the nerves. And visual images are surrounded and informed by tastes, smells, sounds, and palpitations'.[98] Rather than proposing an inverted hierarchy, where smell, touch and taste take priority over sight and hearing, I would suggest that the senses work together, in both contestatory and complementary ways. Whereas Oliver proposes the politically and ethically motivated notion of love (following the

94 Anne McClintock, *Imperial Leather: Race, Gender and Sexuality in the Colonial Contest* (New York and London: Routledge, 1995), p. 38.

95 Ann Laura Stoler, *Race and the Education of Desire: Foucault's 'History of Sexuality' and the Colonial Order of Things* (Durham, NC and London: Duke University Press, 1995), p. 189.

96 By 'familialism' I am referring to the process through which the heterosexual white family is represented as the only viable form of existence (i.e. the ideal mode of social belonging). See, for example, Edelman, *No Future*, pp. 112–15.

97 Meyda Yeğenoğlu, *Colonial Fantasies: Towards a Feminist Reading of Orientalism* (Cambridge: Cambridge University Press, 1998), p. 111.

98 Oliver, p. 191.

feminist tradition of bell hooks and Luce Irigaray), I turn to multisensory histories.[99] Although multiple critics have reclaimed love for its ethical and political potentiality, I see the concept as too tied to romantic ideals and normative values. I therefore turn to the senses to explore how the desire for non-violent modes of coming together may be forged through an embodied ethics.

A shift in paradigms, where subjectivity is multisensory and not only based in visually violent relations of domination, is not only a concern with rethinking how human relations emerge but also a desire to explore the possible ways in which histories of trauma may come forth. It is not about inverting hierarchies or even suggesting that tactility is somehow better or morally superior to vision. On the contrary, touch can be violent, aggressive and sexually intimating – and in the following chapters I explore how colonial hierarchies of race are implemented, reinforced and temporarily rendered shaky through sexual and domestic tactile intimacy. It is an attempt to explore how our sense of being with others is not always or necessarily about violence, domination or distance. Indeed, intimacy, proximity and tenderness are as much a part of subject formation as is the emphasis on aggression and separation found in Lacan's and Hegel's formulations. Irigaray and Julia Kristeva offer alternative theorizations of tactile relationality and subjectivity. Irigaray asks, 'If we keep on speaking the same language together, we're going to reproduce the same history. [. . .] Don't you think so?'[100] In response she turns to the body as a viable epistemology. She states, 'You are there, like my skin. [. . .] Touch yourself, touch me, you'll "see"'.[101] Building on this sense of the skin as simultaneously touched and touching, Shildrick suggests:

> [In] the contact of flesh, we experience our other/self not only as surface feeling, but as an emotion: we are touched. The physiological and psychological processes come together such that the skin is less a boundary than an organ of communication, a passage or crossing point, both for the self and towards the other.[102]

Tactility demonstrates how the self is other to the self and yet does not become the other: we are touched as much as we touch and the overarching sovereign will of who touches whom is destabilized. This other/self is *not* a denial of the self or of the boundaries between self and other. Indeed, the skin is a significant reminder of how important borders, especially fleshy ones, are to our sense of self, and shows how boundaries can be protective, defensive, porous, permeable and changing. Skin is simultaneously a

99 For an excellent analysis of Fanon's writing on love in *Black Skin, White Masks*, see Oliver. hooks has multiple books that deal with love, for example: *All About Love: New Visions* (New York: HarperCollins, 2001); and *The Will to Change: Men, Masculinity and Love* (New York: Simon & Schuster, 2004). More recently, Berlant and Michael Hardt have produced separate and collaborative work on love. See, for example, Michael Hardt, 'For Love or Money', *Cultural Anthropology*, 26.4 (2011) 676–82; and Heather Davis and Paige Sarlin, 'No One is Sovereign in Love: A Conversation between Lauren Berlant and Michael Hardt', *amour* 18 (2011) <www.nomorepotlucks.org/site/no-one-is-sovereign-in-love-a-conversation-between-lauren-berlant-and-michael-hardt> [accessed 29 November 2011].

100 Luce Irigaray, *This Sex Which Is Not One*, trans. by Catherine Porter (New York: Cornell University Press, [1977] 1985), p. 205.

101 Ibid., p. 216.

102 Shildrick, *Embodying the Monster*, p. 116.

sensation of self and a feeling of self through others. This physical and psychic border is essential to bodily integrity and yet testifies to how a sense of wholeness and well-being is not dependent on impermeability or independence. Proximal and tactile relations are as much a part of the process of becoming a subject as are other sensory impressions. Indeed, when Fanon discusses the racialization of the epidermis through a visual politics that denies his humanness, he bears witness to how the refusal to touch, to get close to the other, renders the skin an object of disdain. In becoming an object, his skin is rendered distinct from the flesh that can be touched and thus the lack of touch instantiates his lack of humanness: 'I feel, I see in those white faces that it is not a new man who has come in, but a new kind of man, a new genus'.[103] The self is formed through a visual and tactile epidermal schema that is sensed *and* historically produced. The ethical potentiality is this reconfiguring of our understandings of the border, not to deny or eliminate its existence (an unnecessary pursuit, idealized by those who can live with the fantasy of no borders), but instead to decrease or even stop the violence perpetuated in its name.

Where violence is deemed at the heart of all relations, and where there is a fantasy of wholeness and a misrecognition of self as separate, then what follows is the need to protect and defend the individual body from difference and outsiders. Of course, we have a right to defend ourselves against violence, to demand the right to bodily integrity and to assert individual agency. Yet, when we make such claims we must be mindful that we inevitably speak on behalf of others and invariably make claims that invoke the lives of others.[104] Furthermore, a contemporary rhetoric of defence is dominated by a liberal agenda that wants to protect individual rights, private property, and thus the choice to consume wherever and whenever. It is about defending borders, individual freedom, national boundaries and nation states, and cares little for the protection of those who do not, cannot or will not adhere to the heteronormative and homonormative logic of state technologies. Indeed, rethinking the self and the self's relations (or interdependence) with others is as much about subject formation as it is a concern with how we feel about, experience and defend all borders, including collective ones. It is clear that the rhetoric of the individual (body and self) – where self is separate from (purportedly dangerous) others and where the body's boundary is sealed and closed – has been and continues to be used to justify intimate, public, private, national and transnational abuses. Any attack to the border is seen to violate the essence of national belonging and therefore the response must be violence. Current wars (including those in Afghanistan and Iraq) and the supposed 'war on terror' demonstrate how an account of violence (often against innocent, demonized people) is justified through a rhetoric that claims only to be protecting individual and

103 Fanon, *Black Skin, White Masks*, p. 87.

104 As Butler states: 'If I am claimed by others when I make my claim, if gender is for and from another before it becomes my own, if sexuality entails a certain dispossession of the "I", this does not spell the end of my political claims. It only means that when one makes those claims, one makes them for much more than oneself' (Butler, *Undoing Gender*, p. 16).

national borders.[105] Here, ontology is dependent upon violent exclusions and acts of destroying purported threatening spaces and people (namely anyone *mis*-identified as a (Muslim) terrorist). Being is thus reliant on borderlines of difference, which are racialized and sexualized, and affective orientations of mastery and certainty over vulnerable borders. Butler insists that 'denial of [our] vulnerability through a fantasy of mastery (an institutionalized fantasy of mastery) can fuel the instruments of war'.[106] Shildrick delineates how the desire to expunge a sense of vulnerability is a normalizing process that instantiates the subject as a contained and separate entity.[107] Both Butler and Shildrick argue that the protection of an ideal sealed body – on the national and individual level respectively – involves the production of an outside, a different other, and thus an abject space or state of being. Abjected difference threatens to violate the boundaries of the social and the individual body and in so doing poses a risk (from within) to the body (politic). For both Butler and Shildrick such fears – of potential contagion and traversals – further demonstrate how the prominence of the imagined inviolable body temporarily covers over the lived experience of being in the flesh, which is messy, uncertain, leaky and, most of all, vulnerable.

Rather than seeking to reject this vulnerability, *Queer Postcolonial Narratives* suggests that precariousness is *primary* to becoming human. Vulnerability encapsulates 'that primary tie, that primary way in which we are, as bodies, outside ourselves and for one another'.[108] Thus, vulnerability is not optional, and any affective relation to it is variable (it can be sensed by the subject even while it is that which founds the subject). Instead of vehemently and performatively trying to deny this state of vulnerability, I work with vulnerability as the very ethical ground on which being with others is enacted. Indebted to Levinas, this ethics cannot be that which is worked out once ontology is settled. The question of being can only be thought through one's ethical relation to others. Beginning with questions of ontology reaffirms the subject as autonomous and all-knowing. According to Levinas, 'Knowledge is re-presentation, a return to presence, and nothing may remain other to it'.[109] In other words, 'It is not a relation with the other as such but the reduction of the other to the same'.[110] Levinasian ethics is the possibility of encountering that which is other to one's self without reducing this other to the same or to absolute difference. It is the attempt to avoid the violence of seeing the self reproduced everywhere (the self-same) and to work with the epistemic limits of both self and other. Difference makes being possible, not as a *thing* that can be owned,

105 After the September 2001 attacks in New York and Washington, President George W. Bush stated,

> Terrorist attacks can shake the foundations of our biggest buildings, but they cannot touch the foundation of America. These acts shatter steel, but they cannot dent the steel of American resolve. America has stood down enemies before, and we will do so this time. None of us will ever forget this day, yet we go forward to defend freedom and all that is good and just in our world

<www.pbs.org/newshour/updates/terrorism/july-dec01/bush_speech.html> [accessed 21 September 2010].

106 Butler, *Precarious Life*, p. 29.

107 Shildrick, *Embodying the Monster*, p. 71.

108 Butler, *Precarious Life*, p. 27.

109 Emmanuel Levinas, 'Ethics as First Philosophy', in *The Levinas Reader*, ed. by Sean Hand (Oxford: Blackwell, 1989), pp. 75–89 (p. 77).

110 Emmanuel Levinas, *Totality and Infinity: An Essay on Exteriority*, trans. by Alphonso Lingis (Pittsburgh, PA: Duquesne Press, 1969), p. 46.

manipulated or harmed, but as the very sense of self/otherness, the means through which self and other are constituted. In Butler's words: 'For if I am confounded by you, then you are already of me, and I am nowhere without you'.[111] This interdependence, mutuality, relationality and intersubjective being is less about dependency and more about how our inherent vulnerability ties us to each other in ways that consistently undo the self/other.

We are undone by each other: grief, desire, rage, passion – all potentially political, communal and public entanglements – undo the subject in unthinkable and unknowable ways. This is not an exteriorization to the sense of self, but a destabilization of the certainty of self. In other words, whether in sex, passion, anger, politics, grief or other moments when we may feel *beside ourselves* we sense and sometimes cognitively register how the 'I' is implicated in, dependent upon, entangled with and enthralled by others.[112] This sense of intimate being with others queerly orientates communal belonging away from Hegelian and Lacanian separateness and domination towards the recognition of how our bodies and selves are tied to each other even when they feel separate. The emphasis on multisensory encounters and histories is a turn towards how our bodies may register the unspeakable. As Laura Marks explains, 'What is left out of expression registers somatically, in pain, nausea, memories of smells and caresses. What does not register in the orders of the seeable and sayable may resonate in the order of the sensible'.[113] This is not a return to the body as an authentic source of feeling, or a hope that sensory plenitude will somehow reveal definitive knowledge. Multisensory witnessing draws attention to the unarticulated, to the excess that cannot be assimilated into existing knowledge. It gives attention to the sensorial register without reducing experiences or subjectivities to the body. As Marks argues, 'Tactile epistemology involves thinking with your skin, or giving as much significance to the physical presence of an other as to the mental operations of symbolization. This is not a call to willful regression but to recognizing the intelligence of the perceiving body'.[114] History making is thus as much about trying to hear unspeakable narratives through embodied exchanges as it is about creating linguistic narratives. Multisensory witnessing is the desire to hear when words cannot be spoken. It is also an act of recognition to the body as archive that can be shared if the listener can learn to be with others differently from the colonial and familial order of violence.

Importantly, multisensory engagements do not grant access to the other as if one could *know* the other in an easy graspable form; it undoes the self as the self enters into a mutual process of witnessing. I concur with Oliver that witnessing is formed through 'address-ability' and an infinite call of indefinite 'response-ability' with others.[115] Indeed, 'address-ability' and 'response-ability' are embodied and intimate; they involve

111 Butler, *Precarious Life*, p. 49.
112 For Butler's work on being beside oneself and becoming undone, see *Undoing Gender*, pp. 1–39 and *Precarious Life*, pp. 19–49.
113 Laura Marks, *The Skin of the Film: Intercultural Cinema, Embodiment and the Senses* (Durham, NC and London: Duke University Press, 2000), p. 111.
114 Ibid., p. 190.
115 Oliver, p. 17.

the self in the other and the other in the self so much so that the self may feel ec-static, implicated in the lives of others as much as in one's own life (indeed, in the mutuality of life).[116] This is not a suggestion that one becomes other, a practical and philosophical impossibility, but rather that one becomes other to one's self.[117] In becoming other to the self the parameters of selfhood are undone. This is the possibility of an ethical response, of listening without knowing what lies ahead and without already knowing how the story goes. It is the potential for communications based less on what is already known and already familiar and more on working with and through the limits of (all types of) entanglements. Communication is not about expecting transparency; it is about working with what cannot be articulated in the form of words and what may be translated into narrative. According to Ahmed, an ethics of touch 'would allow what cannot be spoken, or voiced in the present, *to be opened, or reopened*, as that which remains ungrasped and unrealized, as an approach that is always *yet to be taken*'.[118] This is not a temporal future of better communication, but a process of speaking and hearing where one's infinite responsibility is called upon. Here, one cannot measure one's responsibility in knowing one has heard or helped an other, but rather one is always indebted to the call of others. In other words, to begin to take responsibility for that which remains 'ungrasped' is to be called upon to listen over and over again, without ever hoping, wanting or reaching a point of complete knowledge. This unknowability is not hidden knowledge as such but is the imperative to keep listening to and to be touched by others over and over again. Indefinite listening is redolent of how Felman and Laub describe psychoanalytic listening and artistic witnessing. However, in queer postcolonial narratives, the important difference is that space is created for those who cannot be heard within institutional contexts. Recognition, thus, comes about not through institutionalized norms, which are often the source of violence, but through an attempt to hear what is unarticulated and, in so doing, to take responsibility for a past that cannot be known in its entirety. It is a bodily encounter in which the self is implicated in the process of bearing witness to unarticulated, embodied memories. To speak with the body is to suggest that silence is not always disempowering and that listening is an embodied event. Bearing witness is a communally queer event that involves a repeated undoing of selves with others. No one stays intact as the stories unfold and yet the capacity to hear the body makes such painful undoings potentially bearable.

One of the significant contributions that queer theory offers to trauma studies is a serious challenge to the emphasis on individuality, individual stories and individual recovery or reparation. I do not agree with Oliver, Caruth, Felman or Laub that

116 Speaking on the signification of ec-staticness, Butler says that it 'means, literally to be outside oneself, and thus can have several meanings: to be transported beyond oneself by a passion, but also to be *beside oneself* with rage or grief' (Butler, *Precarious Life*, p. 23).

117 It should be clear that there is no possibility of becoming other in this ethical bind of address-ability and response-ability. The desire to become other – a willed position of the subject – is a violation of this ethical relation insofar as it assumes to know the other. The possibility of an address and of a response is part of the process of becoming a subject. Beginning the process of witnessing after experiences of traumatic violence reinstates the possibility of an address, of responding and thus of being taken outside of one's self (as one learns anew).

118 Ahmed, *Strange Encounters*, p. 156.

the capacity to address or respond to a potential, imaginary or real other – which is integral to subject formation – must always lead to the individual entering into linguistic narrativization.[119] Indeed, what we witness in queer postcolonial narratives is the willingness of listeners to take on the responsibility for an endless narrative that they must translate from embodied exchanges into a comprehensible language that is still largely incoherent in form. I therefore want to conclude this section by exploring how these gatherings come into being. Importantly, narratives of trauma are shared queerly, in an orientation that undermines the hold of colonial institutions (especially the school and the home), domestic proprietary, heteronormative and 'white' conjugality, and the disaggregation of the public from the private. Bodies form, de-form, consolidate and undo social space. We are not simply in a body that takes up its (designated) place; through our movements in space in contact with and avoidance of others we create communal alignments, entanglements and detachments. Our bodies may feel 'at home', 'out of place', a sense of communality or exclusion, or a temporary comfort or irritation with others in space.[120] As Ahmed argues histories of getting close to others or pulling away from other others – or of having such acts done to us – serve to instantiate boundaries of commonality or of unbelonging. The body is resensed in these encounters, formed anew in proximity with others and with histories that bring some people together, some potentially closer than previously possible, some distant and others impossibly separate. To this extent, the body is cognitive matter that is formed through and by contact with others and simultaneously is transformative of the spaces into which it enters. This is a social body that is tied to the politics of flesh and to histories of exclusion and belonging (on a regional, national and transnational scale). It is a body that can lay claim to space, can be forced out of place, and that can leave its traces and tracks. In making claims to the body, to the right to be recognized as an embodied subject, to space, to the right to inhabit shared lives and to be in public, we give recognition to the fact that the body 'has its invariably public dimension' and that it is '[constituted] as a social phenomenon in the public sphere'.[121]

Embodiment may feel simultaneously (and somewhat paradoxically) individual and private and collective and social. Yet, how are queer postcolonial gatherings formed and how might they offer a way into remembering unarticulated histories?

As mentioned earlier, evocations of queerness usually distance themselves from identitarian affiliations. An attachment to definitive categories is said to perpetuate the

119 Marianne Hirsch explores how photographs may restore the possibility of address, especially for subsequent generations. On the one hand, Laub mentions the potential of photographs to create an addressee, and yet his emphasis remains on the eventual narrative that emerges. On the other hand, Felman sensitively explores the differences between body and theory and how witnessing is not a theoretical pursuit but an embodied undertaking. However, she never adequately explains the role of the body in witnessing, although she does touch on the role of the reader's body in belatedly bearing witness to unacknowledged events. See Marianne Hirsch, *Family Frames: Photography, Narrative and Postmemory* (Cambridge, MA: Harvard University Press, 1997); and Felman and Laub, *Testimony*, pp. 44–6 and pp. 108–9.

120 See especially chapter two of Ahmed's *Strange Encounters*, pp. 75–134.

121 Butler, *Precarious Life*, p. 26. Increasingly, the right to inhabit a public space is being closed down as commercial properties take ownership over what were formerly publicly accessible areas. See Lauren Berlant, *The Queen of America Goes to Washington: Essays on Sex and Citizenship* (London and Durham, NC: Duke University Press, 1997).

violence of exclusionary practices. In *Queer Postcolonial Narratives* I evoke a sense of belonging that is attached to the family form. Yet it refuses a logic of familial nationalism, which is formed through colonial subjugation, patriarchal domination or intimate abuses. What queer postcolonial narratives seek out is a mode of witnessing that brings ostracized peoples together and yet does not level out differences in experiences or intensities of traumatic events. It is an embodied desire to share histories with others that makes the impossible possible. In other words, taking responsibility for histories that are not one's own but in which one is implicated is the beginning of a reaching out, a touching of an other that shatters the existing frame of reference. This alignment, togetherness and temporary sense of belonging is vulnerable. In Butler's words: 'I think that if I can still address a "we", or include myself within its terms, I am speaking of those of us who are living in certain ways *beside ourselves*, whether in sexual passion, or emotional grief, or political rage'.[122] A sense of being with and for others, especially the imperative to translate into language that which has remained unarticulated and that for which no one has assumed responsibility, is forged through an intimacy of passion, rage and grief. Bearing witness is the performative narrativization of histories; it is the endless repetition of narrating collective and intergenerational stories that reverberate out of and through the bodies of those subjected to intimate abuses. Queer postcolonial narratives forge ethical modes of witnessing insofar as they create literary forms that give space to embodied histories. They evoke the vulnerability of the narrative form, and thus reflect and instantiate the vulnerability of ontology as the foundation upon which a sense of belonging and an ethics of witnessing are imagined.

What is unique about queer postcolonial narratives is the desire to imagine gatherings that remember the joys of being attached to institutions and yet defy the violence of normative belonging. Communal belonging is thus not brought into being through ontological certainty or epistemological uniformity. Coming together is reconceived as the cessation of the repetition of violence through a notion of responsibility that instantiates the subject (where violence is understood as the violation of the very thing that makes us human: our vulnerability). Paramount to the modes of belonging I am describing is not a universal production of happiness or 'better' norms but rather a desire to share knowledge through multiple forms and to give recognition to what cannot be spoken. Coming together to share histories and to bear witness to what the body has being trying endlessly to communicate are vulnerable and often painful tasks. The risk of not being heard can repeat the violence of the originary trauma. However, such risks – often ontological risks – are what found the sense of belonging in queer postcolonial narratives. To quote Ahmed:

> The 'we' of such a collective politics is what must be worked for, rather than being the foundation of our collective work. In the very 'painstaking labour' of getting closer, of speaking *to* each other, and of working *for* each other, we also get closer to 'other others'. In such acts of alignment (rather than merger), we can reshape the very bodily form of the community, as a community that is yet to come.[123]

[122] Butler, *Precarious Life*, p. 23.
[123] Ahmed, *Strange Encounters*, p. 180.

I would add that the speech act of bearing witness to bodies that remember is the *moment* where existing modes of belonging are reimagined. These bodies disrupt the existing frames of reference with their stories, and when these stories are heard they reverberate and transform lives in irrevocable and often painful ways. Sharing these histories is to take on responsibility and to enter into relations that can potentially transform what it means to belong and what it means to inhabit a body that is different and that is often viewed as out of place. Telling these stories is to live with this sensed state of vulnerability, the very sense of ethical being with others. In Shildrick's words:

> To hold open the idea of the other, in whatever form she takes, is to enter into the risk of mutual becoming. In short, it is vulnerability itself, of the one and of the other, and the responsibility that it engenders in the one for the other, that is the provocation of ethical subjectivity.[124]

The risk is that as one listens to an other one may become undone; this uncertainty and disorientation can be and is frightening, but it is also the space where one can begin to experience something other than violent belonging and where one can begin to take responsibility for previously unknown histories of violence. This precarious coming together takes place through the attempt to listen to what remains unsaid, especially by touching, smelling and listening to the body that communicates through all its senses. Bodies speak and, in so doing, a multisensory form of communication is brought into being so as to bear witness to subjectivity itself, to the very relationality of being with others, and to previously unspeakable histories.

Queer postcolonial structure

This book takes a queer postcolonial approach to reading texts insofar as it tries 'to remain supple enough to respond to the various locations of information', and it puts into practice 'a certain disloyalty to conventional disciplinary methods'.[125] Bringing together three authors who have yet to be analysed in conjunction with each other is one small attempt to enact Shildrick's ethics of risk and to convey the ways in which reading is, to use Butler's words, a means of becoming undone. In other words, the texts speak to each other both in terms of their search for forms of remembering that bear witness to the unspoken and in their representation of queer embodiment as opening up intimate belonging to less violent modes of coming together with others. However, the colonial and postcolonial contexts of the three selected novels vary greatly and thus this book is divided into three chapters and a coda. Each chapter explores the intimacy of familial violence in a specific colonial context, and examines varying modes of ethical witnessing.

The first chapter, 'Intergenerational Witnessing in Shani Mootoo's *Cereus Blooms at Night*', critically engages with Mala Ramchandin's refusal and/or inability to speak after being subjected to domestic abuse at the hands of her father. It explores how her carer,

124 Shildrick, *Embodying the Monster*, p. 102.

125 Judith Halberstam, *Female Masculinity* (Durham, NC and London: Duke University Press, 1998), p. 10.

Tyler, tentatively listens to her embodied communication and suggests that silence may be political. The intimacy of the relationship between Tyler and Mala portrays an ethics of multisensory remembering, where Mala and Tyler communicate through the senses. Embodied epistemologies convey unspeakable and unspoken histories of familial and colonial violence. Indeed, Mala's story of sexual abuse is interwoven with a history of Indo-Caribbean indentured labour. Yet, the novel resists the idea that a complete history can exist, and instead portrays how an encounter with epistemic limits can be the potential for a reconfiguration of the writing of history. The chapter therefore examines how queer postcolonial histories may be forged through methods that can bear witness to incomplete knowledge. It concludes by demonstrating how queer postcolonial spaces are imagined into being through intimate multisensory modes of listening to and sharing stories.

Chapter 2, 'Monstrous Witnessing in Tahar Ben Jelloun's *L'Enfant de sable*', explores the ethics of reading queer and disabled bodies in colonial contexts, and puts into question the repeated symbolic and allegorical interpretations of *different* bodies. I show how such readings are available in the novel and yet resisted through its form. This novel is composed of a narrative structure where each storyteller interrupts the previous one and where each narrator claims to have the authentic version of the story. This spectacularization of narrative production, I argue, undermines the possibility of consolidating particular bodies into national symbols. Indeed, because this is a story of a girl raised as a boy in colonial Morocco, I suggest that the materiality of the body is the site that constantly disrupts each storyteller's desire to claim definitive knowledge over the tale. The performative structure of narrative and of gender demonstrates how the process of bearing witness to queer and disabled bodies requires an indefinite and communal gathering of people who refuse to simply accept normative (embodied and literary) forms. Where change in theories of performativity is conceptualized as non-violent, I examine how implementing something different can be violent. The chapter concludes by exploring how the embodied harm the narrators experience only becomes bearable through this collective desire to keep alive a story that has been hidden and silenced by both the family and the nation.

The Coda, 'Eyes at the Tips of the Fingers: Materializing the Self in Tahar Ben Jelloun's *La Nuit sacrée*', addresses the significance of the intertextual act of repetition to the reconceptualization of borders (especially as the boundaries of the first text blur into those of the second). This novel tells the same story of the main protagonist from *L'Enfant de sable* but from the perspective of a woman who claims to be the eponymous hero. I have included this text because it is a performative act of repetition and is generally read as closing down the multiple readings and gender diversity of the first novel. In contradistinction, I argue that the novel's focus on a consolidation of the boundaries of the self through a tactile visuality is a rethinking of how the human comes into being. The self, in this novel, materializes through eyes that cannot only see but can also touch. I suggest that gaining a sense of self through the flesh does not simply foreclose multiple embodiments, as many critics suggest, but instead bears witness to how life may become bearable through a proximity to identity categories and to queer embodiments and desires.

Chapter 3, 'Fossil Witnessing in Ann-Marie MacDonald's *Fall on Your Knees*', examines the relationship between memory and familiar and familial objects. It explores how a proximity to fossils – objects laden with memories – may undo existing (restrictive) familial and national narratives. This chapter examines the materiality of artefacts and emphasizes the act of remembering as not solely a psychological undertaking (i.e. memories as in the mind) but also as a physical process. Memory formation takes place via the body's contact with forms that guard the opacity and untranslatability of the originary events. The physicality of embodied remembering requires a response that is both individual and sociopolitical, and thus a change to the self and the structures that ignore and endorse violence in the home. To this extent, this chapter questions the reading of texts for trauma, and instead suggests that symptoms of trauma may also be creative ways of surviving a life of violence. Sex work, in particular, becomes a form of remembering in MacDonald's text. Indeed, I suggest that harm to the self is an embodied registering of what cannot be spoken or remembered. It is the attempt to share with a witness that which is in excess of language. Through objects and intimacies queer postcolonial histories are felt and shared, and the hidden violence of domestic life is momentarily heard. This chapter demonstrates how the desire for whiteness is tied to sexualized violence, and how national purity is implemented in the home. Finally, I argue that the optical violence of the colonial and familial gaze is undone through a mode of looking that is intimate and shared. To bear witness is to respond to this mutual looking and to take on the responsibility for indefinite narration with others.

The concluding chapter portrays the historical significance of silence to political movements, and questions the current emphasis on speaking out as the main mode of recovery from trauma. I insist on the centrality of the witness to theories of performativity and thus unravel the process through which change may become possible. To this extent, the conclusion insists that the performative structure of power does not guarantee change, and that the technologies of colonial and familial belonging are felt in, on and through the body. The turn to the multisensory body portrays how history is not only about telling stories, but is also a concern with how we hear what falls outside of traditional frameworks. An ethics of witnessing is this response, this act of listening over and over again, and this embodied engagement through which the responsibility for the story is assumed. The conclusion opens up a set of questions concerning where we might take queer postcolonial methodologies, and how we might further create less violent ways of being with others. It turns to further ways in which bodies are cut open and through the flesh literally tied to each. Indeed, in being open to the other, in being irrevocably moved by the other, I suggest that we might hear something unexpected. To bear witness is to be moved such that one ceases to inhabit the same place. This is the possibility of hearing an other and of being moved by the touch, by the smell, by the feel of an other. Multisensory witnessing is an indefinite narrative engagement with others that forges queer modes of belonging by decolonizing epistemologies of the body, the family home and the nation.

1

Intergenerational Witnessing in Shani Mootoo's *Cereus Blooms at Night*

Unknowing pain

> *As we ask to know the other, or ask that the other say, finally or definitively, who he or she is, it will be important not to expect an answer that will ever satisfy. By not pursuing satisfaction and by letting the question remain open, even enduring, we let the other live, since life might be understood as precisely that which exceeds any account we may try to give of it. If letting the other live is part of any ethical definition of recognition, then this version of recognition will be based less on knowledge than on an apprehension of epistemic limits.*[1]
>
> *Physical pain [. . .] is language-destroying.*[2]

At first glance, Shani Mootoo's *Cereus Blooms at Night* confirms Elaine Scarry's assertion that 'Physical pain [. . .] is language-destroying'.[3] After years of sexual abuse at the hands of her father, Mala Ramchandin ceases to use language. On the one hand, such traumatic events appear to lead to Mala's inability to speak and, more specifically, to her incapacity to articulate a sense of her past (and her self) in narrative form. Indeed, when speaking of Mala, her carer confirms this view, saying, 'I detected what I think are symptoms of trauma'.[4] On the other hand, her refusal to use the colonial language of English testifies to her defiance: she refuses to speak the language used to teach her father to hate both himself and his family because of their purported racial inferiority. This is the language of the British, who implemented the indentured labour system through which Mala's grandparents migrated from India to the Caribbean. Mala therefore refuses to live by the rules set down by the British system of trading in people and the Canadian missionaries who seek to convert the Indians on the

1 Judith Butler, *Giving an Account of Oneself* (New York: Fordham University Press, 2005), pp. 42–3.
2 Elaine Scarry, *The Body in Pain: The Making and Unmaking of the World* (Oxford: Oxford University Press, 1985), p. 19.
3 Ibid.
4 Shani Mootoo, *Cereus Blooms at Night* (Toronto, ON: McClelland & Stewart, 1998), p. 14. Hereinafter all references to this novel will be given in the body of the chapter in parentheses.

island in order to raise them out of supposed destitution and backwardness.[5] Thus, although redolent of much feminist and postcolonial work, where the articulation or reconfiguration of the colonial language is a form of resistance, *Cereus* does not so much reimagine linguistic communication (in the way we see many of Mootoo's other characters doing so when using Creole) as affirm silence as a powerful political tool.[6] Mala's resistance manifests itself through her refusal to engage with others within the existing frame of reference. In other words, her abandonment of language is a wilful turn to her surroundings in a search for alternative and less violent ways of being with others. She cultivates a wild (i.e. uncontrolled) garden space, where she coexists with the beauty and ugliness of a decaying house and a flourishing out-of-control garden-home. She actively refuses to harm the bugs, animals and plants around her. She gives into the chaos of not controlling life, self and other, and the ecosystem. In so doing, Mala lives with a sensorial alertness to the simultaneity of putrid stenches and delightful odours, beautiful fauna and rotting bodies, and life and death. Thus, although Scarry may be right to assert that physical pain is 'language-destroying', I would argue that the destruction of linguistic communication can be a politically motivated act and an ethical turn towards non-violent modes of being with others.

In this chapter I examine the embodied potentiality and potency of silence. My analysis is attentive to how silence is 'too common, too institutionalized, and too destructive', especially for those who cannot speak or who are forced into silence as a result of the interrelated violence of colonial rule and family life.[7] Like Wendy Brown I understand that silence may have its limits. It may restrict entry into the public domain where it becomes possible – or even essential – to exercise selfhood and relational needs and desires. However, I also agree with Brown that 'refusing to speak is a method of refusing colonization, of refusing complicity in injurious interpellations or in subjection through regulation'.[8] Indeed, I am focusing on the political and ethical

5 While many of the Indian labourers would have been living in the barracks previously housed by African slaves, the levels of poverty were caused by the structure of the indentured labour system and not by religious belief or practice. *Cereus* makes explicit how missionaries targeted individuals as the cause of their own problems, rather than addressing the systemic inequalities between the white missionaries and the Indian labourers.

6 For postcolonial critiques see, for example, Bill Ashcroft, *Caliban's Voice: The Transformation of English in Post-Colonial Literature* (London: Routledge, 2009); Edouard Glissant, *Poetics of Relation*, trans. by Betsy Wing (Ann Arbor: University of Michigan Press, 1997); and Celia Britton, *Edouard Glissant and Postcolonial Theory: Strategies of Language and Resistance* (Charlottesville, VA: University of Virginia Press, 1999). For feminist work on language as colonial resistance in the Caribbean, see, for example, Denise Decaires Narain, *Contemporary Caribbean Women's Poetry: Making Style* (London: Routledge, 2001); and Kathleen J. Renk, *Caribbean Shadows and Victorian Ghosts: Women's Writing and Decolonization* (Charlottesville, VA: University Press of Virginia, 1999). I would draw particular attention to Audre Lorde on language as a form of resistance. Although my work on silence as resistance may seem to run counter to Lorde's emphasis on 'The Transformation of Silence into Language and Action', my arguments are very much informed by her work on embodied language as central to creating a different kind of language, one that diverges from the language of oppressors and that thereby imagines and builds other possibilities. See especially, *Sister Outsider: Essays and Speeches* (Berkeley: Crossing Press, 1984).

7 Patricia J. Williams, *The Alchemy of Race and Rights: Diary of a Law Professor* (Cambridge, MA: Harvard University Press, 1992), p. 127.

8 Wendy Brown, *Edgework: Critical Essays on Knowledge and Politics* (Princeton, NJ: Princeton University Press, 2005), p. 97.

valency of silence in order to interrogate the current critical attention given to speech as the main (and often sole) means through which political subjectivity is gained. In this chapter I explore how silence is not a refusal of the public or the political, but a demand for change in institutional structures so that the unspoken may be heard. I therefore argue that silence, as Foucault suggests, is not the opposite of discourse but 'an integral part of the strategies that underlie and permeate discourses'.[9] More specifically, I argue that Mala speaks with and through her body. To hear her embodied communication we must listen with more than our ears. Indeed, our eyes must be aware of movements, our nose sensitive to smells, our tongues willing to taste and our bodies open to tactility. I explore both the difficult task of translating such embodied engagement into words and the ethical potentiality of repeatedly failing to know Mala's complete history. An ethics of unknowingness is integral to reimagining knowledge production, how knowledge is authorized, and the meanings of silence and multisensory communication.

With a focus on how the stories of Mala Ramchandin are narrated, I explore the collective and multisensory narrative structure of the novel. That the narrator only hears Mala's stories by being with, close to and attentive to Mala portrays narration as an embodied, intimate and multisensorial endeavour. I further suggest that the queering of both the narrative form – insofar as it cannot quite stay straight, or follow a heteronormative trajectory – and the content – with Tyler desiring to express his feminine gender and Otoh having transitioned from a girl to a boy – is constitutive of the decolonization of knowledge, embodiment and modes of belonging in the novel. Furthermore, I argue that queer is not simply a mode of categorization, whereby we identify queer characters (although the fact that the characters explore multiple and non-normative embodiments, genders, sexualities and desires is important), queer is also a wilful defiance of the normative and violent structures of a religious family life under colonial duress.

To this extent, this chapter explores the spatialization of queer postcoloniality, whereby Mala imagines into being a non-violent mode of being with others. Mala's sequestration in her garden-home is a resistance against and a reimagining of the colonial order that seeks to control and dominate the land and its peoples. Her intimate relation to her environment is the basis upon which an ethics of being non-violently *with others* emerges. Indeed, through the creation of a rather queer gathering – where stories are begun, flowers are smelled, and silence is heard as an embodied form of communication – it becomes possible both to share shards of narratives and to engage with the limits of what can be known. The repetitive and endless telling of the same stories differently, the openness to listening without hoping for endings, and the sensory openness to each other and the environment are central to the ethics of witnessing proposed in this novel. This performative narrative structure gives space to a theory of performativity where change becomes possible as epistemological certainties begin to crumble. Yet, I argue that the performative nature of identity is repeatedly related back to Fanon's epidermal schema. Indeed, a significant aim of the chapter is to reinfuse

9 Michael Foucault, *The History of Sexuality, Vol. 1: An Introduction* (New York: Pantheon, [1976] 1978), p. 27.

Bhabha's work on performativity with a phenomenologically informed Fanonian approach, while also bringing Fanon's work on sexuality and gender into conversation with the queer gatherings, desires, genders and imaginaries forged through this queer postcolonial narrative. This chapter argues that multisensory epistemologies open up the meanings of performativity and its decolonizing and queer potentialities.

Cereus Blooms at Night tells the story of the now old Mala Ramchandin, who is brought to the Paradise Alms House after being acquitted of the murder of her father, Chandin Ramchandin. Tyler – an outsider in this community because he has studied abroad, is feminine and works in a profession dominated by women – willingly takes on the care of this socially ostracized woman. In addition to his role as carer, Tyler assumes responsibility for the acts of listening to and narrating Mala's unarticulated history of physical and sexual violence at the hands of her father. He explains that, despite her unwillingness to speak, Mala is searching for someone to listen: 'I was not sure what I was discovering beyond her voice but I felt it would not be long before I would have the privilege, and honour, of entering her world' (77). Narrated retrospectively and non-chronologically, the novel tells of the events that lead up to and follow Chandin's wife, Sarah, fleeing the fictionalized Caribbean island of Lantanacamara.

Chandin's Indo-Caribbean parents want their son to have a life beyond the plantation, and the Reverend Thoroughly offers this to them in the form of adoption. The white missionaries raise Chandin in their home space, and through Presbyterian pedagogy teach him the racist hierarchical dogmas of religious conversion. Unable to attain the white wife he so desires – his 'adoptive' sister, Lavinia Thoroughly – Chandin marries the only Indian woman at the missionary school, Sarah. Much to Chandin's distress, Sarah leaves him for the sister he has always loved. Where his 'adoptive' father, the Reverend Ernest Thoroughly, dismisses Chandin's longings for Lavinia as incestuous, Sarah and Lavinia's desires for each other queer the normative familial and religious structures to which both Chandin and the Reverend cling. Although Sarah and Lavinia had planned to take Mala and Asha with them, the daughters are accidentally left behind. Certain Sarah will return in the night, Chandin awaits her arrival by sleeping in the same bed as his daughters. However, this intimacy soon extends into a repeated violence towards and raping of his daughters. The novel weaves a connection between the racist tenets of colonial missionary pedagogy and Chandin's subsequent abuse of his daughters. Indeed, Sarah's queer migration with her white lover is linked to – without causing – Chandin's horrific violence towards Mala. Queer desires, migrations, economic and social aspirations, and familial taboos are wrapped up in this colonial system, which not only maintains the order on the island but also perpetuates and silences violence.

However, other stories are being told: Mala's lost love for Ambrose, her blossoming relationship with Tyler, and the latter's growing love for Ambrose's son, Otoh. We learn of Ambrose's passive involvement in the perpetuation of violence towards Mala. Yet, we are also told of Otoh's determination to reconcile Ambrose's unarticulated past by getting close to Mala. This history of colonial and familial abuse is interwoven with Tyler's urgent need to embody his feminine self. To speak of and listen to these imbricated and yet different histories is the collective decolonizing and queer task undertaken by these four characters. How to *hear* Mala and her family's unspoken and silenced histories of intimate and public violence may appear to be an impossibility. If Mala refuses or is unable to speak of her experiences, then how can we hear what she has to share? Scarry describes how a listener may become the narrator of someone else's pain:

> Because the person in pain is ordinarily so bereft of the resources of speech, it is not surprising that the language for pain should sometimes be brought into being by those who are not themselves in pain but who speak *on behalf of* those who are.[10]

However, in contradistinction to Scarry's articulation, I would suggest that Mala's move away from the use of language belies the idea that the one in pain is 'bereft of the resources of speech', where speech is understood as a solely linguistic means of communication. Where other nurses cannot hear Mala's unspoken words, Tyler insists: 'I watched her eyes, which I had come to believe were what she used for communicating' (25). He is attentive to 'her clinched fists, defiant stare [and] stubborn independence' (21). Tyler makes a resolute decision to listen by trying 'to decipher the words in her eyes' (23). This is not an absence of communication – in contrast to dominant (and negative) interpretations of silence – it is a call for an intimate listening and thus for a different form of being with others. Tyler hears snippets of Mala's incomplete stories. He connects her bodily narrative to Otoh's stories and to his memories of his grandmother's tales in order to weave a narrative that he then relates to the reader. The mediation of Mala's tale via Tyler, so that the reader only ever hears his version of the events, is the refusal to let the visceral, damaged body and the broader history of colonial rule fade out of sight. It is also the instantiation of silence as a mechanism of communication that questions how knowledge is produced. According to Ahmed, 'Pain is not simply an effect of a history of harm; it is the *bodily life of that history*'.[11] The body is the paradoxical visceral entity that may remain silent or speechless about pain, and its sometimes traumatic origins, and the living testimony of a life of pain. To testify with the body may sometimes mean employing speech; it is, however, also the desire and need to share one's distress with someone who can hear when words cannot be spoken. To this extent, Tyler – and this could tentatively be extended to the reader – attempts '*to learn how to hear what is impossible*'.[12]

The novel is framed by an appeal from Tyler to the reader. Italicized and interspersed with images of bugs, the plea is distinct from the narrative that follows insofar as it demands a response from the 'you' to whom it is addressed:

> *By setting this story down, I, Tyler [. . .] am placing trust in the power of the printed word to reach many people. It is my ardent hope that Asha Ramchandin, at one time a resident in the town of Paradise, Lantanacamara, will chance upon this book, wherever she may be today, and recognize herself and her family. If you are not Asha*

10 Scarry, p. 6.
11 Ahmed, *The Cultural Politics of Emotion*, p. 34.
12 Ibid., p. 35.

> *Ramchandin [. . .] but know her or someone you suspect might be her or even related to her, please present this and ask that she read it.* (3)[13]

As readers, we are directly called upon to respond and to act. We learn that the story we are about to read is not simply one of entertainment or distraction, but a narrative for which we also have a responsibility. This strategy pulls us into the text by asking us to participate in its circulation to ensure that it reaches Mala's ever-absent sister, Asha Ramchandin. The urgency of the plea simultaneously requires immediate action (to both read the stories and act upon the narrated tales) and conveys the necessity of an indefinite response to the events related (every time the book is read – regardless of the time passed – the plea is always the same). Such a narrative framework encourages the reader to 'recognise the infinite nature of responsibility, *but the finite and particular circumstances in which [we are] called on to respond to others*'.[14] The narrative framing makes apparent that our (real) lives are intertwined with the (fictionalized) ones we are about to encounter. This intersubjective narration – where our sense of self is implicated in and tied to the lives and narratives of others – is not simply an invitation to listen, but is a plea to keep the stories alive (as if our determination to ensure the narrative endures could transform the very world in which we live and participate). This call for immediate action, which can never end, is central to the process of bearing witness to unspoken and often unspeakable histories. Uncertain of what is about to unfold, the readers are not given space to judge whether they might want to accept this task.[15] To bear witness through a mutual sharing of stories is thus redolent of Levinasian ethics where one is held hostage by the other. There is no choice because responsibility for the other is the very condition of being and thus the possibility of subjectivity. To quote Levinas:

> The responsibility for the other cannot have begun in my commitment, in my decision. The unlimited responsibility in which I find myself comes from the hither side of my freedom, from a 'prior to every memory', an 'ulterior to every accomplishment', from the non-present par excellence, the non-original, the an-archical, prior to or beyond essence.[16]

Bound to others through embodied communication and narrative formation, the readers must act on the stories *we* hear. The possibility of preventing further violence to Mala, Tyler, Otoh, Ambrose and even to ourselves is forged through this collective, as well as individual, responsibility to circulate and act upon the stories.

13 The final paragraph of the novel uses a similar technique, but Tyler directly addresses Asha rather than the reader.

14 Ahmed, *Strange Encounters*, p. 147.

15 Eventually the readers learn that should they want to consider the veracity of this one woman's history, then they too are implicated in the violence to which Mala has been subjected (both by her father and by the community that views Mala as complicit in her violent relationship with her father). When Ambrose begins to wonder whether Mala may have been complicit in the violently sexual relationship with her father, the reader witnesses her reliving of a traumatic scene of departure. Such doubts ignore the very ways in which choice may be foreclosed through community norms and institutions.

16 Emmanuel Levinas, *Otherwise Than Being or Beyond Essence*, trans. by Alphonso Lingis (Norwell, MA: Kluwer Academic Publishers, 1991), p. 10.

It is not simply that, as a storyteller, Tyler weaves a connection between his life and that of Mala, but rather that Mala's stories are integral to his sense of self. He tells us:

> Might I add that my own intention, as the relater of this story, is not to bring notice to myself or my own plight. However, I cannot escape myself, and being a narrator who also existed on the periphery of the events, I am bound to be present. [. . .] It is my intent, however, to refrain from inserting myself too forcefully. Forgive the lapses, for there are some, and read them with the understanding that to have erased them would have been to do the same to myself. (3)

His insistence that he cannot erase himself from the story of Mala reveals an interdependence and an intersubjective relationality that does not deny or dissolve their separate identities, but does reinforce their mutually constitutive relationality. Rather than describing Tyler as an 'unreliable and self-involved' storyteller, as does Sarah Phillips Casteel,[17] I would suggest that he expresses his ex-centric (embodied and narrative) style by indulging in talk about himself *and* that he makes a broader philosophical statement which could read as, '*I am only in the address to you*'. In other words and to further quote Butler: '[The] "I" that I am is nothing without this "you", and cannot even begin to refer to itself outside the relation to the other by which its capacity for self-reference emerges'.[18] This relationality – although the word does not quite capture the pre-ontological tie between self and other that is ethical responsibility – is critical in this novel because it undoes the bodily (racial, ability, sexual and gender) divisions enforced by colonial rule and because it puts into practice a mode of being with others that bears witness to this primary tie. Furthermore, it seeks to give recognition to both the multiple ways in which the institutions, including the community in Paradise, have failed Mala and how lives are always and necessarily interlocked.

Tyler, like most of the residents of Paradise, has always been aware of Mala's *perverse* relations with her father and how his own queerness may be equated with such violence. As a child, he asks his Cigarette Smoking Nana:

> Could a nephew be the father of his uncle? I wondered, or could a mother ever be any other relationship to her child? Could she be the father? [. . .] Could your sister be your brother too? Could your brother be your father? (26)

Tyler's interrogatives make apparent how familial taxonomies may conceal violent transgressions of the incest taboo. Through his own uncertainties, Tyler brings our attention to the difficulties of understanding when one *perversion* is a violence and another the living of one's sense of self:

> Over the years I pondered the gender and sex roles that seemed available to people, and the rules that went with them. [. . .] I was preoccupied with trying to understand what was natural and what perverse, and who said so and why.

17 Sarah Phillips Casteel, 'New World Pastoral: The Caribbean Garden and Emplacement in Gisèle Pineau and Shani Mootoo', *Interventions: International Journal of Postcolonial Studies* 5.1 (2003), 12–28 (p. 19).

18 Butler, *Giving an Account of Oneself*, p. 82.

> Chandin Ramchandin played a part in confusing me about these roles, for it was a long time before I could differentiate between his perversion and what others called mine. (51)

On the one hand, Tyler establishes the narrative as a critique of the heteronormative rhetoric that conflates incest with queer modes of existence. On the other hand, he grounds his own queerness and Mala's life narrative in an interrogation of the supposed dichotomy of nature and perversity, questioning the ideological, specifically colonial and religious, basis of such definitions. *Cereus* concerns itself with the language of natural history. The novel questions the purported neutrality of the natural and the perverse, and portrays how this dichotomy is the foundation upon and the rhetoric through which the aims and goals of European colonial expansion and occupation were gained. Natural history is constrainingly prescriptive of bodies, spaces and modes of being (intimately) with others.

Queer encounters and violent relations are everyday occurrences in the evocatively named town of Paradise. Such fictionalized namings (including Lantanacamara and the Shivering Northern Wetlands) create ambiguity around the exact location and time period of the novel – although, the references to a post-Emancipation Trinidad that is economically sustained through Indian indentured labour are aplenty. They also draw attention to the very ways in which histories are written and gain validation. The fantastically named spaces, the narratives that remain untold (such as the histories of migration of Mala's mother and sister) and the magical realist modes of representation convey an impossibility of epistemological definitiveness or finality. The stories exceed reality, in the sense that they cannot be captured through existing representational forms (including language and realism). Thus, the novel does not simply add to the history of the Caribbean – by adding in the often-absent narratives of indentured labour and their entanglement with domestic violence – but rather it questions the arrogance of historiographies that assume the possibility of a conclusive history. I therefore agree with Grace Kyungwon Hong that the novel engages in 'a new mode of historical memory, one that does not privilege totality but brings to light an epistemic crisis'.[19] This crisis questions 'the presumption that a complete record can exist, and in so doing, [identifies] the desire for totality, resolution, or wholeness as fundamentally nationalist and colonial'.[20] This is a historiography that is grounded in, to use Butler's words, 'an apprehension of epistemic limits'.[21] I would add to Kyungwon Hong's theorizing that not only are Mootoo's subtle critiques of natural history integral to her ethics of historical memory, but also that her turn to the senses, the body and fantasy portrays a further dimension to her queer postcolonial modes of remembering. Fantasy is thus the means through which the reader glimpses how narratives fail to translate into words – or to render transparent – the originary violence.

19 Grace Kyungwon Hong, '"A Shared Queerness": Colonialism, Transnationalism and Sexuality in Shani Mootoo's *Cereus Blooms at Night*', *Meridians: Feminism, Race and Transnationalism* 7.1 (2006), 73–103 (p. 76).

20 Ibid.

21 Butler, *Giving an Account of Oneself*, p. 43.

However, fantasy, particularly in the Caribbean, is also linked to the violence of colonial occupation, pedagogy, religious conversion and surveillance. The name of Paradise recalls how colonial expeditions were imagined and enacted as processes of travelling to and living in *uninhabited* tropical spaces where one could recreate fantasies of desire, violence and economic gain in an idealized garden space.[22] Christian beliefs are interwoven with colonial endeavours in a novel concerned with how epistemologies are produced to both subjugate populations and justify (ignoring) varying forms of violence.[23] As Kyungwon Hong suggests, the novel displays a preoccupation with Linnaean, Latinate classifications and thereby exposes natural history as the desire to create order in the natural world by categorizing all life forms. Botany and zoology are the epistemological and empirical foundation for ideological justifications for structuring societies and populations through racist and sexist classifications of bodies. Furthermore, the cultivation of the colonial landscape into an idyllic garden (i.e. ordered, procreative and economically profitable) is transposed onto wider society. Phillips Casteel affirms that the setting of the novel in the town of Paradise is an evocation of the 'early explorers' hopes of recovering the original Garden of Eden in the New World'.[24] The biblical reference, according to Jill H. Casid, evokes Eve's search for knowledge through the apple as the 'familiar associative cluster connecting the sexual regulation of bodies and desires, the supposed dangers of embodied knowledge, and the attendant story of a first diaspora, the expulsion from paradise, envisioned as a garden, into a world of agricultural toil'.[25] Religious, specifically Christian, and colonial knowledge production seeks to manage bodily labour, reproduction, relationality and desires. Colonial natural history's privileging of the taming of gardens, attempting to order nature, is bound to the need to make profit from the landscape, the desire for a paradise absent at 'home', and the wilful regulation of bodies in order to produce a docile and reproductive labour force. Requiring consistent monitoring in order to remain ordered, the garden is a living metaphor for how the colonizer's property (his house, land, workers and the labourers' homes) must be surveilled, reordered and maintained.

In *Cereus* the houses have an 'excellent view of the cane fields' (131), revealing the ties between the characters, their homes and the land on which the enslaved and indentured labourers toiled and continue to work. Just as it does in V. S. Naipaul's *A House for Mr. Biswas*, the colonial home haunts Mootoo's text. Chandin builds a replica of the Reverend's home with 'a library, a pantry, a guest room [and eventually]

22 For texts dealing with the colonial Caribbean garden, see Jamaica Kincaid, 'In History', *Callaloo* 24.2 (2001), 620–6 and *My Garden (Book)* (New York: Farrar, Straus & Giroux, 1999); Helen Tiffin, '"Replanted in this Arboreal Garden": Gardens and Flowers in Contemporary Caribbean Writing', in *English in International Contexts*, ed. by Heinz Antor and Klaus Stierstorfer (Heidelberg: C. Winter, 2000), pp. 149–64; and Elaine Savory, 'Towards a Caribbean Ecopoetics: Derek Walcott's Language of Plants', in *Postcolonial Ecologies: Literatures of the Environment*, ed. by Elizabeth DeLoughrey and George B. Handley (Oxford: Oxford University Press, 2011), pp. 80–98.

23 The two most significant and critical pieces of work on gardens in Mootoo's work are: Phillips Casteel; and Jill H. Casid, *Sowing Empire: Landscape and Colonization* (Minneapolis, MN: University of Minnesota Press, 2005).

24 Phillips Casteel, p. 15.

25 Casid, p. xii.

a modest chandelier' (53–4). The construction of Chandin's own colonial home is not only a copying of the design of the Thoroughlys' house, but is also a mimicry of the Reverend's lifestyle and thus of his white status: '[Chandin] desperately wanted [the labourers] to see the inside of the Reverend's house so they could embrace not just the Reverend's faith but his taste' (33). Chandin's idealization of colonial familialism, of a whiter life, promises to be a public display of socio-economic and cultural superiority. However, his house is haunted by colonial legacies of racial and sexual violence. The hierarchies of racialized labour are transposed on to his home life where the women, who are 'too dark' (55), must create an ideal space and are punished when it fails to materialize. McClintock notes a paradox in the labour of the Victorian home where a 'wife's vocation was not only to create a clean and productive family but also to ensure the skilled erasure of every *sign* of her work'.[26] Yet labour in the colonial home is not only about performing an ideal gender role where the work is erased (and thus not understood as work), but it is also about colonial injunctions of Indian women's behaviour enforced through a hierarchization of home labour as the proper role for decent (i.e. aspiring middle-class) women.

I agree with Gopinath that, 'the colonial state, in conjunction with Indian immigrant male interests, sought to legislate and naturalize hierarchical nuclear family arrangements within this newly constructed space of the Indian immigrant home'.[27] Private rooms (and sometimes houses) were designed for heterosexual, reproductive families, to discourage Indian women from becoming independent labourers, and to encourage them to become wives.[28] This policy of 'housewifization'[29] was not only proposed and implemented by colonial officials, but was also endorsed by proponents of the campaign for Indian independence who saw women labourers and those who crossed the *kala pani* as a threat to the image of middle-class India.[30] Therefore, Mala's residence in a wild garden that is taking over the (failed) colonial home of Chandin – her literal moving into the garden-as-home – displays her undoing of the violently constraining ideals of British colonialism and Indian nationalism. Redolent of and yet a queering of Eve's search for knowledge, Mala seeks out alternative ways of living by only taking fruit and vegetables into her body and by living with the forbidden (the unclean and unruly). These acts of 'un-housing' are queer and postcolonial in

[26] McClintock, p. 162.

[27] Gopinath, p. 180.

[28] This sense of propriety of the type of labour that is suitable for women is not only to do with the so-called need for women to marry the male labourers and therefore the colonizer's desire to keep peace on his land (i.e. that the proportion of men to women is so high that the men are fighting over women), but is also tied to the Indian independence movement which promoted 'Indianness' through particular class values (particularly the supposed correct ways of being a wife and mother). See Tejaswini Niranjana, 'Left to the Imagination: Indian Nationalisms and Female Sexuality in Trinidad', in *A Question of Silence? The Sexual Economies of Modern India*, ed. by Mary John and Janaki Nair (New Delhi: Kali for Women, 1998), pp. 111–38.

[29] Gopinath, p. 181.

[30] The *kala pani* signifies black water and taboo and, in relation to indentured labourers, refers to the taboo of crossing the oceans, leaving the sacred Gangetic plain, and therefore, especially for Brahmins, being contaminated by such a journey (largely in terms of caste). See Mariam Pirbhai, *Mythologies of Migration, Vocabularies of Indenture: The Novels of the South Asian Diaspora in Africa, the Caribbean and Asia-Pacific* (Toronto, ON: University of Toronto Press, 2009).

that they seek out alternative ways of thinking about and enacting non-violent and non-hierarchical modes of being in the world with others. I use the term 'un-housing' because of its queer dimensions, specifically how it evokes the need to imagine and create alternative forms of belonging that give recognition to non-heteronormative living. I also use it to uncouple belonging from the colonial idealization of the family home as the natural space in which to reproduce replicas of self and labouring other. I therefore concur with Gopinath that Mala enacts a form of un-housing by carving out 'an alternative space of "not-home", one that explodes the gendered and racialized terms of the domestic as set forth under indentureship'.[31] Yet, un-housing also refers to the effect of the narrative on the listeners and readers. In Ahmed's words, un-housing calls for 'a different kind of inhabitance'.[32] It 'is not a healing', if healing is understood as the assimilation of newly acquired knowledge into the status quo.[33] It is both an unlearning of the world and bodies as we might know them, and a living with the potentially unknowable. Instead of taking on her expected gender role, which has already been violently restructured by Chandin who forces her to be his 'wife' (213), Mala lets the garden, which her mother and Lavinia lovingly nurtured, grow around her and slowly allows her body do as it pleases.[34] She actively cultivates a living and embodied space that defies the ordinances of the colonial domestic order.

Where colonial practices in the Caribbean included enslaving and forcing mainly African, Indian and Chinese populations to labour the land, Mala's turn to nature is neither a search for mastery nor a romanticized ideal. Mala, 'the gardener who does not attempt to domesticate or tame nature's uncanny power to decompose',[35] creates 'a Gothic landscape [of] overripe fruit, rotting vegetation, and pungent odours of decay'.[36] I would add that the odours of this un-home reflect Mala's desires to keep memories alive in the earth, and to bear witness to the intimacy of life and death:

> The scent of decay was not offensive to [Mala]. It was the aroma of life refusing to end. It was the aroma of transformation. Such odour was proof that nothing truly ended, and she revelled in it as much as she did the fragrance of cereus blossoms along the back wall of the house. (138)

Mala's un-housing is both a willed defiance of the life chosen by her father *and* her attempt to remember. Whereas the colonial order seeks to suppress all unpleasant odours as offensive, repulsive and situated in the body of the other, Mala nurtures these smells to encourage out into the open what has been hidden by her father's (and thus the Reverend's) domesticity. The smells of 'decay' as much as the aromatic and dazzling scent of the cereus plant testify to Mala's strength and her determination to survive with others. These odours bring forth traces of memories unavailable in other forms. Indeed, the only touchable, material memory that the old Mala has – beside her

31 Gopinath, p. 183.
32 Ahmed, *The Cultural Politics of Emotion*, p. 39.
33 Ibid., p. 38.
34 The younger adult Mala wonders whether 'Ambrose had ever figured out that her father pretended she was the wife who had many years ago run out on him' (213).
35 Casid, p. xx.
36 Phillips Casteel, p. 19.

body, to which I return – is a photograph of her with her sister, mother and Lavinia that she not only stares at but also raises to 'her nose' (125). Marks describes the impact of smells on the memory of the perceiver as 'a kind of image that contains the material trace of the past within it'.[37] Smells are an embodied access to memories that might otherwise remain inaccessible:

> When we smell, we are able to re-create this sense of past in our own bodies – lucky for us, because these are memories that often can't be apprehended any other way; unlucky, because the memories smell brings us can be overwhelming.[38]

Smell is the *body's* way of remembering. If Mala could be described as actively cultivating a life full of death where the 'pungent odours' keep alive what others do not remember, then I would suggest that the odoriferous opens up the possibility of an embodied epistemology. Smells contain and release memories, but these opaque sensations cannot be easily translated into words or narrative forms. Like Tyler and Otoh, we – as readers – might have to use our bodies to get close to the possibly elusive meanings of these smells. The eponymous cereus plant, which releases its 'dizzying scent' (144) only once a year, is an entangled mess of nothingness and a beautiful wild odorous plant. Through its migratory channels in the novel it bears witness to, literally carries within it, the traces of the various love stories, family violence, colonial abuse and the unspoken. It is the scent that releases love into the air and that promises trusting intimacies and shared memories. It is these shared stories and trusting gatherings that allow the process of witnessing to begin for Mala, her friends Tyler and Otoh, and her first love Ambrose. In another garden space, to where the cereus that was once in Mala's garden has now been transplanted, these four friends and lovers wait to feel the dazzling sight and smells – and thus the corporeal effects – of the flowers on their intimate lives.

Historicizing responsibility

Relating snippets of a history often absent from dominant narratives of the Caribbean, Tyler interweaves a narrative of purported benevolence (establishing an education system for children of Indian indentured labourers with the intention of converting them and their families from Hinduism to Christianity) with the violence of the idealized colonial home. *Cereus* could be described as historical fiction, with its focus on and rewriting of a specific historical period from a decolonizing queer perspective.[39] However, my aim is not to categorize a text that employs techniques from many genres

37 Laura U. Marks, *Touch: Sensuous Theory and Multisensory Media* (Minneapolis, MN: University of Minnesota Press, 2002), p. 114.

38 Ibid.

39 Although Linda Hutcheon does not discuss queer, her understanding of historiographic metafiction comes close to what I am referring to as historical fiction: The characters of historiographic metafiction 'are the ex-centrics, the marginalized'; historiographic fiction 'acknowledges the paradox of the *reality* of the past but its *textualized accessibility* to us today'; and it has an 'overt (and political) concern for its reception, its readers' (*A Poetics of Postmodernism: History, Theory, Fiction* (London: Routledge, 1988), pp. 114–15).

(including the magical real and gothic), but rather to emphasize how the novel rethinks the relationship between ethics and history. It grapples with the idea that fictionalized testimonies, with their ellipses, multivocalities and disruptive temporalities, offer ethical accounts of historical events. As Felman suggests, '[narrative] has thus become the very writing of the impossibility of writing history'.[40] In other words, the urgency to write these histories – of indentured labour and its violent intergenerational effects – demands the reimagining of the very form, language and imaginary through which histories have been constructed. Indeed, narrative renders visible the very impossibility of a coherent and complete history.

When Bhabha posits mimicry as a challenge to colonial knowledge production, he stresses how the performative structure of power creates 'the subject of colonial discourse [who] is a subject of [. . .] affective ambivalence and discursive disturbance'.[41] In creating narrative gaps and in positing racialized identity as performative, Mootoo portrays the very ways in which the subject of colonial discourse feels this ambivalence and disturbance as a shameful failure to be white. Thus, although Chandin comes close to Bhabha's formulation of colonial mimicry as '*[almost] the same but not white*',[42] *Cereus* shows the effects of desiring to be an ideal colonial mimic and the impossibility of challenging such authority. Agency does not, as Bhabha suggests, emerge in this gap (where the ambivalence of colonial discourse becomes apparent), but rather is often foreclosed through a shaming of those who fail to embody whiteness. Indeed, Chandin fears not pleasing the Reverend: '[He] had the uncomfortable feeling he was about to be sent back, a failure, to the cane fields, to live forever in the midst of his parents' shame and disappointment' (38). As Ahmed suggests, '*we feel shame because we have failed to approximate "an ideal" that has been given to us through the practice of love*'.[43] It is this desire to please, to fit in and to get close to white power that Bhabha ignores when he posits mimicry as 'the signs of a much deeper crisis'.[44] Knowledge production is thus not only the opening up of signifiers to change, but also a corporeal experience where our psychosomatic structures of knowledge are irrevocably undone. In other words, attachments to the normative values of the missionaries constrain Chandin through a shaming love.

The introduction of the indentured labour system to the Caribbean came about as a direct result of the abolition of slavery.[45] While these systems are not equivalent,

40 Felman and Laub, *Testimony*, pp. 200–1.

41 Bhabha, pp. 137–8.

42 Ibid., p. 128.

43 Ahmed, *The Cultural Politics of Emotion*, p. 106.

44 Bhabha, pp. 143–4.

45 For a general history of the Caribbean during the period of indentured labour, see K. O. Laurence, *A Question of Labour: Indentured Immigration into Trinidad and British Guiana 1875–1917* (Kingston, Jamaica: Ian Randle Publishers, 1994); David Northrup, *Indentured Labor in the Age of Imperialism, 1834–1922* (Cambridge: Cambridge University Press, 1995); and Kay Saunders (ed.), *Indentured Labour in the British Empire, 1834–1920* (London and Canberra: Croom Helm, 1984). For a much more nuanced analysis of women during the indentured labour period, see Tejaswini Niranjana, *Mobilizing India: Women, Music and Migration between India and Trinidad* (Durham, NC: Duke University Press, 2006). On the impact of missionaries and their role during Trinidad's colonial period, see Hemchand Gossai and Nathaniel Samuel Murrell (eds), *Religion, Culture and Tradition in the Caribbean* (Hampshire: Macmillan Press, 2000); and Gerhard Stilz (ed.), *Colonies, Missions, Cultures in the English-Speaking World: General and Comparative Studies* (Tübingen: Stauffenburg Verlag, 2001). More specifically on the politics of the representations of the Caribbean, see Belinda J. Edmondson (ed.), *Caribbean Romances: The Politics of Regional Representation* (Charlottesville, VA and London: University Press of Virginia, 1999).

the search for a replacement labour force after Emancipation in 1833 resulted in the introduction of a sometimes violent and certainly oppressive structure of recruitment and work. Walton Look Lai maintains that the objectives of British West Indian immigration policies post-1838 were

> to introduce a fresh laboring population whose purpose would be to act as a competitive element against the Black labor force and thereby to depress wages to what the plantocracy would consider manageable and reasonable levels. Thus the main recommendations [of the Stanley Committee in 1842] were not for a new pioneer farmer class, but a new estate labor force, and as the policy debates evolved, not even a free labor force, but one that was tied to the estates by legal and contractual mechanisms that severely constricted its nominal freedoms.[46]

What was agreed upon as a civil contract in India proved, in the Caribbean, to be a legal document that bound the labourers to the plantations on which they worked. This state-funded, -regulated and -supervised system ensured that there was little or no freedom of movement permitted for the labourers and that the plantation owners had easy recourse to the legal system should workers commit any 'offences'.[47] Indeed, in the early years, indentured labourers took 'over not merely the jobs but also the dwellings of the emancipated slaves'.[48]

However, the promises of economic betterment; of the levelling out of the hierarchical Indian caste system (which many historians agree did often occur on the passage from India to Trinidad); and of returning to India free of charge at the end of the contract or, as was the case post-1870, of purchasing land under the 'land-for-return-commutation program' (i.e. the money for the return trip being commuted into land ownership) were significant factors in encouraging migration from India and possible settlement in Trinidad throughout the whole period of indentured labour, 1838–1917.[49] Yet, this promise of social betterment, within the context of the British colonial system, is central to Chandin's eventual deterioration into an alcoholic who physically and sexually abuses his daughters. Chandin's father is represented as spending his evenings worrying whether 'enough funds might be accrued to send Chandin to a college in the capital, or even abroad to study a profession' (28). The emphasis on education,

46 Walton Look Lai, *Indentured Labor, Caribbean Sugar: Chinese and Indian Migrants to the British West Indies, 1838–1918*, intro. by Sidney W. Mintz (Baltimore, MD and London: Johns Hopkins University Press, 1993), p. 12.

47 Some of the 'offences' that Look Lai notes are: absence from work, improper performance, habitual idling, drunkenness, abusive or insulting language, wilful disobedience, threatening language or behaviour and damage to plantation property. See chapter three of Look Lai, pp. 50–86.

48 Northrup, p. 106.

49 Look Lai, p. 229. This undoing of the hierarchy of the caste system was also seen as a major deterrent in migrating to Trinidad. For those who wished to return to India, there was the risk, on return, of being seen as contaminated by the crossing of the *kala pani* and thus as an outcast. In terms of land rights, many East Indians in the West Indies took possession of land illegally, effectively squatting, prior to 1870, while others were given land on the plantation as free labourers so long as they continued to work for the plantation owner. For a detailed analysis of the many reasons indentured labourers decided to stay in Trinidad and under what conditions, see Look Lai's chapter eight, pp. 217–313.

especially education through migration, represents his parents' wish for him to move beyond the existing indentured labour system:

> Old man Ramchandin thought about life in the barracks and life in India before his recruitment to Lantanacamara. There was no difference. But by making the long journey across two oceans, he hoped to leave behind, as promised by the recruiter, his inherited karmic destiny as a servant labourer – if not for himself, at least for his son who had been born just before they left India. In Lantanacamara it was easier to slip out of caste. He planned to work hard, save money and educate Chandin out of the fields. (28)

Caught up in one of his reveries about Chandin's future, Old man Ramchandin is interrupted by the arrival of the Reverend Ernest Thoroughly, who offers not only a free education for Chandin but also a place for him in the Reverend's own home. The simultaneity of these events – Old man Ramchandin's dreams of a brighter future for Chandin and the Reverend's arrival – powerfully indicates the Reverend's promise of fulfilling the dreams of the first generation of indentured labourers and his role in the eventual devastation of the lives of Chandin and his children.

Although explored in greater detail in her later works, the divisions and tensions between Afro-Caribbeans and Indo-Caribbeans are touched upon as reasons for accepting the Reverend Thoroughly's interventions. As one of the labourers observes:

> Since the Africans let go from slavery, all eyes on how the government treating them. It have commissions from this place and from that place making sure that the government don't just neglect them. They have schools, they have regular and free medical inspection. Now, you see any schools set up for our children, besides the Reverend's school? When we get sick and we have pains, who looking after us? We looking after our own self, because nobody have time for us. Except the Reverend and his mission from the Shivering Northern Wetlands. All he want from us is that we convert to his religion. If I had children, I would convert! Besides, nobody but you really know which god you praying to. Convert, man! (30)

Conversion to Christianity is thus the only way for the Indian labourers to potentially move away from the sugar cane fields and ascend the economic and sociocultural ladder. There is an uncanny historical accuracy between the (fictionalized) Reverend Thoroughly and the (real) Reverend John Morton, who was one of the only missionaries in Trinidad to attract the children of Indian indentured labourers to attend Christian schools. The missionaries are not named as the Canadian Presbyterian Mission and most critics assume the fictionalized place of origin, the Shivering Northern Wetlands, to be Britain. While the plantation owners in Trinidad were mostly British, the missionaries working with the Indo-Caribbeans would have been Canadian.[50] The narrator in Mootoo's earlier short story 'Out on Main Street' affirms that the missionaries who targeted their conversion work on Indo-Trinidadians were Canadian: 'In de ole days when Canadian missionaries land in Trinidad dey used to make a bee-line straight for Indians from down South'.[51]

However, the ambivalence created in the novel, as to whether the colonizers, missionaries and educators might be Canadian or British, purposefully confuses the reader (especially as Canada is later named) and conflates Canadian and British colonial histories in the Caribbean. Mootoo implicates the British plantation owners, policymakers and missionaries, and the Canadian missionaries in forging a path that leads directly to Mala's abuse and eventual isolation. In addition, such ambiguity also suggests that responsibility cannot be isolated in *only* these two national spaces. Walking a line between historical accuracy and deliberate confusion, the narrative makes apparent that Chandin is the perpetrator of familial sexual violence, and that the British endorsed and ran and the Canadians supported a violent labour system and an education service based on these hierarchies.[52] Yet, such uncertainties show how the narrativization of violent transnational histories should not only be a concern with revealing which individual, institution or nation did which particular wrongdoing. In other words, pointing the finger of blame is not equivalent to taking responsibility for historical violence. Rather, responsibility is an indefinite and communal process that acknowledges the institutional structures and the individuals that support, endorse and continue such practices. It is a search for state or supra-state justice, but a recognition that this is not enough and that the work for justice continues. This labour takes place through a questioning of the production of knowledge and the impact of existing knowledge (and norms) on contemporary living. The history of Mala, of violence in the home, is the history of Indian social hierarchies, indentured labour, Canadian missionaries, British colonialism and Caribbean sociopolitical tensions. To take responsibility for such complex, partially unspoken histories is to condemn the actions of Chandin, the Reverend Thoroughly, Britain and Canada, but it is also to make a broader critique of contemporary global trends that are built on the institutions and ideologies of enslaved and indentured labour. In other words, this is a critique of a colonial past and an engagement with how present transnational relations are haunted

50 The one critical exception to the consensus regarding where exactly the Shivering Northern Wetlands are geographically situated is Vijay Mishra who argues:

> So as to differentiate between a nineteenth-century Canada committed fully to British colonial practices (the Presbyterian mission was clearly an instrument of colonization that managed the evangelical side of Empire) the 'Shivering Northern Wetlands' is distinguished from the real Canada which also exists in the novel. This real Canada is, of course, enlightened and multicultural in the way in which the earlier never was. (Vijay Mishra, *The Literature of the Indian Diaspora: Theorizing the Diasporic Imaginary* (New York: Routledge, 2007), p. 157)

51 Shani Mootoo, 'Out on Main Street', in Shani Mootoo, *Out on Main Street and Other Stories* (Vancouver, BC: Press Gang Publishers, 1993), pp. 45–57 (p. 46).

52 For an analysis of the Canadian endorsement of the recruitment of cheap labour from India to Trinidad, see Kathleen Firth, 'Resisting the Bible and the Whip: Trinidad's East Indians and the Canadian Presbyterian Missions', in *Colonies, Missions, Cultures in the English-Speaking World: General and Comparative Studies*, ed. by Gerhard Stilz (Tübingen: Stauffenburg Verlag, 2001), pp. 168–77.

by and rooted in nineteenth-century Lantanacamaran histories. It is an articulation of history as an encounter with epistemic limits, where these limits point to (and challenge) how national and familial histories may conceal the continued prevalence of these violently unequal structures in contemporary society.

How is it possible to make an intervention into histories that are repeated throughout or that haunt subsequent generations? In other words, how is change imaginable? Bhabha proposes the act of mimicry – the possibility of a performative intervention, where the copying of the colonizer produces a slippage between the original and the copy – as the point where a challenge becomes possible. However, such interventions are more complex than Bhabha suggests. Chandin's father's desire to move beyond the constraining hierarchical system of Indian society is enabled by the indentured labour system which is dependent upon colonial technologies of racialization (and while migration to the Caribbean transformed the Indian caste system for South Asians in the Caribbean, the prevalent system of class in contemporary Trinidad is haunted by these strict hierarchical divisions).[53] This focus on the desire for change through an equally restrictive system adds an important dimension to theories of performativity: it shows how the process of questioning norms, hierarchies and divisions is not simply about destabilizing them but is more specifically about the modes of coming together that are imagined into being. In other words, the desire for social mobility (expressed by both Chandin and his father) cannot become enabling performative acts, as Bhabha wishes, because the indentured labour system itself is based on a belief that some beings are naturally superior to others and that this is determined by visual markers (the skin as referent). Bhabha fails to engage with how the act of defying social norms in order to climb the socio-economic ladder does not necessarily undo but may actually reinforce hierarchical and prejudicial sociopolitical structures.

Chandin feels an increasing sense of alienation from both his Indo-Caribbean family and his adoptive Wetlander home. In an attempt to embody whiteness, because for Chandin 'there is only one destiny [and] it is white',[54] he tries desperately to distance himself from all that he understands as 'Indian' and to associate himself with everything he perceives as 'Wetlander'. However, his mimicry of the missionaries does not produce the slippage, the somewhat romantic undercutting of colonial authority, desired by Bhabha. Instead, it becomes apparent that Chandin comes close to Fanon's notion of mimicry:

> Chandin seemed to be well liked by the taller, fair, heavily accented men, but he wondered constantly whether it was because he was the Reverend's adopted son and Lavinia's brother, or because he was of the race that it was their mission to Christianize. [. . .] He copied their manners and dressed like them in the white shirts and trousers the Wetlanders considered the height of tropical fashion. (41)

53 See my work on class and sexuality in 'Illicit Intimacies'.

54 Fanon, *Black Skin, White Masks*, p. 4.

Where Chandin desires to be read as the white 'son' (33) of the Thoroughlys,[55] his parents demonstrate an active resistance towards the evangelical assimilating arm of colonialism:

> [Chandin] inquired after the foot-long brass crucifix the Reverend had given [his mother] to put above the doorway, she shyly said that she had wrapped it carefully in a clean white cloth and put it away, for safe-keeping, in a trunk. However, he noticed that the number of statues of Hindu gods and goddesses lining the walls had increased since his move to the Reverend's house. Sometimes sacred camphor and incense used in Hindu prayers coloured the air, and always a faint cloud of pooja smoke permeated his parents' hair and clothes, replacing the odour of coals and spices that used to emanate from his mother's body. He was embarrassed by his parents' reluctance to embrace the smarter-looking, smarter-acting Reverend's religion, and there soon came a time when, to his parents' dismay, he no longer visited. (31–2)

Historically, many Indo-Caribbean labourers resisted conversion to Christianity and as late as 1931 '83 percent of [Indians] in Trinidad were still adherents of their traditional religions'.[56] Brinsley Samaroo argues, 'The East Indian in Trinidad, therefore, was prepared to use the mission schools as levers for upward economic mobility, but was unwilling to forsake his ancient faith'.[57] The continuation of certain cultural practices regardless of public declarations or affiliations could be said to approximate Bhabha's mimicry.[58] Chandin's parents assert a certain 'cultural tenacity' by acting as if they have converted to Christianity in order for their son to rise out of the plantation system through education.[59] Their mimicry – '*almost the same, but not quite*' – succeeds insofar as they achieve their ends (education and social mobility for Chandin), but fails in that they lose their son to the Reverend and his moralistic religion.[60] The first generation of labourers creates an effective strategy of survival and resistance, but it is taken on as a form of shame by the subsequent generation (expressed, in the above quotation from the novel, through the sense of smell). For Chandin, the dream of social mobility – with its promise of white ascendency – is distorted through the racialized hierarchies

55 Chandin is represented as embodying the contradictions of assimilation and supposed progress insofar as he is taught to 'aspire' to whiteness through impossible desires and hurdles: he wants to be the 'son' of the Reverend so that he can be white and a part of that supposed superior world – encouraged by the Reverend and his ideals – and he wants to marry his 'sister' so as to create a 'whiter' household – discouraged by the Reverend as it would 'contaminate' the whiteness of the Thoroughly bloodline.

56 Look Lai, p. 259.

57 Brinsley Samaroo, 'The Presbyterian Canadian Mission as an Agent of Integration in Trinidad during the Nineteenth and Early Twentieth Centuries', *Caribbean Studies* 14.4 (1975), 41–55 (p. 51).

58 Certainly Look Lai attests to the defiance of Indo-Caribbeans:

> [The] cultural tenacity of the Indian immigrants represented simultaneously a form of confident self-assertion against the forces of Westernization and the colonialist order [. . .] and an umbrella of self-protection against the social derision which plantation society and the larger Creole value system had reserved for them. (Look Lai, p. 259)

59 Ibid.

60 Bhabha, p. 122.

taught in the Reverend's school. In other words, unlike his parents, Chandin cannot question the colonial moralism of the system through which he rises; instead, he grows to embody its values. It is this embodiment of colonial religiosity that Bhabha does not discuss and that is central to Chandin's inability to interrogate the very structures that are harming him. Unlike Bhabha, I would suggest that the psychic structure of racism is experienced through the body and therefore affects how agency is expressed and foreclosed.

Chandin's orientation towards an embodiment of whiteness is not simply one man's desire to be accepted within the Christian family of white ascendancy. As Fanon explains: 'Then I will quite simply try to make myself white: that is, I will compel the white man to acknowledge that I am human'.[61] Fanon captures how only whiteness grants access to the privileges of humanness, and thus how the dominant sociopolitical (in the case of Chandin, the colonial) logic enforces whiteness as a necessary aspiration if one wants to be recognized within the existing system.[62] The significance of returning to Fanon in order to flesh out Bhabha's theories is that what we witness with Chandin is that his orientation towards whiteness is felt so deeply that his sense of self is inseparable from the fantasy of belonging to the white missionary family. To violate his attachment to the white fantasy that is skin deep would be to damage the ego, the self, that is lived and felt through the skin: Chandin '[hates] his looks, the colour of his skin, the texture of his hair, his accent' (36). His sense of irreversibility and thus of inevitability (52) surfaces after the Reverend scolds him for being sexually attracted to his adoptive sister:

> Look here. You are to be a brother to Lavinia and nothing more. A brother. She is your sister and you her brother. A brother protects and helps and supports and comforts his sister. There is no harm in loving your sister. Or your mother or your father. But that love must remain pure, as pure as God's love is for his children. [. . .] You cannot, you must not have desire for your sister Lavinia. That is surely against God's will. (39–40)

The interdiction of interracial desire, through the invoking of the incest taboo and the supposed natural laws of religion, is later revealed as the Reverend's own fear of miscegenation. The latter is made patently apparent when he explains to Chandin that Lavinia is to marry her first cousin:

> He is not truly her cousin. You see, my brother married a woman who had been married once before and brought with her a child – Fenton. My brother was good enough, wouldn't you say, to bring him up as his own child, give him his name and all that sort of thing . . . but as you can see he is not a true relation. He is a marvellous gentleman by every standard, and on maturing he is slated to inherit a rather large estate from his blood father. He is a medical student. (48)

61 Fanon, *Black Skin, White Masks*, p. 73.

62 Of course, Fanon argues against these structural inequalities, and Oliver builds on Fanon's argument to argue against the logic of recognition.

The mirroring of family adoptions – Chandin's adoption by the Reverend and Fenton's adoption by the Reverend's brother – reinforces that the Reverend's prohibition of Chandin's attraction to Lavinia is less to do with incest and more with cultural origins, wealth, skin and family honour.

While Brinda Mehta suggests that Chandin has a 'predilection to indulge in incestuous thoughts and feelings', I would argue that the incest taboo is only invoked to keep the colonial hierarchy of whiteness in place.[63] It is not that his desires for Lavinia are necessarily incestuous, but rather that Chandin has so readily absorbed the Thoroughlys' racist hierarchical values that he wants to put these into practice by marrying a white woman. As Fanon states, 'By loving me [the white woman] proves I am worthy of white love. I am loved like a white man. I am a white man'.[64] Chandin's attachment to the Reverend's teachings is both intellectual and bodily. Confirming his bodily attachment to whiteness, his bodily ego's proximity to the Reverend's fantasies of white ascendancy, Chandin tries to get closer to and sexually intimate with whiteness (embodied by the Reverend's daughter). Mootoo's text breaks down the racist stereotype of men of colour as simply lusting after white women (as if it is a problem of uncontrollable sexuality on behalf of men of colour). Here, sexual desire is formative of the epidermal schema. In other words, the possibility of coming close to, of marrying the ideal, is integral to the psychic structure of the self. In terms of Bhabha's notions of mimicry and performativity, Chandin cannot challenge the Reverend's teachings because he seeks not to recognize and embody the gap between the copy and the original. Instead, he seeks to wipe out the differences between colonizer and colonized by becoming whiter, by marrying a white woman.

On hearing Lavinia is to marry Fenton, Chandin hastily decides to marry the only woman of South Asian origin at the Reverend's school, Sarah. He stops '[imitating] the Reverend's posture of confidence and power' (47) and his bodily shape begins 'to accede to its inherited nature' and to develop a 'faint echo of his father's curvature' (53). Mootoo represents his embodied nature not in terms of biological determinism but precisely through this colonial religiosity that constrains his sense of his self. Chandin resigns himself to non-whiteness, and his body acquiesces to what he understands and feels is his destiny: an intimate sense of racial inferiority and a public image of success. I agree with Gopinath that his marriage is 'a failed attempt at replicating the domestic idyll of the missionary home [and] an attempt to reproduce the patriarchal nuclear family as it took shape under indentureship'.[65] It is also his need to assuage the 'flames of anger and self-loathing' (36). The reader's inaccessibility to Chandin's thoughts and reasoning goes some way towards capturing his unexpressed humiliation and his inability to challenge the Wetlander teachings, beliefs and practices. This lack of articulation suggests that the effects of his adoptive family's racism remain unknown and emphasizes the unavailability of a language in which to speak of these injustices.

63 Indeed, the Reverend does not intervene with such strong moral values and actions in Chandin's own family life, despite Chandin's raping of Mala being public knowledge. Brinda Mehta, *Diasporic (Dis)locations: Indo-Caribbean Women Writers Negotiate the Kala Pani* (Kingston, Jamaica: University of West Indies Press, 2004), p. 200.

64 Fanon, *Black Skin, White Masks*, p. 45.

65 Gopinath, pp. 182–3.

The silencing and constraining hold of the religious family is stressed as Chandin screams 'in the silent space of his own head' (42). Without there being a causal relation, his physical violence and self-destructive acts give momentary access to Chandin's emotional expression of what cannot be spoken: institutional racism and its intergenerational effects. To some extent, Mootoo is reiterating a prevalent stereotype of South Asian men in the Caribbean as drunk and violent wife murderers.[66] In so doing, however, she situates familial abuse and alcohol dependency in a wider history of colonial violence, rather than representing these acts as specific only to men who are of South Asian origin. These are not 'biological' traits; they are individual actions that are situated in, but not determined by, the unequal and unjust sociopolitical structures of the colonial nation. Cvetkovich claims, 'The chain of causality is complicated to trace because the motives that produce incest are portrayed in a historically located fashion that verges on sympathy'.[67] Chandin is unable to question the very structures that make him ashamed of his family, his origins and his own self. He is unable to take responsibility for the violence he continues to inflict through the teaching of a theology that is reiterating and reinforcing the inferior status of himself and other South Asian Caribbeans. As a colonial missionary, Chandin knows only how to teach self-hatred, shame and hierarchies (through a doctrine that claims to be about peace, equality and love). One could go so far as to say that Chandin's failure to embody the colonial and religious dream of whiteness gives him the framework

[66] Look Lai describes the need for legislation against 'wife murders' as a form of protection for women:

> The internalization of this violence within the family was a form of social response by the Indian immigrants which became almost a stereotype of Indian male behavior towards their women. The phenomenon of 'wife murders' among the Indians was so widespread that the immigration ordinances had to legislate for the physical protection of women from spouse violence, as well as against the practice of seduction of immigrants' wives. (Look Lai, p. 144)

In contrast, Gopinath suggests that colonial legislation was less to do with helping avoid domestic violence and more with the monitoring of South Asian women's comportment:

> Significantly, this period [1870–1900] saw a tremendous increase in violence perpetuated by Indian men against Indian women, often in the form of murder. Madhavi Kale argues that violence was used as a major method of control against Indian women who sought to assert their sexual autonomy in the face of increasing legislation that would keep them firmly within the confines of conjugal domesticity. (Gopinath, p. 180)

Mehta states:

> The high incidence of rape, domestic abuse and murder during this period testifies to the attempts made by men to restrict and subjugate women within the narrow confines of rigid familial ties. Violence against women became a rationalized purging of 'female bad intent' and an effective elimination of the stigma of whoredom and social marginality that was attached to sexually independent women who tried to rewrite patriarchal scripts of Hindu womanhood through their individual and deliberate acts of self-affirmation. (Mehta, p. 19)

Although the problem of male violence towards women was a heightened phenomenon during the indentureship period and the colonial authorities legislated against it, I want also to express some caution especially towards Mehta's work. I do not understand the expression of violence by Chandin, or by men in general, as the direct result of emasculation. While the destabilization of masculinity may contribute to violent attitudes, it is simplistic to suggest it is the cause. It seems to me that Mootoo is attempting to demonstrate the ways in which some men resort to violence through a history of maltreatment. Even so, not all men who are disempowered resort to violence.

[67] Cvetkovich, p. 147.

through which to feel repulsion for his wife and children, who are 'too dark and their manner of talking too crude' (55). Again, it should be apparent that Mootoo does not portray a cause and effect relation between violence in the home and colonial religiosity, and the novel does not suggest that violence is perpetuated throughout generations because of institutional mistreatment. Indeed, Mala comes to embody the very refusal of the subsequent generations to follow in the violent footsteps of their parents. Chandin's violence towards his daughters is situated in a history of colonial racism that has continually failed to recognize the destructive and negative impact it has on the most intimate of bodily levels. Chandin cannot challenge the Reverend not because he is intellectually incapable of doing so, but because his skin burns with the shame of having failed to embody his adoptive father's religious and colonial dream of whiteness.

Unsettling reality

If the bodily ego is damaged by and distorted through the Reverend's pedagogical, missionary and domestic pursuits, then the challenge to his teachings and practices must also emerge through a re-experiencing of the bodily sensorium. In other words, imagining and enacting change is simultaneously a literal decolonizing of the matrix of heteronormative whiteness and a forging of queer belonging through a multisensory witnessing *with others*. Mala's lover Ambrose embodies the potentially transformative element of performativity *and* its simultaneous powerful ability to foreclose change. Through a focus on the mirroring of Chandin and Ambrose, we see how a challenge to the structures of violence destabilizes prevailing norms. However, to question norms by reinstating another form of knowledge that similarly makes life unbearable for those whose lives remain outside the realms of the 'real' is to violate the notion of responsibility central to my understanding of performativity. It is a closing down of the self to the other, an act of distancing self from other, which denies one's vulnerability and indebtedness to the other. The correlation between the representations of Ambrose and Chandin remains unexplored by critics, yet it offers an understanding of the way in which change emerges and is easily foreclosed throughout the generations. It also adds a much needed dimension to Bhabha's distinction between the performative and the pedagogical in showing that the latter's force exists in its capacity to keep the image of the domestic order in place as supposedly natural and organic. The correlation between these two characters further captures how a lack of communal response to institutional violence results in its perpetuation.

Chandin and Ambrose are 'successful' Indo-Caribbean students at the Reverend Thoroughly's school, where they both train as missionaries. Ambrose is raised, like Chandin, in the barracks in a 'mud house' (33 and 100). Ambrose, just as was Chandin, is the star pupil who, unlike Chandin (as there was no such scheme in place), wins a scholarship to study theology in the Shivering Northern Wetlands (209).[68] The description of the 'foreign-accented' Ambrose (207), who 'except for his skin colour [. . .] looked like a man in a foreign magazine, and with a little twist of her imagination [Mala] could picture him fair skinned' (212), is strikingly similar to the earlier one of Chandin, who 'would turn [the Wetlander] accented phrases over and over in his mind until he was brave enough to air them' (41) and who looked 'very foreign in spite of his dark skin' (31). The aspirations of Indo-Caribbean men from one generation to the next are caught up in the Christianizing mission of the colonial project that is rooted firmly in the need for a cheap and violent labour system. As Look Lai attests, 'The training of native teachers, preachers, and catechists, especially in Trinidad, produced a vigorous middle layer of Christian Indians, who carried on the work of the mission with dedication and sacrifice'.[69] The repetition of Ambrose following Chandin's path emphasizes the constraining hold of the plantation-based economy through its moral representatives, the Christian missionaries and their schools.

However, there are distinct differences between Chandin and Ambrose, which indicate a glimmer of hope that intergenerational change may happen. Ambrose, importantly, is not physically violent and, following Mala's example, he protects bugs from harm: 'We fancied ourselves protectors of snails and all things unable to defend themselves from the bullies of the world' (128). Importantly, he questions and refuses to repeat the racist, hierarchical foundation upon which theology is constructed:

> Look. At the heart of theology there is a premise – they will try to tell you otherwise, but if one listens carefully there is a premise that we humans are the primary sun around which the entire universe revolves. Unstated but certainly implied is the assumption that humans are by far superior to the rest of all nature, and that's why we are the inheritors of the earth. Arrogant, isn't it? What's more, not all humans are part of this sun. Some of us are considered to be much lesser than others – especially if we are not Wetlandish or European or full-blooded white. (214)

Ambrose rejects the ideology of Christian religiosity that reasserts the power of the colonizers on the island. Indeed, instead of using his scholarship to study theology, as was expected, he studies entomology. Under Mala's tutelage, Ambrose turns to nature to challenge the hierarchical structures upon which colonial taxonomies are built. Mala and Ambrose see the natural world as the site through which colonial religiosity can be challenged.[70] Ambrose embodies Butler's description of the power of intervention where there is a disruption of 'what has become settled knowledge and knowable reality'.[71] Amusingly, he does so by focusing on the very beings that the missionaries

68 Although, we should remember that Chandin's father had high hopes that Chandin might study abroad:

> [Old man Ramchandin] had, as usual, whipped himself up a headache with his obsessive predictions of what the state of his finances could be if he and his wife, Janaki, were to work one hour more, or even two hours more per day, so that enough funds might be accrued to send Chandin to a college in the capital, or even abroad to study a profession. (28)

69 Look Lai, p. 261.

70 Whereas natural history has been employed to endorse and justify colonial and religious violence, Mala and Ambrose turn it on its head and use it to question these ideologies and practices.

71 Butler, *Undoing Gender*, p. 27.

insist are at the bottom of the evolutionary ladder: insects (215–16). Just like Mala, who seeks to be with and not control nature (in its beautiful and disturbing forms), Ambrose gives his attention to supposedly insignificant beings in order to challenge the Reverend's teachings.

In stark contrast to the descriptions of Chandin's violence, the coming together of Mala and Ambrose is a tentative engagement of all the senses:

> Ambrose breathed in the sugary aroma of her sweat. Her scalp had a faint scent of coconut oil. Even though he wore a concoction of clove oil, bay leaves and cardamom, the natural fragrance of his sweet-and-tangy skin rose from his shirt. She knew now the taste of his skin by its smell. [. . .] He didn't smell like her father, of rum and stale genitals, the shrill severity of soured secretions. (234)

Their intimacy is a sensual olfactory delight where proximity is a reaching out to the other to express a mutual attachment. To avoid subjecting Mala to any distress, even that of being looked at, 'Ambrose would drop his eyes and stare at his own dancing feet and imagine the taste and texture and smell of her lips and tongue' (226). Their appreciation of the other's body, especially the feel and smell of the skin, portrays the potential for a different type of relationship from the violent, invasive touch of her father.[72] The emphasis on the textures, smells and tastes shows a desire for intimacy without sensorial harm. It is a turn to the body, to its senses, to portray both trust and openness.

However, Ambrose clings to the sexual norms that Tyler desperately seeks to question. He clings to an understanding of knowledge that is produced through empirical and linguistic means. He therefore fails to hear the story he is being told 'in code' by Mala (228). Although Mala 'desperately hoped that [Ambrose], of all people, might understand the things she couldn't say' (213), his inability to hear her bodily expressions is emphasized through the consequences of his doubt and inaction:

> [Ambrose] looked feebly around for a knife to protect himself, all the while feeling shame for her and for himself – as though he had been betrayed by Mala, and at the same time wrestling with the notion that she could not possibly, not conceivably have been agreeable to intimacies with her father. In that instant of hesitation he so distanced himself from Mala that, like an outside observer, he saw the world as he had known and dreamed it suddenly come undone. (246)

Ambrose's doubt, his inability to bear witness to the unspeakability of familial abuse, inflicts further violence; by failing to listen, he reinforces Mala's isolation (and continued abuse) and the impossibility of her narrative. As Ambrose flees the scene of violence, destruction and potential death, Mala relives the day her mother left without her (247). The repetition of this original traumatic departure, which is directly related to but cannot be said to have caused her father's abuse of her, forcibly demonstrates

72 It is in the following chapter on Tahar Ben Jelloun's *L'Enfant de sable* (Paris: Éditions du Seuil, 1985) where I explore, on a philosophical level, the relationship between non-violent and violent touch.

Ambrose's connection to Mala's extreme maltreatment.[73] To return to Butler, while able to question the reality constructed through and implemented by theological teachings and conversions, Ambrose is unable to question the idealized 'settled knowledge' of the family.[74] In terms of Bhabha's distinction between the pedagogical and the performative, Ambrose is the ideal colonial mimic in the challenge he poses to colonial ideology. However, his role in the continued subjugation of Mala, by leaving her alone with her violent father and not trying to help, shows how mimicry does not stop familial violence. For there to be a performative intervention, there has to be an undoing of all structures of belonging, as well as a willingness to render the self vulnerable to having one's own parameters of reality disrupted. In seeking to understand how to unsettle reality, the encounters between Mala and Ambrose show that to make a successful challenge one must learn to listen to those whose stories cannot be articulated through speech. Ambrose fails to question the silencing power of the very structures he seeks to interrogate and in so doing repeats their violence. Mala's body will remember and survive, as will that of Ambrose, but Mala's derealized life will only become a realized narrative through witnessing narrators who can listen to the body's expression of pain.

To render bearable his moral judgement of Mala, Ambrose sleeps the rest of his life away, waking only once a month to send her provisions. His body literally takes on the responsibility of his actions towards Mala and, in so doing, shuts itself down. The possibility of performative change is foreclosed as Ambrose closes down his senses. He tells Otoh that he 'slept to avoid the nausea that seemed to sour [his] insides and the weight of defeat crushing [his] heart' (254–5). Ambrose refuses to feel his body, to sense the impact of his actions and to bear witness to a collective (if passive) violence towards Mala. This absence of sensorial experiences reinforces that the body is central to the possibility of achieving change (and to maintaining the status quo). Ambrose embodies the continuation of violence throughout the generations not so much as the physical violence of Chandin but as the inertia and inaction of accepting the status quo. Communal lethargy and apathy are how the villagers respond:

> While many shunned [Chandin] there were those who took pity, for he was once the much respected teacher of the Gospel, and such a man would take to the bottle and to his own child, they reasoned, only if he suffered some madness. And, they further reasoned, what man would not suffer a rage akin to insanity if his own wife, with a devilish mind of her own, left her husband and children. Whether they disliked him or tolerated his existence, to everyone Chandin was Sir. (211)

73 Although Ambrose does not fight in this scene, indeed it is Mala who protects him by tackling Chandin to the floor, it is Ambrose who, on fleeing, hits Chandin on the head with the door. Mala returns to the scene and repeatedly hits Chandin on the head with the door. She then takes him down to the basement and leaves him locked in there. It is unclear who kills Chandin or even if he dies alone in the basement unable to get help. It is, however, clear that Ambrose knocks Chandin unconscious and that Mala ensures he does not wake up until at least after she has locked the basement door.

74 Butler, *Undoing Gender*, p. 27.

In order to transform Paradise there must be an intergenerational wilfulness that disrupts the acceptance of an anaesthetized inertia. If it is to defy the constraining hold of the colonial regime over intimate relationships, this disruption must be bodily, an opening up of the senses and the self to the other, as we witnessed in the intimacy between Mala and Ambrose. It must follow Mala and Ambrose's decolonizing epistemologies, where nature does not serve the pedagogical arm of the missionaries. Yet, change requires more than what Ambrose and the community can offer.

Embodied survival

Where Ambrose closes down his senses through his almost-permanent state of sleepiness, Mala remains awake, with all her senses alert to the smells, colours, sights, textures and sounds of nature. Her mode of being with the world does not require language:

> The wings of a gull flapping through the air titillated her soul and awakened her toes and knobby knees, the palms of her withered hands, deep inside her womb, her vagina, lungs, stomach and heart. Every muscle of her body swelled, tingled, cringed or went numb in response to her surroundings – every fibre was sensitized in a way that words were unable to match or enhance. (136)

Mala coexists with the earth and its inhabitants, while remaining isolated away from all human life:

> Mala's companions were the garden's birds, insects, snails and reptiles. She and they and the abundant foliage gossiped among themselves. She listened intently. With an ear pressed to the ground she heard ant communities building, transporting food and breeding. She listened to worms coiling arduously from place to place. She knelt on the ground and whispered to the grass and other young plants, encouraging them to grow, and then she listened as they stretched up to her. She did not intervene in nature's business. When it came time for one creature to succumb to another, she retreated. (137)

Her intimacy with the natural world is an active imagining of other ways of being, which do not cause harm to either herself or others. Mala communicates with her surroundings in a way that may be considered out of the ordinary or even ab-normal. Cvetkovich argues that 'Mala weaves traumatic memory into a protective fantasy whose creative logic is only reductively described as insane'.[75] This narrative of ability or disability – of Mala's strategies for survival – is queer in its turn away from institutional intervention and towards unknown possibilities. I agree with Cvetkovich that Mala creates a world different from that of her father. However, I would insist that she does

[75] Cvetkovich, p. 148.

this to remember, to find ways of communicating that bear witness to her daily life of ordinary survival. Mala's creative reconstructions of household furniture further testify to her reconfiguring of the home, her experience of sexual trauma and her need to remember. In other words, she forges memories in and on the form taken by everyday objects. She creates new meanings by transforming how we engage with and read the (no longer useful) objects.

In her un-home, Mala witnesses daily pain, death, life and survival. Just as she bears witness to nature's ugliness and beauty, nature grows around Mala, giving a sense of closeness, of touching and of being present. Mala remembers her pain and appeals for a witness of her own by inflicting pain on her body:

> She thrust her finger into the bottle, scooped out a heavy clump of raw pepper and shoved the finger into her mouth. [. . .] She didn't swallow, keeping the fire on her tongue, by then so blistered that parts of the top layer had already disintegrated and other areas had curled back like rose petals dipped in acid. [. . .] Her flesh had come undone. But every tingling blister and eruption in her mouth and lips was a welcome sign that she had survived.
>
> She was alive. (143–4)

Damaging the tongue is Mala's embodied means of remembering, of bearing witness: 'Her body remembered' (188). Jane Kilby argues, 'Self-harm is a naked testimony risking itself for a reading, and even though it cannot secure it, it appeals, nevertheless, for a careful leap of witnessing'.[76] What is important here is not so much the categorization of the act but how damage to the self is testament to the body's capacity to communicate without recourse to language. The need for the flesh to testify to survival and to continued life demonstrates Mala's risking of her own physical self in order to be heard, to sense her self and to bear witness to pain. It is a way of feeling a body that has been denied sensory expression by her father's repeated sexual and physical abuse. The undoing of the tongue, as the main tool of communication, is also Mala marking 'her memory on her tongue, but by disabling it, rather than by using it for speech'.[77] Pain can only be communicated through a manifestation of pain. Her memories are alive in her body but the tongue offers only a glimpse of her life. Mala is searching for someone who can hear this body and bear witness to the intensity of the memories, which is manifested as physical damage and visceral communication. Mala's tongue is a tangible trace of a history that has failed to be recorded in words.

From a young age, Mala is attentive not only to a natural world where life and death coexist, but also to what Gopinath calls 'impossible desires'. Despite having 'no words to describe what she [. . .] realized was their secret' (60), Mala recognizes the attraction between her mother and Lavinia. Although Mala protects Sarah and Lavinia

[76] Jane Kilby, 'Carved in Skin: Bearing Witness to Self-Harm', in *Thinking Through the Skin*, ed. by Sara Ahmed and Jackie Stacey (London and New York: Routledge, 2001), pp. 124–42 (p. 141).

[77] Kyungwon Hong, p. 93.

from Chandin by warning them whenever he returns home,[78] she is unable to prevent him from eventually *seeing* this unimaginable desire:

> [Chandin] watched through the lens. In the midst of their laughter and frivolity, he did not fail to see Lavinia place herself behind Mama, and he saw Mama press herself against Lavinia. Through the lens he watched carefully and saw Lavinia's hands rest tenderly on Mama's waist. He saw it all only because, that day, he intended to. And Pohpoh [Mala] watched him as he did. (62)

Chandin needs an aid – the lens of a camera – to visualize and recognize queer desires. If, in the colonial order of things, the camera – like the gaze – is a method of control and subjugation, then this scene portrays Chandin's scopic attempt to reassert power over these women. Cvetkovich describes this photograph as 'like the flash of traumatic experience or memory, condensing social relations into a single still image that has the power to shock'.[79] The event as photograph serves to freeze the image as that which haunts this family for the rest of their lives. After Sarah flees with Lavinia and the two girls are inadvertently left behind, Chandin destroys all photographs except for this one that, unbeknown to him, Mala guards close to her body. The only remnant that remains of these two women and their 'secret' is this photograph, almost as if what cannot be said, what cannot be known, can only be pointed to through an image of intimacy. As Marianne Hirsch iterates, '[Family photographs are] eloquent witnesses of an unspeakable history, in themselves stubborn survivors'.[80] The photograph is a material remnant that, despite the invisibility of the relationship in Paradise, shows Mala's determination to remember both what has not been named (through the unspeakability of the relationship) and the traumatic absence of her mother. Prosser, in *Light in the Dark Room*, describes photographs as 'evidence of absence'.[81] He states, '[Offering] insight into the inexorable loss that *is* life, photography captures a reality that we would otherwise not see, that we would choose *not* to see'.[82] Where the taking of the photograph captured a previously unseen queer relationship, the destruction of all the photographs by Chandin is the refusal to see what has happened: that his wife has eloped with the woman he has always loved. In contrast, Mala's act of taking secret possession of the one remaining photograph, the one image that served to reveal to Chandin what was happening between Sarah and Lavinia, is her ability to accept loss as part of life. The photograph is Mala's act of bearing witness to her mother's queer desires, to the loss of protection from the violence of her father and to the material traces of her lost family.

78 Mala is represented as not quite cognizant of her behaviour and yet aware enough to recognize that when Chandin returns home she must make lots of noise to ensure her mother is disturbed and therefore not close to Lavinia.

79 Cvetkovich, p. 146.

80 Hirsch, p. 13.

81 Jay Prosser, *Light in the Dark Room: Photography and Loss* (Minneapolis, MN: University of Minnesota Press, 2005), p. 1.

82 Ibid., p. 2.

This cataclysmic moment, which leads to Sarah and Lavinia fleeing the island without the children, shatters Chandin's reality and frames (without causing) the events that ensue:

> One night [Chandin] turned, his back to Asha, and in a fitful, nightmarish sleep, mistook Pohpoh [Mala] for Sarah. He put his arm around her and slowly began to touch her. Pohpoh opened her eyes. Frightened and confused by this strange, insistent probing, she barely breathed, pretending to be fast asleep. She tried to shrink away from under his hand. Suddenly, awakening fully, he sat up. Then he brought his body heavily on top of hers and slammed his hand over her mouth. She opened her eyes and stared back at him in terror. A sweat covered his face and neck, and dripped on her. Glaring and breathing heavily like a mad dog, he pinned her hands to the bed and forced her legs apart. (70)

Chandin defies the Reverend's interdiction of incest by raping his own daughter. Unable to challenge the Reverend's racist invocation of the incest taboo, Chandin responds not by questioning the ideas or power of the Reverend and his school (or even by ceasing to be a missionary). Instead, Chandin turns to his daughter's young body as a site over which he can assert not only his own authority, but also his desires. He clings to the categories through which we make sense of the world by replacing one woman (his daughter) for another (his wife), because both are his 'property' (238). However, Mala uses her own body to protect her sister, Asha, from her father's sexually abusive touch. Even when her father calls for Asha, Mala presents her body to him and thus refuses to accept that Chandin can abuse her younger sister. Although Asha is present in the above scene, I would argue that she does not bear witness to what takes place. The traumatic breaking of the familial frame of reference means both daughters cannot acknowledge the events as they unfold. Asha's inability to bear witness at the time is reinforced by her continued absence even at the close of the narrative. The lack of witness, the non-presence of a person who can bear witness to the destructive violence to which Mala is subjected, is further emphasized when the judge later dismisses Mala as not responsible for the death of her father because, in his words, '[There] are no witnesses. No witnesses! And there is no evidence that a crime was ever committed' (8). As Mehta rightly points out what unfolds is that Mala should never have been on trial for the murder of her father but that Chandin should have been tried for his abuse of Mala.[83] The absence of any case against Chandin indicates the judicial system's unwillingness to deal with a history of familial violence. The attempt to prosecute Mala for murdering her father powerfully portrays the idea that there is no institutional justice. In other words, another type of justice must be sought or, more specifically, a different type of witnessing must be imagined into being and enacted if the violation of Mala's life is to be recognized.

[83] Mehta, p. 199.

Intergenerational witnessing

I want to conclude this chapter with a focus on the multisensory engagements that are the foundation for queer postcolonial epistemologies, and intimate and trusting gatherings. After Ambrose abandons Mala, leaving her alone with her almost-dead father, she 'all but rid herself of words' (136). Whereas Ambrose fails to hear 'the things [Mala] couldn't say' (213), Tyler recognizes 'the words in her eyes', the 'pleading' in them (23). He becomes 'accustomed to reading, as if by Braille, her twitches and her gasps' (107). When Tyler first meets the silent Mala in the alms house he touches her and tells the reader: 'This one touch turned her from the incarnation of fearful tales into a living human being, an elderly person such as those I had dedicated my life to serving' (11). Furthermore, his nose is pricked as he becomes 'aware of her odour'. He adds: 'She had a curiously natural smell' and 'She did not have the sweet yet sour smell I had come to expect whenever close to an old person. Instead, an aroma resembling rich vegetable compost escaped from under the sheet' (12). Mala returns to being read, understood and connected to as a 'human being'. Here, to be physically touched is to be recognized as human again. Tyler is reading Mala as belonging to the category of the human, like other human beings, and yet as distinct and individual, as not smelling like others.[84] It is Tyler's multisensory reading that opens up avenues of communication between these two queer characters, just as it did between Mala and nature. Their vulnerability – and thus their acute engagement with their embodied smells, sounds, movements and tactility – is the possibility of bearing witness.

Tyler coexists with Mala because he senses that his 'actions spoke more eloquently than any words' (18). Similarly, when Mala gives Tyler a female nurse's uniform, she does not give recognition through an appropriating gaze but instead continues piling pieces of furniture:

> The reason Miss Ramchandin paid me no attention was that, to her mind, the outfit was not something to either congratulate or scorn – it simply was. She was not one to manacle nature, and I sensed that she was permitting mine its freedom. (83)

Just as Tyler realizes he 'had become her witness' (107), Mala bears witness to his embodied desires by encouraging him to express himself without the need for external (namely visual) recognition. If recognition is understood through optical relations where the power dynamic of master and slave dominates, then *Cereus* approximates Oliver's critique of recognition as 'a symptom of the pathology of oppression itself'.[85] Mala extricates her relationships with others from this dominant mode of recognition, the one within which her father was trapped, where 'the pathology of oppression

[84] This movement between Mala being recognized as belonging to the general human category as well as being distinctly individual is reinforced through the psychic splitting of her sense of self in two: the child Pohpoh and the adult Mala. We are told in the novel that '[Pohpoh] was a common nickname affectionately given to children' (50). In contrast, Mala is the individual adult character, distinct from others.

[85] Oliver, p. 9.

creates the need in the oppressed to be recognized by their oppressors, the very people most likely not to recognize them'.[86] Instead, Mala gives to Tyler a material gift, which expresses her understanding of his embodied needs and desires. Their response-ability – their ability to respond to and with both self and other – is an address to the other that opens up the possibility of communication.[87] This form of recognition is not based on objectification of the other or on one subject conferring humanness on an other. Rather it is an embodied and material process, and a sensorial and uncertain engagement. Multisensory recognition is integral to an ethics of witnessing and becomes possible through bodily communication and the exchange of objects that have touched multiple histories and bodies.

In order to bear witness to the unarticulated, there must be a bodily risk and an ontological unravelling. In Shildrick's words:

> It is in the embodied gesture of touch that we may sustain a reciprocal sense of solicitude and intimacy that is grounded in the mutual instabilities and unpredictability of our corporeal becoming. To touch and be touched speaks to our exposure to, and immersion in, the world of others, and to the capacity to be moved beyond reason, in the space of shared vulnerabilities.[88]

To risk one's self is not to sacrifice who one is, as if there is an already predetermined and unchanging self, or to invite violence; it is to be open to the touch of others and to being transformed by this intimacy. Otoh willingly tries to show to Mala his own sense of vulnerability and therefore his capacity to listen in a way that differs from his father. After Ambrose falls down the stairs, Otoh takes on 'his inherited task' (119) and delivers food parcels to Mala once a month. In contradistinction to his father, Otoh repeatedly tries to gain contact with Mala in order to understand the attachment between her and his father; to protect Mala, in a way his father has failed to do so; and to potentially reunite the childhood friends. Defying his masculine body in an attempt to meet Mala, Otoh puts on his mother's dress and risks being seen by the community in Paradise not as himself but as a man who is cross-dressing in women's clothes (130). He does so, as he later explains to Tyler, to convey his vulnerability and openness towards Mala:

> I felt as though she and I had things in common. She had secrets and I had secrets. Somehow I wanted to go there and take all my clothes off and say, 'Look! See? See all this? *I am different!* You can trust me, and I am showing you that you are the one person I will trust. And I am one person, for sure, for sure, that you can trust. I will be your friend.' (133)

Otoh stresses that his feelings of being 'different' and of having 'secrets' should allow Mala to trust him. As with Tyler when he meets Mala, Otoh wants to reassure her that she can trust him.[89] To this extent, the above passage conveys a vulnerability, a

86 Oliver, p. 9.
87 Ibid., p. 15.
88 Shildrick, *Embodying the Monster*, p. 117.
89 At the beginning of the novel Tyler similarly states to Mala, '[. . .] trust me. You must, you *must* trust me!' (22).

riskiness, a willingness to be open and to be transformed in the very contact of the encounter with Mala. As Simon Critchley argues, 'The end of certainty can be the beginning of trust'.[90] Thus, to become undone, and to thereby give up the certainty of knowledge, is the potential to imagine into being a collective space of trust. This sense of belonging is tentative and changing; it emerges through the embodied and collective process of storytelling.

After failing to meet Mala in his mother's dress, Otoh puts on the clothes his father wore to visit Mala on his return from the Shivering Northern Wetlands. In terms of Bhabha's mimicry, Otoh intervenes in history to bring about a different outcome. In other words, the story is repeated and resignification occurs. More importantly, I would suggest that his openness to the unknown is what makes his act performative. No one has ever come face to face with Mala since she isolated herself away in her garden. Otoh is willing to take the risk because he wants to rectify his father's unarticulated wrongdoings (Otoh has very limited knowledge of what his father has done). He wants to apologize for the unknown by taking responsibility in the present. His determination to get close to Mala is a desire to bear witness to her repeatedly ignored existence by recognizing their intertwined queer lives. Otoh's act is performative insofar as he seeks to creatively re-enact the past by donning another man's clothes, which Mala should recognize. In so doing, he acknowledges the power of material objects to unsettle reality. It is through a shared, intergenerational touching – where the clothes that brushed against the skin of both Ambrose and Mala, now touch Otoh, who seeks to reach out to Mala – that another outcome becomes a reality.

It is impossible for Otoh, wearing his mother's dress, to meet Mala, as such a sartorial act is the embodiment of a woman who is deeply perturbed by Mala's haunting presence in her married life with Ambrose. More importantly, Otoh cannot meet Mala dressed as a woman as she is 'not one to manacle nature' (83) and would not ask for a vulnerability that might undermine his sense of self. Furthermore, the donning of Ambrose's suit is an attempt to step back in time and embody the memories of those who aspired to climb the Lantanacamaran social ladder by participating in an education system based on sexist, racist and homophobic hierarchies. Otoh tries to touch the past through his contact with its material remnants, that is the suit, and by bringing together this artefact with the woman who loved the man who wore it. By putting himself into the material space of memories, Otoh seeks to bring the past back to life in order to transform the present. If this act can thereby be described as performative, it is not simply because it is the narration of a different version of the past. It is performative in that it both refuses to accept the status quo *and* is the beginning of an unknown communal gathering that attempts to collectively articulate the unspoken.

Otoh's stepping into a past of which he has little knowledge is a queer act that decolonizes the myth of Mala (as a woman who lived as a wife to her father). Not only is the repetition of the past an attempt to understand the present, it is also the queering of the past. Otoh traverses a generational division in order to become other to his self. In so doing, he queers the supposedly immutable boundaries of the past

[90] Simon Critchley, 'Introduction', in *The Cambridge Companion to Levinas*, ed. by Simon Critchley and Robert Bernasconi (Cambridge: Cambridge University Press, 2006), pp. 1–32 (p. 26).

and present, father and son, and man and woman. This queer postcolonial time, which cannot quite stay straight, is also an instance of traumatic memory that is repeatedly relived. Unlike many critics who write on *Cereus*, I would suggest that trans embodiment is not a simple metonym for the fluidity of gendered being in a globalized world;[91] rather, Mootoo's turn to the body is an exploration of how queer (i.e. non-normative) embodiments are an existing part of Caribbean realities. The text also portrays the search for modes of being with others that do not forget the process of transitioning and that bear witness to the diversity of queer identities. Otoh's embodied transition portrays an interrogation of the normative categories of belonging that have played a significant role in Mala's isolation. He steps into his father's life not as Mala's lover but as the one who hopes to protect Mala in a way that his father failed to do: 'I wanted to go up there, to meet her and apologize for [Ambrose] and say that even though he was my father I wasn't a coward like him and that I would take care of her' (134). The unknown is what makes Otoh's action ethical. In Butler's words:

> Perhaps most importantly, we must recognize that ethics requires us to risk ourselves precisely at moments of unknowingness, when what forms us diverges from what lies before us, when our willingness to become undone in relation to others constitutes our chance of becoming human.[92]

He recognizes the need for action and responds to Mala's sequestration not by refusing to acknowledge it like everyone else but by facing the unknown. On seeing Otoh dressed in his clothes, Ambrose whispers to him,

> I remember now, son. You are indeed a reincarnation but not of a person per se, merely of a forgotten memory. You are a perfect replica of me in my prime. [By] appearing in front of me like this you have given me the gift of remembering. I am sure I cannot thank you enough. (155)

Through a sartorial reminder of himself and his past, Ambrose begins to remember. Nevertheless, Ambrose also warns Otoh, 'You go and make death restless dress like that today' (157). On the one hand, Otoh does symbolically wake Ambrose up from the dead and, similarly, brings Mala back into the present. On the other hand, when Mala shows Otoh the decomposing body of her dead father, telling him that, 'He can't hurt us now, Ambrose' (176), it is clear that the dead will not rise. Otoh has not revived the dead but rather has, as his father later tells him, 'unleashed the business of an ugly, lurking phantom' (183).

Otoh enters Mala's garden carrying the gramophone Ambrose brought back for Mala from the Shivering Northern Wetlands. He plays the music along to which she

91 See, for example, Howells, *Contemporary Canadian Women's Fiction*; Vikki Cook, 'Basking in a Cloudless Sky: Refiguring National Identity in Shani Mootoo's *Cereus Blooms at Night*', *Canadian Studies in Europe: The Making of Canada*, vol. 4 (2005), 41–51; and Heather Smyth, 'Sexual Citizenship and Caribbean-Canadian Fiction: Dionne Brand's *In Another Place, Not Here* and Shani Mootoo's *Cereus Blooms at Night*', *ARIEL* 30.2 (1999), 141–60.

92 Butler, *Giving an Account of Oneself*, p. 136.

and Ambrose used to dance. James Baldwin describes the link between music and time emphasizing the materiality of memory:

> Music is our witness, and our ally. The beat is the confession which recognises, changes and conquers time. Then history becomes a garment we can wear and share, and not a cloak in which to hide; and time becomes a friend.[93]

Prior to Otoh's arrival, Mala is represented as deep in memories of her past, and thus when she finally hears the music she sees not Otoh but Ambrose (172). The music reinforces the sense of another time, and history is forged through this shared 'garment'. Their sensorial intimacy as they dance to the music comes close to Paul Gilroy's description of how music, especially for those subjected to racial inequalities and violence, can be used as a form of political agency.[94] Mala, living multiple times and seeing the man who originally wore the suit, shows Otoh the dead body of her father. While Mala hopes the body reassures Ambrose that her father can no longer do any 'harm' (173), Otoh bolts away from her garden and she relives Ambrose's original traumatic departure.[95] While Otoh's intervention into Mala's past results in the police entering her house, her being forcibly moved out of her garden-home, and the destruction of her gothic, fairy-tale garden, it is also the catalyst that brings her together with Tyler, Ambrose and Otoh. Music, dancing and decaying bodies destabilize time, and Mala's queer world is destroyed.

The sense of belonging subsequently and tentatively forged by these four characters coheres around the olfactory sense. The centrality of the senses to their gathering is reinforced by Otoh's act of retrieving the cereus plant from Mala's garden before burning the house down to destroy any evidence. This 'uninteresting tangle of leafage' (23) is a trace of the migrations of the Ramchandin family and its connections to the Thoroughlys: the cereus is transplanted from Lavinia's mother's (Chandin's adoptive mother's) well-ordered garden to the more unruly Ramchandin one, where eventually it supports the back of the house, and Tyler will recognize it as something he 'had seen [. . .] in the Exotic Items Collection of the SNW National Botanical Gardens' (23). Otoh brings it to the alms house as a gift to Mala: it is a surviving remnant of her mother's relationship with Lavinia and an odoriferous trace of the memories contained in her garden-home. The plant mirrors Mala's life history, testifies to the strength of her survival, and keeps alive the traces of all the unarticulated and unknown memories.

The plant, with its overwhelming smell, is a sensory evocation of the various places it has inhabited and a material artefact touched by the unspoken histories of colonial, familial violence. As Marks suggests, 'Objects, bodies, and intangible things hold histories within them that can be translated only imperfectly'.[96] Otoh is 'a witness to her past' (173) as he reaches out to touch her. His act of setting Mala's house alight recognizes that Mala should not be tried for the murder of her father. His gesture of

93 James Baldwin, 'Of the Sorrow Songs: The Cross of Redemption', as cited in Paul Gilroy, *The Black Atlantic: Modernity and Double-Consciousness* (London: Verso Books, 1993), p. 203.

94 See Paul Gilroy, *The Black Atlantic: Modernity and Double-Consciousness* (London: Verso Books, 1993).

95 It is also important to remember that Mala experiences Ambrose's original departure as a traumatic reliving of being left behind by her mother, when Sarah fled the island with her lover Lavinia.

96 Marks, *The Skin of the Film*, p. 131.

retrieving the cereus plant gives to Mala a memory of what she has lost. As an explicit symbol of blossoming love, the gift of the cereus expresses what he failed to do in his original encounter with her: to protect her and express a deep attachment. He ensures the continued life of the historically mobile, variously transplanted and mesmerizingly odorous cereus plant. Its beauty (seen only once a year for one night) is testament to the cycle of life and death, and thus to the tentative intimacy between Mala, Otoh, Tyler and Ambrose.

If, as I have suggested, Otoh bears witness to Mala's survival, he alone cannot take responsibility for the histories of indentured labour, of the colonial missionary education system, of forced and chosen migrations and separations, and of the familial violence that have all contributed to Mala's present isolation. Otoh sets in motion an embodied process of bearing witness to the physical violence to which Mala has been subjected and the disastrous consequences of his own father's inertia. It is Tyler who goes on, after Otoh's encounter with Mala, to bear witness to Mala's story through the acts of listening, caring and eventually narrating the stories we – as readers – have just heard. Similarly, Mala enables Tyler to publicly embody his femininity, or, as he says, 'to unabashedly declare myself, as it were' (268). To take responsibility is bound up in the acts of listening, narrating, waking up and expressing the body; it is to enter into a collective gathering where recognition is a multisensory engagement with others; and it is queer in its decolonizing of the colonial home by living with a constant undoing of assumed knowledge. Unlike Laub's description, there is no single listener but rather a community of witnesses, who through a mutual vulnerability begin to translate into words histories of violence.

The sense of belonging forged through their multisensory intimacies and storytelling is best explained by Ambrose, who, after waking up from a life-long slumber, tells his son: 'I slept because I couldn't face myself. [. . .] In a way I didn't merely lose Mala Ramchandin. I lost myself also' (254–5). When Butler asks, 'Who "am" I, without you?', she suggests in her response an entanglement so deep that where 'I' begin and 'you' end is not so evident. In her words: 'I think I have lost "you" only to discover that "I" have gone missing as well'.[97] Ambrose describes this 'tie', this unbearable loss and this passionate love, as not only the loss of an other but also the indescribable loss of self. It is the same tie – what Shildrick calls 'the mutual instabilities and unpredictability of our corporeal becoming' – that prompts Otoh into action and Tyler into listening to Mala through her bodily communication.[98]

As the four characters await the blossoming of the cereus plant, Mala speaks 'her first public words' (269). The 'whispering' of 'Poh, Pohpohpoh, Poh, Poh, Poh' (269) recalls her creative act of splitting herself in two in order to protect her younger self and to live adventures the adult Mala would never experience. The act of speech reminds the reader that although Mala has said little throughout this novel, to say she has been silent would fail to describe her defiance and determination to be heard. Her silence has brought about the necessity for other, less violent, ways of listening and

97 Butler, *Precarious Life*, p. 22.
98 Shildrick, *Embodying the Monster*, p. 117.

communicating. The telling of Mala's tale may bring about change, as Bhabha would suggest happens with postcolonial literature. Yet the novel insists that narratives of the past can only bring about change when they are connected to the present. Such stories must unravel how such historical violence is connected to contemporary unequal sociopolitical structures. Thus, at the end of the novel, we learn that Asha's repeated epistolary attempts to contact Mala failed 'because the righteous postman, deeming the Ramchandin house to be a place of sin and moral corruption, refused to go up there' (263). The absence of Asha speaks to a history untold, to the gaps in knowledge, and to the sadness and violence of separation. These gaps are what necessitate an indefinite response, not only to tell more stories, but also to recognize what counts as history. This encounter with epistemic limits reinforces that the translation of Mala's tale into the narrative form is an incomplete act. There is yet more to tell. The risking of the self in coming close to Mala and to her stories, along with a willingness to assume an infinite responsibility for the narration of the tale, is what makes these encounters performative. Performativity is thus the undoing of the self and of existing parameters of knowledge in a multisensorial engagement with others. These embodied histories challenge the colonial structure of knowledge and queerly seek out forms of belonging that undo such normatively violent institutions. As the cactus bears the promise of awakening all the senses, for at least one night, Tyler and Otoh's love blossoms. The four characters congregate around the plant not only to publicly demonstrate their communal ties but also to bear witness to the histories contained within it and about to be opaquely released through its scent. Mala, Ambrose, Otoh and Tyler bear witness to the silence of what is yet to be known, yet to be imagined and yet to be realized. The blossoming of the cereus will release odours containing traces of many memories but in order to translate them the listeners will have to become undone by what their bodies sense.

2

Monstrous Witnessing in Tahar Ben Jelloun's *L'Enfant de sable*

Embodied stories

> *[It] is in the very power to disturb and unsettle, to resist final intelligibility, that the monstrous beckons to a more open future.*[1]
>
> *Ce livre, je l'ai lu, je l'ai déchiffré pour de tels esprits. Vous ne pouvez accéder sans traverser mes nuits et mon corps. Je suis ce livre. Je suis devenu le livre du secret ; j'ai payé de ma vie pour le lire. Arrivé au bout, après des mois d'insomnie, j'ai senti le livre s'incarner en moi, car tel est mon destin.*[2]
>
> *[This book, I have read it. I have deciphered it for others. You cannot gain access to it without traversing my nights and my body. I am this book. I have become the book of the secret; I have paid with my life to read it. Having reached the end, after months of sleepless nights, I felt the book become embodied within me, for such is my fate.]*[3]

In the above epigraph from Tahar Ben Jelloun's novel *L'Enfant de sable* [*The Sand Child*], the first storyteller claims there is no separation between his own body and the life story of the main protagonist. He embodies the book and, therefore, if the audience is to understand the narrative it must listen to his authoritative perspective. As each storyteller claims to have authority on this tale of gender uncertainty, gender inequality, French colonial rule, and Moroccan nationalism and independence, the

1 Shildrick, *Embodying the Monster*, p. 130.

2 Tahar Ben Jelloun, *L'Enfant de sable* (Paris: Éditions du Seuil, 1985), pp. 12–13. Hereinafter all references to this novel will be given in the body of the chapter in parentheses.

3 For an English version of this text, see Tahar Ben Jelloun, *The Sand Child*, trans. by Alan Sheridan (Baltimore, MD: Johns Hopkins University Press, 2000). However, all translations throughout this chapter are my own. I concur with both Suzanne Gauch and Robert Harvey that Sheridan's translation of the novel, while invaluable, often leaves out sentences and passages or gives a rather unnuanced version of the language employed. The novel, thus, loses its multi-interpretational possibilities. See Suzanne Gauch, *Liberating Shahrazad: Feminism, Postcolonialism and Islam* (Minneapolis, MN: University of Minnesota Press, 2007), p. 152; and Robert Harvey, 'Purloined Letters: Intertextuality and Intersexuality in Tahar Ben Jelloun's *The Sand Child*', in *Articulations of Difference: Gender Studies and Writing in French*, ed. by Dominique D. Fisher and Lawrence R. Schehr (Stanford, CA: Stanford University Press, 1997), pp. 226–45 (p. 227).

audience witnesses a steady disintegration not only of the physical text within which the story is alleged to be contained but also of the narrative itself and those who try to contain its possibilities. Unfolding in an unnamed square redolent of Jemaa al Fna in Marrakech, the narrative of Ahmed's life takes over the psychosomatic existence of both the storytellers and the listeners. Challenged by a member of the audience, the first storyteller concedes the narrative to this second narrator who similarly asserts:

> Fragmentaire mais non dépourvu de sens, l'événement s'impose à ma conscience de tous les côtés. Le manuscrit que je voulais vous lire tombe en morceaux à chaque fois que je tente de l'ouvrir et de délivrer des mots, lesquels empoisonnent tant et tant d'oiseaux, d'insectes et d'images. Fragmentaire, il me possède, m'obsède et me ramène à vous qui avez la patience d'attendre. (108)
>
> [Fragmentary, but not without meaning, the story is stamped on every part of my consciousness. The manuscript I wanted to read to you falls to pieces whenever I try to open it and free its words, which poison so many birds, insects, and images. Fragmentary, it possesses me, obsesses me, and brings me back to you who have the patience to wait.]

The storytellers cannot quite contain the story, as they claim they would like to. Each storyteller attempts to construct a logical and chronological narrative whereby Ahmed's life story is rendered understandable and entertaining, and a clear metaphor for Moroccan politics during and after French colonial rule. Ahmed's struggle to comprehend his sense of self and his sense of maleness, after being born female and raised a boy, is an allegory for the transition from French protectorate rule to the post-1956 independent state of Morocco, *and* the effects of both colonialism and nationalism on psychosomatic existence. Concomitantly, his attempt to forge an identity not determined by his father begins as he steps outside the family home, and this search for a post-masculine sense of self parallels Morocco's own search for a post-independence identity.

However, the incessant impulse and desire to make sense of the story and to produce a definitive version (of individual and national self) is foiled. Words literally escape the storytellers' grasp, leading to a loss of control over the narrative and their selves. *L'Enfant* makes a spectacle out of the impossibility of lording authority over texts, language and bodies. In its incessant repetition of the same story, its emphasis on collective stories, and its insistence that language and texts are embodied, the novel makes a turn towards ethics. While the story may slip out of their hands, it never leaves their bodies. Audience members are not passive listeners; instead, they actively take up the story and reinvent it with, albeit temporary, authority. Divisions between storytellers and audience members are blurred, and the line between fiction and reality suspended when some speakers not only claim to have known Ahmed but also assert that they are the main protagonist of the story being relayed. The possibility of narration of a rather *queer* tale is bound up in a body possessed by a story of which it cannot rid itself. Incessant, infinite and psychosomatically disruptive storytelling with others in a public space makes a spectacle of difference not only to entertain, but also to grapple with how individual and national identities are formed through violently exclusionary processes. Yet the intimacy of the storytelling process – the embodied sense of being a part of the story – and the repetitive impulse to keep the story going also suggest an ethical imperative whereby self and other (storyteller's life and main protagonist's life story) are intertwined and interdependent. Searching for the final truthful version of Ahmed's history and its correlation to Morocco's own search for an independent identity, the storytellers reveal a narrative form that is dependent upon collective sharing and listening, embodied and psychic undoings, and infinite uncertainty and responsibility.

In this chapter, I explore how narration is experienced through the body. To feel physically perturbed by the story, I argue, necessitates a communal response. This collective sense of responsibility for the story, the compulsive desire to keep the story alive with others, opens up the possibility of bearing witness to the multiple, discordant histories of colonial and familial violence. Where the repetitious narrative form gives space to yet more versions of the main protagonist's life and therefore has been read by some critics through the lens of performativity, I argue that the interminable repetition of history is painful and difficult to bear. The sharing of narrative responsibility with others lightens the weight of the story and opens up the possibility of bearing witness. Where *Cereus* creates a mode of witnessing where each character's sense of self is intertwined with the histories relayed by Tyler (namely the history of colonialism on the island and Mala's disturbing tale of familial abuse), *L'Enfant* imagines an ethics of witnessing that is much more physical and where language is experienced through, in and on the body. Similar to Mootoo, Ben Jelloun reinvents both which histories are heard and the very ways in which we may listen. Building on the figure of the traditional Moroccan storyteller, Ben Jelloun creates a public gathering that is as much concerned with rewriting histories and memories as with how epistemologies are forged. I argue that the storytellers and audience members carve out a heterogeneous and ephemeral collectivity through a sensorial language and an embodied historiography. My emphasis on the embodied experiences of narratives, especially on how the senses inform and are formed by histories, is a desire to question the numerous readings of *queer* (and by queer I mean morphologically diverse, disabled, non-normative desires and gender expressions, and perverse and freaky practices) characters solely through a metaphorical or allegorical lens. While I agree with most critics that the novel conveys Moroccan independence through bodily difference, I also suggest that the material representations exceed this symbolic level. The staging of each narrative event – where the reader's attention is repeatedly drawn to the production of the story – renders visible and, I would argue, critiques how *queer* bodies are reduced to metaphorical readings, encouraging readers to reflect on how bodies come to be lived, perceived and thought of as viable modes of existence. Thus, the performative structure of the narrative and of queer bodies coincides not solely to reveal how nations and bodies are constructed, but also to enact the very vulnerability of being. Unable to stabilize the narrative or the queer bodies, the narrators describe their own sense of vulnerability of form and matter. I would suggest that Ahmed's tale makes apparent the vulnerability of the human and bears witness to those whose existence reminds others of this originary vulnerability.

L'Enfant de sable is narrated by a series of largely unreliable storytellers who assert an authentic or personal connection to the main protagonist of the tale, Ahmed/Zahra. They tell of a man whose wife gave birth to only daughters and of how he devised a plan to raise the next child, regardless of its sex, as a boy, as a man. Ahmed, the eighth child, is declared 'un homme, un homme, un homme' (26) [a man, a man, a man], despite the fact that the mother gave birth to a girl. Hadj Ahmed Souleïmane is portrayed as simultaneously supporting a system that values only male children and trapped by a hatred of his brothers who would inherit two thirds of his wealth on his death. The narrative is framed by a critique of both the unjust inheritance laws in Morocco, where daughters cannot inherit the major part of their parents' wealth, and the virulent masculinity to which Hadj Ahmed Souleïmane clings. His assertion of male virility is further rendered public through his declaration of political allegiance to the Moroccan nationalists in the struggle for independence from the French protectorate: 'Cette naissance annonce fertilité pour la terre, paix et prospérité pour le pays. Vive Ahmed! Vive le Maroc!' (30) [This birth will bring fertility to the land, peace and prosperity to the country. Long live Ahmed! Long live Morocco!]. Here, the storytellers invite the listeners to reflect on how colonial policies and practices emasculate colonial subjects, and how nationalism may emerge out of a masculinity that reasserts dominance, aggression and virility (especially the reproduction of sons) as traditional and aspirational values in a postcolonial nation. Raised as a boy, as the pride of the family, Ahmed takes his father's decision further than the latter anticipates by deciding to marry. In a moment that openly mocks his father's plan, Ahmed tells his father, 'Père, tu m'as fait homme, je dois le rester. Et, comme dit notre Prophète bien-aimé, « un musulman complet est un homme marié »' (51) [Father, you made me a man. I must remain one. And, as our beloved Prophet says, 'A complete Muslim is a married man']. Simultaneously defying his father's desire to achieve a public image of idealized masculinity and ridiculing his uncles' inheritance-focused greed, Ahmed chooses a woman who is represented as unmarriable: his disabled cousin Fatima (the daughter of one of Hadj Ahmed Souleïmane's much-despised brothers). After her death and that of his own father, Ahmed falls into a series of crises. Unsure of his identity, of the connection between his psyche and soma and of his sexual desires, Ahmed leaves the family home and sets out on a journey in search of a sense of (a post-masculine) self.

The intra-diegetic narrative ends abruptly when the storyteller mysteriously disappears. The flow of the narrative is forestalled just as we learn that Ahmed is working in a circus routine where, under the name of Zahra, a name given to him by the owners of the circus, he enacts the role of 'L'homme aux seins de femme' (111) [The Man with a Woman's Breasts] and 'La femme à la barbe mal rasée' (125) [The Woman with the Badly Shaven Beard]. As Ahmed grows increasingly uncertain of his sense of self, the narrative also begins to disintegrate. The first storyteller asserts authority over the text by claiming to be reading from Ahmed's diary, but his version is contested by the second storyteller who reassures the audience that he is Fatima's brother and therefore has the real version of Ahmed's diary. When the crowd is eventually disbanded by the authorities who want to modernize the bustling square, three committed listeners take the story into their own hands; le troubadour aveugle [the blind troubadour], who claims to have come 'd'un autre siècle' (172) [from another century], intervenes and tells of his own encounter with someone he suspects might have been Ahmed; and the novel ends with an earlier narrator, who had supposedly died, returning to tell us that Ahmed's diary has been wiped blank by the moon except for a few remaining traces. On leaving, this storyteller lays the almost blank book before the audience – and, thus, the reader – and says, 'Moi, je dépose là devant vous le livre, l'encrier et les porte-plume [*sic*]' (209) [I now lay down before you the book, the inkwell and the pens]. By laying these writing tools, along with Ahmed's almost blank diary, on the ground the storyteller invites the listeners to participate in creating yet another version of Ahmed/Zahra's almost invisible history. He places responsibility for the tale in the hands of the listeners.

As with Tyler in *Cereus*, the storyteller in *L'Enfant* draws the reader into the narrative, encouraging the audience to take responsibility for the continuation of this story. He invites the reader to bear witness to the interwoven histories of bodily and colonial violence, morphological diversity, and the search for an independent, postcolonial nation. He does this by handing over to the audience the tools with which to narrate a tale that has no end, that could cause immense physical and psychological disturbances, and that may result in chaotic (but not meaningless) multiplicity. In contrast to *Cereus*, *L'Enfant* does not call upon the reader to circulate the story in order to find a missing relative. Instead, this novel portrays the potentially destructive, repetitive and interminable pain that may be felt when bearing witness to histories of violence that can never be resolved or rendered digestible. To bear witness is not only to be present and therefore recognize (and write into existence) the gaps and violences of colonial, nationalist and familial histories, it is also to act belatedly upon what is heard and felt in and on the body. Such potentially painful sensations are the burdens of unknowable and unnarratable histories that become the ethical foundation for not only building new epistemologies, but also new (namely multisensory) knowledge structures.

All narrators repeatedly turn to a gender-transitioning body to understand the current political situation in Morocco, but the body cannot be contained by coherent, chronological narratives of the nation. The viscerality of the body literally forces them to keep revising the same story. Just as Bhabha reads Derrida's supplement as that which exceeds the pedagogical and therefore that which renders national structures unstable and changeable, I read Ahmed's material body as excess.[4] That is, Ahmed's simultaneous certainty and uncertainty about the relation between his sense of self and his sense of embodied being is not only Ben Jelloun's attempt to render the individual body symbolic of the body politic. Instead, Ahmed's embodied histories necessitate an ethical imperative where the reader comes close to him, his words, and narratives about him, but must also act on what is not known and what may not be knowable. From unknowability emerges the necessity to keep on narrating with others, to keep transforming the story and to bear witness to what has yet to be articulated. It is the

[4] Bhabha, pp. 221–2.

very act of narrative production through intimacy with others, through the body and through words that is the possibility of bearing witness to embodied violence.

L'Enfant enacts narrative repetition as the agonistic meeting point of the narrators' desires to reduce the ambiguously gendered protagonist and the disabled characters to allegorical or symbolic readings, and the body's morphological refusal and inability to cohere neatly. The incessant narrational repetition is pedagogical insofar as the individual, collective and authorial desire is to tell a tale of embodied and colonial transitioning. Yet, such narrative repetition is performative insofar as it manifests the incessant discursive production of embodied existence and, while so doing, renders apparent the impossibility of reducing flesh to language. No author can contain the story. Thus, to begin to translate Ahmed/Zahra's story is both to narrate and to yield to the fact that no amount of narration could produce a complete history. To recognize this unknowingness is to enter into an indefinite, never-ending process of all-consuming narration and listening with others. Translation of an embodied history is not only to speak but also to listen and, in so doing, to forge a sense of history and belonging as vulnerable, uncertain and incoherent. In other words, the very breaking down of the narrative, its vulnerability to change and multiplicity, suggests that in being open to another version, to an other, is to conceive of belonging and humanness as vulnerable from the start.

Vulnerability of form and matter, monstrous embodiment and incontrollable stories are central to my own reading of Ben Jelloun's *L'Enfant*. However, I want to briefly address the position of the author in the production of postcolonial novels, largely because what we witness with Ben Jelloun's literary oeuvre are the (normativizing) moral and political demands placed on particular, namely postcolonial, writers. This novel has received hugely positive academic attention, with most literary scholars cohering around the idea that Ben Jelloun's work has seriously declined in quality since the publication of this novel.[5] His oeuvre is simultaneously critiqued for exoticizing Morocco and North Africa, and celebrated for revealing the inequalities and injustices of Moroccan society. Similar to Salman Rushdie in the English-speaking world, Ben Jelloun is also criticized (in largely non-academic work) for his supposedly negative representations of Islam. In light of the events that have unfolded since 11 September 2001, I want to comment specifically on the role of Islam in Ben Jelloun's novels.

I am not seeking to centre my readings on an event that is unnecessarily coalescing into the pivotal point of contemporary historiography. However, I do want to draw out how *L'Enfant* proposes ethical modes of encountering others through a multisensory, embodied and communal storytelling that moves between the particular and the infinite. To this extent, I want to address the *particular* and emphasize how it is intimately tied to the broader ethics of his novels. My concern with some of the critical work on Ben Jelloun's novels is the insistence that the reader can see how Islam and particularly Muslim societies are anti-feminist, violent and largely backward (in a teleology that moves forward through modernity in a mimicking of the Global North). John Erickson suggests that the 'woman in traditional Arab societies like that of Morocco [. . .] is

[5] I discuss this academic quandary in the coda that follows this chapter.

in many ways silenced and silent. She is traditionally veiled and draped'.[6] Erickson assumes the burqa to be a garment symbolic of women's oppression. Yet, in *L'An Cinq de la révolution algérienne* [*A Dying Colonialism*], Fanon explicates how French colonial officials sought first to conquer women by convincing them they were cloistered, silenced and disempowered by Algerian men.[7] Erickson thus repeats this colonial ideology by targeting women, their clothes and the spaces in which they circulate, suggesting that scholarly and literary interventions might 'liberate' these women from 'the state of aphonia in which [they exist] in traditional Arab society'.[8] Evincing certainties about women, democracy and freedom is historically and contemporaneously tied to the justification of both violent acts towards whole populations and the occupation of territories and countries. I would argue that postcolonial criticism of Islam in Ben Jelloun's novels is often redolent of Gayatri Spivak's description of colonialism where 'white men are saving brown women from brown men'.[9] Furthermore, technologies of the state and media engage in a facile othering of Muslim men, whereby their bodies and rights are targeted and violated because they are deemed a threat to national security. As Puar argues, 'Religion, in particular Islam, has now supplanted race as one side of the irreconcilable binary between queer and something else'.[10] For many critics of Ben Jelloun's novels, reform of a so-called Islamic society, namely Morocco, would invariably result in better conditions for women. This critique remains prevalent, despite the insistence of many women, involved in the struggles for independence, who maintain that religious practices were integral to an independent and feminist Morocco. Fatima Mernissi and Alison Baker delineate how changes in external, public clothing became central to women involved in the nationalist cause in North Africa.[11] Baker stresses that the women she interviewed 'say that everything they did was done for their King, their country and their God'.[12]

As we witness each storyteller asserting her or his own political agenda through the body of the main protagonist, we are invited as readers to reflect on the ramifications and consequences of interpretation. Undoubtedly the novel encourages

[6] John Erickson, *Islam and Postcolonial Narrative* (Cambridge: Cambridge University Press, 1998), pp. 71–2.

[7] Frantz Fanon, *L'An V de le révolution algérienne* (Paris: Éditions La Découverte & Syros, [1959] 2001). The text was subsequently translated into English in 1967 as *A Study in Dying Colonialism* and republished in 1970 as *A Dying Colonialism*, trans. by Haakon Chevalier (London: Pelican Books, 1970).

[8] Erickson, *Islam and Postcolonial Narrative*, p. 71.

[9] Gayatri Spivak, 'Can the Subaltern Speak?', in *Colonial Discourse and Post-Colonial Theory: A Reader*, ed. by Patrick Williams and Laura Chrisman (Hertfordshire: Harvester Wheatsheaf, 1994), pp. 66–112 (p. 93).

[10] Puar, *Terrorist Assemblages*, p. 13.

[11] Mernissi delineates a shift away from the *haïk* towards the lighter *djellaba* (mainly worn by men, but taken on by Moroccan women during French protectorate rule) and also shows, like Fanon, that what women wore during French colonial times was not quite as homogenous as the French authorities suggested. See, Fatima Mernissi, *The Harem Within: Tales of a Moroccan Girlhood* (London: Doubleday, 1994), pp. 119–28. Alison Baker's interviews with Moroccan women involved in the nationalist movement for independence include many of the women speaking about their decision to continue wearing or (sometimes to temporarily) not wear the hijab. See, Alison Baker, *Voices of Resistance: Oral Histories of Moroccan Women* (Albany, NY: State University of New York Press, 1998).

[12] Baker, p. 11.

multiple – potentially even endless – readings, but it also represents how reading is a public, communal and engaged process. It is something to be undertaken in dialogue with others, and with the possibility of constant revisions and rethinkings. However, what circulates as (acceptable) knowledge may feed into, destabilize or even potentially challenge the contemporary forms of distantiation, prejudice and violence we are witnessing on a global scale. As readers, we have a responsibility to consider the impact of our work both inside and outside of academia. Ben Jelloun does not set moral parameters around the reading practices of his collective audience members, but in *L'Enfant* he does insist that readings are felt on the body and that they may create or shut down spaces for queer bodies. In our engagement with Ben Jelloun's work, we also have responsibilities to recognize how the creation of false dichotomies exacerbates contemporary dominant power relations, and reinforces colonial ideas that countries in the Global North are modern and liberal in contrast to those of the Global South, which are deemed to be religious and therefore not quite modern. Such rhetoric assists in justifying violent intervention in countries thought to be in need of progress, even where the aim may be to render visible sociopolitical injustice. I would therefore suggest that the ethics that emerges from *L'Enfant* moves between a critique of inequalities, injustices and violence towards difference, and an attention to how such questioning may enable the repetition of colonial violence in newer forms.

Linguistic touching

Reading from what he claims to be the diary of Ahmed, the first narrator searches for coherence and asserts knowledge by turning to a supposed authentic source:

> Il avait besoin d'un long moment, peut-être des mois, pour ramasser ses membres, mettre de l'ordre dans son passé [. . .] et faire le propre dans le grand cahier où il consignait tout : son journal intime, ses secrets – peut-être un seul et unique secret – et aussi l'ébauche d'un récit dont lui seul avait les clés. (9)
>
> [He needed time, perhaps months, to gather himself up, to put some order into his past [. . .] and sort out the big notebook to which he consigned everything: his private diary, his secrets – perhaps a single and unique secret – and also the sketch of a story to which he alone held the keys.]

Lynette Hunter describes the diary as 'a place to sort out one's life by sorting out one's words'.[13] Following Enlightenment traditions, the storyteller explains that the written word enables the diarist to know and therefore to master the 'I'. As Felicity Nussbaum says, '[The diary] is a way to expose the subject's hidden discourse, in the hope of "knowing" the self when the subject is still the sole censor and critic of his or her own discourse'.[14] Yet,

13 Lynette Hunter, *Literary Value/Cultural Power: Verbal Arts in the Twenty-First Century* (Manchester: Manchester University Press, 2001), p. 107.

14 Felicity A. Nussbaum, 'Toward Conceptualizing Diary', in *Studies in Autobiography*, ed. by James Olney (New York and Oxford: Oxford University Press, 1988), pp. 128–40 (p. 135).

it becomes evident that Ahmed sought neither to learn to 'know' himself, as Nussbaum suggests might be the function of a diary, or to become intelligible as such. Language is not the reorganization of the self for the sake of clarity but an end in and of itself. The search for who Ahmed *really* is is foiled at every turn even by the documents that promise insight.

Describing Ahmed's adolescence as he reads from the diary, the storyteller turns to his enraptured audience and tells them: '[C'est] une période bien obscure. [. . .] Dans le livre, c'est un espace blanc, des pages nues laissées ainsi en suspens, offertes à la liberté du lecteur. A vous!' (41–2) [It is a very obscure period. [. . .] In the diary, it is a blank space, naked pages left hanging, offered freely to the reader. For you!]. While four audience members offer their brief thoughts on Ahmed's adolescence, the fifth calls for a return to the book and thus to Ahmed's words. Compliant, the storyteller states, 'J'ouvre le livre, je tourne les pages blanches . . . Ecoutez!' (43) [I open the book, I turn the blank pages . . . Listen!]. On the one hand, I agree with Gauch that the audience members 'ally themselves with a view of history that sets its sights on narrative resolution rather than on an analysis of their involvement in a particular narrative's constitution'.[15] On the other hand, I would argue that the self-reflexive structure of the narrative encourages the reader to question why the audience would cede authority to a blank text. To this extent, where the reference to the blank pages may evoke the absent recordings of histories, the continuation of the story suggests a persistent public and communal desire to remember what has failed to be recorded. The purposefully blank pages, rather than just an absence of a period of years (i.e. that there are material blank pages and not simply a diary that is full but which does not record all stages of his life), portrays how this period cannot be recorded in words and cannot be contained by the narrative form. One may read the return to the absent words as a recognition of how Ahmed cedes authority over his own tale; how he did not wish to reveal knowledge to prying eyes; how he was not able to narrate the inaccessible; that he could not put into words what he was living; and/or his assertion that not having the language to describe who one is is not the same as not existing.

I would suggest that the act of reading the blank pages conveys to the listeners and readers that, although there 'is nothing to see, there may be a lot to feel, or to smell'.[16] The sensory emphasis in the diary descriptions suggests there is indeed more than can be captured by the eye and confirms that although nothing has been written this is not the same as having nothing to remember. The narrator forges an epistemology that is bound to the senses, where language is a sensual experience that expresses Ahmed's body. That is, the body is made manifest through a sensorial language, and thus without always recourse to meaning (to a signified) or to narrative. Ahmed's body is completely hidden from view by both the fog and the words that grow dense in the

[15] Suzanne Gauch, 'Telling the Tale of a Body Devoured by Narrative', *differences: A Journal of Feminist Cultural Studies* 11.1 (1999) <http://muse.jhu.edu/journals/difference/v011/11.1gauch.html> [accessed 6 November 2004], 179–202 (p. 191).

[16] Marks, *The Skin of the Film*, p. 231.

women-only space of the hammam (33).[17] He imagines the words rising in the heat, falling from the ceiling and collecting on his body:

> Curieusement, les gouttes d'eau qui tombaient sur moi étaient salées. Je me disais alors que les mots avaient le goût et la saveur de la vie. [. . .] Là, ils tombèrent comme une pluie et je me faisais un plaisir de les ramasser et de les garder secrètement dans ma culotte ! [. . .] Je ne pouvais pas les garder longtemps sur moi car ils me chatouillaient. Lorsque ma mère me savonnait, elle était étonnée de constater combien j'étais sale. Et moi je ne pouvais pas lui expliquer que le savon qui coulait emportait toutes les paroles entendues et accumulées le long de cet après-midi. (34–6)
>
> [Curiously, the drops that fell on me were salty. I told myself that words had the taste and smell of life. [. . .] There, they fell like rain and I took great pleasure in collecting and keeping them secretly in my underpants! [. . .] I could not keep these words on me for a long time as they tickled. When my mother washed me, she was surprised at how dirty I was. I could not explain to her that the soap was washing away all the words that I had heard and collected that afternoon.]

Collecting the words in his 'culotte' suggests a physicality of language, a sense that it can be touched, felt and can even tickle. That Ahmed collects these words not in his hands but close to his supposedly defining sex also indicates a proximity between normally unspoken or, indeed, forbidden words and what is kept in his underwear.[18] Or, in other words, Ahmed is represented as taking hold of language not to master it but to feel the pleasure of it on his body. This scene establishes language as containing inaccessible meanings; words as, in and of themselves, delightful; and narrative as not the only way of understanding the body and language. According to Marks, the 'memory of the senses [is] a nontransparent and differentially available body of information' that is crucial for all but especially for those 'not represented in the dominant society'.[19] Ahmed's diary entries portray his embodied memories as sensorial experiences. He creates an embodied language that the reader comes close to feeling, tasting and smelling. Histories are not being written, but are being sensed through, in and on the body of Ahmed, the storyteller, the fictive audience and the readers. We are invited to sense what cannot be spoken or written into familial and national histories.

Captivating the audience's interest by focusing extensively on Ahmed's adolescence, the storyteller draws our attention to how Ahmed moves between and within gender-segregated spaces. Employing a fantastical narrative form to describe this difficult time, the storyteller transports his audience to the mosque:

> J'escaladais la colonne, aidé par le chant coranique. Les versets me propulsaient assez rapidement vers le haut. Je m'installais dans le lustre et observais le mouvement

17 Ahmed is allowed in this space until the age where he is deemed to be watching women in a sexual way and then he must move on to the male-only baths. This prohibition is celebrated, later in the novel, as a triumph of Ahmed's masculinity (37).

18 The words Ahmed reaches out for are those not of the everyday events such as getting hot or cold water but the ones he does not always understand, the ones that relate specifically to the body and to sex.

19 Marks, *The Skin of the Film*, p. 199.

des lettres arabes gravées dans le plâtre puis dans le bois. Je partais ensuite sur le dos d'une belle prière :

ان ينصركم الله فلا غالب لكم

'Si Dieu vous donne la victoire,

personne ne peut vous vaincre.'

Je m'accrochais au Alif et me laissais tirer par le Noun qui me déposait dans les bras du Ba. J'étais ainsi pris par toutes les lettres qui me faisaient faire le tour du plafond et me ramenaient en douceur à mon point de départ en haut de la colonne. Là je glissais et descendais comme un papillon. (38)

[I scaled the column with the help of the Qur'ānic chant. The verses lifted me quickly to the top. I settled on the light and observed the movement of the Arabic letters engraved in the plaster and the wood. Then I set off on the back of a beautiful prayer:

ان ينصركم الله فلا غالب لكم

'If God gives you victory,

No one can defeat you.'

I clung to the *'alif* and let myself be pulled by the *nūn*, which laid me in the arms of the *bā'*. Thus I was taken, by all the letters, on a tour of the ceiling, and brought gently back to my starting point at the top of the column. There, I fluttered down like a butterfly.][20]

Although Ben Jelloun employs multiple languages, this is the only moment that Arabic appears in this novel.[21] The space of prayer and community stifles Ahmed, whose presence puts on display his father's prowess and success as a man.[22] The poetics of

20 Among the many absences in the official translation of the novel, the non-presence of the prayer in Arabic is striking.

21 He quotes a poem in Spanish on p. 198. It is worth noting that the official English translation includes the Spanish version. See *The Sand Child*, p. 156.

22 Through the child, Ben Jelloun is able to make a critique of a certain devotion to Islam as the creation of a public, masculine image. The child's revelling in the mistreatment of the sacred text is, one could suggest, a strategy on the author's behalf to avoid further criticism of his novels as blasphemous; he places the act in a child's world and, therefore, implies that not being an adult could be the reason for this lack of respect for all that is sacred. Ben Jelloun repeatedly iterates that his critique of Islam is specifically of fundamentalist interpretations. He also criticizes those who follow religion uncritically or who use it for violent ends, suggesting these practices are not necessarily related to spirituality. Ben Jelloun maintains his affinity to Islam and the Arabic language as sacred. Speaking of his own literary critique of religion, he says,

> I think that I also take a critical look, not at Islam – I'm not crazy enough to criticize a religion, no matter which one it is, by the way, because I respect people's convictions – but I do take a critical look at the manipulators of religions, whether they're Jews or Muslims or Christians. I don't like people who manipulate the convictions of others for political ends, for temporal ends, if you like. I think that religion is an affair of personal conscience, morality, ethics, and no one has the right to generalize it into a political ideology. (Miriam Rosen, 'A Conversation with Tahar Ben Jelloun: Toward a World Literature?', *Middle East Report* 163 (1990), 30–3 (p. 32))

Giving his reaction to the condemnation of his texts as sacrilegious, Ben Jelloun states,

> There are sermons against me in the mosque. I'm occasionally the bête noire of integrationists. Whether they are political or religious fundamentalists. [. . .] I've never asked a fanatic to like

the Qur'ān gives Ahmed temporary reprieve from his father's paternalism. He literally holds on to the straight line of the character *'alif* [ا], is pulled up by the u-like shape of the character *nūn* [ن], and the latter places him securely and comfortably in the closing arms of the convex of the character *bā'* [ب]. The storyteller is critical of the men who use this religious space for their own – personal, sexual, financial or egotistical – gains, and yet portrays to the reader the embodied power of poetic spirituality. Arabic words are felt intimately and allow Ahmed to convey his life experiences in a body that is undergoing significant changes. Ben Jelloun may be offering a romanticized or perhaps even an exoticized image of Arabic; this may be a representation that appeals to a Western audience that seeks distinct and definitive differences. Yet, the turn to language, specifically Arabic, also conveys a refusal to let the body be defined in French colonial terms and a desire to find meaning through Islamic poetry. Ahmed is seeking to understand his embodied transformations, and turns to the senses to create an epistemology that is firmly grounded in tradition and religion. Such sensorial knowledge structures remain equally critical of unjust practices and firmly question how history itself is recorded.

Describing the relationship between narrative and embodied transitions, Prosser states:

> [Transition] always requires that narrativization of the life, there is no other way in which the subject – indeed, surely the point is any subject – could come to naming, to realization of his or her categorical belonging except through some form of narrative.[23]

In contrast to Prosser, Steven Connor describes such entries into signification (as a subject – *assujettissement*) as moments of 'violence', confirming the injustice of the patriarchal imposition to which Ahmed has been subjected.[24] Indeed, Jarrod Hayes insists that Ben Jelloun is drawing out the violence at the heart of gender acquisition, and he describes the paternal imposition of the male gender as indicative of a larger 'violent stamping of the body by language'.[25] However, I want to ask: is narrative ever

> what I've written. That would be unthinkable. That would be like asking him to disown his mother. All I want is simply to have nothing to do with them; I'm not trying to provoke them. I don't force them to read my books. But, without even reading my books, they attack me in the mosques. (Thomas Spear, 'Politics and Literature: An Interview with Tahar Ben Jelloun', *Yale French Studies* 83.2 (1993), 30–43 (p. 42))

Here is an example of one of the many times Ben Jelloun has had to justify why he does not write in Arabic:

> I often say that the fact of writing in French is a way for us [Maghrebian writers] to be somewhat bold and also to be relevant, because, when one writes in Arabic, one is slightly intimidated by the language of the Koran. To my knowledge, there is no writer in Arabic, at least no modern writer, who has tried to do violence to the Arabic language. It's hard to do. There is no tradition in Arabic of *work* on language, as there is, for example, with Joyce or even Faulkner [. . .]. Arabic is a very beautiful language, very strong and solid. It is not at all an easy language to twist, either. (Ibid., p. 34)

23 Prosser, *Second Skins*, p. 125.
24 Steven Connor, *The Book of Skin* (London: Reaktion Books, 2004), p. 72.
25 Hayes, p. 174.

enough to create a subject and a bearable life? While I agree that narrative is central to subjectivity, especially for marginalized peoples (including queers, colonial subjects, people of colour, the disabled and women), I want to ask: what could the ascription of blank pages to the diary (from which the storyteller nonetheless goes on to read), of Ahmed's maturation into adulthood, signify in this quagmire of representational violence and the acquisition of subject status?

Ahmed's first experience of menstruation destabilizes his sense of self, and creates an anxiety around the possibility of an incoherent sense of being:

> Je suis l'architecte et la demeure ; l'arbre et la sève ; moi et un autre ; moi et une autre. Aucun détail ne devrait venir, ni de l'extérieur ni du fond de la fosse, perturber cette rigueur. Pas même le sang. Et le sang un matin a taché mes draps. Empreintes d'un état de fait de mon corps enroulé dans un linge blanc, pour ébranler la petite certitude, ou pour démentir l'architecture de l'apparence. [. . .] C'était bien du sang; résistance du corps au nom ; éclaboussure d'une circoncision tardive. [. . .] Une sorte de fatalité, une trahison de l'ordre. (46–8)
>
> [I am the architect and the house; the tree and the sap; me and a male other; me and a female other. No detail, not from the outside or from the bottom of the grave, must disturb this rigour. Not even blood. And one morning blood stained my sheets. Imprints of a fact about my body, rolled up in white linen, to shake the tiny certainty or give the lie to the architecture of my appearance. [. . .] It was certainly blood; resistance of the body to the name; the splash of a tardy circumcision. [. . .] A fate, of sorts; a betrayal of order.]

I agree with Gauch that Ahmed's confrontation with his menstrual blood at this stage is 'not an insight into a hitherto repressed female identity, but a confrontation with the materiality of a body that does not conform to social and scientific definitions of masculinity'.[26] His reaction manifests how viscera are integral to the sense of self. We witness how a story of boyhood begins to unravel, not because biology is stronger or more truthful than his embodied life as a boy, but because the sensation of menstruation is culturally and socially tied to the concept of womanhood. His knowledge of women is so distinct from his own sense of being in the world that connecting menstruation to his sense of maleness causes a disjuncture.

Ahmed begins to question whether it is possible to access that which has never been known. Trying to capture the unspeakable, he turns to the sense of smell. The traces of memories are compared to 'une odeur d'étable abandonnée, ou bien l'odeur d'une blessure non cicatrisée qui se dégage [. . .] une dégénérescence physique avec cependant le corps dans son image intacte, car la souffrance vient d'un fond qui ne peut non plus être révélé' (43) [the smell of an abandoned stable, or even of an open wound which emits the smell of physical degeneracy, while the image of the body remains intact, because the suffering comes from a depth which can no longer be accessed]. The scent of decay shows that something has gone awry. Smell is also the sense most

[26] Gauch, 'Telling the Tale of a Body Devoured by Narrative', p. 183.

'associated with emotion'.[27] The 'olfactory sense is able both to preserve memory and even, as in Proust's reveries, to redeem lost time'.[28] This sense memory 'faintly present in the body itself' both uncovers a certain knowledge about the protagonist and yet, as a smell, creates a screen between Ahmed and the audience (and the reader) to 'protect [him] from casual consumption'.[29] Ahmed's menstruating body represents the potential violence of signification: to be labelled female or a woman, when he is both publicly and privately a man, would be to enter into a state of incoherence in a space that demands bodily certainty. In other words, Ahmed is threatened with familial and national unbelonging should he fail to cohere. He therefore marks his identity on the blank pages by refusing to reveal or render spectacular his bodily dissonance.

The storyteller's turn to the olfactory makes apparent an embodied trauma that haunts Ahmed's present:

> [La] résistance du corps au nom [. . .]. C'était un rappel, une grimace d'un souvenir enfoui, le souvenir d'une vie que je n'avais pas connue et qui aurait pu être la mienne. Etrange d'être ainsi porteur d'une mémoire non accumulée dans un temps vécu, mais donnée à l'insu des uns et des autres. (46)
>
> [The resistance of the body to the name [. . .]. It was a reminder, a grimace of some buried memory, the memory of a life that I had not known and that could have been mine. Strange to be the bearer of a memory that had not been experienced during my lifetime, but given unbeknown to all.]

Haunted by a memory he cannot quite remember, Ahmed turns to the senses to describe his emotions and the intangible. On the one hand, his 'inability to know' the event and the sense of 'belatedness and incomprehensibility that remain at the heart of this repetitive seeing' suggest that Ahmed is reliving a traumatic moment that remains outside his referential framework.[30] There is an ethical demand for others to not only listen, as Laub suggests, but also to publicly reconstruct the story in dialogue with each other. On the other hand, Ahmed's refusal or inability to write his life narrative and to articulate his memories in anything other than sensorial language conveys a political engagement with knowledge production. Leigh Gilmore argues that 'autobiographical writing about chronic pain breaks from humanism and branches into a posthumanist inquiry'.[31] She adds that 'it exposes the self-sufficient and masterful "I" as both deception and error [. . .] and it shifts the focus from the study of exemplary selves to an engagement with selves in conditions of alteration and relations of interdependence'.[32] Ahmed senses the awakening of an embodied memory that coincides with and could even be prompted by his bodily changes. However, such hauntings portray Ahmed's and the storyteller's refusal (or even inability) to repeat humanist ideologies and philosophies. Both the protagonist and the narrator are imagining into being a

27 Connor, p. 216.
28 Ibid.
29 Marks, *The Skin of the Film*, p. 230.
30 Caruth, *Unclaimed Experience*, p. 92.
31 Leigh Gilmore, 'Agency without Mastery: Chronic Pain and Posthuman Life Writing', *Biography* 35.1 (2012), 83–98 (p. 84).
32 Ibid.

monstrous subjectivity that bears witness to unspoken and sometimes unspeakable memories. Yet, they are determined to make the public listen by bringing histories and subjects forth in previously unimagined ways.

Monstrous encounters

As the first storyteller begins to describe Ahmed's intimate epistolary correspondence with a (potentially fictive) unknown other, another storyteller interjects. The latter asserts his narratorial authority by claiming to be the brother of Ahmed's deceased wife, Fatima. The public story of Ahmed traces a queer history of a man who appears to perfect his father's dream of an ideal son. Sara Ahmed suggests that the act of following well-trodden paths is performative, insofar as these inlets are produced through and productive of conventions and norms. These repetitive acts are therefore 'a form of commitment as well as a social investment'.[33] The crowd gathered in the public square shows a commitment and investment in the story of Ahmed, just as the latter is determined to fulfil his father's plan. Yet, the acquiescence of the narrative to another storyteller portrays a disorientation, which is further reflected in Ahmed's decision to marry a woman. It is both an affirmation of heteronormative and nationalist masculinity, as desired by his father, and a deviation from the trodden path, as his father remains concerned that such intimacies might 'reveal' a 'truth' about Ahmed's sex. What we witness, as readers, is 'a politics of disorientation', which sustains 'wonder about the very forms of social gathering' and of embodiments that may emerge.[34] Ahmed defiantly breaks from the normative demands and further exacerbates his father's anxieties by choosing to marry his disabled cousin Fatima.

The second storyteller focuses on sexuality, and the lack of sexual desire between Ahmed and Fatima. He makes a spectacle out of difference by connecting non-normative embodiment (physically disabled and trans bodies) to 'freakish' sexualities.[35] Redolent of Foucault's work on sexuality and building on Freud's account of sexuality in women, David Serlin suggests that psychologists and sexologists often monitored physically disabled women to confirm a correlation between sexuality and the '"truth" of the self'.[36] Although the story of Fatima may be said to be a 'narrative prosthesis'[37] that

[33] Ahmed, *Queer Phenomenology*, p. 17. In order to avoid any confusion between the main protagonist and the critic, I use Sara Ahmed's full name.

[34] Ibid., p. 24.

[35] I am specifically building on Rosemarie Garland-Thomson's work on the processes through which non-normative embodiment is rendered freakish, as something to stare, laugh or be disgusted at. See Rosemarie Garland-Thomson, 'Introduction: From Wonder to Error – A Genealogy of Freak Discourse in Modernity', in *Freakery: Cultural Spectacles of the Extraordinary Body*, ed. by Rosemarie Garland-Thomson (New York and London: New York University Press, 1996), pp. 1–19.

[36] David Serlin, 'Touching Histories: Personality, Disability and Sex in the 1930s', in *Sex and Disability*, ed. by Robert McRuer and Anna Mollow (Durham, NC and London: Duke University Press, 2012), pp. 145–62 (p. 152).

[37] See David T. Mitchell and Sharon L. Snyder, *Narrative Prosthesis: Disability and the Dependencies of Discourse* (Ann Arbor, MI: University of Michigan Press, 2000).

reveals Ahmed's emotional state and the predicament of women in Morocco,[38] it is also concerned with the sexualization of disability. In other words, this story unravels the process through which disabled embodiment is thought to preclude or render abnormal the possibility of sexual desire.[39] Unlike Hayes, I do not read Ahmed's encounters with women through a lens that emphasizes 'the possibility of lesbian desire', largely because Ahmed is living as a man.[40] Instead, I would suggest that Ahmed's and Fatima's sexualities are queer in a sense that echoes Mala's queerness. That is, there is a refusal and sometimes an inability to adhere to heteronormative configurations of national propagation. On the one hand, their marriage appears to destabilize the status quo, in its capacity to threaten the coalescing of the national able-bodied family. On the other hand, their sexualities make manifest histories of medicalized oppression where queers and the disabled are pathologized through an ocularcentric rhetoric of difference. Such historical repetitions render apparent both how monstrous bodies emerge through a reiterative practice of normalization and how the boundaries of normative embodiment appear to temporarily cohere. Rather than a politics of tolerance or equality, where Ahmed and Fatima appeal to be accepted as normal, I would suggest that the novel reveals the vulnerability of the human form and its inability to definitively congeal. What the second storyteller narrates is a fear of openness and an anxiety about the vulnerability of form and matter. Reacting to this sense of precariousness, he speaks of the human as bounded and separate. Like Shildrick, I am not seeking to expand the category of the human to include morphologically different or ab-normal bodies, but to revise understandings of humanness as morphologically uncertain, as vulnerable.[41] Such vulnerability is manifested through the narrative disorientations where the inability to create a coherent story opens up unimagined possibilities of collective narration, and of queer and disabled embodiments and desires. Vulnerability is thus not specific to certain bodies but is the very condition of becoming human.

Describing Fatima's ostracization from her family and her isolation, the storyteller focuses on her body as the source of their rejection:

> Son corps la trahissait, la lâchait en pleine jeunesse. Les démons de l'au-delà lui rendaient souvent visite, s'introduisaient dans son sang, le troublaient, le faisaient

38 Prominent readings of Fatima suggest that she displays how 'sick' Ahmed and their marriage are (Odile Cazenave, 'Gender, Age and Narrative Transformation in *L'Enfant de sable* by Tahar Ben Jelloun', *The French Review* 64.3 (1991), 437–50 (p. 440)). She is read as 'quite symbolic of the whole unsound situation' (ibid.) and 'un signe de la détresse morale dans laquelle Ahmed se trouve' [a sign of the moral distress in which Ahmed finds himself] (Michèle Chossat, *Ernaux, Redonnet, Bâ et Ben Jelloun: Le Personnage féminin à l'aube du XXième siècle* (New York: Peter Lang, 2002), p. 145). Ibnlfassi states, 'Her physical disability, and the epileptic seizures she is prone to, are mere metaphorical displacements for Ahmed's consideration of his femininity as a deformity' (Laïla Ibnlfassi, 'The Ambiguity of Self-Structure; Tahar Ben Jelloun's *L'Enfant de sable* and *La Nuit sacrée*', in *Francophone Voices*, ed. by Kamal Salhi (Exeter: Elm Bank Publishers, 1999), pp. 157–69 (p. 165)). My own reading does not seek to deny the metaphoricity of bodies in literature, but to explore how some bodies are reduced to metaphors even in texts that give social space to non-normative identity formation.

39 For an excellent exploration of sexuality and disability, see McRuer and Mollow.

40 Hayes, p. 167.

41 Shildrick reads monstrous embodiment as 'hopeful' and as 'the potential site of both a reconceived ontology, and a new form of ethics' (Shildrick, *Embodying the Monster*, p. 131).

> tourner trop vite ou de manière irrégulière. Son sang perturbait sa respiration, elle tombait et perdit connaissance. Son corps s'en allait, loin de sa conscience. Il se livrait à des gesticulations incontrôlées, se débattait tout seul, avec le vent, avec les démons. On la laissait seule débrouiller les fils de tous ces nœuds. Son corps, lentement, revenait à elle, reprenait sa place, fatigué, battu, endolori. Elle restait étendue à même le sol et se reposait. (73–4)
>
> [Her body betrayed her, deserted her in the fullness of youth. The demons of the beyond often visited her, slipping into her blood, disturbing it, making it circulate too quickly or in an irregular way. Her blood would disturb her breathing; she would faint and fall. Her body went away, far from consciousness. It was given to uncontrolled gesticulations, as if fighting itself, the wind or the demons. She was left alone to untangle the threads of all those knots. Slowly her body came back to her, resumed its place, exhausted, beaten, pain-ridden. She stayed lying on the ground to rest.]

Using a pseudo-religious lens to describe Fatima's epilepsy and physical disabilities, the storyteller presents her as somewhat animalistic, out of control and therefore as not quite human. Her not so human status is confirmed through her family's mistreatment of her. She lives outside the confines of the familial nation (which necessitates compulsory able-bodiedness); her disability marks her as not marriage material and therefore as a burden on her family (and also a hindrance in terms of the marriageability of her siblings). Ahmed's choice of wife is presented to the audience as logical: he chooses to marry a woman who has no control over her body, is all alone in the world, and is outside the confines of the nation and the family. He also gets to avenge his father by transferring his familial inheritance to the daughter of his father's brother. Nancy Mairs highlights the relationship between the nation and the need for 'healthy' populations:

> When it comes to sexuality in the disabled, dismissal is apt to turn into outright repression. Made uncomfortable, even to the point of excruciation, by the thought of maimed bodies (or, for that matter, minds) engaged in erotic fantasy or action, many deny the very possibility by ascribing to them the innocence of the very young. (In this, of course, they are as wildly mistaken about immature as about adult sexuality.) Perhaps this disgust and denial stem, as the sociobiologists would probably have it, from the fact that such bodies are clearly less than ideal vehicles for the propagation of the species.[42]

Bodily coherence is married to the demands of the heteronormative, reproductive nation. On the one hand, Fatima's brief presence reiterates a literary trope where people with disabilities are excluded from societies. On the other hand, the novel plays with an orientalist gaze that is repeatedly spectacularized by the narrators and thus is open for critique. Where Nicole Markotić and Robert McRuer see inclusive images

[42] Nancy Mairs, 'Sex and Death and the Crippled Body: A Meditation', in *Disability Studies: Enabling the Humanities*, ed. by Sharon L. Snyder, Brenda Jo. Brueggemann and Rosemarie Garland-Thomson (New York: The Modern Language Association of America, 2002), pp. 156–70 (p. 162).

of people with disabilities as also reiterative of nationalist exclusionary rhetoric, I see the negative descriptions of Fatima's disabled body as interrogative of a nationalist grammar that demands compulsory able-bodiedness and heteronormativity.[43] These monstrous bodies evoke an erotics that must be dismissed and in so doing emphasize the national familial dependence on clean propagation.

Fatima's role as wife to Ahmed brings the latter closer to monstrosity; their proximity reinforces the other as 'in-valid' bodies in this society. However, the storyteller describes a process of normalization whereby Ahmed tries to create a separation and distinction between himself and Fatima by isolating her away in a room far from his own private space.[44] As Garland-Thomson suggests freakish bodies are 'fundamental to the narratives by which we make sense of ourselves and our world'.[45] Ahmed takes on the position of the normativizing figure who seeks to consolidate his sense of self through an expulsion of the monstrous other.[46] Through the act of *watching* Fatima's out-of-control body, which displays his 'lack of affective engagement' and a 'minimisation of interconnection', Ahmed seeks to separate himself as a self-complete subject.[47] He employs a gaze that acts not only to distance him from Fatima, but also to render her an object of study, fascination and exotic fantasy:

> J'essayais un jour de voir pendant qu'elle dormait si elle ne s'était pas excisée ou cousu les lèvres du vagin. Je soulevai doucement les draps et découvris qu'elle portait une espèce de gaine forte autour du bassin, comme une culotte de chasteté, blindée, décourageant le désir ou alors le provoquant pour mieux le casser. (76–7)
>
> [One day, as she lay asleep, I tried to see if she had been circumcised or if the lips of her vagina had been sewn together. I gently lifted the sheet and found that she was wearing a sort of girdle around her pelvis, like a chastity belt, armoured, discouraging desire or provoking it to destroy it all the more.]

The second storyteller places Ahmed in a position of power where he orientalizes difference, imagining that Fatima may have undergone bodily procedures which colonial practitioners and Western feminists sought to render visible as barbaric and backward practices, and which are not performed in Morocco.[48] Difference is not

43 Nicole Markotić and Robert McRuer, 'Leading with Your Head: On the Borders of Disability, Sexuality and the Nation', in *Sex and Disability*, ed. by Robert McRuer and Anna Mollow (Durham, NC and London: Duke University Press, 2012), pp. 165–82.

44 Gauch, 'Telling the Tale of a Body Devoured by Narrative', p. 188.

45 Garland-Thomson, 'From Wonder to Error', p. 1.

46 Ahmed's desire to make sense of his self through a normativizing impulse towards Fatima is further confirmed by his desire 'l'emmener consulter de grands médecins, la guérir, lui donner sa chance' (69) [to take her to consult great doctors, get her cured, give her a chance].

47 Shildrick, *Embodying the Monster*, p. 103.

48 This description also evokes the acts of infibulation and genital cutting as much discussed in the context of the continent of Africa. Ben Jelloun is often criticized for representing female circumcision as if current in North Africa, especially for the very violent scene in *La Nuit sacrée*, given it is not practised in Morocco or the Maghreb. In *L'Enfant de sable*, this description betrays more about the assumptions of the reader of Fatima's body, namely Ahmed, but also, of course, the reader of the novel. Ben Jelloun seems to be invoking stereotypes of African women not to criticize the practice of circumcision as such but to demonstrate how Ahmed's social imaginary is formed through rumours, male desires and a lack of intimate contact. This issue is discussed further in the coda on *La Nuit sacrée*.

simply put on display, but serves to instantiate Ahmed's sense of self as both detached from non-normative embodiment (and therefore to establish him as 'normal') and in control of the patriarchal, normative and imperial gaze. He seeks knowledge of Fatima, to find her true self, by seeking access to her vagina. He mimics the storytellers – who seek knowledge of Ahmed by trying to gain access to the latter's true sense of self via his body – by believing that the answer to who Fatima really 'is' lies in the most intimate areas of her body. The storyteller puts on display not only the very processes through which difference is hierarchized, but also how sex and disability are mutually constitutive in producing a monstrous image of exotic difference. Keith L. Walker reads the above scene as '[dramatizing] thwarted sexuality' from which, he claims, nearly all the characters suffer.[49] However, Walker's analysis ignores how sexuality is produced through normative embodiment, which the storytellers tie to nationalist values. I would suggest that, on the one hand, Fatima's presence as the only disabled character in the novel makes manifest how disability precludes sexuality in a rhetoric where national propagation necessitates normative embodiment. On the other hand, the spectacularization of difference to which Ahmed is subjected is not undermined by him but rather is reinforced as he takes on the role of viewer. Fatima haunts Ahmed by rendering apparent their similarities: Fatima cannot have a sexuality, just as Ahmed cannot, in a society where only morphologically stable and healthy bodies are the norms to be reproduced.

The appeal of seeing monstrous bodies, according to Elizabeth Grosz, betrays a 'perverse kind of sexual curiosity'[50] that makes 'the bounded, category-obeying self possible'.[51] Yet, if Ahmed attempts to secure his self by coming closer to visible bodily difference, he fails to realize that Fatima, unlike himself, is not attached to achieving gender conformity or gendered recognition. In Gauch's words:

> Desiring to divest herself of her corporeality rather than contest the limitations imposed upon the female body, Fatima dismisses the femininity Ahmed holds out to her like a reward and increasingly compels him to question the validity of the narrative of masculinity he has so willingly mastered [. . .].[52]

Fatima seeks a spiritual transcendence of her body and thus to divest herself of the matter that defines her relationships with others. She represents the impossibility of a life in this society, but also gives a glimpse of a refusal to accept the existing conditions (especially those of womanhood on Ahmed's terms). Fatima is not the only character to seek bodily transcendence through spirituality, but her motives for taking this path are portrayed as influenced, if not determined, by her sexualized disability. However, I would still argue that Fatima is not reduced solely to the metaphorical or allegorical level. She affirms a gender-based politics in her refusal to adhere to the contract offered

[49] Keith L.Walker, *Countermodernism and Francophone Literary Culture: The Game of Slipknot* (Durham, NC and London: Duke University Press, 1999), p. 154.

[50] Elizabeth Grosz, 'Intolerable Ambiguity: Freaks as/at the Limit', in *Freakery: Cultural Spectacles of the Extraordinary Body*, ed. by Rosemarie Garland-Thomson (New York and London: New York University Press, 1996), pp. 55–66 (p. 64).

[51] Ibid., p. 65.

[52] Gauch, 'Telling the Tale of a Body Devoured by Narrative', p. 188.

by Ahmed, while still hoping for an outlet that is disembodied and otherworldly. Furthermore, if Ahmed sought to consolidate his sense of self by watching Fatima – rendering her different, freakish and monstrous – he does not succeed. Her death provokes a crisis in Ahmed because Fatima tried to take him to the depths of her despair and to make him feel the pain of having used her 'pour parfaire [son] apparence sociale' (79) [to perfect [his] social appearance]. His loss provokes the realization that life as a dominant patriarch is becoming psychosomatically unbearable and that other ways of coming together than those based solely on a visual economy are necessary if he is to survive in his increasingly uncertain body. Fatima dies and disability as embodied by her disappears from the text. Yet disability haunts Ahmed as the monstrous process through which embodiment is realized when value is placed on wholeness, normative reproduction, nationalist ideals and able-bodied sexual desires.

Tactile correspondence

The 'detachment of the specular' – not only the lack of physical contact but also the purposeful creation of distance and distinction through watching – reinforces both the isolation of and boundary between Ahmed and Fatima.[53] However, even after Fatima's death, Ahmed does not seek intimacy by trying to get physically close to an other. Instead, he enters into an epistolary correspondence with an anonymous other. The materiality of language – including the paper on which it is written – offers Ahmed a temporary reprieve from the external and often violently appropriating gaze:

> Cette voix lointaine, jamais nommée, l'aidait à vivre et à réfléchir sur sa condition. Il entretenait avec ce correspondant une relation intime ; il pouvait enfin parler, être dans sa vérité, vivre sans masque, en liberté même limitée et sous surveillance, avec joie, même intérieure et silencieuse. (85–6)
>
> [That distant voice, never named, helped him to live and reflect upon his condition. He developed an intimate relationship with this correspondent; at last he could speak, exist in his truth, live without a mask, in a certain freedom, however limited and subject to surveillance, even with joy, if an inward silent joy.]

The storyteller insists that the physical absence of this other opens up the possibility of intimate proximity. Yet there is a constant doubt about the origin of these letters: 'Sont-elles d'un correspondant ou d'une correspondante anonyme ? Ou sont-elles imaginaires ? Se serait-il écrit à lui-même dans son isolement ?' (59) [Are they from an anonymous correspondent? Or are they imaginary? Or did he write to himself in his isolation?]. The second storyteller cannot assure the audience of the veracity of the other, or whether this other ever existed. Trust, as Derek Attridge suggests, is 'born of uncertainty and uncertainty alone'.[54] We are given over to the storyteller in ways that we

53 Shildrick, *Embodying the Monster*, p. 103.

54 Derek Attridge, 'Trusting the Other: Ethics and Politics in J.M. Coetzee's *Age of Iron*', *The South Atlantic Quarterly* 93.1 (1994), 59–82 (p. 65).

do not fully understand, and this trust founds the possibility of ethical narrativization. The uncertainty of the letter writer's existence also portrays how Ahmed's search for an interlocutor may not mean a reaching out to an external other. This doubt, however, does not undermine the gesture of entering into dialogue with an other, so much as establish letter correspondence as the opening up of a discussion between self and other or even self as other to the self. In other words, the letters create the possibility of an address, where the address, as Oliver insists, is foundational to subjectivity.

In contrast to Ahmed's distant relationship with Fatima, his intimacy with this letter writer is sensual and arousing:

> Quand je relis certaines de ses lettres, je suis traversé par des frissons. On dirait que ses phrases me caressent la peau, me touchent aux endroits les plus sensibles de mon corps. Ah ! J'ai besoin de sérénité pour réveiller ce corps ; il est encore temps pour le ramener au désir qui est le sien. (96)
>
> [When I reread certain of the letters, a shiver runs through my whole body. It is as if the sentences were stroking my skin, touching me on the most sensitive parts of my body. Ah! I need serenity to awaken this body; there is still time to bring it back to the desire that belongs to it.]

Language – not fleshy contact – is felt on the body and reawakens bodily desires. Ahmed reaches out to an other and is literally touched by the language of the other. Entering into correspondence with an other is thus a search for a viable existence, for a sense of self. The power of language to touch the body has such an impact that Ahmed almost drowns as he feels the body sensing the touch of the other:

> Un homme est venu, il a traversé la brume et l'espace et a posé sa main sur mon visage en sueur. Les yeux fermés, je me laissais faire dans l'eau déjà tiède. Il passa ensuite sa main lourde sur ma poitrine, qui s'éveilla, plongea sa tête dans l'eau et la déposa sur mon bas-ventre, embrassant mon pubis. J'eus une sensation tellement forte que je perdis connaissance et faillis me noyer. (95)
>
> [A man came into view; he crossed the mist and the space and laid his hand on my damp face. My eyes closed, I let him continue as I lay in the already tepid water. He put his heavy hand on my breasts, which awoke, plunged his head into the water, and placed it on my pudendum, kissing my sex. What I felt was so strong that I lost consciousness and almost drowned.]

Redolent of the scene in the hammam, Ahmed's (imaginary) encounter portrays sensuality as an almost unbearable and somewhat deadly touch. Language perturbs his body and creates unimagined sensations that cause Ahmed to further question his sense of self. Here, words are concrete physical sensations that give life to a body that could not feel. The multisensory language arouses the body in a way that proximity to people has failed to do so. To this extent, language is not a simple cognitive undertaking; language is a sensorial, embodied experience. Indeed, here, the self is not formed through the comprehension of words, but through its intimate contact with how words make the body feel.

Tactile correspondence, which provokes unimagined bodily reactions, portrays how intimacy may be experienced non-violently and how the self may emerge through a sensuality that is not reiterative of the well-trodden path of nationalist and familial rhetoric (as espoused by Ahmed and his father). The potential fictionality of the correspondence is a manifestation of the impossibility of a definitive story. It also displays Ahmed's refusal and/or inability to present a transparent and coherent self. In Butler's words:

> I might try to tell a story here about what I am feeling, but it would have to be a story in which the very 'I' who seeks to tell the story is stopped in the midst of the telling; the very 'I' is called into question by its relation to the Other, a relation that does not precisely reduce me to speechlessness, but does nevertheless clutter my speech with signs of its undoing. I tell a story about the relations I choose, only to expose, somewhere along the way, the way I am gripped and undone by these very relations. My narrative falters, as it must.[55]

On one level, Ahmed's loss of Fatima and of his father shakes the stable foundation of his masculine self. On another level, Ahmed's sense of vulnerability to the other's touch creates space for a self that is not determined by the narrative of his father or the violence to which Ahmed has subjected Fatima. These letters bear witness to his changing body and to an intimate erotics that provokes narrative dialogue. Finding a sense of self through the body, outside the confines of the family home and of the father's control, involves the giving up of the certainty of masculinity and living with a bodily vulnerability. This is not a denial of Ahmed's masculinity or a celebration of something feminine, but an opening up of the body to a linguistic touching that puts into question the integrity of the subject as independent and secure.

Ahmed's diary interrupts and disorientates the audience. It does not have a linear trajectory and thus does not mimic the form of historical narratives. Indeed, it is not progressive and one might say that it resists the impulse of futurity. The diary is not marked by heteronormative and able-bodied events, such as marriage or childbirth. Time is queer in the way that both Edelman and Halberstam describe. It is not governed by the logic of the institutions to which Ahmed's sense of self is tied, but rather is more spatialized and embodied. Queer time and alternative temporalities to those of the nation and the family are written into Ahmed's diary and made apparent through the long periods he spends alone masturbating. This autotelic act, like the storytelling itself, is a pleasurable and disorientating sensation that is felt in the present. This intimacy of self brings the past into the present and reverberates through the self opening up the possibility of not following a future-orientated, progressive path, and of searching out intimacies with others that do not mimic the violence to which he has been subjected and that he has inflicted on others. In other words, Ahmed feels his present self by trying to remember what has been foreclosed by his need to perfect the image of an ideal son. This is not a search for femaleness or womanhood, as if this could be available in some pure or originary form. Rather, this is a desire to remember how to both feel a self that is not determined by a father and sense a body in transition.

[55] Butler, *Precarious Life*, p. 23.

One could say that Ahmed is coming into being just as is the narrative of his life, and yet such emergence remains vulnerable and precarious:

> Ces caresses devant le miroir devinrent une habitude, une espèce de pacte entre mon corps et son image, une image enfouie dans un temps lointain et qu'il fallait réveiller en laissant les doigts toucher à peine ma peau. [. . .] Mon corps était cette page et ce livre. Pour le réveiller, il fallait le nourrir, l'envelopper d'images, le remplir de syllabes et d'émotions, l'entretenir dans la douceur des choses et lui donner du rêve. (116)
>
> [These caresses in front of the mirror became a habit, a sort of pact between my body and its image, an image buried long ago that had to be awoken by letting my fingers lightly touch my skin. [. . .] My body was that page and that book. In order to awaken it, it had to be fed, wrapped in images, filled with syllables and emotions, maintained in the sweetness of things, and given dreams.]

Kamel Ben Ouanes suggests that the representation of the body in Ben Jelloun's novels 'n'est pas autre chose qu'une configuration verbale' [is nothing other than a verbal configuration].[56] While I agree that language is central to the formation of subjectivity in his texts, I see this language as much cerebral and linguistic as it is sensual, tactile, intimate and sexual. Masturbation is historically associated with the queer, the a- or anti-social, the disabled, the ex-centric, the childlike and the oversexed racialized woman.[57] It is a (sometimes temporary) turning away from the path of reproduction, as endorsed by nationalist familial values. Ahmed's sexual acts portray that his body's desires and sense of self cannot be confined to the demands of his father. Just as the words in the hammam and the mosque opened up the possibility of bodily pleasure and support beyond his existing world, masturbation furnishes his mind and body with thoughts, feelings, images and words that exceed the narrative forced upon and endorsed by him thus far. His sexual desires do not seek to ratify 'the narrative of containment of sex into one of the conventional romantic forms of modern consumer heterosexuality'.[58] As Thomas Laqueur says, '[Masturbation] has been understood as the paradigmatic sex of the mind, specifically of fantasy, of its capacity to imagine something other than the here and now; therein lay its pleasure and creative possibilities but also its dangers'.[59] Laqueur intimates that the dangers and pleasures of solitary sex are due to its separation from and repudiation of the established social order.[60] Where colonial discourse and practices sought to ensure white ascendency, racial purity and able-bodied populations who would reproduce replicas, onanism keeps 'men and

56 Kamel Ben Ouanes, 'L'Itinéraire de la parole dans l'œuvre romanesque de Tahar Ben Jelloun', in *Tahar Ben Jelloun: stratégies d'écriture*, ed. by Mansour M'Henni (Paris: Éditions L'Harmattan, 1993), pp. 35–49 (p. 40).

57 See Thomas Laqueur, *Solitary Sex: A Cultural History of Masturbation* (New York: Zone Books, 2004); Serlin, 'Touching Histories'; Vernon A. Rosario (ed.), *Science and Homosexualities*, (London: Routledge, 1997); and Sander Gilman, *Difference and Pathology: Stereotypes of Sexuality, Race and Madness* (Ithaca, NY and London: Cornell University Press, 1985).

58 Berlant, *Queen of America*, p. 62.

59 Laqueur, *Solitary Sex*, p. 218.

60 Ibid., p. 224.

women from the appropriate venue of pleasure that was the marriage bed, or at the very least the bed of heterosexual union'.[61] This act, which Laqueur insists has long been represented as a social problem or, more specifically, as a problem of inadequate socialization, represents the ineffectuality of institutional structures to curb the desires of the mind and the body.

These solitary sexual encounters address an other who is both self and other, both Ahmed and (maybe fictive) correspondent. Indeed, the categories of self and other do not grasp the representation of self, and self as other to the self, in these masturbatory awakenings and epistolary encounters. Here, touch is a reaching out to an other and feeling the other's response (both through the letters and through the self's touch). Ahmed uses his imagination as an embodied, sensorial experience to create different ways of being with himself and with others. Touch is no simple act of self-fulfilment, although it is a pleasure; solitary sex creates a time different from his father's linear, progressive narrative. Ahmed gives time to himself, to his body, and lives the present moment in pleasure and in contact with his flesh.

An ethics of touch

Although *L'Enfant* offers a critique of vision, it does not give priority to touch (as a superior or less violent sense). Similar to the works of Iris Marion Young and Marks,[62] Ben Jelloun's texts portray a visuality that is not determined by a desire for mastery, dominance or control. This optical politics is concerned with the intersubjective relationality of existing with others through our intellectually perceiving bodies. *L'Enfant* is therefore cautious in its portrayal of touch as a modality that will not violate the vulnerability of corporeal existence. The colonial and gendered gaze creates distance (even when close to others) through a politics of racialized difference and an erotics of able-bodied heteronormativity. Yet touch is not its opposite. As Sara Ahmed explains:

> We could consider how some forms of touch have been means of subjugating others, or of forming the other as a place of vulnerability and fear (colonial and sexual histories of touch as appropriation, violation and possession). We could also begin to deal with the relationship of touch implicit in the very fear of touching some others: such a refusal of touch is also a means of forming and de-forming some bodies in relationship to other bodies.[63]

Touch is one of the principal senses through which violence is enacted. Ontologically, touching others is not only constitutive of self with others, but is also the possibility of violating the ethical tie that is foundational to coexistence. Asserting the primacy

[61] Laqueur, *Solitary Sex*, p. 255.

[62] Iris Marion Young, *On Female Body Experience: 'Throwing Like a Girl' and Other Essays* (Oxford: Oxford University Press, 2005).

[63] Ahmed, *Strange Encounters*, p. 49.

of separateness and boundedness by violating an other is to seek to disavow the vulnerability of matter and form and of being with others. The colonial pursuit of knowledge is not only attached to a penetrating and constricting gaze, but is also connected to touch. Scientific research reaches to the body and into the flesh in search of truth and, especially in the colonial search for knowledge of difference, often subjects different others to irrevocable violence.[64]

Having left the confines of the familial home, Ahmed now leaves the parameters of his hotel room. His first encounter is with 'une vieille femme, mendiante ou sorcière, vagabond rusée' (112) [an old woman, a beggar or witch, a cunning vagabond] who asks, 'Qui es-tu ?' (113) [Who are you?]. Dissatisfied with Ahmed's response, she tears open his djellaba and 'passa ses mains sur [sa] poitrine, approcha de [lui] sa tête et posa ses lèvres sur le bout du sein droit, l'embrassa, le suça. Sa bouche n'avait pas de dents ; elle avait la douceur des lèvres d'un bébé' (114) [moved her hands over his chest, came closer to him with her head and then put her lips to the nipple of his right breast, kissed it, sucked it. Her mouth was toothless; it had the softness of a baby's lips]. After pushing her away from him and fleeing, Ahmed admits, 'La sensation physique que j'éprouvai aux caresses de cette bouche édentée sur mon sein fut, même si elle ne dura que quelques secondes, du plaisir. J'ai honte de l'avouer' (115) [The physical sensation I felt as that toothless mouth caressed my breast was pleasurable, even if it lasted only a few seconds. I am ashamed to admit it]. His second encounter is with a woman who becomes Ahmed's employer, Oum Abbas. Coercing Ahmed into following her, Oum Abbas corners him against a wall and begins to search his body:

> Je compris vite qu'elle ne cherchait ni argent ni bijoux. Ses mains tâtaient mon corps comme pour vérifier une intuition. Ma poitrine minuscule ne la rassura point, elle glissa sa main dans mon séroual et la laissa un instant sur mon bas-ventre, puis introduisait son médium dans mon vagin. J'eus très mal. Je poussai un cri qu'elle étouffa en mettant l'autre main sur ma bouche, puis me dit:
>
> - J'avais un doute.
> - Moi aussi ! dis-je entre les lèvres. (118)
>
> [I soon realized that she was looking neither for money nor for jewellery. Her hands roamed over my body as if to verify an intuition. My tiny breasts did not reassure her; she slipped her hand into my seroual and left it a moment on my sex, then inserted her middle finger into my vagina. It hurt a lot. I uttered a cry, which she stifled by putting her other hand over my mouth, saying,
>
> 'I wasn't sure.'
>
> 'Nor was I!' I said between my lips.]

64 An excellent example of how the gaze is penetrating and structured through unequal relationships is Michel Foucault's *The Birth of the Clinic*, trans. by Alan Sheridan (London: Routledge, [1963] 2004). See also, Ann Laura Stoler, *Race and the Education of Desire* and *Carnal Knowledge and Imperial Power: Race and the Intimate in Colonial Rule* (Berkeley, CA: University of California Press, 2002).

I agree with Hayes that Ahmed's contact with these women conveys how the 'answer to gender ambiguity [is thought to lie] in the *sex* of the body'.[65] In contradistinction to Butler's exploration of the ethical implications of the question 'Who are you?', this witch-like woman's question seeks epistemological certainty and definitive bodily answers.[66] The act of sucking on his breast, in a gesture that replicates and reverses the supposed nurturing relationship of mother and child, is the search for knowledge through an understanding of body parts as referential. Ahmed's arousal (he goes on to masturbate after this encounter) by a woman on the margins of society reinforces him as a visually monstrous other who is not constrained by the moralistic sexual norms of the familial nation. His libido is not directed towards reproductive sex and is awakened by a violent cross-generational intimacy.

The second encounter is much more aggressive and has a definitive aim of finding a body that can be used as a spectacle in a circus to replace 'l'homme [qui] joue à la danseuse sans se faire réllement [*sic*] passer pour une femme, où tout baigne dans la dérision, sans réelle ambiguïté' (120) [the man who plays a female dancer without really passing himself off as a woman, where there is an atmosphere of derision, without any real ambiguity]. That the orifice *is* knowledge for Oum Abbas is a forewarning of the violence to which she and her son subject their employees. The doubt Ahmed expresses about the presence of the vaginal canal, after his intense moments of masturbation, some taking place in front of a mirror, portrays his psychosomatic adherence to maleness. Gender identity is not solely based in the visual, but is significantly formed through the imaginary. Ahmed feels and perceives his body to be mainly male, while having knowledge that his body menstruates. Therefore that this woman can insert her finger is both a surprise and uncertain in meaning. That this intimate contact is distancing and violating is confirmed when she uses Ahmed as a spectacle in a circus show, reducing his body to one of visual fascination. The correlation of this circus environment with the freak show draws attention to the colonial practice of putting exoticized and eroticized difference on display as well as to the scientific interest in in-betweenness.[67] It highlights the connection between the exploitative visual fascination of colonial rule and the social hierarchization of bodily markers. Through a sexualized touch, the novel draws a parallel between the violation of an unreadable body and the bodily violence of colonial oppression. Touch is as susceptible to violent exploitation as the historical colonial and masculine use of the gaze. Touch, in the above encounters, is a denial of vulnerability. When unknowingness, vulnerability and opacity are rejected then the ethical potentiality of these encounters and of touch is foreclosed.

65 Hayes, p. 167.

66 For Butler's discussion of this question in relation to Hannah Arendt's work, see *Undoing Gender*, p. 35.

67 David A. Gerber, 'The "Careers" of People Exhibited: The Problem of Volition and Valorization', in *Freakery: Cultural Spectacles of the Extraordinary Body*, ed. by Rosemarie Garland-Thomson, foreword by Leslie A. Fiedler (New York: New York University Press, 1996), pp. 38–54 (pp. 44–5).

Embodied allegories

The second storyteller fails to return and is reported to have been found dead with Ahmed's diary in his hands. The square in which the audience was gathered is subsequently 'nettoyée' [cleaned up] and the entertainers replaced by 'une fontaine musicale où, tous les dimanches, les jets d'eau jaillissent sous l'impulsion des Bo-Bo-Pa-Pa de la *Cinquième Symphonie* de Beethoven' (135) [a musical fountain where, every Sunday, jets of water play to the accompaniment of the Da-Da-Da-Dum of Beethoven's *Fifth Symphony*]. In reference to the restructuring of public spaces in North Africa during French colonial rule, Fanon insightfully comments, 'Colonialism made no mistake when from 1955 on it proceeded to arrest these storytellers systematically'.[68] Ben Jelloun is building on this potential for anti-colonial resistance through the act of sharing narratives in public spaces. Yet the dispersal of the crowd and the modernization of the square, while redolent of colonial policies and practices, take place in post-independent Morocco. Indeed, the novel portrays a continuation of colonial modernization (implemented by the first resident general of Morocco, Marshal Louis-Hubert Lyautey) in the postcolonial period. Both the colonial administration and the postcolonial regime aim to dissipate culturally specific spectacles in an attempt to make the cities of Morocco 'clean' and therefore 'modern' (where modernity is in opposition to what might be considered 'traditional' practices).[69] At the moment when Ahmed most visibly embodies gender ambiguity (where the narrator admits to no longer knowing which pronoun or name to employ) the narrative thread is temporarily lost. Cleansing the square poses a threat to the existence of the tale; the listeners are left in a state of uncertainty and with a further realization of the power of the technocrats to continue the colonial project as a postcolonial endeavour. Responding to the state's acts of cultural cleansing through the process of modernization, three avid listeners take responsibility for keeping the story alive and resolve to each tell her/his own version of the Ahmed/Zahra story. A collective determination to bear witness to the as yet unarticulated histories of Ahmed/Zahra drives the listeners to speak despite the state's attempt to silence narrative through spatialized 'development'.

These three responses by the dedicated audience members have in more recent critical readings of *L'Enfant* largely become the lens through which the novel is interpreted. There is a contemporary critical shift to reading this novel, through Fanon's *The Wretched of the Earth*, as a postcolonial text. In this context, Ahmed/Zahra's body is largely reduced to the allegorical level where his/her body stands in for the postcolonial politics of the Moroccan nation. However, I would argue that the novel resists its own process of allegorization by continually presenting an embodied tale

68 Frantz Fanon, *The Wretched of the Earth*, trans. by Constance Farrington (New York: Grove Press, 1963), p. 241.

69 See McClintock's work on the fetishization of cleanliness, especially in the Victorian period, in *Imperial Leather*, pp. 207–31.

that is in excess of and therefore uncontainable by the narrative form. The narrators focus on violated, aroused and multisensorial bodies. Indeed, the only woman narrator in the novel insists that she is the main protagonist Ahmed/Zahra. While I agree that the novel explores the emergence of dichotomous national narratives by portraying the uncertainty of gender through queer embodiments, I would also suggest that the text necessitates a reading that addresses why the materiality of the body – the viscerality of the story – remains at the fore. I agree with Stephen Slemon that postcolonial allegories generally build 'the provisional, discursive nature of history into the structure and narrative mode of the text so that it becomes approachable only in an act of reading'.[70] Indeed, these three storytellers make visible how queer bodies are useful political tools for telling their own histories of Morocco. Yet, each version of this tale shows a deep-seated concern for how life could be rendered livable for the main protagonist and thus explores how living a queer life within the available narratives may result in violence, invisibility and/or the creating of unimagined modes of being with others. It is the very materiality of gender and sexual desire that repeatedly brings the audience and the readers back to the question of how the protagonist will live a viable life in post-independent Morocco.

Describing the function of the three audience members who become narrators, Lisa Lowe focuses on the national allegory they each offer:

> In the novel's allegory, which figures colonialism, nativism, and nomadism in the register of sexuality, the *topos* of forced transvestism corresponds to the cultural *topos* of French colonial domination of Morocco, while the possibility of realizing an 'authentic' female identity, which preoccupies a number of the narrators, corresponds to an idealized return to precolonial nativism. [. . .] Thus, the protagonist's nomadic cross-dressing suggests a relationship to sexuality in which there are no stable, essentialized gender sites, in which the undetermined wandering from identity to identity, and desire to desire, is a strategy for resisting the fixed formations of either fixed masculine or feminine subjectivities, and allegorically, the overdetermined opposition of colonial rule and nativist reaction.[71]

Gauch adds to Lowe's formulation by suggesting that the 'text upsets the very idea that sexual or national identity naturally follows from biology or an authentic cultural essence'.[72] According to Lowe, Salem, the first of the three to begin and the son of a

70 Stephen Slemon, 'Post-Colonial Allegory and the Transformation of History', *The Journal of Commonwealth Literature* 23 (1988), 157–68 (p. 160).

71 Lisa Lowe, 'Literary Nomadics in Francophone Allegories of Postcolonialism: Pham Van Ky and Tahar Ben Jelloun', *Yale French Studies* 82.1 (1993), 43–61 (pp. 56–7). For further readings of Ahmed's body as an allegory of the nation, see Gauch, 'Telling the Tale of a Body Devoured by Narrative', 179–202; Rebecca Saunders, 'Decolonizing the Body: Gender, Nation and Narration in Tahar Ben Jelloun's *L'Enfant de sable*', *Research in African Literatures* 37.4 (2006), 136–60; and Hayes, especially the chapters 'In the Nation's Closets: Sexual Marginality and the Itinerary of National Identity', pp. 120–35 and 'Becoming a Woman: Tahar Ben Jelloun's Allegory of Gender', pp. 165–81. Despite the overlap of these critics' readings of Ahmed's body as an allegory of the Moroccan nation, it should be clear that how they each read the physicality of Ahmed's body differs significantly. I discuss some of these divergences later in the chapter.

72 Gauch, 'Telling the Tale of a Body Devoured by Narrative', p. 181.

slave brought from Senegal, 'allegorizes the worst extreme of colonial domination, and implies that resistance to colonialism is as ill-fated as Zahra's violent end'.[73] Gauch, also using Fanon's thesis from *The Wretched of the Earth*, draws a slightly different conclusion: 'Salem's position echoes Fanon's writings when he insists on the necessity of engaging in violent resistance to put an end to the social violence afflicting Moroccan society'.[74] Lowe focuses on the destruction and violence of colonial rule through slavery, whereas Gauche stresses the violence necessary to achieve independence from colonial rule. Despite their different interpretations of the violence in this account, both critics focus mainly on Salem's history as the son of a slave. Yet Salem spends a significant amount of his narrative explaining Ahmed's afterlife, telling us he was canonized after his death as 'le saint de la fécondité bienheureuse, car il assure aux femmes d'accoucher d'enfants mâles' (138) [the saint of blessed fertility, for he could ensure that women gave birth to male children]. Salem makes a national hero, a martyr, out of Ahmed and, in so doing, makes him the sanctified one who can ensure the reproduction of physical maleness and the evident values attached to this necessity. He betrays his adherence to the same values as Ahmed's father in recognizing the need for a saint who can assure the birth of boys, but asserts this through a figure (Ahmed) who has struggled throughout his own life with the violence of strict gender imposition.

Salem, however, openly admits that Ahmed's sainthood is merely a rumour, thus undermining the surety of his own narrative and pointing to the somewhat fictive way in which value may be attributed to dead bodies. If Salem's is a nationalist tale of anti-colonial struggle, then his reference to Ahmed/Zahra's posthumous life is an indication of his own belief that there are 'autant de questions sans réponses' (139) [so many questions without any answers]. Although he valorizes the one who dies in fighting against the violence of colonial rule, and I explain this in detail below, Salem takes a somewhat confusing political position, insofar as the Moroccan nationalists had long made clear their thoughts on sainthood:

> Moroccan neo-Salafiya theorists concluded that the neglect or misinterpretation of Islam were both due to ignorance (*jehaliya*), and that this ignorance began in the family. Therefore, in order to rebuild Muslim society, the first step was to fight against false traditions and ignorance within the family. [. . .] Thus, a large part of the social reform movement was directed against superstition – the lively religious life centered around saints [*sic*] tombs (*zaouiya*) – and against extravagant spending during celebrations. [. . .] The nationalists saw the education of women as one of the most effective means of fighting ignorance in the family.[75]

Furthermore, as the nationalist Oum Keltoun El Khatib states, '[The] colonialists [. . .] sponsored *zaouiya* [saints' celebrations] and everything else that would make Moroccans even more ignorant'.[76] Thus, while giving an anti-colonial stance, Salem aligns himself with practices outlawed by the pro-independence fighters and endorsed

[73] Lowe, p. 58.
[74] Gauch, 'Telling the Tale of a Body Devoured by Narrative', pp. 194–5.
[75] Baker, pp. 21–2.
[76] Ibid., p. 124.

by the French colonizers. The beatification makes a spectacle out of Ahmed, reinforces that male children are more valuable than female ones (and thus that gender divisions are central to postcolonial nationalism), and undermines Salem's adherence to a post-independence nationalism that demands a cessation of such colonial practices (namely the worshipping of saints).

As Salem moves on to speak of how Ahmed/Zahra died, he tells not only of a nationalist hero but also of a transnational method of fighting against colonial oppressors and of stopping the maltreatment of workers:

> Une nuit de pleine lune, Zahra eut l'intuition qu'Abbas allait se jeter sur elle. Ses mains libres ramassèrent deux lames de rasoir jetées dans la cage par des spectateurs. Elle se déshabilla, mit les deux lames dans un chiffon qu'elle plaça en évidence entre ses fesses et attendit à plat ventre la visite de la brute. Elle avait lu dans un vieux magazine que les femmes pendant la guerre d'Indochine avaient recours à cette méthode pour tuer les soldats ennemis qui les violaient. C'était aussi une forme de suicide.
>
> Zahra reçut comme une masse d'une tonne le corps d'Abbas qui eut la verge fendue. De douleur et de rage, il l'étrangla. Zahra mourut à l'aube étouffée, et le violeur succomba des suites de l'hémorragie.
>
> Voilà comment est mort Ahmed. Voilà comment s'est achevée la vie – courte – de Zahra. (143)
>
> [One night with a full moon, Zahra felt that Abbas [the son of the circus owner] was going to attack her again. With her free hands she picked up two razor blades that had been thrown into the cage by spectators. She undressed and put the blades between her buttocks; lying on her belly, she awaited the brute's visit. She had read in an old magazine that during the Indochinese war women had used this method to kill enemy soldiers who raped them. It was also a form of suicide.
>
> Abbas's body fell on Zahra's like a ton weight. His member was cut. Yelling with pain and rage, he strangled her. Zahra died at dawn, and the rapist later died from loss of blood.
>
> That is how Ahmed died. That is how Zahra's – brief – life came to an end.]

Zahra's choice of weapon is situated in a wider global context where women, and it is specifically women, have sought to bring an end to the sexual violence of colonial domination through death. The magazine reference recalls how it was in Indochina that the first resident general of Morocco, Marshall Louis-Hubert Lyautey, was to learn about, and later attempt to violently implement in Morocco, French protectorate rule rather than 'outright colonial annexation and direct French rule'.[77] Salem's version asserts that if practices of colonial warfare, domination and rule migrated along with the army leaders from country to country, then the techniques of fighting against these also travelled. Zahra, here, stands in for the many women who died in the colonial

[77] William A. Hoisington, Jr, *Lyautey and the French Conquest of Morocco* (London: Macmillan Press, 1995), p. 6.

wars of independence, not as a passive or cloistered woman but rather as someone able to use the tools available to her – the very blades thrown at her to harm her. Violent intimacy destroys self and other in an act that is redolent of the suicide bomber as described by Mbembe. She undermines – even destroys – the force (and violence) of the occupiers in an attempt to further the nationalist cause and thereby bring an end to colonial violations. As Zhor Lazraq, staunch nationalist and founder of the Association for the Protection of the Moroccan Family, says, 'The Moroccan woman was up to the task. She was a warrior, a nationalist, and she made all kinds of sacrifices'.[78] Salem's narrative thus both commemorates what has often been written out of nationalist history books and critiques the literary critic's tendency to read Moroccan women as passive tools of male manipulation. In addition, Salem recognizes Ahmed/Zahra as both the man he was and the persona of Zahra he took on as part of a circus routine. Salem does not simply reduce Ahmed/Zahra's body to an allegory of violent anti-colonial nationalism. Rather, he bears witness to history as a narrative act full of uncertainties that defy the logic of colonial *and* nationalist ideals. He seeks to give agency to anti-colonial protestors, especially women, and to Ahmed who defies the sexualized violence of colonial rule, exemplified through the freak show. The necessity of violence for independence is apparent, but Salem's narrative is full of gaps, ambiguity and conflict, and thereby opens up a space for the other listeners to create a different future for Ahmed/Zahra.

As Salem terminates his version of Ahmed/Zahra's life story, Amar contests his words saying, 'Je connais la fin de cette histoire. J'ai trouvé le manuscrit que nous lisait le conteur' (144) [I know the end of this story. I found the manuscript that the storyteller was reading to us]. According to Gauch, this reference back to the official document indicates this storyteller's desire to 'return to the texts of the Arab golden age and the cultivation of the mind as a way of combating the restrictions currently placed upon their bodies'.[79] Lowe describes this as a return to a 'nativist' tradition[80] and Hayes suggests it is a quest for 'national origins'.[81] Amar certainly valorizes the ancient Islamic texts (that 'plus personne ne lit aujourd'hui' (158) [nobody reads nowadays]) for their poetry and sensuality. He does, however, refuse to assign the protagonist anything other than his male name:

> Moi, je ne l'appellerai pas Zahra. Parce que sur le manuscrit il signait par son unique initiale, la lettre A. Bien sûr ce pourrait être Aïcha, Amina, Atika, Alia, Assia. . . . Mais admettons qu'il s'agit d'Ahmed. (147)
>
> [I shall not call him Zahra. Because the manuscript was signed with his single initial, the letter 'A'. Of course, it might have been Aïsha, Amina, Atika, Alia, Assia. . . . But let's say it meant Ahmed.]

According to Gauch, Hayes, Lowe and Saunders, through his refusal to acknowledge the possibility of another initial, Amar is dismissing a time prior to both maleness and

78 Baker, p. 92.
79 Gauch, 'Telling the Tale of a Body Devoured by Narrative', p. 195.
80 Lowe, p. 58.
81 Hayes, p. 180.

the birth of the independent nation. In other words, they argue that he is wiping out the period of French colonial rule from Moroccan history. He is thereby reiterating a narrative of origins that seeks to implement a nationalist ideology through a fixed idea of how society was prior to colonial rule: an 'authentic', precolonial way of being Moroccan.[82]

However, Amar discusses how French protectorate rule has exacerbated the social, economic and political inequalities between men and women in contemporary Morocco. Stating that the manuscript is signed with the letter 'A' creates a vagueness around the signatory and also emphasizes a process of stigmatization:

> The one marked, whether with a D, a K or an A, is marked for life. His life becomes a mere punctuation mark in time; he becomes characterized, stigmatized, for ever, unchangeable.[83]

That the only trace of Ahmed is the physical presence of the letter 'A' suggests an association between his body-as-narrative and the branding of slaves and criminals, as described by Connor. It reinforces Ahmed as socially ostracized and as physically wearing a label of difference. Furthermore, as do all the storytellers, Amar attempts to create an association between his own life and that of the main protagonist, through this stress on the initial 'A' which they both share. While refuting Salem's version as perverse, he returns to the focus on anal sex to contemporize this act in the sex tourism of the British in Morocco. Where Salem suggests anal intercourse is a defiant anti-colonial and suicidal act, Amar speaks of the taboo of male same-sex desire and its direct relation to the Europeans' stronger economic position. Amar shows how neocolonial oppression continues, despite the achievement of national independence. To this extent, he is concerned with the contradictions of a post-independence identity and the search for sexual relations that do not repeat the violence of colonial and national power struggles. He recognizes that independence has been achieved on a national level, but that French colonial values and technologies structure everyday life in Morocco. His focus on Ahmed's contradictory affiliation to and repudiation of his male and female body reinforces his willingness to narrate a bodily tale of incoherence.[84] Most importantly, Amar terminates his tale by refusing to stay faithful to the text: 'ce que je vais vous lire ne figure pas dans le manuscrit, c'est de mon imagination' (159) [what I am going to read you is not to be found in the manuscript; it comes from my own imagination]. His idea of reading is to repeat the words on the page faithfully and to be led by the imagination.

Amar displays a highly self-reflexive quality as he sums up his and Salem's interests in the tale:

82 It is difficult to agree with these critics that Amar's emphasis on the initial 'A' is a wiping out of colonial history in a narrative of origins. The initial 'Z' of Zahra would represent not the inclusion of Morocco's colonial history in the creation of a post-independent nation, but the desire to return to an identity that reflects the pre-masculine self, the pre-independent nation.

83 Connor, p. 76.

84 Amar highlights these ambiguities, describing Ahmed's 'corps de femme' [woman's body], 'petits seins' [small breasts], 'voix d'homme' [man's voice] and 'visage fin [. . .] couvert par une barbe' [delicate face covered in a beard] (152–3).

> [Je] me demande ce qui m'a passionné [de cette histoire]. Je crois savoir que c'est d'abord l'aspect énigmatique, et ensuite je pense que notre société est très dure, ça n'a pas l'air, mais il y a une telle violence dans nos rapports qu'une histoire folle, comme celle de cet homme avec un corps de femme, est une façon de pousser cette violence très loin, à son extrême limite. Nous sommes intrigués par le pays qui s'exprime ainsi . . . (160)
>
> [I wonder what I found so fascinating about this story. I suppose it was, first of all, its enigmatic quality, and then I think our society is very harsh. I know it doesn't seem that way, but there's such a violence in our relationships that a crazy story about a man with a woman's body is a means of carrying that violence to its absolute limit. We're intrigued by a country that would express itself in such way. . . .]

He is lucidly aware of employing Ahmed's life story to discuss his own dismay at the way in which Morocco is being mistreated and disfigured.[85] He understands the story of Ahmed as the staging of the violence that exists between the genders, and between the colonizers and the colonized. Amar moves between allegory, fiction and sociopolitical critique, while carving out a viable (narrative) space within which Ahmed can survive. Although Salem and Amar express views that overlap with the two Fanonian poles (of anti-colonial violence and nativism), their narratives offer nuanced reflections on how queer bodies move within the national space. They are self-reflective critics of a society that they want to see change, and they do this by staying attentive to the embodied effects of and resistance to state technologies of control. They employ art to articulate what is too difficult to discuss about their contemporary lives and, if their views betray a biased historical angle, they also demonstrate an astute awareness that they are open to other interpretations of the story and, thus, to others. Amar thereby brings us back to the structure of the tale. He admits his usage of Ahmed's body and, in so doing, actively draws our attention to how queer bodies – particularly Ahmed's gender uncertainty – are employed as prosthetic narrative tools in fiction and literary criticism. Ahmed/Zahra is, in the stories of Salem and Amar, a fictional character who helps them understand their own careers, their histories and the contemporary political state of Morocco. They are readers with an open political agenda but, unlike what critics such as Gauch, Hayes, Lowe and Saunders suggest, their readings exceed Fanon's political analysis of struggles for independence from colonial rule. For these two storytellers, fiction becomes the medium through which what cannot be said can begin to be translated, heard and retranslated. Furthermore, they repeatedly return to the exploitation of the body through a sexualized touch in order to trace the ways in which bodies are controlled and coerced to conform to and endorse colonialist, nationalist and neocolonial agendas. Their reflections on their own stories encourage a self-reflexive reading practice from the listener, and invite the readers to contemplate their own interpretations of the stories constructed through the use of queer bodies.

85 Amar states, '[. . .] moi, qui suis un vieil instituteur retraité, fatigué par ce pays ou plus exactement par ceux qui le maltraitent et le défigurent [. . .]' (160) [I'm an old, retired schoolteacher, tired of this country, or, to be more precise, by those who mistreat and disfigure it].

Where Salem and Amar continue the storytelling tradition established in the novel through the use of the third person singular, the only female storyteller, Fatouma, employs the first person singular. This rhetorical device not only creates a parallel between Ahmed/Zahra's life and Fatouma's, establishing her as possibly the protagonist of the story narrated thus far, but also further 'strips the character of Ahmed of his uniqueness' and 'renders [Fatouma's] story collective'.[86] She takes on the narrative as if it is her own and, in so doing, does not simply appropriate the story of an other, but instead insists on its personal and intimate dimensions. It is her story and yet a tale of and for others. Embodying the narrative entails not simply a dominance or a taking control of the story, but also an openness to the story altering the self. Lowe reads Fatouma's narrative as offering Fanon's 'third alternative – neither neo-colonialism nor a nativist inversion – which would break with the old logic, structures, and narratives of colonialism, and would persist in collectively criticizing the institutions and apparatuses of rule'.[87] She states,

> Fatouma's story provides a narrative position from which to resist the other narratives in *L'Enfant*, which suggest that Ahmed/Zahra must choose between 'masculinity' and 'femininity', and allegorically, which imply that postcolonial struggles must either reproduce colonialism or take the form of nativist nationalism.[88]

Gauch is much more cautious in her reading of Fatouma suggesting that 'the discordant memories and experiences of these [disaffected] women and children [of whom Fatouma speaks] demand a reevaluation of the manner in which post-independence nationhood is being formulated'.[89] I concur with Gauch that Fatouma could be said to represent the disillusionment of post-independence life especially for women. Baker explains how, prior to independence, the nationalist movement, especially through the king and his vocal daughters, supported the education of women in order to 'reinforce social cohesion against the menace of colonialism'.[90] She emphasizes the aspirations of the women involved in all aspects of the liberation struggle:

> Everyone had high hopes for the future in an independent Morocco. But this national solidarity and unity of purpose quickly disintegrated. For many of the women who participated in the armed resistance (who had hoped that after independence their lives would somehow be different and better than before) the optimism gave way to disappointment, anger, and finally, resignation.[91]

She stresses how post-independence hope was dissipated once it became apparent that the gaining of power was the sole goal of all political parties:

> There was no discussion of the relationship between the emancipation of women and larger social change; and there were no women in the leadership of the parties who might have raised these issues.[92]

86 Gauch, 'Telling the Tale of a Body Devoured by Narrative', pp. 195–6.
87 Lowe, p. 44.
88 Ibid., p. 59.
89 Gauch, 'Telling the Tale of a Body Devoured by Narrative', p. 197.
90 Baker, p. 22.
91 Ibid., p. 32.
92 Ibid., p. 39.

There is, as Gauch and Lowe insist, a critique of the current political climate that uses a limited notion of tradition as a means of enforcing a system based on inequality of the genders and a family-focused national identity. However, contra Lowe, Fatouma's choice to now live as a woman suggests that identitarian positionalities may sometimes play a role in eradicating social, economic and political inequalities.

I would suggest that Fatouma's emphasis on mass mobilization as a vehicle for change stresses an historically located and geographically specific critique of colonial rule, rather than a generic theory of anti-colonial struggles. She speaks of the women who helped her when she was shot by the French authorities, after being caught up in a protest march of which she was not a part. As Saunders specifies, these events reference directly 'les semaines sanglantes' [the weeks of blood] when, as a result of the assassination of the Tunisian trade union leader Farhat Hached, a general strike was declared.[93] In many of the major cities on the night of 7 December 1952, the unarmed crowds clashed with the colonial security forces, who opened fire creating a 'scene of civilian slaughter'.[94] According to Baker, the 'dead and the wounded were too numerous to count'.[95] Fatouma situates her political mobilization in the events that mirror the unduly violent acts of the French authorities during 'les semaines sanglantes'. She speaks also of 'ceux qui ont été chassés des campagnes par la sécheresse et les détournements d'eau' (168) [those driven out of the countryside by drought and irrigation projects which diverted the flow of water], signalling the 'drought [that] devastated Morocco (exacerbated by certain colons' impudent diversion of public water to their own farms)' in 1937.[96] Her emphasis on the colonial forces' motivation 'nettoyer le pays de la mauvaise graine pour empêcher de nouvelles émeutes' (170) [to rid the country of the bad seed in order to prevent new riots], displays the violence the colonial regime exerted in the name of order. Historical memory is a painful embodied experience that listens to the voices of women and their fight against the French occupiers. It is also a remembering of the details of the fight for national independence so as to question how a post-independent space can be built on oppressive and exclusionary, so-called traditional, values.

Fatouma brings her self into the narrative to describe how the fight against colonial occupation has been felt on women's bodies. Yet, she also focuses on how memories are eclectic and stored within objects. She claims that a cardboard box full of random objects contains 'la clé de notre histoire' (167) [the key to our story]. These objects, like the visual erotics Marks describes, 'remain inscrutable'.[97] They evoke 'an encounter

93 While Saunder's article is unique in the historical analysis of specific events, some of the narrative around the violent events of December 1952 is unclear and confusing. For a clear analysis of the events leading up to the violence, see Jim House, 'L'Impossible contrôle d'une ville coloniale? Casablanca, décembre 1952', *Géneses* 86 (2012), 78–103. For example, Saunders suggests that the strike broke out as a result of the arrest of the Istiqlal leaders, but House makes apparent that the general strike was declared to protest against the assassination of the Tunisian trade union leader Farhat Hached. The Istiqlal leaders were eventually arrested as a result of these protests. The Istiqlal were the main movement fighting for independence from the French protectorate.

94 Saunders, p. 137.

95 Baker, p. 27.

96 Saunders, p. 137. Saunders uses the French term 'colons' to signify the French colonizers.

97 Marks, *Touch*, p. 18.

[. . .] that delights in the fact of its alterity'.[98] There is a trace of memories on and in these objects, but these things remain tangible only through Fatouma. History, for Fatouma, is the mobilization of the population on the streets to fight against injustice and the desire to remember through objects that give no definitive meaning. In other words, to learn about the past is to tell of one's own implication in it, to build memories through the body, and to give others access to random disparate things that provoke questions, bewilderment and the imagination. To this extent, Fatouma is represented as establishing history not as located in all-revealing artefacts of the past but in the inscrutable objects and bodies that remain unknowable. Like Salem who focuses on unanswerable questions and Amar who reads the endlessly deferred meaning of poetical texts, Fatouma leaves her audience with questions *and* with further knowledge of colonial and postcolonial violence.

Fatouma terminates her version by telling her listeners:

> Entre-temps j'avais perdu le grand cahier où je consignais mon histoire. J'essayai de le reconstituer mais en vain ; alors je sortis à la recherche du récit de ma vie antérieure. La suite vous la connaissez. J'avoue avoir pris du plaisir à écouter le conteur, puis vous. J'ai eu ainsi le privilège, vingt ans plus tard, de revivre certaines étapes de ma vie. (170)
>
> [Meanwhile, I had lost the big notebook to which I had consigned my story. I tried to reconstruct it, but in vain; then I went out in search of the story of my earlier life. The rest you know. I admit that I took great pleasure in listening to the storyteller and then to you. It gave me the privilege of reliving certain stages of my life, twenty years later.]

The claim that she is the protagonist of the intra-diegetic narrative is never disputed. Fatouma accepts the previous storytellers' words as the narratives of her life. She dissolves the boundaries between storyteller and intra-diegetic fictional character, and fiction and reality. In so doing, she demonstrates why storytelling is important for those who listen: it gives them the possibility of remembering, of subsequently bearing witness to a life that may have gone unnoticed and of recognizing their own existence. That is, their words create space for yet another life that may have been lost in the post-independent, familial narrative. She specifically gives her listeners yet another version of Moroccan history, of Ahmed/Zahra's life, and hope that the protagonist, through her, may have found a shared and collective space in which to exist without being subjected to violence.

Although the three avid listeners and now narrators of the story of Ahmed/Zahra focus on Morocco's history of colonial subjugation, they also emphasize how life can be made unbearable for those who transition between genders and for those who cannot or who refuse to conform to strict gender norms. The arrival of the troubadour aveugle [the blind troubadour] from Buenos Aires further disrupts the national allegories one might want to read in the text. As Gauch suggests:

> [He] is unencumbered by personal experience of [Morocco's] recent history and culture and thus by the limitations they might pose on fictions generated there.

[98] Marks, *Touch*, p. 18.

> [. . .] In these closing pages of *The Sand Child*, then, he impossibly perverts Ahmed's origins by relating a multilayered tale in which his/her doubles figure everywhere.[99]

The troubadour's presence makes manifest how all the narrators pursue a creative, performative and ethical engagement with Ahmed/Zahra's narrative. He highlights how the process of allegorization and of historiography is an act of storytelling. He speaks of his arrival as a character in a book who throws the reader off track, of falsifying memories according to the audience's needs and of indecipherable objects left by someone he believes may have been Ahmed/Zahra. He brings the story back to the question of how the self comes into being and how it can live a viable existence. He states, 'Peut-être que je finirai par savoir qui je suis. Mais cela est une autre histoire' (185) [Perhaps, in the end, I shall know who I am. But that is another story]. If, as I have suggested, Ahmed/Zahra's life is represented as a search for a sense of self and an understanding of the human as coming into being over and over again, then the troubadour aveugle affirms that to 'know' who one is is to narrate yet another story. Echoing his words, Butler states,

> My account of myself is partial, haunted by that for which I can devise no definitive story. I cannot explain why I have emerged in this way, and my efforts at narrative reconstruction are always undergoing revision.[100]

Knowledge production is an endless narrative engagement with others. Bearing witness to histories of violence involves a constant undoing of the self and of one's epistemological parameters. It is to enter into shared dialogue with others, where the opacity of the other necessitates a never-ending narrative responsibility. In this openness, what is imagined into being is a narrative production that in its failure to cohere suggests a vulnerability of form, of bodily morphology, where the human and the story of belonging are always becoming. *L'Enfant* implicates us all in the lives of others and, thereby, situates the possibility of becoming human in an ethical indebtedness to others. To be human is to be responsible for an other, to be open to an other and to be interdependent. In the viscerality of sharing histories we remember how language is embodied, how state technologies intervene through the intimate and how the body is a tool of resistance. We are also reminded that embodied allegories are testimonies to queer, disabled lives that exceed the symbolic. The flesh of these stories demands an attention to how both Fatima and Ahmed/Zahra forge disabled and queer identities and selves by refusing and being unable to conform to the normative scripture of abled-bodied, heteronormative nationalism.

Performative pain

I want to conclude this chapter with a focus on the return of the second narrator at the end of the novel, who tells us, 'Ni vous ni moi ne saurons jamais la fin de l'histoire' (204) [Neither you nor I will ever know the end of the story] and who, more specifically, speaks

99 Gauch, *Liberating Shahrazad*, p. 77.
100 Butler, *Giving an Account of Oneself*, p. 40.

of the distress he suffered when his life reached breaking point as a result of his telling of the tale. In the previous chapter I suggested that Tyler's narration of Mala's life story approximated Scarry's idea that because pain is so unbearable and unshareable it often requires someone else to speak '*on behalf of*' the one in pain.[101] In contradistinction, Ben Jelloun's novel suggests that the one who takes on the story of pain in turn becomes inhabited by and, thus, unable to detach her/his own self from the story. To begin to translate what one has heard – both to begin to speak and to attempt to comprehend what has been read or narrated orally – is to undergo a somatic disruption that is painful and traumatic. Where the storytellers and listeners experience pain as they try to narrate Ahmed's story, I would suggest that this is not an appropriation of an other's pain in order to take it on as one's own, as if an other's experience is directly accessible. Rather, it is a bodily vulnerability that allows each storyteller to come close to Ahmed's tale, to both touch it and be touched by it, to feel the pain of becoming undone. Sara Ahmed elaborates on how this attempt to understand an other's pain might be able to avoid appropriating the other's inaccessible feelings:

> [The] ungraspability of my own pain is brought to the surface by the ungraspability of the pain of others. Such a response to her pain is not simply a return to the self (how do I feel given that I don't know how she feels?): this is not a radical egoism. Rather, in the face of the otherness of my own pain, *I am undone, before her, and for her*. [The] ethical demand is that I must act about that which I cannot know, rather than act insofar as I know. I am moved by what does not belong to me. If I acted on her behalf only insofar as I knew how she felt, then I would act only insofar as I would appropriate her pain as my pain, that is, appropriate that which I cannot feel.[102]

In *L'Enfant* the speakers and listeners often describe feeling the stories in and on their bodies. They cannot let go of the tale and often stress that the story will not release them. While disturbing and disruptive, this engulfment is the ethical and shared responsibility for narrating silenced, unarticulated or unknowable histories of violence.

There has been a recent critical move where the reiteration of the same story over and over again is read as directly related to theories of performativity. Critics such as Gauch, Hayes and Saunders propose this critical framework as essential to our understandings of *L'Enfant*. Hayes suggests that Ben Jelloun and other North African writers, such as Mohammed Dib, Tahar Djaout and Leïla Sebbar, are working at the intersections of Butler's and Bhabha's work on performativity through a focus on the correlation between sexual identity and national belonging. In his words:

> Writing the Nation is always a rewriting, and in rewriting, there is room for subversion. Butler's performance of gender roles, then, parallels Bhabha's

[101] Scarry states:

> Because the person in pain is ordinarily so bereft of the resources of speech, it is not surprising that the language for pain should sometimes be brought into being by those who are not themselves in pain but who speak *on behalf of* those who are. (Scarry, p. 6)

[102] Ahmed, *The Cultural Politics of Emotion*, p. 31, emphasis added.

> performance of the Nation. Her parody, inserting a slight difference from the original, exploits what Bhabha characterizes as the splitting between the ideal and its performance and offers a way of transforming national identity and proliferating it beyond its narrow definition in dominant discourse. If this splitting can be used to challenge dominant models of gendered identity, perhaps it can also be exploited to challenge official models of nationality.[103]

Hayes suggests that through the representation of the ever-increasing number of narrators, each with their own specific version of Ahmed/Zahra's story, Ben Jelloun teases out how national discourse is deeply intertwined with narratives of the family and heteronormative models of gender. In Hayes's reading, Ben Jelloun is enacting a queering of the nation, through a character whose gender fluctuates, and thus rewriting and revising assumed normal complementary, gender-dyad narratives of the nation. That is, Ben Jelloun puts on display the very production of national discourse, and proposes in its place a queering, where belonging is not restricted to two unobtainable gender norms.

Saunders suggests something similar to Hayes insofar as she reiterates that identity categories are 'effects of regulatory practices that produce the bodies they then "represent" and govern'; that performativity conceptualizes how reiterative practices of 'a sexed body or a native culture' are 'never quite complete'; 'that bodies and cultures never quite comply with the norms by which their materialisation is impelled'; and that 'it is precisely because identity comes into being through repetition that it can be altered'.[104] Where Hayes concludes by discussing 'a method of rewriting national identity in heterogeneous and inclusive ways',[105] Saunders focuses on what she refers to as the decolonization of both gender and Morocco that is 'largely synonymous with a tolerance of uncertainty – of, for example, narrative irresolution, ambiguous genders, and national ambivalence'.[106] Although their emphasis is on proliferation, multiplicity, revision, heterogeneity and uncertainty, they stress a widening of existing parameters of belonging and of sexed and gendered identity so that no one is excluded. It is possible to read the collective listening represented in *L'Enfant* as an openness to allowing others the space to speak and be heard and therefore, to some extent, to argue that the novel proposes an inclusive society where difference is accepted and tolerated. Nonetheless, I would suggest that the return of the psychosomatically disturbed narrator at the end of the novel does not propose a narrative of inclusion where Ahmed/Zahra's gender ambiguity can be tolerated. Instead, he tells of the effects of the story and its incessant telling in and on the bodies of those who speak and those who listen. Storytelling is a literal bodily investment, where self, other and narrative are implicated in and tied to each other. The performative structure of the narrative shows how bodies and spaces of belonging come into being through shared narratives. However, any change to the narrative, any desire to participate in telling the story, could have irrevocable

103 Hayes, pp. 134–5.
104 Saunders, pp. 142–3.
105 Hayes, p. 135.
106 Saunders, p. 143.

psychosomatic effects. The performative structure of memory is potentially painful and destructive in its failure to produce coherence, and can thereby become too much of a burden. This weight *may* be rendered bearable through the determination of the narrators to take collective responsibility for each other and for the continuation of the story. In this novel, the performative form of national and gendered belonging and embodiment portrays how the desire for change requires a collective engagement in a rethinking of the very form histories may take. It also shows how this undertaking is endless, painful and embodied.

Performativity (and this includes narrative reiteration) is not only the potential for change as the copy fails to live up to the original, as bodies fail to approximate norms and as the pedagogical fails to contain everyday practices. It is also an acknowledgement and enactment of Laub's idea that 'no amount of telling seems ever to do justice' and that there 'are never enough words or the right words'.[107] Repetition for Laub is both the necessary narrative conducted by the survivor in relation to an other in order to belatedly bear witness to an event and the more problematic compulsion to tell the same story incessantly because 'very little was heard'.[108] He describes the 'imperative to tell and to be heard' as a potentially 'all-consuming life task'.[109] Laub frames this compulsion as potentially destructive, as negatively skewing the survivor's view of her/himself, and as necessitating 'the obliteration of the audience'.[110] Yet, Ben Jelloun represents this repetitive, compulsive and sometimes destructive narrative production as the *creation* of an audience, as the potential for forging connections between others, and as the possibility of being heard through the acts of mutual listening and narrating. In *L'Enfant*, this compulsion to repeat demonstrates the inability of language and narrative to do justice, as Laub describes. However, instead of suggesting a listener who can take the narrative forward and who can help the speaker reinterpret the event through a different, non-destructive lens, as Laub insists is necessary, Ben Jelloun's novel proposes a publicly embodied storytelling that undoes the self in both productive and destructive ways.

Although Ahmed/Zahra might be said to 'carry an impossible history' within him/her or even to have become a 'symptom of a history that [s/he] cannot entirely possess', s/he is not alone in being burdened by this unknowable history.[111] The obsessive return to the same story conveys its incomprehensibility in the present and that it 'cannot be placed within the schemes of prior knowledge'.[112] This disruptive form is 'the refusal of a certain framework of understanding [and therefore] a refusal that is also a creative act of listening'.[113] In *L'Enfant*, access to Ahmed/Zahra's life story, to a

[107] Felman and Laub, *Testimony*, p. 78.
[108] Ibid., p. 79.
[109] Ibid., p. 78.
[110] Ibid., p. 79.
[111] Cathy Caruth, 'Trauma and Experience: Introduction', in *Trauma: Explorations in Memory*, ed. by Cathy Caruth (Baltimore, MD and London: Johns Hopkins University Press, 1995), pp. 3–12 (p. 5).
[112] Cathy Caruth, 'Recapturing the Past: Introduction', in *Trauma: Explorations in Memory*, ed. by Cathy Caruth (Baltimore, MD and London: Johns Hopkins University Press, 1995), pp. 151–7 (p. 153).
[113] Ibid., p. 154.

history of Morocco, to a story of gender imposition, to a history of gender violence, is not an accumulation of knowledge through a pre-existing framework but an opening up of language to the pleasure of bodily sensuality, of one's self to an infinite listening and of one's body to potential pain. In contrast to Laub, the 'symptomatic' return to the repetitive narration of the main protagonist's life conveys a refusal to move on from this event by reintegrating it into a coherent and cogent interpretation. Just as Ahmed/Zahra embodies incoherence and a movement between coherent genders, the story of his/her life offers glimpses of familiar matter and is narrated through an unimagined form. It is this refusal to heal, to yield a clear story, that is the ethical potentiality of bearing witness to queer postcolonial histories.

As the final storyteller lays down the almost blank book in front of the listeners and the readers, and tells them he cannot bear the burden of the book and so is going to read the Qur'ān, one could suggest he seeks a return to an established, authoritative text that might ease his pain. Yet this would be to ignore the pleasurable bodily impact evoked earlier through the language of the Qur'ān on the walls of the mosque. It would also be to forget how this sacred text is represented, especially by Amar, as a book of poetry open to endless translations. Nevertheless, the storyteller is attempting to unburden himself of this story and, thus, I would conclude that this weight can be understood as the interminable impossibility of doing justice to the personal, subjective histories of transnational colonial domination and bodily morphological uncertainty in societies that demand definitive embodied and communal boundaries.

The visual artist Tina Takemoto describes how, when her friend and colleague began treatment for cancer, she tried to register the pain of invasive medical intervention on and through her own body. She interprets this 'mimicry' as '[making] visible the inadequacy of its own repetition and [demonstrating] the impossibility of direct equivalence between sign and referent, self and other'.[114] According to Takemoto, repetition in art, where the piece is trying to understand one's relation to an other, especially an other who is ill, demonstrates that 'any attempt to re-present or re-member the past only makes clearer the futility of this gesture'.[115] Takemoto's artistic productions reproduce the necessity of destruction in being able to hear an other's tale of pain. She emphasizes the 'inadequacy of one's own memory'[116] and recalls Sara Ahmed's words that 'the ethical demand is that I must act about that which I cannot know, rather than act insofar as I know'.[117] Brought to a deep state of reflection as a result of the harm she inflicts on her body, Takemoto displays the way in which the body expresses itself when it cannot find the words or signs to understand. Bodily harm is not straightforwardly destructive; it is an attempt to remember through the body and therefore to mark memories through a multisensorial epistemology.

Like Ben Jelloun, Takemoto opens up the possibility that what could be read as a destructive pattern of remembering is in fact an ethical turn towards an other that

114 Tina Takemoto, 'Open Wounds', in *Thinking Through the Skin*, ed. by Sara Ahmed and Jackie Stacey (London and New York: Routledge, 2001), pp. 104–23 (p. 111).
115 Ibid., p. 115.
116 Ibid., p. 114.
117 Ahmed, *The Cultural Politics of Emotion*, p. 31.

calls for an other to listen to the pain of the bodies of those who are ill, have died, *and* those who survive as friends, listeners and storytellers. This bodily impact evokes responsibility as the particular demand to bear witness to a personal story of pain and an infinite call to keep history open to further interpretation. In *L'Enfant*, the narrators respond to the urgent need to tell the tale of Ahmed's life, to tell of a history of trauma, to reply to the previous storyteller, to give their version, while also committing to a more infinite involvement as they listen indefinitely and sometimes even take the narrative up again at a later date. In other words, there is a finite call to respond to a history that must be told and heard, but there is also an infinite call to take responsibility for this narrative by keeping the telling going and by being open to different, even infinite, versions. The performativity of pain portrays the potentially harmful ways in which our bodies may remember, as well as the deeply destructive effect narration may have on the body. Repetition does not offer narrative resolution, does not unburden the teller and certainly does not ensure a brighter life for the one who has spoken. To begin to tell the tale of an other is to subject the body to a disruption. To become undone, in Butler's and Sara Ahmed's words, is to have one's pre-existing frame of reference displaced. Here, it is literally to feel the body come unleashed from the reality of which it was so certain. The effects of this are uncertain and violent. Despite the story remaining inaccessible, the responsibility to keep it going is integral to the survival of the listeners, storytellers and the story. In approximating the narrative of bodily incoherence, then, the listener might expect to feel something like what Ahmed/Zahra lived, while never living his/her pain. One can leave the pens and paper on the ground, as does the final narrator, only with the greater burden that what is lost is the possibility of a communal listening and narrating. In so doing, one could lose the potential to reimagine the violent constraints imposed through the familial ideologies of the colonial and post-independent nations. Performative repetition thus opens up the possibility for change when the body comes undone in response to the call of an other; when the narratives of history and the process of knowledge production are kept open to other interpretations; and when the body feels the intersubjective pain of keeping alive stories that must be told. To put the body at risk is to begin to translate a painful tale where incoherence may be understood as how the human comes into being. Despite the psychosomatic harm it may inflict, such a risk is the possibility of coming together with others to forge unimagined ties while bearing witness to the unknowable.

Coda: Eyes at the Tips of the Fingers: Materializing the Self in Tahar Ben Jelloun's *La Nuit sacrée*

> *The body's physical surface or encasing provides the anaclitic support for the psychic apparatus: the ego, the sense of self, derives from the experience of the material skin. The body is not only not commensurable with its 'mental' projection but responsible for producing this projection. The body is crucially and materially formative of the self.*[1]
>
> *On peut oublier un visage mais on ne peut tout à fait effacer de sa mémoire la chaleur d'une émotion, la douceur d'un geste, le son d'une voix tendre.*[2]
>
> *[You can forget a face but you can never really wipe out the memory of the warmth of an emotion, the sweetness of a gesture, the sound of a tender voice.]*

Asserting the materiality of the body as central to the theorization of sex and gender, Prosser refutes Butler's idea in *Gender Trouble* that the 'body itself [is] commensurable with the psychic projection of the body'.[3] Following Freud's work on the bodily ego and Didier Anzieu's work on the skin ego, Prosser argues that the experience of the skin is not, as Butler would have it, a mental projection of the self but the material reality through which the self emerges.[4] The sensation of the physical surface, the flesh that extends into space, thus produces the projection of self; the image of the body is not solely visual but one that emerges through a sense of touch. Building on Sack's proprioceptive model, Prosser suggests that, in contemporary gender theory,

1 Prosser, *Second Skins*, p. 65.

2 Tahar Ben Jelloun, *La Nuit sacrée* (Paris: Éditions du Seuil, 1987), pp. 174–5. Hereinafter all references to this novel will be given in the body of the chapter in parentheses. All translations are my own.

3 Prosser, *Second Skins*, p. 41. See also Butler, *Gender Trouble*, p. 163.

4 See, specifically, Sigmund Freud, 'Mourning and Melacholia', *The Standard Edition of the Complete Psychological Works*, vol. 14, ed. by James Strachey (London: Hogarth, [1917] 1968); Sigmund Freud, *The Ego and the Id*, trans. by Joan Rivière, ed. by James Strachey (New York: Norton, [1923] 1989); and Didier Anzieu, *The Skin Ego: A Psychoanalytic Approach to the Self*, trans. by Chris Turner (New Haven, CT: Yale University Press, 1989).

the body 'image' has become synonymous with 'the body in the eye of the other' and that this fails to account for 'the subjective experience of the body, the body as it is (or is not) felt'.[5] For Butler, flesh is naturalized through the heterosexual matrix rather than being pre-existing matter through which one interprets the surrounding world.[6] Performativity, as a result, is coextensive with an understanding of the body not as emerging through its materiality, or what is felt, but through a reiterative process of external constraints where the power of the gaze attempts to hold the other in place according to existing norms. Prosser argues that for Butler sex was 'gender all along' and performativity is the attempt to uncover how it is 'that gender comes to pass so effectively as sex'.[7] In the performative gap that emerges in this continual process of reiteration, sex and gender are shown to be neither complementary nor concomitant insofar as body morphology determines neither gender behaviour nor sexual desire. A correlation between sex and gender would risk reinforcing biological determinism and/or hegemonic citations of sexuality as bound to a dyadic morphological structure of the body, resulting in an anti-deconstructive, essentialist view of the body. Within this performative model, recognition of the other is a persistent – and often violent struggle between those who have (and generally withhold) power and those who are disempowered and seek recognition from the more powerful.

Without returning to an idea of the body as determined by biology, I want to build on Prosser's work on the skin and explore how a multisensory touch is constitutive of the self in Tahar Ben Jelloun's *La Nuit sacrée* [*The Sacred Night*]. I have chosen to include this text because it reiterates the same story of Ahmed/Zahra (from Ben Jelloun's previous novel, *L'Enfant de sable*) from the vantage point of a female public storyteller who claims to be the eponymous *l'enfant de sable*. The novel offers yet another version of the sand child's story, but with a specific focus on one woman's account of how her sand-like self came to feel its flesh. Claiming to be Zahra, the storyteller describes her intimately queer relationship with the blind Consul. If, as Oliver argues, '[subjectivity] is founded on the ability to respond to, and address, others' then the relationship between Zahra and the Consul restores subjectivity through a multisensory intimacy (what Oliver calls witnessing).[8] More specifically, and central to this coda, is that multisensory witnessing materializes both the self and, for Zahra, the sense of flesh as integral to the self. Speaking as a woman, Zahra narrates her search for a post-Ahmed and therefore post-masculine sense of self. I am therefore arguing that this novel, unlike *L'Enfant*, reinstates identitarian positionalities as integral to being without reaffirming categories as static biological or unchanging sociocultural essences.

I want to briefly situate my reading of *La Nuit* in its critical context in order to highlight the novel's significant academic unpopularity for purportedly reinforcing neocolonial, sexist ideologies.[9] I include this context to draw attention to the highly

5 Prosser, *Second Skins*, p. 79. See Sacks's two texts: *The Man Who Mistook His Wife for a Hat* (New York: Harper, 1990) and *A Leg to Stand On* (London: Picador, 1991).

6 Butler's point is that the body is generally formulated as a pregiven, natural entity through which we can interpret the world. In contrast, her idea is that the body is interpreted and hailed into being, and this includes the flesh, through institutional norms.

7 Prosser, *Second Skins*, p. 35.

8 Oliver, p. 15.

9 Despite its academic unpopularity, the novel is very popular with the general public and *L'Académie française*, as exemplified by the fact that Ben Jelloun was awarded the *Prix Goncourt* for this work.

sensitive debate within which the novel is situated and to indicate what is at stake in a novel that walks a line between critiquing and eroticizing religiously motivated violence against women.[10] Hayes sums up the general critical impression of this novel:

> Though [Zahra's relationship with the Consul] is unconventional in that it is not sanctified by marriage, it would be possible to read it as the closure *L'enfant de sable* lacks. *La nuit sacrée* is a first-person narrative told by Zahra herself and *resembles a more traditional narrative*; it is linear, has an ending, and does not contain competing versions of events or an audience to contest the story. It would seem that Ahmed's search for being in *L'enfant de sable* is resolved in *La nuit sacrée* as s/he takes on a woman's name (and the name of woman) as part of a heterosexual relationship, in Ahmed/Zahra's 'becoming-woman' (Orlando 123). In this case, the consolidation of heterosexuality and closure would be one and the same. [. . .] This rereading of *L'enfant de sable* through the lens of *La nuit sacrée* uses the latter to answer questions left unresolved by the former and eliminates the challenges posed by the former to the narrative of gender.[11]

Erickson, more specifically, accuses Ben Jelloun both of pandering to the higher echelons of literary critics who guarantee economic success and of falling into a trap of literary exoticization of Morocco.[12] Evelyn Accad elaborates on the particular neocolonialist

[10] I want to highlight the prevalent readings of this novel mainly because, in this coda, I am diverging significantly from this work. It is not that I categorically disagree with these critics; it is more that I do not think their criticisms can be sustained in an analysis that focuses on both the textual content and form. If the themes could be described as exoticizing Morocco, then the ways in which they are narrated and contextualized undermine this process. Furthermore, I think that the existing criticism displays a tendency to demand certain themes and ways of writing from postcolonial authors. This, to me, comes at the expense of engaging with a text that is extremely complex, problematic, exciting and challenging.

[11] Hayes, p. 171, emphasis added. Hayes's reference to 'becoming-woman' is from Valérie Orlando, 'Beyond Postcolonial Discourse: New Problematics of Feminine Identity in Contemporary Francophone Literature' (PhD diss., Brown University, Providence, 1996). Orlando's doctoral work has subsequently been reworked and published as a book, *Nomadic Voices of Exile: Feminine Identity in Francophone Literature of the Maghreb* (Athens, OH: Ohio University Press, 1999). Hayes distinguishes his reading of the novel from most other critics, stating, 'My reading of the two novels does the opposite, reading *La nuit sacrée* through the lens of *L'enfant de sable* and reopening questions that *La nuit sacrée*, at first glance, might seem to close' (Hayes, p. 171). While Hayes does make a departure from the views of most critics on the way in which the second novel closes down the open-ended questions of the first, it is important to note that the second text is not quite as straightforward as Hayes implies. First, there is an audience who could contest the story, even though they do not intervene. Second, Zahra tells different versions of the same events: for example, she is uncertain whether the excision of the clitoris and the sewing up of the labia was an act committed by her sisters or an instance of self-harm. Finally, it would be difficult to describe this novel as linear, especially as the tale begins with the now-old Zahra telling a tale about her past life. The presence of the narrator indicates that this story is a reflection on the past, not the unfolding of a linear life. Also, events do not unfold in a way that could be described as linear, given there is little progress towards an end, as such. Indeed, that the text ends in an after-life space is simply confusing, given we know Zahra is telling this tale in a public square in Marrakesh. It seems that even when trying to stress the openness of the text, it is quite easy to miss out or not highlight its contradictory and confusing use of dreams, hallucinations, fantasies and uncertainties.

[12] John Erickson, 'Veiled Woman and Veiled Narrative in Tahar ben Jelloun's *The Sandchild*', *boundary* 2.20.1 (1993), 47–64 (p. 48). Mustapha Marrouchi engages with both Erickson's and Rachid Boujedra's criticisms of Ben Jelloun. See Mustapha Marrouchi, 'My Aunt is a Man: Ce « je »-là est multiple', *Comparative Literature* 54.4 (2002), 325–56 (p. 346). See also Rachid Boujedra, 'Pour le Bonheur du public français', *Le Monde* (15 décembre 1987), 4; and André Rollin's interview with Ben Jelloun: '*La Nuit sacrée* au peigne fin', *Lire* 146 (1988), pp. 147–59.

strategies that she suggests are prevalent in the representations of the main protagonist. She reads Zahra as asking to be raped and as being unable to express her sexual desires; women as represented in conflict with each other; 'genital mutilation' as an 'erotic performance'; and the novel, as a whole, as using images to 'titillate male's fantasy of women'.[13] In contradistinction, this novel, for Valérie Orlando, is 'an act of solidarity [. . .] with all those who have no voice' and an opening up of 'a new politics of the body for oppressed women'.[14] Hayes is the most resistant to available readings of this novel, claiming to 'challenge the very interpretation Ben Jelloun seems to authorize'.[15] Although, like Erickson, Gauch concludes by making a sweeping generalization about the whole of Ben Jelloun's oeuvre as losing its 'nuanced complexity' after *L'Enfant*, she highlights 'the particularly complex set of socio-political and moral obligations incumbent on any writer who today wishes to facilitate the circulation of stories between the global South and the global North'.[16] Indeed, accused of inaccurately representing Morocco and of not producing a postcolonial text of multiple narratives or of multiple storytellers in the image of the ('exotic') public *conteur*, Ben Jelloun offers yet another version of the same story not, according to many critics, to challenge existing forms of authority, but to reinforce his authorial, public power by becoming the official storyteller *par excellence*.[17]

I would suggest that it is no coincidence that Ben Jelloun's act of textual repetition is read as closing down the endless reading process of *L'Enfant* and as thereby constraining gender possibilities. Indeed, the novel gives voice to a woman as an act of public defiance and therefore portrays the storyteller as needing and wanting to occupy a readable identitarian position. The novel creates uneasy tensions: it does not condemn or condone sexual violence; it presents female genital circumcision as a violent act between women, while asserting that such practices never occur in Morocco; and it portrays Islam as both an institutionalized religion used to justify violence, and a poetical and creative process of learning to be peacefully with others. Critical attention to *La Nuit* vacillates between the 'prevailing moralism of current theoretical writing

13 Evelyn Accad, *Sexuality and War: Literary Masks of the Middle East* (New York: New York University Press, 1990), pp. 157–8. Accad fails to discuss the fact that Zahra's first sexual encounter as a visible woman, while violent, is committed in the name of religion. Framing the scene through a religious incantation serves to critique the way in which women are subjected to violence at the whim of men and how violence can be justified through a recourse to religion.

14 Orlando, *Nomadic Voices of Exile*, p. 77.

15 Hayes, p. 172.

16 Gauch, *Liberating Shahrazad*, p. 57.

17 What is, of course, interesting about the virulent criticism and outstanding praise for Ben Jelloun is how certain representations are valorized, and, therefore, interpreted as not 'exotic', such as the multiple storytellers, and others, such as female circumcision, are devalorized as an example of neocolonial writing. It is also worth noting that Ben Jelloun, although popular with *L'Académie française* and therefore able to sell lots of books, is attacked by those from the Global South and the Global North. It seems his unpopularity crosses borders. Much of this unpopularity is due to his refusal to represent Morocco 'accurately' or realistically and to the fact that his work crosses the disciplines of journalism, literature and politics. Indeed, Ben Jelloun, through his outspokenness on many issues, has in the media come to represent *the* voice of the Maghreb. With so much power to influence the media and the French population at large, it is perhaps unsurprising that his inaccurate or negative representations of Morocco are met with vehement hostility.

[of] kinda subversive [or] kinda hegemonic'.[18] We witness in *L'Enfant* the violence to which Ahmed/Zahra is subjected because of his/her gender ambiguity, and yet the second novel is never read in the context of these repeated bodily violations. In other words, the second novel is never interpreted as a response to this violence and thus an attempt to imagine into being a non-violent space of belonging for the sand child. Indeed, I would suggest that *La Nuit* offers many lines of flight that may be simultaneously hegemonic and subversive, but that importantly offer potentialities for Ahmed/Zahra to feel his/her flesh and thus his/her self. Bringing together psyche and soma, this text shows how subversion is not only or always the way to achieve change. It also shows that the search for recognition is not synonymous with forcing one's self to conform to hegemonic categories or to being visually defined. Zahra's reaching for an embodied sensation with others does not offer the endless proliferation of gender possibilities, although s/he does continue to embody an ambiguous gender;[19] it does, however, portray that in the endless repetition of performative power structures witnessing is essential to the survival of those who fail to be recognized within existing parameters.[20] Zahra finds a momentary sense of self in a multisensorial relationship with the blind Consul. Morphological diversity, queer and disabled embodiments, and queer heterosexuality open up the possibility of ethically being with others and bearing witness to the self through the flesh.

Although the same story, *La Nuit* offers a different version of the events narrated in *L'Enfant*.[21] After the death of his father, who has just begged for Ahmed's forgiveness and given him the name Zahra, Ahmed is swept away on a horse by 'un prince envoyé par les anges' (40) [a prince sent by the angels] who takes him to his kingdom where he frees children of their pain. However, Zahra is thrown out by these children for making their leader cry. Alone, she is subsequently raped in the name of the prophet Muhammad and meets the devil and his wife in a hammam.[22] As a result of the latter encounter, the Assise, the socially ostracized woman who sits at the entrance to the

18 Eve Kosofsky Sedgwick and Adam Frank, 'Shame in the Cybernetic Fold: Reading Silvan Tomkins', in *Shame and Its Sisters: A Silvan Tomkins Readers*, ed. by Eve Kosofsky Sedwick and Adam Frank (Durham, NC and London: Duke University Press, 1995), pp. 1–28 (p. 5).

19 Zahra continues to wear both women's and men's clothing, and she is repeatedly addressed as 'monsieur' and is happy to be recognized as a man (175).

20 It should be clear that there are different levels on which performativity could be said to be functioning: first, the repetition of the same story with a difference in the second novel; second, the existence of a narrator who presents herself as the now female Zahra and who tells the tale of Zahra's post-Ahmed life – this is the continuation of the *halqa*, where a crowd gathers in a public place to listen to the storyteller, and thus the suggestion that this is yet another version of the same tale and that the narrator is the character of the intra-diegetic story; and third, a process of change that emerges through a multisensorial witnessing.

21 Many of the chapters from *L'Enfant de sable* are repeated in this novel and many of the intra-diegetic characters reappear under different names. For example, the Consul and the Assise are redolent of Um Abbas, the circus owner, and her son from *L'Enfant de sable*, and there is an association between the Consul and the troubadour aveugle, in terms of their blindness.

22 Although I am using the term 'rape' here, I see the scene between Zahra and the man whose face she does not see as rather more complex than him forcing her to have sex with him. This scene is one of the main focuses of Accad's criticism, in that Zahra is represented as accepting this man's violent desire to have sex with any woman he chooses. However, as with *Cereus*, the novel removes the issue of choice from the scene in order to suggest that the debate around sexual coercion and rape needs different parameters of discussion. In other words, choice is misleading, especially in

baths, offers her a place to stay, on the condition that she take care of the Assise's blind brother, the Consul. Zahra moves in with this couple who are described as monstrous, especially as they are engaged in an incestuous mother/son relationship (although they are brother and sister, she breastfeeds him and bathes him like her baby). While Zahra spends her time working hard at forgetting the past and grows increasingly close to the Consul, the Assise, plagued by jealousy, finds Zahra's paternal uncle and brings him to the house to expose Zahra's duplicitous nature. As a result, Zahra kills her uncle and is condemned to 15 years in prison, where her sisters are alleged to have cut off her clitoris and sewn up her vaginal lips. On leaving the prison, Zahra embarks on a journey that leads her to an idyllic after-life space where she is reunited with the Consul, now the Saint, whom she greets erotically.

Where I have suggested that *L'Enfant* presents the possibility of remembering as a painful and endless repetition of the same story with others, I would argue that *La Nuit* offers the condensing of the story into one version as an attempt to bring together psyche and soma. With the emphasis on fantasy – dreams, hallucinations and her inability to know whether the events she narrates actually happened or if she imagined them – the novel places Zahra's life beyond the communally disputed reality of her previous world as Ahmed and into a much more obscure nightmare-esque space. *La Nuit* teeters between utopian, peaceful places and hell-like spaces full of evil spirits. Just as Amar and Salem in *L'Enfant* use fiction to understand contemporary Morocco, Zahra seeks out another mode of being with others by imagining a, previously absent, connection between her flesh, her self and her sexual desires with others. In Butler's words:

> [Fantasy] is part of the articulation of the possible; it moves us beyond what is merely actual and present into a realm of possibility, the not yet actualized or the not actualizable. The struggle to survive is not really separable from the cultural life of fantasy, and the foreclosure of fantasy – through censorship, degradation, or other means – is one strategy for providing for the social death of persons. [. . .] These practices of instituting new modes of reality take place in part through the scene of embodiment, where the body is not understood as a static and accomplished fact, but as an aging process, a mode of becoming that, in becoming otherwise, exceeds the norm, reworks the norm, and makes us see how realities to which we thought we were confined are not written in stone.[23]

Fantasy is thus the mode through which Zahra is represented as coming together with an other in mutually constitutive, highly tactile encounters. It allows her to imagine into

a situation where it is simply not possible to exercise free will. That Zahra is represented as not distressed by this encounter is not necessarily feeding into male fantasies of rape or the novel's endorsement of rape. Rather, this encounter shows, as Hayes suggests, that as a woman Zahra can be subjected to many more forms of violence than men. Perhaps, most importantly, this man never looks at her and this for Zahra becomes a means of thinking about her body differently. Again, it is not that rape is idealized as another way of thinking about coming into being but that the lack of ocular contact is represented as not as violent as the eyes that condemn ambiguity. Evidently, touch, here, is violent.

23 Butler, *Undoing Gender*, pp. 28–9.

being a different type of encounter from those of the ocularcentric institutions of the family and the nation. Through a persistent desire to match the material impressions of her body with her psychic understanding of herself, Zahra gives flesh to her self (but does not consolidate herself as a woman). Flesh and psychic coherence is, thus, not the consolidation of gender and sex as concomitant or complementary but the affirmation that the 'body is crucially and materially formative of the self'.[24] To this extent, the reiterative process of bodily becoming, central to Butler's formulation of fantasy as the medium through which change can be imagined and achieved, is also composed of a sensorial impression of bodily being and of being in the flesh.

In the space of their home, the Consul and the Assise create a world where they hyperbolically 'perform' the identities they wish to inhabit. In an attempt to deal with social ostracization, they take on grandiose identities. The Consul's name is bestowed on him by the Assise as they play the 'jeu théâtral' (72) [theatrical game] that is their life. His authority extends not over the French Republic, like the first Consul's (Napoleon Bonaparte), but only over 'une ville imaginaire d'un pays fantôme' (71) [an imaginary city in a ghost country]. They walk through their house 'saluant une foule imaginaire' (72) [waving to an imaginary crowd] and eventually Zahra learns 'à jouer le jeu et à être cette foule immense levée très tôt pour saluer le couple princier' (73) [to play the game and to stand in for this huge crowd that rose early to greet the princely couple]. Drawn into their world of fantastic reality, Zahra decides she will accompany the Consul to the brothel where, in the place of his sister, she will be his eyes and describe the physicality of the women he cannot see. Zahra, however, goes on to present herself as the only beautiful option, and the Consul knowingly chooses her as the one with whom to have sex. Although the reader is told that the Consul knows he is having sex with Zahra and that she is aware of his knowledge, part of the charade is that they silently agree to pretend they are unaware of what is happening. The Consul's recognition that Zahra needs this anonymity brings them closer together.

'La comédie du bordel' (130) [the brothel charade] is the pact that seals the 'complicité' [complicity], which binds their bodies 'dans le silence et le secret' (126) [in silence and secrecy]. Zahra is represented as having great sex with the Consul in a brothel where no words are spoken. The brothel gives this encounter, which is repeated many times, a sense of anonymity, just as the letters did in *L'Enfant*. That is, these anonymous encounters in both novels create a space where the main protagonist can open him/herself out to an other. Where the letters touched Ahmed/Zahra intimately without him/her having to literally get close to an other, *La Nuit* represents a mutually risky encounter where Zahra gives her body over to an other, just as the Consul gives himself over to her. Touch is not simply an erotic awakening; it is the entering into a mutually vulnerable bodily engagement through a physical proximity and intimacy. However, where touch captures Ahmed's desire to reach out to an other who is both self and other in *L'Enfant*, Zahra in *La Nuit* is represented as finding a fleshy other with whom she can begin to feel an interdependent bodily sensibility. Situated outside the family home, perverse in itself in this novel, the context of the

24 Prosser, *Second Skins*, p. 65.

brothel gives this intimacy a form of illegitimacy and illegality. Sex is kept to a space where, whether legally or illegally, it is expected to happen, but it does not mimic the reproductive demand of nationalist familial rhetoric. One could suggest that this sex-focused choice of setting both emphasizes the bodily aspect of eroticism and attempts to extract emotional attachment from their intimacy. At the same time, the space keeps to the fore how sex is often about power and manipulation, especially through economic means. The setting, thereby, reinforces erotic touch as their primary mode of communication and pleasure; as different from the national and familial monitoring and fixing function of the gaze; and as an intimate connection where each is vulnerable and open to the other.

The description of the sex they have emphasizes the ec-static pleasure they both enjoy and its impact on the constitution of selfhood:

> J'étais heureuse que le premier homme qui aima mon corps fût un aveugle, un homme qui avait les yeux au bout des doigts et dont les caresses lentes et douces recomposaient mon image. Ma victoire je la tenais là ; je la devais au Consul dont la grâce s'exprimait principalement par le toucher. Il redonna à chacun de mes sens sa vitalité qui était endormie ou entravée. Quand nous faisions l'amour il passait de longs moments à dévisager tout mon corps avec ses mains. Non seulement il éveillait ainsi mon désir, mais il lui donnait une intensité rare qui était ensuite superbement comblée. Tout se passait dans le silence et la lumière douce. (137)
>
> [I was happy that the first man who loved my body was blind, a man who had eyes on the tips of his fingers, and whose slow and gentle caresses recomposed my image. That was my victory; I owed it to the Consul, whose grace was expressed mainly through touch. He had restored vitality to each of my slumbering, fettered senses. When we made love he spent long moments staring at my whole body with his hands. Not only had he thus awakened my desire, but he also gave it a rare intensity that he satisfied magnificently. Everything happened in silence and soft light.]

With an evident allusion to his friend and muse Jorge Luis Borges, Ben Jelloun represents the blind Consul – in a vein similar to Derrida's reading of visual representations of blind men – as 'a seer', a 'visionary' and, thus, as someone who can see differently due to his disability.[25] In this narrative of exceptionality, his disability enables him to be different from the other characters who have subjected Zahra to harm. Similarly, Abbes Maazaouri suggests that the representation of the Consul shows a devalorization of vision in the novel and that it is, thereby, symbolic of 'un hommage au sens tactile'

[25] Jacques Derrida, *Memoirs of the Blind: The Self-Portrait and Other Ruins*, trans. by Pascale-Anne Brault and Michael Naas (Chicago, IL and London: Chicago University Press, 1990), p. 2. Although not unproblematic, Ben Jelloun, somewhat similarly to Derrida, wants to acknowledge the greatness of Borges and other partially sighted and blind writers to whom he is indebted, including James Joyce. On Borges in *L'Enfant de sable*, see Marie Fayad, 'Borges in Tahar Ben Jelloun's *L'Enfant de sable*: Beyond Intertextuality', *The French Review* 67.2 (1993), pp. 291–9; and Marc Gontard, 'Le Récit meta-narratif chez Tahar Ben Jelloun', in *Tahar Ben Jelloun: stratégies d'écriture*, ed. by Mansour M'Henni (Paris: Éditions L'Harmattan, 1993), pp. 99–118. The Consul is also an allusion back to the troubadour aveugle in *L'Enfant de sable*.

[a homage to the sense of touch].[26] Blindness represents and stands in for all that is negative about the appropriating and, in Maazaoui's terms, misogynistic gaze. However, like Ahmed/Zahra in both novels, the Consul's ever-present body is not reducible to a symbolic function. Sex with Zahra opens up a social space different from the violence of the familial home. Forced to live like a child, the Consul has been dependent on women who control him and over whom he exerts his own violent power.[27] Through his blindness – not despite it – he reaches out to Zahra and through touch he feels another mode of being with others emerge. Their anonymous sex, where no words are spoken, gives sense to their bodies and their selves in a world where thus far there has been largely only psychosomatic violation. Zahra's decision to move their relationship from a domestic setting to the sex context of the brothel portrays how their intimacy arises in an anonymous encounter that is intensely focused on the flesh and on visceral feelings.

Maazaoui's suggestion that there is a 'valorisation du toucher au détriment du regard' [a valorization of touch to the detriment of the gaze] fails to account for the importance of the eyes in this scene and for the position of the Consul, who succeeds in carving out a non-violent space of belonging for himself.[28] I would suggest that the novel does not denigrate vision but reworks it as a tactile, proximal sense. Therefore, the text portrays tactile visuality as both embodied and a subjective and constitutive mode of being in the world. Just as Derrida describes the artists with eyes at the tips of their fingers to articulate a synaesthetic knowledge and epistemological form,[29] Ben Jelloun describes the Consul's tactile vision as artistically constitutive of Zahra's flesh and thus of her self:

> Il m'avait sculptée en statue de chair, désirée et désirante. Je n'étais plus un être de sable et de poussière à l'identité incertaine, s'effritant au moindre coup de vent. Je sentais se solidifier, se consolider, chacun de mes membres. (138)
>
> [He had sculpted me into a statue of flesh, desired and desiring. I was no longer a being made of sand and dust, of uncertain identity, crumbling at the slightest gust of wind. I felt each of my limbs grow strong and solid.]

The implication that the Consul is the artist who produces flesh out of fleeting and transient dust and sand gives the hands that both touch and see not the authority of creation but the sensorial capacity to render feeling to a body that had little image of itself, little sense of self. As the eyes touch, they give priority to proximity and not distance (as associated with the gaze); they risk the impact of the touch of the other; they feel the pleasure of a body awakening to a different type of embodiment; and,

26 Abbes Maazaoui, '*L'Enfant de sable* et *La Nuit sacrée* ou le corps tragique', *The French Review* 69.1 (1995), pp. 68–77 (p. 74).

27 The Consul is bullied by his sister and easily taken advantage of in the brothel due to his blindness. As a result, he is often described as reacting aggressively and violently towards the women he encounters. He is not reduced to a romantic notion of blindness (where the loss of the gaze brings about a rethinking of how he encounters others); rather, we are often presented with images of him as being able to exert his authority as a result of his superior status of maleness.

28 Maazaoui, p. 74.

29 Derrida, *Memoirs of the Blind*, p. 4.

as George Bataille has clearly shown, they become aroused.[30] The erotic pleasure of the eyes at the tips of the fingers is much more vulnerable than that of the remote gaze as they open out to touch an other. Zahra expresses the consolidation of the physical body, the dissolution of uncertainty, as strength that gives sexual pleasure. In an able-ist and heteronormative national context, disability and queer trajectories merge and the search for self slowly materializes through queer sex. A multisensorial intimacy, where they simultaneously feel beside themselves and in their selves, gives a momentary glimpse of how a multisensory touch opens up the possibility of bearing witness to queer and disability histories of violence and to the continued existence of self and other. Indeed, in this encounter, where the eyes on the hands meet an other's body, there is a breakdown in the referent of the visual as it merges into touch and becomes a tangible flesh deeply connected to that of the Consul's. They do not lose their individuality, but they do feel their pleasurable intersubjective relationality.

The intensity of the synergetic experience of sex as a non-violent encounter with an other is temporarily brought to an end not only because Zahra and the Consul are separated when she is imprisoned but also because Zahra's sisters try to ensure she cannot have sexual pleasure. The text displays an ambiguity towards the sense of touch and towards the ethical potentiality of tactility, and I would argue refuses to hierarchize or prioritize one sense over another. Zahra's sisters subject her to a horrifying scene of violence and do so as the 'cinq doigts d'une main' (158) [five fingers of the same hand].[31] Nelly Lindenlauf explains that the hand in Maghrebian culture, 'la main de Fathma' [the hand of Fatima], is a 'porte-bonheur' [good luck charm] that 'symbolise la protection, le pouvoir, la force' [symbolizes protection, power, strength] and recalls 'les cinq dogmes de l'islam' [the five pillars of Islam].[32] This evocation of the 'la main de Fathma', the hand that deflects evil through the presence of the eye in its centre, is contrasted with the hand as a vehicle for violence. The hand connected to the eyes, where more than one sense is alive and where it is intimately engaged with the poetics of Islam, is a moment of potential non-violence. The strict division of the senses, where there is an attempt to actively close down one's sensorial connection with others,

30 Bataille creates a direct correlation between the eye and sex, reinforced, for him, by the fact that syphilis led to his father's blindness. See George Bataille, *Histoire de l'oeil* (Paris: Gallimard, 1967), especially pp. 103–10.

31 This description is all the more remarkable given Zahra has seven sisters. The text, thereby, emphasizes the importance of both the number five and the hand.

32 Nelly Lindenlauf, *Tahar Ben Jelloun: Les Yeux baissés* (Brussels: Éditions Labor, 1996), p. 91. Although Lindenlauf is speaking specifically about Maghrebian culture, it is clear that the hand with the eye in the centre is not unique to North Africa or Arab culture. For example, it is also a prevalent symbol in Jewish culture. Claude Gandelman states,

> In the Middle East and North Africa an amulet called a *khamssa*, or sometimes 'Fatima's hand' has existed for centuries; indeed, one might consider it a translation into popular visual language of the long-forgotten *âri* hieroglyph. [. . .] The idea inherent in the *khamssa* doubtlessly is that of exorcising the evil eye. It embodies the sort of thinking which anthropologists call sympathetic magic. The very representation of the evil eye on the hand is believed to cause the look of any actual evil eye in one's vicinity to ricochet back on itself. The magic hand, the *khamssa*, mirrorlike, will hurl the evil spell back upon itself and blind the evil look. (Claude Gandelman, *Reading Pictures, Viewing Texts* (Bloomington and Indianapolis, IN: Indiana University Press, 1991), p. 4)

portrays the violence of being. Moreover, Ben Jelloun connects the closing down of one's sense of vulnerability to the wilful misinterpretation of the Qur'ān for one's own abusive ends.[33] It is not that there is a good or a bad touch, but rather that embodied openness might allow us to assume over and over again 'our collective responsibility for the physical lives of one another'.[34]

Subjected to a violent touch that seeks to mark her body as not male and not female, and therefore as not human, Zahra is forced to sign an official document that states the act was one of self-harm.[35] Without this paper she cannot receive the much needed medical treatment. Yet, Zahra later expresses doubt about the presence of her sisters and wonders if she may have inflicted this harm on herself. Her ensuing fever conveys bodily (self-)harm as a form of remembering memories that are not her own. She tells the doctor that she dreamt of a hangar where sick and poor people were left to die, gathered off the streets that were 'cleaned' 'parce qu'un visiteur important, un étranger allait faire quelques pas dans les rues' (162) [because an important visitor, a foreigner was going to walk briefly through the streets]. She tells of the mounds of bodies and of one, not quite dead, speaking to her. As was the case for the narrators in *L'Enfant*, the

[33] Similar to the man who rapes Zahra, the sisters perform this act in the name of Islam. However, the novel states quite categorically that Islam has never endorsed such practices: 'J'appris aussi que jamais l'islam ni aucune autre religion n'ont permis ce genre de massacre' (163) [I also learnt that never had Islam or any other religion permitted this sort of massacre]. Ben Jelloun has also felt it necessary, in an interview, to assert that this practice does not take place in the Maghreb:

> I must make it perfectly clear that there is no female excision in the Maghreb; it simply isn't done there. There is no female excision in Islam; it is expressly forbidden. It is a practice that has been imported from Africa. In the terrible world of my heroine, it belongs to the realm of her nightmares. Even so, this allows me to write that excision can exist in an act of extreme violence . . . but not in a sociological tradition as is the case in certain African nations. When I wrote this scene, I was terrified. (André Rollin, '*La Nuit sacrée* au peigne fin', *Lire* 146 (1988), 147–59 (p. 139))

Given his desire to situate this practice in Africa, which he does in this interview and in both novels, specifying that the idea originates from the Sudanese prison guard, it is worth noting Ben Jelloun's own response to the question about whether he identifies as African:

> No. In Morocco one tends to feel more Arab than African. We're really in the northernmost part of Africa and we have a very different history. Personally, I don't feel at all African. That's not a pejorative or mean statement, but I don't feel African because I have no ties to Africa. (Spear, p. 31)

[34] Butler, *Precarious Life*, p. 30. My reading of Ben Jelloun's novels is attentive to the inequalities of contemporary global relations, particularly the atrocities that occur during occupation and war. Openness, following from Butler and Shildrick, is foundational to being and therefore the very way in which we become human. I agree with Butler that attention to this vulnerability could change how global politics operates, especially how those in and with power respond to acts of violence. I would also stress that current anti-Islamic rhetoric may build on the tendency of authors and critics to emphasize how religion, largely Islam, has been used to disenfranchise women. I would, however, also stress that this novel searches for ethical ways of being that are poetical and therefore informed by Qur'ānic teachings, where the poetic may exceed the known and/or the knowable.

[35] Evidently, the cutting off of one's genitals does not necessarily undermine one's sexed or gendered identity. Indeed, in some cases, it reinforces it. However, the sisters explicitly state that their desire is to render Zahra sexless and therefore a nobody: 'On va te débarraser de ce sexe que tu as caché. [. . .] Plus de désir. Plus de plaisir. Tu deviendras une chose' (159) [We are going to rid you of this sex that you hid. [. . .] No more desire. No more pleasure. You will become a thing].

burden of the narrative and the compulsion to bear witness are felt on her body and force her to speak:

> Pour m'en libérer je devais raconter ce que j'avais vu dans le hangar. [. . .] Ces images et les paroles du mourant me pesaient mentalement et physiquement. Chaque mot était comme un cristal à l'aiguille fine me perçant les points sensibles du corps. (164–5)
>
> [In order to free myself, I had to speak of what I had seen in the hangar. [. . .] The images and the words of the dying man weighed heavily on me mentally and physically. Every word was like a sharp glass needle piercing all the sensitive parts of my body.]

These memories are confirmed by the doctor not as a personal nightmare, but as an unrecorded incident that took place many years earlier (165). The intensity of the bodily sensations creates a correlation between the severing of genital parts and the remembering of what fails to enter into official recordings of History. As we saw in *L'Enfant*, the pain of remembering an unlived event comes about through the undoing of the narrator's body. The sexualization of the memory, through the slashing of the clitoris and the binding of the labia, draws out a correlation between the closing down of the body to external stimuli and the act of remembering. The hand inflicts harm on the body, cuts into its flesh and as a result causes both great pain and the possibility of articulating what has hitherto been unnarrated and unnarratable. I am not arguing that self-harm is integral to memory formation. However, these scenes, where the origin of sexual violence is unclear, convey how cutting the flesh is not straightforwardly destructive; rather, it is also a wilful desire to remember what is felt in the body and what has thus far remained inexpressible in narrative form. The novel does not endorse self-harm as a collective mode of remembering, but it does suggest that a depathologization of self-harm may be necessary. Thus, self-harm is sometimes a form of embodied remembering. In *La Nuit*, such embodied histories express narratives that have been silenced by the nation. As we saw in *Cereus* and in *L'Enfant*, the body remembers and feels the intense pain of these memories.

The textual vacillation between the hands that are sensitively, artistically and erotically capable of making flesh out of sand and those that are destructively and aggressively violent and vengeful creates, as I have shown above, a tension in the representation of touch. The five sisters who work together as one hand form a relationship where touch works to distance the one who touches from the one being touched. There is a refusal to acknowledge that when touching one is touched, and this becomes apparent through the sisters' use of an object – the blade – to distance self from other. I do not want to suggest that there are two different forms of touch or that a single sensory experience is always and necessarily violent. Rather, this tension between a violent touch and a caressing touch shows how tactility is not superior or inferior to the gaze. Instead, sensorial experiences that shut down relationality and that refuse to feel what Marks calls an 'intersubjective eroticism' often result in violence.[36] Thus, when the Consul, after learning what Zahra's sisters have done to her, explains to her that he must leave her alone and head southward, he tells her:

> Sachez enfin que j'ai appris votre beauté avec mes mains et que cela m'a donné une émotion comparable à celle de l'enfant qui découvre la mer. Mes mains, je les préserve, je les couvre d'un tissu fin, car elles gardent comme un secret l'empreinte de votre beauté. Je vous dis cela parce que j'ai appris aussi que cette émotion a la particularité d'être unique. Je ferme mes yeux et mes mains sur elle et je la garde, éternelle. Adieu, amie ! (170–1)
>
> [I want you to know that I have learned your beauty with my hands, and that this has moved me like a child who first looks upon the sea. My hands, I will take care of them, I will cover them with a fine cloth, for they bear the imprint of your beauty like a secret. I am telling you this because I have also learned that the peculiar quality of this emotion is that it is unique. I close my eyes and my hands around it and keep it, forever. Farewell, my friend!][37]

Zahra is a trace on his body. She has literally marked herself on his hands and eyes, and he treasures these marks as a form of intersubjective commingling. The physical trace is a bodily memory of their mutually constitutive erotic relationship. Zahra and the Consul do not lose a sense of self in coming close to and being touched by the other; rather tactile proximity allows them to bear witness to themselves and to each other. It thereby opens them up both to feel their own flesh as self with other, and to carry the other on the self as a witness to the flesh that now feels.

The importance of intersubjective eroticism – to allow one's sense of self to be undone in order to get close to an other – is further emphasized as the Consul and Zahra are reunited at the end of the novel in a dreamlike, after-life space:

> A mon tour je me levai et me mis dans la file des femmes. Puis, j'eus envie de jouer, je rejoignis la file des hommes. Avec ma djellaba je pouvais passer pour un homme. Quand je fus face au Saint, je m'agenouillai, je pris sa main tendue et, au lieu de la baiser, je la léchai, suçant chacun de ses doigts. Le Saint essaya de la retirer mais je la retenais de mes deux mains. L'homme était troublé. Je me levai et lui dis à l'oreille:
>
> - Cela fait très longtemps qu'un homme ne m'a pas caressé le visage . . . Allez-y, regardez-moi avec vos doigts, doucement, avec la paume de votre main.

36 Marks, *The Skin of the Film*, p. 183.

37 Heading south is a key idea in both of Ben Jelloun's novel, but also in many of his other works, including for example *La Prière de l'absent* (1981). In *L'Enfant de sable*, the storyteller who returns at the end, who was thought to be dead, has been south, wandering through the desert. To head south into the desert generally represents a character's search for her/his self, insofar as the self is represented through the image of the non-solidified and ever fleeting matter of sand. However, it is also read by some critics as the refusal to settle in one space and the move towards a more nomadic lifestyle. It is, thus, a way of theorizing modes of belonging, especially through Gilles Deleuze's work. For a reading along the latter lines, see Lowe, pp. 43–8. For a broader interpretation of the desert and the characters' motivations for going there, see Amar, pp. 77–83. Amar connects the ephemerality of the traces in the sand to the breaking down of the narrative in Ben Jelloun's novels and the instability of identitarian positions.

Il se pencha sur moi et me dit

- Enfin, vous voilà ! (189)

[I too got up and joined the line of women. Then, in a playful mood, I crossed to the line of men. In my djellaba I could pass for a man. When I reached the Saint, I knelt, took his outstretched hand, and, instead of kissing it, I licked it, sucking each of his fingers. The Saint tried to pull his hand away but I held it in both of mine. He was troubled. I rose and whispered in his ear:

'It has been a very long time since a man caressed my face. . . . Go ahead, look gently at me with your fingers, with the palm of your hand.'

He leaned towards me and said,

'At last, you are here!'][38]

In a sacrilegious moment, where the encounter between Saint and supposed worshipper is eroticized, Zahra affirms an intersubjective connection to the Saint as she takes his fingers into her mouth, inside her body. A seemingly irreverent moment of worship, this encounter, in actual fact, displays Zahra's deep attachment to the constitutive power of their relationship. Furthermore, by taking his hands, on which the trace of her is marked, into her mouth, Zahra reawakens both the Saint's bodily memories of her and the need for recognition through a commingling of self and other. The evident sexual connotation of the licking and sucking of his fingers and the way in which this troubles him serve to stress the whole body (and not just the genitalia) as a sensorial site of arousal and desire. Neither the Consul nor Zahra is locked into a position of difference, but rather they approximate Irigaray's description of the unassimilability of the other: 'I caress you, you caress me, without unity – neither yours, nor mine, nor ours'.[39] Here, tactile visuality and gustatory tactility portray an ontological vulnerability as the foundation for their ethical encounter. Mutual openness to each other and an irreverence for institutionalized practices give space to their flesh to feel itself in contact with each other. Inside and outside they touch, smell, taste and generally sense their flesh as self and as other. Yet they do not become other but remain other to themselves.

The crossing over into the male line is described as a playful gesture that nonetheless displays Zahra's remembering of a time that is still integral to her sense of self. Unlike the vehement denial of her male past that led to the Assise being able to take on such

38 See my discussion of the ambiguous position of saints in Morocco during the pre-independence period in the chapter on *L'Enfant de sable*. That the previous chapter of the novel entitled 'L'Enfer' [Hell] also represents Zahra as a saint could suggest they both occupy a similar position in society as symbolic of something other than being simply human. Although the sanctity of the representation could be read as involving a form of transcendence, I read this as a reimagining of space and identity in order to redefine their previous encounters, and, potentially, as offering them an imaginary space of belonging. It is not that the move from the brothel to an after-life space is a purification of their encounter but rather a perverting of the notion of purity. I read the sanctity of the situation as a final move to fantasy in order to suggest that the space in which they can exist must be outside existing parameters of belonging. One could further suggest that the taking on of the role of sainthood is a continuation of the theatrical lifestyle represented earlier in the novel.

39 Luce Irigaray, *Elemental Passions*, trans. J. Collie and J. Still (London: Athlone Press, 1992), p. 59.

a vengeful plan against her, Zahra manifests an acceptance of her uncertain identity of having been raised a man and spent her adult life wondering whether she is of another gender and/or sex. The identitarian position, often asserted as dominating the text through the presence of the main female narrator at the beginning of the text, is neither undermined nor confirmed in this final encounter: it remains possible that the playfulness of the crossing unduly, given the context of *L'Enfant*, represents identity as fluid and maybe even affirms a prior, more serious, chosen state of womanhood; but the desire to cross over to another position also, importantly, refers back to a previous sense of self fundamental to, and thus not separate from, the present. This negotiation – between a past that was determined by a dominant patriarch, and wilfully accepted as who he was by Ahmed, and the search for what it means to have been told and to feel that his/her body may be different from the way in which s/he has understood it all his/her life – suggests both a need for categories of belonging in order to find a sense of self and a willingness to encounter bodies as inconsistent, changing and porous entities. Change has become not only imaginable but also possible through an intimate moment of recognition where self commingles with other without becoming other. To feel the Consul is to feel her flesh, to remember and to bear witness to their erotic awakening intimacy.

Where the chapter on *L'Enfant* emphasized the repetitive undoing of the self and of narrative in order to remember and to begin to narrate a traumatic history, this coda on *La Nuit* has focused on the way in which the main protagonist of the intra-diegetic narrative emerges through a multisensory relationality. I therefore want to conclude by elaborating on how the performative act of intertextual repetition, the same story with a difference in a second novel, intersects with the idea that 'embodiment is as much about feeling one inhabits flesh as the flesh itself'.[40] Both novels draw the reader's attention to the importance of the process of becoming undone (including on a bodily level) in an attempt to remember what remains unspoken. *L'Enfant* emphasizes narrative proliferation as an ethical engagement with both the impossibility of full knowledge and the possibility of recognizing a body that falls outside existing taxonomies of national familial life. In contrast, *La Nuit* situates this mode of recognition – the undoing of the self in relation to an other in order to come close to or rub up against this other and her/his history – in the representation of the intimate and erotic encounter between the Consul and Zahra. The constrained performative act of the second novel displays what Prosser describes as 'the sobering realization of [the] foundational power' of gender categories.[41] That is, if *L'Enfant* has been highly praised for its supposed representation of gender as fluid and easily changeable, *La Nuit* asserts that life in a body, the realization of one's gender and one's sense of belonging, demands a theorization and a literary representation that resist such unobtainable celebrations. The representation of the intimacy of Zahra and the Consul thus captures the way in which the self, in order to find a space for itself in the world, requires a connection between what one feels as flesh and sociopolitical categories of belonging. I would stress that gender transitioning may *read* as a transgressive act but sometimes transitioning bodies and

40 Prosser, *Second Skins*, p. 7.
41 Ibid., p. 11.

selves may begin to crumble or break down when they fail to be recognized as human. To this extent, taxonomical recognition is represented as crucial to any theorization of gender performativity. I am not suggesting that a body must conform to existing gender categories as such, but rather that in order to find a viable mode of existence one needs a communal recognition to give feeling to one's flesh and one's self. This mode of recognition approximates Butler's ideas in her recent work on ethics:

> Thus, it is at a moment of fundamental vulnerability that recognition becomes possible, and need becomes self-conscious. What recognition does at such a moment is, to be sure, to hold destruction in check. But what it also means is that the self is not its own, that it is given over to the Other in advance of any further relation, but in such a way that the Other does not own it either. And the ethical content of its relationship to the Other is to be found in this fundamental and reciprocal state of being 'given over'.[42]

To be recognized is not, therefore, understood as the gaze of the other asserting one's existence. Rather, the mutuality of the encounter, where one is 'given over' to an other, in the sense that one's existence depends on this other and vice versa, entails a vulnerability of self and other. Recognition is not entrenching the self in certainty for ever, although it may require a momentary occupation; it is an openness to an other where the sense of proximity serves to recall one's indebtedness to and one's responsibility for the other. Ben Jelloun offers intersubjective eroticism, or the eyes that touch, as one possible mode of recognition for Zahra and the Consul. The lack of multiplicity of stories gives not a definitive consolidation of gender and/or sexed identity but the possibility of feeling the flesh anew through an erotic contact with an other. The body is not determined through the flesh but is constituted as visceral through an erotics of touch. A synergy of the senses is represented as one possible way of avoiding the reiteration of violence to which the gender-transitioning protagonist has been subjected. It also opens up the possibility of a sustaining moment of fleshy pleasure with self and others.

[42] Butler, *Undoing Gender*, p. 149. It should be clear that Butler herself is not currently making these connections between gender performativity and multisensory recognition. She discusses performativity in her chapter, 'The Question of Social Transformation', *Undoing Gender*, pp. 204–31.

3

Fossil Witnessing in Ann-Marie MacDonald's *Fall on Your Knees*

Unknowing the family

> *Materia went upstairs to the attic. She knelt down, opened the hope chest and inhaled deeply. James thought Materia hadn't filled the hope chest because she had nothing to put in it. But she kept it empty on purpose, so that nothing could come between her and the magical smell that beckoned her into memory. Cedar. She hung her head into the empty chest and allowed its gentle breath to lift and bear her away . . . baked earth and irrigated olive groves; the rippling veil of the Mediterranean, her grandfather's silk farm; the dark elixir of her language, her mother's hands stuck with parsley and cinnamon, her mother's hands stroking her forehead, braiding her hair . . . her mother's hands. The smell of the hope chest. The Cedars of Lebanon. She stopped crying, and fell asleep.*[1]

> *A fossil is the indexical trace of an object that once existed, its animal or vegetable tissue now become stone. [. . .] Created in one layer of history, the fossil witness is gradually covered with more sedimental layers. But instead of disintegrating it solidifies and becomes transformed. So when some earthquake happens years later or continents away, these objects surface, bearing witness to forgotten histories.*[2]

In *Fall on Your Knees*, Materia Piper comes close to, touches and smells the hope chest made from cedar. Immersing her senses and thus her self in fading memories of her lost home of Lebanon and her (now broken) relationship with her mother, Materia finds comfort in the sensorial object that circulates in the novel as a symbol of (failed) hope. When her husband James Piper presents the hope chest to her, he dreams of a wife like his mother.[3] His hope is that, like his mother, his child wife

1 Ann-Marie MacDonald, *Fall on Your Knees* (Toronto, ON: Vintage, 1997), pp. 25–6. The novel will be referenced in the body of the chapter in parentheses.

2 Marks, *The Skin of the Film*, p. 84.

3 What is tragic about this dream of marital bliss and James's desire to have a wife like his mother is that James mimics his father's actions. Rather than treating Materia as he would have liked to see his father treat his mother, he subjects her to abuse that is similar to his father's domestic violence.

will fill the box with everyday maternal niceties – where these material objects are, both for James and wider society, condensed affective sites of an imaginary idyllic family life. Materia's refusal to fill the chest and James's inability to comprehend her multisensory proximity to the object indicate, on the one hand, Materia's inability to live up to James's colonial-informed familial ideals and, on the other hand, the couple's estrangement from each other. Locked away in the attic by James, the chest is used by multiple generations of the Piper family as a literal space in which to leave precious, haunting or traumatic objects and memories. After the eldest daughter Kathleen dies in the attic while giving birth to her father's children, James and other members of the family refuse to enter this supposedly haunted space. In contrast, his other daughters – namely Frances and Lily – repeatedly play in the attic unencumbered by adults. Ritualistically, the sisters 'honour the story' of their unmentionable dead sister (203), breathe in the smell 'of cedar', and touch objects that resonate with familiar and otherworldly histories. Like Materia, their senses are alert, and the odour of the chest allows and encourages them to speak of subjects that would 'hurt [James] terribly' (204). Constantly disturbing the fossilized layers of unarticulated histories, the daughters do not uncover narrative coherence. Instead their bodies are open to the unspoken histories that are contained within and yet not necessarily accessible through this multisensorial object and its contents. Because they are searching for histories that have been silenced or rendered invisible by the patriarchal father figure, they turn to non-institutionalized methods for remembering and recording the unspoken and the unspeakable.

This chapter explores the role of familiar and familial objects in memory formation. I am interested in how the materiality of memory – its tactile, auditory, odorous and tasteful intimacies – interrupts the narrative flow, and thus how these sensory engagements are indexical traces of that which is both translatable into words and outside of the knowable. In the colonial spectacle of difference, the gaze renders the other distinct and separate from the self. In contrast, the encounter with objects in *Fall* comes close to Bettina Pappenberg and Marta Zarzycka's description of a feminist and synaesthetic aesthetic: 'It takes into account the (often fearful) collapse of distance between the viewer and the art object, fostering an immersive approach where the viewer is no longer only a viewer, but rather the subject of an embodied encounter'.[4] This synaesthetic looking undoes the distancing distinction between subject and object, and binds self to other. Where *Cereus* portrays a queer postcolonial sensibility through both Mala's garden-home and Otoh's embodiment of the past (through his father's suit), *Fall* conveys a queer postcolonial aesthetics and politics through a multisensory intimacy with familial and familiar objects. Thus *Fall* figures decolonization as an embodied, queer and public engagement with others where knowledge is not restored (although we may glean more information and details), but rather where we interrogate how we hear the histories that are in and on objects and bodies.

4 Bettina Pappenberg and Marta Zarzycka, *Carnal Aesthetics: Transgressive Imagery and Feminist Politics* (London: Palgrave Macmillan, 2013), p. 3.

This chapter therefore examines the task of historiography – the art *and* mischief of storytelling – and is specifically concerned with a crisis in 'the art of storytelling'.[5] Where Benjamin and Felman emphasize a loss in the capacity to share experiences or stories post-First World War, I examine how '*it has become impossible to tell a story*' of everyday domestic and familial abuses.[6] More precisely, I explore the impossibility and possibility of *hearing and responding* to histories of familial sexual trauma. Like Kilby I am concerned by how sexual trauma (concerning women, girls and queers) is simultaneously silenced and, amid a popular culture of intimate public disclosure, a constant noise that despite its prevalence fails to be heard.[7] Similar to Cvetkovich, I am interested in how sexual trauma in the domestic arena gives 'rise to different ways of thinking about trauma and in particular to a sense of trauma as connected to the textures of everyday experience'.[8] That everyday life continues and that sexual violence may be a normal part of this existence challenges us to think through how we may recognize the ordinary (and somewhat non-catastrophic) traumatic events with which we live daily. In other words, how do we bear witness to the failure of justice as integral to institutional norms? Thus, where Kilby takes on the challenge of how feminism may deal with the multifaceted issue of false memory syndrome, I argue that *Fall* grapples with fictionality as a creative, necessary and ethical response to the repeated violations of women's, girls' and queer bodies.[9] I suggest that the novel does not shy away from how memories and narratives of remembering are produced through fictional forms – indeed, the novel openly interweaves such experiences and memories with fictional texts. Instead I examine how the repeated fictionalization of trauma openly bears witness to the unrepresentability, opacity and untranslatability of the originary event. While I agree with Freud and Laub that fantasy is integral to memory formation, I do not read fantasy as testifying to a truth that is as yet to be recovered and that will emerge in the interpretive psychoanalytic encounter. Rather, I turn to fiction – the creative fictionalization of memory through, for example, literature, theatre, sex, painting, photography and music – as a call for an individual *and* a sociopolitical response that questions and reworks the very structures that supposedly determine truth from lies

5 Walter Benjamin, 'The Storyteller: Reflections on the Works of Nikolai Leskov', in *Illuminations*, trans. by Harry Zorn, intro. by Hannah Arendt (London: Pimlico, [1955] 1999), pp. 83–107 (p. 83).

6 Shoshana Felman, *The Juridical Unconscious: Trials and Traumas in the Twentieth Century* (Cambridge, MA and London: Harvard University Press, 2002), p. 26 (emphasis in original).

7 In her most recent book Kilby discusses the political potentiality of popular culture (especially, although not exclusively, talk shows) and how public conversations may be political tools for fighting against, coping with, and surviving sexual and physical trauma in the home. Kilby is challenging and working with feminist criticisms of public disclosure (mainly popular) culture, and in many ways is seeking to recuperate a public culture that can effectively respond to the unspeakability or the untranslatability of sexual trauma (and within this I am including the inability of audiences to hear the words and experiences of trauma survivors). See Kilby, *Violence*.

8 Cvetkovich, pp. 3–4.

9 Butler defines false memory syndrome as 'a wish transmuted into memory' (*Undoing Gender*, p. 154); Cvetkovich explains it as 'recovered memories of sexual abuse [that] can be implanted in overly suggestible clients' (p. 33); and Kilby, although expanding considerably on this issue, is working with the idea that the charge of false memory syndrome is mobilized against therapists and children when 'therapists are [thought to be] responsible for "suggesting" to their clients that they have forgotten a history of abuse' (*Violence*, p. 17).

and fact from fiction. The fictionalization of memory is not a process towards truth, as if eventually a definitive fact will be revealed; fiction is the possibility of narrative, particularly for those silenced by institutionalized violence. Indeed, as Morrison states, fiction makes 'it possible to remember'.[10] Fiction, in *Fall on Your Knees*, is the narrativization of truths that cannot be heard within the normative structures of the colonial household.

Fall on Your Knees tells the tale of Gaelic-speaking James Piper's illicit elopement with and marriage to Lebanese-born Materia Mahmoud, and his subsequent hatred for his 'dark' and 'fat' (37) child wife. Relying on the texts of Freud and Darwin, James believes he has been manipulated by an over-sexualized and therefore racial flaw in Materia. While readers may want to question James's interpretations of these authors' texts, the novel stresses the real consequences of textual interpretation on lived lives. Colonial-informed theories of evolution dominate domestic and community life, and whiteness is idealized through a narrative concerned with the purported purity of blood relations. As a consequence of his fear of having come too close to Materia's supposed racially inferior body, James endeavours to raise their first daughter Kathleen as a beautiful 'white' (35) princess classically trained in opera. Reliving his initial desire for his young bride, James's intense love for and intimacy with Kathleen soon manifest as sexual desire. In order to escape his fear that he could harm his pure teenage daughter, James enlists to fight in the First World War and is later honourably discharged.[11] On Armistice Day, James brings Kathleen, who has been training as an opera singer in New York, back to Cape Breton. Unbeknown to the reader until the end of the novel, James rapes Kathleen after he finds her having sex with her black lover Rose. Kept in the attic for the duration of her pregnancy, Kathleen dies in childbirth after Materia stabs her with the kitchen scissors in order to deliver the breached twins, Lily and Ambrose. The chaos that ensues on this night haunts the house and the characters for the rest of the novel: James beats Materia for killing Kathleen, and Frances, knowing it the 'right' thing to do, takes the twins to the creek to baptize them. Ambrose dies in the creek and Lily contracts polio. The delay in conveying basic knowledge reflects James's inability to register his violent actions at the time of their occurrence, the absence of familial knowledge in the Piper/Mahmoud household and the novel's search for a witness. The novel centres on Frances's desire to remember what happened on this night and who Lily's parents might be.

Set at the turn of the twentieth century, the novel presents a narrative about the purity of origins in a space where migrants of varying generations are coming together. Taking place in the town of Waterford on Cape Breton Island, the text portrays a multi-ethnic space that differs from the traditional representation of the East Coast of Canada as a primarily white Anglophone community of Gaelic, Celtic and English

10 Danille Taylor-Guthrie (ed.), *Conversations with Toni Morrison* (Jackson, FL: University Press of Mississippi, 1994), p. 248.

11 James is suffering from post-traumatic stress disorder, but this is not acknowledged when he is discharged because of the purported shame it would bring on him (114).

descent.[12] Racial hierarchies and gender-based sexual violence are justified through an evolutionary rhetoric. The foundation of the celebrated multicultural Canadian nation is built on an idealized whiteness that is stabilized through hierarchies of class, ability, sexuality and gender.[13] In this novel, the Canadian mixed-race home is not idealized as a national paradigm of belonging. Instead, a white imperial imaginary is repeatedly implemented through physical violence, which seeks to obliterate difference by assaulting the one who – in this imperialist logic – embodies difference. The final pages of the novel reveal the extent of the family's adherence to religious and national narratives of racial and sexual purity: Frances's older sister, Mercedes, unable to accept the purported shame of her unmarried sister giving birth to a mixed-race child, lies to Frances by telling her that her baby boy died of sudden infant death syndrome. In actual fact, Mercedes had him placed in a care home for 'coloured' children (547). Mercedes institutes a mode of communal belonging that is violently exclusive and that denies her own mixed-race heritage. How to read between the lines of official histories is, to a certain extent, what this novel explores. More importantly, it also portrays how alternative, namely multisensory, epistemologies may be necessary if we are to hear the unsayable.

In its narrative complexity, the novel demands a committed engagement and a reading practice that does not repeat the embodied violence justified through reference to canonical literature. Whiteness, as an embodied norm that founds familial belonging for James, is enforced through a cultural heritage that reaches back to canonical texts. Thus what to do with these texts if the violent interpretations are to be undone is a significant concern of the novel. Frances reinvents literature, and Lily learns from her sister to be a creative storyteller. At the end of *Fall*, we learn that the stories we have just heard are about to be retold, or maybe have just been told, to Frances's supposedly dead son Aloysius/Anthony.[14] The temporality of the narrative is haunting: a circular structure that will never end, may only expand and

12 For an engaged analysis of Atlantic literature, see Margaret Conrad and James K. Hiller, *Atlantic Canada: A Region in the Making* (Toronto, ON: Oxford University Press, 2001); Marta Dvorak and Coral Ann Howells (eds), *The Literature of Atlantic Canada*, Special issue of *Canadian Literature* 189 (2006); and Danielle Fuller, *Writing the Everyday: Women's Textual Communities in Atlantic Canada* (Montreal: McGill-Queen's University Press, 2004). See also, Herb Wyile and Jeanette Lynes, 'Surf's Up!: The Rising Tide of Atlantic-Canadian Literature', *Studies in Canadian Literature* 33.2 (2008) <www.journals.hil.unb.ca/index.php/scl/article/view/11226/11978> [accessed 13 October 2011].

13 For an analysis of the problematics of multiculturalism in Canada, see Smaro Kamboureli, *Making a Difference: Canadian Multicultural Literature* (Oxford: Oxford University Press, 2006); and Gillian Roberts, *Prizing Literature: The Celebration and Circulation of National Culture* (Toronto, ON: Toronto University Press, 2011).

14 Mercedes insists that Frances give birth to her baby at the convent infirmary at Mabou (423). While she tells Frances and the rest of the family that Aloysius/Anthony died of sudden infant death syndrome, she arranges for him to be raised (Catholic) in the first Nova Scotia (Baptist) Home for Coloured Children (547). While Frances is away from the family home, Lily and James decide her baby boy should be called Aloysius, but Mercedes has him baptized as Anthony. Anthony is appropriately named after the 'patron saint of lost objects' (555). Aloysius is a more ambiguous name and could be an intertextual reference to multiple fictional characters, including Mr Snuffleupagus from *Sesame Street* and Lord Sebastian Flyte's teddy bear in Evelyn Waugh's novel *Brideshead Revisited.*

is as alive as the dead family members who refuse to stay dead. The historical time of the narrative is not linear, but is repeatedly haunted by bodies that refuse to be silent or buried. On the one hand, haunting time shows how the national family of Canada cannot hide or forget its unspoken or unspeakable histories (as it may prefer to do).[15] On the other hand, time is postcolonial and queer in its refusal to follow a path of progress through national heteronormative whiteness. In this potentially interminable narrative, time is discontinuous, in the Benjaminian sense, and comes close to Bhabha's description of Derrida's supplement.[16] Time is repeatedly interrupted by another time, and the order of time, just like the order of events, is disrupted. Indeed, that the novel ends where it began – insofar as we are invited, along with Aloysius/Anthony, to sit down and listen (again) to the story of Frances – portrays *an indefinite communal narration*. Thus, this story of intimate family life in a small Canadian town of multiple and mixed heritages is a call not simply for history to be rewritten, but also for historiography to be rethought. In other words, how we articulate histories and how knowledge is consolidated as authoritative are as important as the content itself.

Joel Baetz suggests that *Fall* 'raises a much-ignored regional history of Cape Breton, and retrieves a portion of a long-forgotten national past'.[17] Jennifer Andrews concurs that MacDonald's 'narrative strategically displaces simplistic constructions of Canada as a country colonized by two nations'.[18] Melanie A. Stevenson similarly emphasizes how the novel shows that Canada 'never was as monolithically white and European as history books and literature often painted it'.[19] To summarize much of the critical reception on this novel, the narration of a multicultural Cape Breton history is not only a 'desire to emphasize the fictive nature of history, its repression of certain cultural stories in an attempt to preserve a narrow and exclusive version of communal (oftentimes national) identity'[20] but also to 'recreate history in a pluralistic and provisional fashion'.[21]

While these critics produce diverse and often divergent readings of the novel, my concern is how performativity – the politics of repetition that opens up the potential for change – is theorized as a politics of diversification. Although such a politics makes evident the need for more (and different) stories, it suggests that recovery (in

15 See, for example, Laura Moss's introduction, 'Is Canada Postcolonial? Introducing the Question', in *Is Canada Postcolonial? Unsettling Canadian Literature*, ed. by Laura Moss (Waterloo, ON: Wilfrid Laurier University Press, 2003), pp. 1–26.

16 Bhabha, p. 223. Benjamin describes the linearity of history in the following way: 'The continuum of history is that of the oppressors.' In contradistinction, he suggests: 'The history of the oppressed is the discontinuum' (Benjamin, 'Paralipomènes et variantes des *Thèses "Sur le concept de l'histoire"*', as cited in Felman, *Juridical Unconscious*, p. 31).

17 Baetz, p. 62.

18 Jennifer Andrews, 'Rethinking the Relevance of Magic Realism for English-Canadian Literature: Reading Ann-Marie MacDonald's *Fall on Your Knees*', *Studies in Canadian Literature* 24.1 (1999), 1–19 (p. 11).

19 Melanie A. Stevenson, 'Othello, Darwin and the Evolution of Race in Ann-Marie MacDonald's Work', *Canadian Literature* 168 (2001), 34–54 (p. 34).

20 Baetz, p. 66.

21 Andrews, p. 9.

all senses of the term) is sufficient for a postcolonial and/or queer politics.[22] Here, the emphasis is on responsibility for uncovering hidden (mainly national) histories (which is important), but there is no questioning of how responsibility can be assumed for that which remains inaccessible, unspeakable and/or a psychosomatic sensation. There is also little engagement with how the production of more histories does not necessarily produce less violent or less hierarchical societies or relationships. Furthermore, diversification often entails what Howells describes as 'wholeness'.[23] In Laura M. Robinson's words:

> In speaking the silences, in revisiting history to tell the tales that are often not told – such as stories of lesbians at the turn of the [twentieth] century or of incest or of racial oppressions in Nova Scotia – the abuse can finally be addressed and redressed.[24]

Neta Gordon insists on the 'curative capacity' of both Frances's storytelling and the novel as a whole.[25] I would argue that this politics is non-performative. Ahmed describes non-performatives as working 'as if they bring about what they name. Or to be more precise, such speech acts are taken up as if they are performatives (as if they have brought about the effects that they name)'.[26] On the one hand, a politics of diversification (where performativity produces, for example, multiple narratives, genders, sexual identities) brings about what it names by claiming the text produces both multiplicity and diversity as desired ends. On the other hand, while multiple histories must be narrated to challenge the monolithic image of Canada as a multicultural and thus equal space, the production of more histories cannot be the ultimate goal of politics. These readings ignore the interminable nature of the ethics of storytelling, which is integral to the rewriting of histories in this novel. As Oliver insists, 'Only a response that opens rather than closes the possibility of response is a responsible response. And while a responsible response begins in acknowledging another person's reality, it also *performs* the dialogic constitution of reality itself'.[27] In other words, it is the ethical responsibility for interminable narrative, and the immediate and indefinite response to the other that open up the possibility for change. Thus, the diversity of historical narratives may be an important political aim, but to what we are prepared to listen (or even accept) as evidence and how we might hear are also integral to the process of historiography.

22 Much critical work on MacDonald reinforces performativity as that which returns differently because it does not conform to a pre-existing norm. While my emphasis is on how such readings could be said to depoliticize performativity, my critique is indebted to the inspiring work produced by scholars who write on MacDonald.

23 Howells, *Contemporary Canadian Women's Fiction*, p. 104.

24 Laura M. Robinson, '"Crossing Nature's Divide": Miscegenation and Lesbianism in Ann-Marie MacDonald's *Fall on Your Knees*', in *Identity and Alterity in Canadian Literature*, ed. by Dana Puiu (Cluj-Napoca: Risoprint, 2003), pp. 213–25 (p. 223).

25 Neta Gordon, 'Twin Tales: Narrative Profusion and Genealogy in *Fall on Your Knees*', *Canadian Review of American Studies* 35.2 (2005), 159–76 (p. 163).

26 Sara Ahmed, 'The Non-Performativity of Anti-Racism', *borderlands e-journal* 5.3 (2006) <www.borderlands.net.au/vol5no3_2006/ahmed_nonperform.htm> [accessed 1 January 2012].

27 Oliver, p. 108.

In these non-performative readings of the novel, there is also a normativizing tendency that seeks to heal the wounds of history, largely by healing Frances. Here, Frances must stop her so-called destructive behaviour, in the form of sex work, in order for the restorative transformation to occur. There is no critical exploration in readings of MacDonald's novel of how sex work may be the very means through which Frances finds a space in which to work with her memories and with what she cannot remember. Yet, Frances is queer in her exuberant and public sex acts, for which she is paid, and is similar to Mala in her refusal to conform to the heteronormative script of how women and girls should behave. Similarly, Frances's younger sister Lily refuses to adhere to Mercedes's Catholic-informed desire to take Lily to Lourdes to cure her 'little leg' (251).[28] When disability is understood as a 'personal tragedy', 'the person with [the] disability is placed under an obligation to want to get well'.[29] The normative logic of ameliorating people's lives, I would argue, is repeatedly destabilized through the decolonizing of queer and crip embodiments, desires and modes of belonging. These sisters – Frances and Lily – come together to depathologize queer, crip and mixed-race embodiments in ways that undo and exceed Mercedes's compulsive able-bodied whiteness and James's compulsively white heteronormativity.[30] I therefore interrogate, in a vein similar to Puar's recent work, the critical and ethical drive towards 'getting better'.[31] *Fall* simultaneously mobilizes and resists narratives that pathologize difference. Although I follow Cvetkovich's exploration of queer spaces that open up possibilities for dealing with trauma in ways that differ from the norms of trauma studies, I supplement her ideas from a disability studies' angle:

> Thinking about trauma from the same depathologizing perspective that has animated queer understandings of sexuality [*and disability studies' understandings of morphological and cognitive difference*] opens up possibilities for understanding traumatic feelings not as a medical problem in search of a cure but as felt experiences that can be mobilized in a range of directions, including the construction of cultures and publics.[32]

Queer, crip and postcoloniality do not accept the normative compulsion of medical and psychoanalytical models, where difference requires corrective interventions and where difference is defined in relation to imperialist able-bodied, heterosexual and white norms.

Current readings of literary texts, where trauma is a prevalent issue or theme, are often 'lost in a diagnosis that finds the same symptoms everywhere'.[33] Thus, Pilar Somacarrera

[28] Mercedes tells Lily, 'Well, God has provided. There's more than enough money for us to go together [to Lourdes] and to stay as long as it takes to petition Our Lady for a cure.' Lily responds, 'I'm not sick.' When Mercedes questions her further, asking, 'Lily. Don't you want to have two good legs?' Lily simply answers, 'No' (445).

[29] Ato Quayson, *Aesthetic Nervousness* (New York: Columbia University Press, 2007), p. 2.

[30] See 'Introduction' to Robert McRuer, *Crip Theory: Cultural Signs of Queerness and Disability* (New York and London: New York University Press, 2006), pp. 1–32.

[31] Jasbir K. Puar, 'The Cost of Getting Better: Suicide, Sensation, Switchpoints', *GLQ* 18.1 (2011), 149–58.

[32] Cvetkovich, p. 47. The italicized words are my own.

[33] Ibid., p. 32.

suggests that Frances 'enters the sex trade as a teenager after being a victim of childhood sexual abuse'.[34] I would argue that while Frances's turn to paid sex work may be a sign of a childhood trauma, it is also a creative (and not straightforwardly destructive) act that allows Frances to assert agency and even control over a body that has been repeatedly violated within the safe space of the home. The representation of Frances '[cuts] through narratives of innocent victims and therapeutic healing to present something that [is] raw, confrontational, and even sexy'.[35] Frances's irreverent, humorous and purposefully provocative responses to the abuse to which she is subjected by her father portray, as I argue in previous chapters, a need to rethink acts that are traditionally defined solely through the lens of self-harm or self-destruction. Turning to the body and taking it out into the public arena is a political act. It is also an ethical engagement as Frances learns to use her body to remember and to share her memories with Lily. Frances refuses to keep her trauma hidden in the home and Lily rejects the possibility of amelioration. Their public embodiment of difference is an orientation towards a depathologizing path where they both fight against the logic of institutionalized normalization. There is a resistance to testimony as only a private or public narrative. This is a call for a witness, who can hear what is also expressed through the body. Lily is an attentive listener to and narrator of Frances's outlandishly fictionalized tales. Lily bears witness to the histories Frances cannot quite remember, and Frances lovingly and somewhat demonically cares for Lily (protecting her from Mercedes's Catholicism). It is Lily's capacity to hear Frances's fictional truths and Frances's determination to tell Lily about her unspeakable brother that bring these two sisters together to remember the unarticulated. Their ethics of storytelling is a decolonizing of bodily epistemologies and a search for knowledge through a multisensorial engagement with each other and their surroundings. The novel seeks a witness to Frances's chaotic expressions and to Lily's interminable narrative, and portrays to the reader the impossibility and yet absolute necessity of assuming responsibility for this infinite process.

Witnessing photographs

Outside the nine books of which the novel is comprised, the prelude functions as an introductory framework through which we read the narratives. The intimate address to 'you', which often fades out of focus as we move into the main books of the novel, is calling upon someone to listen and bear witness and, in so doing, creates an interrelational testimonial process. The narrator is, thus, seeking 'to recruit and act upon that someone',[36] who is both Aloysius/Anthony, as revealed at the end of the novel, and the reader.[37] The narrator insists on showing us photographs that are

34 Pilar Somacarrera, 'A Madwoman in a Cape Breton Attic: "Jane Eyre" in Ann-Marie MacDonald's *Fall on Your Knees*', *Journal of Commonwealth Literature* 39.1 (2004), 55–75 (p. 67).

35 Cvetkovich, p. 4.

36 Butler, *Giving an Account of Oneself*, p. 63.

37 Howells reads the ending of the novel, where Lily says to Aloysius/Anthony, 'sit down and have a cuppa tea till I tell you about your mother' (566), as confirmation that 'it is Lily's voice that begins the narrative as it loops back into the past' (Howells, *Contemporary Canadian Women's Fiction*, p. 103).

unavailable to the reader. The novel is thus framed by a desire to give an account to an other and, yet, by beginning with unseeable photographs establishes the project itself as an impossibility. This impossibility structures the necessity and urgency of the account that follows.

The prelude takes a visual medium and describes it through language, and thus simultaneously deprives us of one sense (the visual) and demands that we experience a multisensory engagement (that we both recreate our own images from words and feel the materiality of the absent objects). The narrator proceeds to show a series of family photographs. Hirsch describes the family album as a normalizing tool:

> Because the photograph gives the illusion of being a simple transcription of the real, a trace touched directly by the event it records, it has the effect of naturalizing cultural practices and of disguising their stereotyped and coded characteristics. As photography immobilizes the flow of family life into a series of snapshots, it perpetuates familial myths while seeming merely to record actual moments in family history. [The] family photograph [. . .] can reduce the strains of family life by sustaining an imaginary cohesion, even as it exacerbates them by creating images that real families cannot uphold.[38]

Family photographs create and consolidate a (multigenerational) life trajectory marked by linear and progressive time and events. They give coherence to a form that is often chaotic, and tend to wipe out what may tarnish an ideal narrative. In repeating and normalizing this imagined structure, such images also constrain how others should behave, and reveal to yet others their failure to be a normal (and, of course, happy) family. Yet, Hirsch explains that 'meta-photographic textuality [can] disrupt a familiar narrative about family life and its representations, breaking the hold of a conventional and monolithic familial gaze'.[39] In other words, composite prose pictures may disrupt the conventions of the family album through the narration of what the photographs cannot or will not tell.[40] The prose surrounding the absent photographs seeks to record who and what the family has purposefully left out of the picture in its attempt to render the family's image perfect. Rather than presenting a chronological view of family life as a neat flow of snapshots, these prose pictures display the disjointed, fragmentary and absent memories that make up family life.[41] Through the visual absence, the narrator in *Fall* places the onus on the listener (and reader) to imagine another way of seeing and of remembering what is not accounted for in this constrained national familial medium.

Similar to Roland Barthes's description of mourning in relation to the photographs of his mother, this narrator could be described as telling of 'that rather terrible thing which is there in every photograph: the return of the dead'.[42] The first photograph is of

38 Hirsch, p. 7.
39 Ibid., p. 8.
40 Ibid. Prose pictures are absent images that exist only in prose form.
41 See W. J. T. Mitchell, *Picture Theory: Essays on Visual and Verbal Interpretation* (Chicago, IL: University of Chicago Press, 1994).
42 Roland Barthes, *Camera Lucida: Reflections on Photography*, trans. by Richard Howard (New York: Hill and Wang, 1981), p. 9.

'Mumma', Materia, on 'the day she died' (2).[43] The narrator describes a photograph of 'Daddy [who is] not dead, he's asleep' and then tells us there 'are no pictures of Ambrose, there wasn't time for that. Here's a picture of his crib still warm' (2). Death defines these photographs, including those of the living, and the absence of an image of Ambrose speaks to his silenced position in the family, as Lily's drowned twin brother. However, there is an image of 'Other Lily' – Materia's daughter who died before Kathleen's daughter Lily was born – who is 'in limbo' and that is 'why this picture of Other Lily is a white blank' (2). Here, the act of recording the family history through photography establishes for the reader the parameters of knowledge available in traditional media of recollection: Ambrose is absent except for the image of where he lay and Other Lily is there in a non-visualizable form. In other words, there is no or little official record of their lives. The words surrounding the photographs, the 'meta-photographic' text, become a form of recognition of what is not there.[44] The 'white blank' suggests a whitewashing of Other Lily's story – and whitewashing must be understood as both the rendering of something invisible and making white that which may not have been so – and the failure of the camera, as an instrument of the imperial familial gaze, to register her physical presence.

Barthes describes the relationship between the physicality of the person who has been photographed, the remaining photograph and the one who looks as follows:

> I call 'photographic referent' not the *optionally* real thing to which an image or a sign refers but the *necessarily* real thing which has been placed before the lens, without which there would be no photograph. [. . .] The photograph is literally an emanation of the referent. From a real body, which was there, proceed radiations which ultimately touch me, who am here; the duration of the transmission is insignificant; the photograph of the missing being, as Sontag says, will touch me like the delayed rays of a star. A sort of umbilical cord links the body of the photographed thing to my gaze: light, though impalpable, is here a carnal medium, a skin I share with anyone who has been photographed.[45]

The 'white blank' photograph infers that Other Lily was never a 'real thing [. . .] placed before the lens', and the Catholic Church confirms this in its affirmation that Other Lily was 'unbaptized and therefore no one' (82). Despite this invisibility, the whiteness confirms light as 'a carnal medium' that touches the one who looks upon it and who is moved by its physicality into remembering. Other Lily is not visualized through the family frame but emanates out of the material skin of the photograph and is recognized through this tactile visuality by Lily and the listeners.[46] This multisensory reading of

[43] The photograph of Materia is accompanied by a smell – 'all the eggs in the pantry went bad – they must have because you could smell that sulphur smell all the way down Water Street' (2) – suggesting memory lives on in sensory form and in the materials that remain. The strong, putrefied odour is also an indication of or, more precisely, a cover for the tragedy of the events that surround Materia's death.

[44] Hirsch, p. 8.

[45] Barthes, pp. 76–7, 80–1.

[46] The overexposed element of the photograph also reflects Materia's interpretation that sudden infant death syndrome occurs because 'they arrive, look around with their little blind eyes and decide not to stay' (82).

the material object shows that the 'photograph is the ghost of the photographed body, a revenant of the referent's lost skin'.[47]

Despite the correlation between these photographs and loss, the narrator also portrays the constative force of this medium: those pictured were alive and continue to haunt the present through this carnal medium. She tells of Mercedes 'holding her opal rosary, with one finger raised and pressed against her lips. She's saying, "Shshsh"' (3). An immediate connection is created between the practice of religion and the act of silencing others. Furthermore, these supposedly 'Silent Pictures' can speak, but paradoxically what is said serves only to reinforce the silence. The photographic recording of Mercedes as the one who silences others is a glimpse of her function in the family order. It also indicates one of the difficulties with which Frances and Lily must struggle to articulate what cannot be seen or said aloud.

In contrast to all the other photographs, the one of Frances 'is a moving picture' (3). The narrator describes a creek and then the surface of its water breaking. She describes 'a real live soaked and shivering girl rise up from the water and stare straight at us. Or at someone just behind us. Frances' (3). It is as if Frances is born out of the creek and, indeed, her actions on this night of Kathleen's death do determine the rest of her life and that of the family's. The incomprehensibility of what Frances is doing in the creek with a 'dark wet bundle' (3) reflects the uncertainty of memory and the inability of the camera to capture in full the events of that night. There is a correlation between the camera's impartial recollection and the narrator's own hesitancy when she asks, 'What are you doing, Frances?' (3). Although the narrator addresses Frances directly, we are told that even if Frances were to answer we would not hear anything because '[the moving picture] is also a silent one' (3). In other words, in the family album, Frances has no voice. Candida Rifkind describes Frances here as an 'actor in a silent film' and suggests that the movement of the snapshot shows 'Frances is alive' and not 'frozen in time'.[48] It is evident that Frances is moving and, thus, 'alive' in a way that the others pictured are not. However, Barthes's idea that the 'photograph is literally an emanation of the referent' would also suggest this medium is not frozen in time but instead has the literal capacity to emanate light and thus create contact across time.[49] Yet Rifkind's observation of the non-static quality of the image of Frances is important. This suggests Frances is different, uncontainable by a static medium or too boisterous to be framed by a still image. The movement also suggests a move in time towards, as Rifkind suggests, the silent movie era. In other words, Frances cannot and refuses to be represented solely through the familial medium and, thus, the image hints that the reader will not be able to use the same tools to read Frances as to read the other characters. Just as the prelude is outside of the diegesis and the photographs are visually absent but present in words, the medium through which Frances is represented exceeds the existing parameters of the family album. Frances is 'out of time [and] out of sync',[50]

[47] Prosser, *Light in the Dark Room*, p. 179.
[48] Candida Rifkind, 'Screening Modernity: Cinema and Sexuality in Ann-Marie MacDonald's *Fall on Your Knees*', *Studies in Canadian Literature* 27.2 (2002), 29–50 (p. 30).
[49] Barthes, p. 80.
[50] Halberstam, *In a Queer Time and Place*, p. 108.

in that she cannot quite conform to and refuses to be contained by the restrictive gaze of the familial frame.

However, the recording of this particular event (along with some of the others to which the narrator refers) through a photographic lens is an impossibility: the family has not photographed this traumatic occurrence. More precisely, the description attempts to literalize a memory into material form, so as to allow an other to see what the family has sought to render invisible. The filmic imagery attempts to both bring to life what is already dead or lost and remember Frances's love of silent films. It figures memory as a camera, as an imperfect but literal recorder, and places a witness back in the picture. In other words, the prose pictures decolonize and queer the familial gaze by remembering what was never recorded in the original family album. The photograph of Frances also creates the possibility of multiple looking as we are invited to look at the picture of Frances '[staring] straight at us. Or at someone just behind us' (3). This mutual exchange of looks is distinct from all the other images where no one holds the power of the gaze. It demonstrates not only Frances's own determined agency and defiance, but also a more subtle searching out for an other. That is, this initial memory picture of Frances staring out of the frame reinforces that this narrative is addressed to this onlooker (and the reader as onlooker), and that Frances needs this presence if the events around that night are to be narrated. One could suggest that in this multiple and mutual looking, where those looking at the image are touched by the light emanating from the surface and by Frances's gaze, we are called upon to take responsibility both for what we are about to learn and for what is in excess of and thus absent from the narrative.[51] This gaze, which is simultaneously powerful and pleading, bears witness and seeks at least another witness. This prose picture resists constructing a monolithic gaze that could be all-powerful and possessive. It does this by describing the image, thereby denying the onlooker the power of sight and by making the reader as much the object of the gaze as the agent of looking. It thereby establishes the listener, the onlooker and the reader in positions of uncertainty by inviting us to both look at the absent images and listen to the unsaid. The prose pictures create a relationship of interdependence between the one who is looking at what cannot be seen, the one describing what is absent and the one looking out from the frame. Intersubjective and multisensory looking is the vulnerability of bearing witness to unspoken and unspeakable material histories. Historiography is thus the task of listening to the unsaid and seeing the unseeable.

The prelude – a series of familial images that are familiar and yet disturbing in their hauntingly close relationship with death and uncertainty – condenses into minimal words the key events around which this extensive novel unravels. The final lines of the prelude tell us, 'All the pictures of Kathleen were destroyed. All except one. And it's been put away' (4). If photographs record familial reality, then the destruction of the images of Kathleen is an attempt to wipe her from memory and to consolidate a sanitized image of the familial past. Yet, the preservation of one photograph shows a desire to

[51] This reading is informed by Hirsch's interpretation of Barthes's winter-garden image. See the introduction to *Family Frames*, pp. 1–16.

hold on to a physical memory and is symbolic of Kathleen's own material refusal to disappear from this family life. Hidden and supposedly irretrievable, this forbidden photograph is like Marks's fossil with its tangible traces to unmentionable people and unspeakable events. Kept firmly in Mercedes' copy of Charlotte Brontë's *Jane Eyre* (and subsequently in the hope chest), the photograph literally disturbs the normative and imagined linear flow of everyday life and history itself (438). This photograph, like a 'revenant of the referent's lost skin',[52] is Frances's carnal connection to her sister and to her own embodied memories.

Having destroyed all images of Kathleen, James does not want to be reminded of the daughter he loved and raped, and who then died giving birth to his children. When Mercedes leaves the photograph of Kathleen on the piano (another object that carries within it the histories of familial abuse, care and love), Frances asks James questions that she knows will stoke his upset and anger: 'Kathleen was my sister and I'd like to see her now and then. [. . .] Why can't we, anyhow? Was there something wrong with her? Was she a lunatic or something? [. . .] Was she a slut?' (261). Frances uses James's own rhetoric of evolutionary prejudice to provocatively question why Kathleen must not be seen. After a disturbingly beautiful scene where Frances is a 'modern dancer' (263) and James composes the music, Frances feels 'restful' (263) because she *knows* that such a reaction means there is truth in her fictions. Refusing to be a passive victim, she insists that the beating 'lets [her] get back at him' (264). Material memories give rest only after they have torn the body apart. As in *Cereus*, *L'Enfant* and *La Nuit*, remembering can be a violent experience, but one that gives space to other narratives, images and even non-violent potentialities. Witnessing is '*in one's own body*'.[53] Although Felman and Laub are not exploring the physical violence of remembering and the physicality of memories, I would argue that Frances's embodied relation to objects portrays how 'Witnessing itself becomes thus not a passive function, but an *act* (an *art*) partaking of the very physicality of Resistance'.[54] As Frances bears witness to embodied and material memories and Lily bears witness to Frances's life, the reader bears witness to a familial history that is both catastrophic and ordinary. The prelude tells – possibly warns – all who read and try remember that witnessing is not simply about telling stories, it is a disturbing (which can be pleasurable) process where listeners must 'hear [the stories] with their skin, with their flesh'.[55]

Painting memories

The events described in 'The Prelude' are revisited in Book 2 through a further pictorialization of the memory process. Where the impossibility of seeing the photographs (that the narrator describes to the reader in 'The Prelude') calls for a

52 Prosser, *Light in the Dark Room*, p. 179.
53 Felman and Laub, p. 108.
54 Felman and Laub, pp. 108–9, note 9.
55 Melanie Lee Lockhart, '"Taking Them to the Moon in a Station Wagon": An Interview with Ann-Marie MacDonald', *Canadian Review of American Studies* 35.2 (2005), 139–57 (p. 147).

witness to see the unseeable, Book 2 describes a repeated seeing and not seeing of a painting that re-presents the unavailable reality before the eyes. According to Caruth, belatedness is at the heart of traumatic experience.[56] An inability to register events as they take place attests, on the one hand, to disbelief in the face of survival after such violence and, on the other hand, to that which 'resists simple comprehension'.[57] To a certain extent I agree with Caruth insofar as witnessing an image (rather than the event itself) portrays the very inaccessibility of the event to the eyewitness. I also concur with Hirsch that absent visual texts (the fact that the reader cannot see the painting) lay 'bare the levels of mediation that underlie *all* visual representational forms'.[58] And, as Derrida suggests, painting is only an 'adequate' re-presentation of truth and cannot 'manifest [truth] *itself*'.[59] Thus memory as painting portrays a textual concern with the unassimilability of the event, post-trauma re-presentation (often in narrative form), and truth.

However, I would argue that painting as memory is also a literalization of the act of remembering into a material and artistic form. The fossilization of memories into material objects – that may or may not literally exist – creates a sensory (and not only a psychological) relationship between the one looking and the scene witnessed. The painting, which is described from multiple perspectives, encourages the reader to both reflect on and engage with the multisensory, idiosyncratic and communal ways in which memories are formed. History is thus not only a recollection and subsequent narrativization of events, it is also a multisensorial engagement with objects that carry traces of the inaccessible and the unspoken. Sam Durrant suggests that Freud's work shows the 'materiality of the collective unconscious'.[60] What is at stake in queer postcolonial remembering is how we *respond* to the very material form taken by memories. In queer postcolonial narratives, unlike in (both Freudian and Lacanian) psychoanalysis, the physicality of memory reconfigures the relationship between self and other. It is not a mastery of the image or the memory as image by either self or other, rather self and other are undone by and for each other. To this extent, material remembering demands a corporeal giving of the self that is the risky potential of witnessing with others.

When James brings Kathleen back to Cape Breton pregnant with his twins, no information is given to the reader about the father of her children. With James insisting on Kathleen's racial inferiority and her blood (and thus behavioural) inheritance from her mother, the reader is led to believe that Kathleen had a black boyfriend in New York:

> James is grateful that all his girls turned out so fair. But there's obviously a morbid tendency in the blood they inherited from Materia that made Kathleen lean towards colour. [. . .] He has dipped into Dr Freud in an effort to discover where

56 Caruth, *Unclaimed Experience*, pp. 17–18.
57 Ibid., p. 6.
58 Hirsch, p. 25.
59 Jacques Derrida, *The Truth in Painting*, trans. by Geoff Bennington and Ian McLeod (Chicago, IL and London: University of Chicago Press, 1987), p. 5.
60 Sam Durrant, *Postcolonial Narrative and the Work of Mourning*, (Albany, NY: State University of New York Press, 2006), p. 81.

> to lay the blame for Kathleen's perversity. Freud calls women 'the dark continent'. James couldn't agree more. He doesn't hate blacks, he just doesn't want them near his bloodline. (359)

Furthermore, Frances mistakenly believes that Lily's father is 'a black man from The Coke Ovens' (321). James's judgement of Kathleen is formed through colonial ideologies of evolution where sexual degeneracy is, in this logic, a result of racial backwardness. As Stoler argues, 'the middle-class impulse to prescribe children's social, and specifically sexual, behaviour was based on a racialized language of class difference'.[61] His colonial reading of Kathleen's body and desires dominates the novel as a rhetoric through which he views the women in his family. Yet, his violently damaging perspective is repeatedly challenged and reworked by a text that not only offers further knowledge of Kathleen's true love (and how she came to be pregnant) but also invites the witnesses to visualize the events differently. In other words, how we see the events, the very form through which they are rendered apparent and not fully available, is the means that questions the patriarchal and imperialist authority of James.

The scene begins with Kathleen in labour in the attic and Materia forced to make a decision about whose life should be prioritized now that one of the twins is breached. As Kathleen's sight is 'extinguished', the first version of events is presented 'through her mother's eyes' (137). Materia is the only character who sees the events, not a painting, and who 'looks straight out from the picture at the viewer' (143). Redolent of Frances who '[stares] straight at us. Or at someone just behind us' (3), this act of looking (at someone who is looking back) creates a connection between mother and daughter in their search for someone who cannot simply *see*, but who can also bear witness to these events. They both look 'out from the picture' (143) at this unnamed viewer, who we soon learn is James. The momentary confusion regarding whether 'we' (as readers) are being looked at and whether 'we' are somehow connected to James (as the one being looked at) produces a heightened awareness about how 'we' might respond to what we see and whether we will align ourselves with James's response. The determination to look out of the picture also suggests a defiance (especially as Kathleen's 'eyes are closed' (143)) where Materia and Frances refuse to be solely visualized through the father's colonial-informed familial frame.

However, I would argue that Materia's open eyes – the witnessing of the events as they unfold – is central to her 'creative' act of suicide (145).[62] It is as if she sees too much and has no protection, and her belief in Catholic dogma reinforces that her role in Kathleen's death is too much of a burden with which to live: Materia knew that Kathleen 'preferred to die and [she] allowed her to do so. [. . .] Looked at from this angle, Materia has not saved two babies, she has mercy-killed one young woman, and therein lies the mortal sin' (138). Materia cannot live with the fact that she enabled her daughter's wish to die in order to protect Kathleen from James (in a way that Materia

61 Stoler, *Race and the Education of Desire*, p. 151.
62 Suicide is described as an act 'too creative [for James] to initiate' (145).

knows she failed to do during Kathleen's short lifetime).[63] Having sight, and in this case insight, into how Kathleen ended up in the attic is physically and psychically unbearable.

Contrary to Materia's sight, James sees only 'an overdone, tasteless, melodramatic painting': '*Death and the Young Mother*' (143). As James realizes that 'this is not really a painting but a moment freeze-framed by [his] eye' (144), he tries to take control by putting the painting out of sight:

> What can you do with such a picture? You never want to see it again yet you can't bring yourself to burn it or slash it to dust. You have to keep it.
>
> *Put it in the hope chest, James. Yes. That's a good place for it. No one ever rummages in there.* This is crazy, of course. You can't stuff a memory of a moment into a real-life hope chest as if it were a family heirloom. But for a second James feels as though that's what he's looking at – an old portrait that he hid in the hope chest many years ago and just stumbled upon again. This temporary confusion is a premonition; it tells him that he will never get over this sight. That it will be as fresh fourteen years from now, the colours not quite dry, just as it is today. (144)

Baetz comments:

> The irony is that he does stuff this picture into his mental hope chest and it does become a family heirloom, a burden that his daughters, especially Frances, will have to live with for the rest of their lives. [. . .] The pattern is by now a familiar one: psychological repression (i.e., stuffing the picture into his hope chest) and resurgence (i.e., the colours will be just 'as fresh fourteen years from now') leading to a feeling of horror, dread, or 'temporary confusion'.[64]

While Baetz situates the scene within the frame of trauma and psychoanalysis, the representation of the events through the painting resists a solely pathological diagnosis. The painting is a piece of art created through the inability of James to bear witness to what he is seeing. The object is stored not simply within his mind, but is also quickly placed in the symbolic hope chest. The chest connects the painting to both familial traditions of white heteronormativity (embodied by James and his mother) and the loss of familial connections and national home (for Materia). The physicality of the memory portrays how this event is tied to broader sociopolitical histories of familial migration and racist gender-based violence in the home. Its material form suggests a connection to a sensory epistemology (specifically the chest) that contains the traces of unspeakable and unspoken histories. This memory is tangible and therefore when James's daughters rummage in the *real* hope chest they sense remnants of histories. When dialogue is not possible (James refuses to speak about what he saw), then such

63 Materia 'watched' when James unwittingly hit Kathleen and then felt aroused as he comforted her. Although James tries to outrun what is called 'the demon' (62), Materia can *see* that his desires for Kathleen do not wane. Indeed, Materia acts 'the harlot with him' (63) to keep him away from Kathleen and believes that her prayers for James to go away are tragically answered when the First World War is declared (78). Her sight is insight into the unarticulated and the unspoken.

64 Baetz, pp. 70–1.

embodied intimacies are often the only way to learn that other forms and structures of knowledge exist (even if inaccessible). As Marks suggests, 'The "radioactive" aspect of these [fossilized] objects is that they may arouse other memories, causing inert presences on the most recent layer of history themselves to set off chains of associations that had been forgotten'.[65] Furthermore, the painting does not dry not only because, as Baetz stresses, it is a repressed memory that haunts the one who cannot face it, but also because what needs to be seen is always incomplete. Because he leaves the wet painting in the hope chest James can no longer assert his ultimate control over the familial framing. Indeed, just as she does with Mercedes's copy of *Jane Eyre* (224), Frances will rework this piece of art and create many different stories.

Frances, who is 'going on six' (140), manages to see 'everything':

> The difference between Frances and James is that, although she sees a version of the same horrible picture, Frances is young enough still to be under the greater influence of the cave mind. It will never forget. But it steals the picture from her voluntary mind – grand theft art – and stows it, canvas side to the cave wall. It has decided, 'If we are to continue functioning, we can't have this picture lying around.' So Frances sees her sister and, unlike her father, will forget almost immediately, but, like her father, will not get over it. (146)

Howells, like Baetz, reads the 'cave mind' as 'a process of repression'.[66] Although not defined, the cave mind does enter 'into a creative collaboration with the voluntary mind, and soon the two of them [. . .] cocoon memory in a spinning wealth of dreams and yarns and fingerpaintings. Fact and truth, fact and truth . . .' (151). The painting is stored in a literal space where facts – often figured as the socially sanitized version of events – and truth – the multiple, contestatory and not always coherent interpretations of what took place – further blur the incomprehensibility of the originary event. I would argue that the cave mind resonates and fractures with psychological and psychoanalytical approaches to memory formation. It evokes, along with James's readings, Freudian interpretations. Yet, the literality of the space (and later in the novel Frances and Lily will enter the French mine) where a fossilized object touches its walls suggests a *physical response* may also be necessary. Frances sees 'everything' and it all 'gets filed under "Normal"' (146), portraying Frances's creative and queer alliance with normality and thus how a therapeutic response may not be necessary or sufficient. Although she sees the events and forgets, Frances does not yet know the prejudicial violence that brought about Kathleen's incarceration and the death of both the latter and Materia. She must therefore begin to grapple with histories that bind the family to violence but that far exceed the limits of the familial home. It is this need for a response that exceeds the immediate circumstances and that can question the norms of familial life, even when words are absent, that renders this encounter queer and postcolonial.

The cave is thus a turn to the material, environmental and embodied histories that form, influence and exceed the individual and the individual household. It is a call for a

65 Marks, *The Skin of the Film*, p. 91.

66 Howells, *Contemporary Canadian Women's Fiction*, p. 116. See Baetz, p. 71.

response that is in excess of trauma as narrative or as accessible object, and therefore a call for another response that engages the materiality of memory, history, and individual and collective being. In MacDonald's play *The Arab's Mouth*, the Scottish scientist Pearl uncovers fragments of her family's bestial (her sister who is hidden in the attic has dog-like ears) and Arab heritage through the fossils collected from the shoreline.[67] They mark the hands of those who touch them, burning on the body an Egyptian hieroglyph as a trace of a silenced heritage. An embodied epistemology emerges that has always been present but that now demands to be recognized as its scars the flesh. Similarly, in MacDonald's latest novel, *The Way the Crow Flies*, the cave is a space that holds forgotten and silenced histories.[68] The earth remembers and bears witness to what has been written out of histories of post-World War Two science.[69] I would therefore suggest that the cave mind is as much a psychological as a physical space and thus that responses to unspeakable memories must also involve an engagement with multiple sites of memory (and not focus solely on the eventual articulation of trauma into words). Therefore we may want to rearticulate our approaches to trauma by not only asking how we gain access to more knowledge, but also how we can listen to what already exists and to the unspeakable. We may have to unlearn our search only for multiple or diverse histories, and begin to work on how to do justice to unavailable memories and how to engage with sensorial memories (whether in objects or bodies).

Frances's response to the painting shows a vision in which 'the looker is also implicated'.[70] Having seen James beat Materia to prevent her from seeking out the priest to baptize the twins, Frances *knows* the babies must be baptized to prevent them from suffering the same fate as Other Lily who is stranded in limbo. Displaying her ability to improvise, take control and pervert (in this case, religious) norms, Frances carries the babies down to the creek to baptize them. She takes responsibility for their lives as she knows they will be 'no one for all eternity' (147) if unbaptized. Frances's perceived petulance, as she 'wrongly' took the babies out of their safe space in the attic, is an act of love to protect them and ensure their humanness. Blame for who kills Ambrose, given James interrupts Frances and drags her out of the water and she dashes back to the creek against his strict instructions, is impossible to discern. Responsibility is figured not as naming the one who killed the child but as the possibility of telling Lily and Ambrose's story. Whereas James wants to keep this event hidden, as he wraps Ambrose in Frances's nightgown and 'tucks him into the shallow earth' (159), Frances is determined to remember. Indeed, Frances is the one who names this unnamed, dead

67 Ann-Marie MacDonald, *The Arab's Mouth* (Winnipeg, MB: Blizzard Publishing, 1995).

68 Ann-Marie MacDonald, *The Way the Crow Flies* (Toronto, ON: Alfred A. Knopf, 2003).

69 My understanding of the distinction between fact and truth in these two novels is as follows: facts are used to convey the minimal information that reinforces the dominant image of the family and the nation – so, for example, in the case of Dora, we are told that it existed and that the Jews were liberated from Nazi oppression and violence by the allies; in contrast, the truth would tell how many of the countries that 'liberated' Germany went on to employ the scientists involved in the creation of these concentration camps and in the violence which took place within. *The Way the Crow Flies* complicates the distinction between fiction and fact suggesting that fiction tells the truth whereas facts tell lies. At the age of six, Frances realizes that 'the facts of a situation don't necessarily indicate anything about the truth of a situation' (142).

70 Marks, *The Skin of the Film*, p. 184.

and unspeakable twin (141). That Ambrose is shrouded in her nightgown conveys the strong material connection that will enable Frances to stay in contact with the memory of Ambrose. Where James sees the burial as a secure way of keeping the death a secret, the nightgown conveys how secrets remain attached to objects and to those with intimate ties to the object. The earth and the nightgown (that touched Frances and now shrouds Ambrose) function as vessels for unarticulated memories. These bodies and objects ensure the earth never settles.

How the characters *respond* to what they see portrays how they begin to take *response*-ability for the events that led to and that follow this night. In a chapter entitled 'See No Evil', Mercedes hears the commotion upstairs and thinks that perhaps 'they're hanging a picture' (153). Although a new picture has been hung in the attic room, insofar as James and Frances see an imaginary one, Mercedes has no desire to see it because she 'can hold out against trouble, against curiosity, someone has to' (155). Her repeated invocation of God and goodness hints at how Mercedes will refuse to *see* anything that could destabilize her colonial-informed religious familial frame.[71] Although Mercedes does not see what happened to her elder sister or her mother, she feels its effects in her body: 'Mercedes' almost-seven-year-old nerves are still tender but tonight begins a process that will eventually turn them into steel' (155). The coldness and inflexibility of this matter reflect her unwavering faith in a Catholic God who can take away insecurities and doubts, and give her the strength to 'support' (155) anything.

However, Mercedes does see Frances in the creek:

> It's Frances, down there in the creek. She's holding something, cradling it – a bundle. And on the embankment there's something moving. A small animal. A kitten. That must also be a kitten she's holding. Frances dunks the bundle, then dives after it. What's she doing? No! No, Frances loves kittens, she wouldn't be drowning them. She's giving them a bath. That's what she's doing. She puts the one kitten down and picks up the other one, but Mercedes doesn't see what happens next because Daddy comes into the yard and up to the creek, blocking her view. Uh oh, Frances is really going to get it now. Well, she shouldn't be up playing in the creek at this hour anyhow. In fact, no one's allowed to play in the creek ever. It's not a beach. Mercedes sees the struggle, the extent of Frances's disobedience in running back to the creek, leaping in. Why is she so bad? Some people are just made that way. (155–6)

The repetition of the baptismal scene – which we have already seen from Frances's perspective and which we therefore know is an inaccurate description of the events – conveys 'a suspicion of visuality'.[72] Mercedes sees a childlike vision of kittens and is thus unable to register what is happening before her eyes (i.e. she is unable to imagine that Kathleen has given birth and that Frances is baptizing the babies). Mercedes is like her father in her unwillingness to question Frances's motivations for taking the twins to

71 For Mercedes's early devotion to God and religion, see pp. 153–6. For an example of how Mercedes inherits her father's colonial-informed racism, see p. 393.

72 Marks, *The Skin of the Film*, p. 21.

the creek. This similarity is reinforced when James later echoes Mercedes's critique of Frances in the above quotation, asserting that he 'just knows she's bad' (169). Mercedes's inability and/or unwillingness to search out knowledge and to listen to the other are exacerbated by her belief in the unwavering rightness of her religiosity. She will only see and allow others to see what maintains the image of the whitened ideal family.

Although Mercedes attempts to maintain her stiff embodiment of the '*Old-Fashioned Girl*' (175), she does remember. On the night of Kathleen's funeral, Mercedes leaves her bed and goes downstairs to find Frances on her father's knee on '*The Rocking Chair*' (167):

> It's all right. Frances is alive alive-o. She is in the rocking-chair with Daddy. It's funny that Frances seems already to have been looking at Mercedes even before Mercedes arrived in the doorway. It's daddy making the puppy sound. He is sad because Kathleen died. He needs his other little girls all the more now. Frances is sitting nice and still, not squirming for a change. Mercedes waits until the rocking-chair stops and Frances slides from Daddy's lap to join her in the doorway. As they walk upstairs hand in hand Frances says, 'It doesn't hurt.' Mercedes says, 'I don't like that smell of kidneys cooking.' And Frances says, 'Me neither.'
>
> Back in bed with Frances cuddled once more at her side, Mercedes starts to feel afraid. And a bit sick to her stomach although she can't understand why. She rises, goes over to the wash-basin and throws up. It must have been the smell of kidneys cooking [. . .]. (167–8)

Frances looks at Mercedes, or is looking for her, even before Mercedes arrives. Frances searches for a witness, someone to be there and watch. Recalling her own memories of sexual abuse, the main protagonist, Madeleine, of *The Way the Crow Flies* describes the importance of watching: 'We think of "witness" as a passive role, but it's not, it can be terribly difficult. That's why we say "to bear witness". Because it can be so painful. *Watch me*'.[73] She explains why watching her childhood self is so important: ''Cause I can't change it. But at least, if I watched it, she wouldn't have to be alone'.[74] Like Mala's act towards Pohpoh, Madeleine puts herself back in the original frame to bear witness to the unacknowledged violence. Frances searches for this viewer, someone to watch as an intimate presence who can see differently and therefore bear witness. Nonetheless, the presence of Mercedes does not give Frances the witness for whom she searches, despite the former seeing Frances. Rather, Mercedes's response to Frances, when Frances tells her it does not hurt, is to elide the subject and to move into an olfactory realm that portrays a repulsion. The smell could be said to be Mercedes's sensory registering of something untoward. It does, however, also convey that Mercedes has not (quite) heard, is incapable of understanding or is not listening to what Frances is saying. Despite this failure to respond with words, there is a bodily recognition, a knowledge in the body, that manifests itself through the pervading smell of 'kidneys cooking' and her vomiting. As James does when he recognizes his sexual attraction to

[73] MacDonald, *The Way the Crow Flies*, p. 615.
[74] Ibid.

Kathleen (61), Mercedes throws up what she does not want to know. The body tries to expulse what has been recorded in and on it. Indeed, Mercedes's body effectively and affectively tries to rid itself of that with which she cannot cope but keeps a trace of what she really saw.

A few years later Mercedes experiences a resurfacing of this memory in the form of a painting that has '[torn] itself from its frame':

> It was here in the living-room. The painting from the junk pile is called *Daddy and Frances in the Rocking-Chair*. But there never was a rocking-chair, in this room or any other. [. . .] To the left is the dark kitchen and a smell like the inside of someone's body. [. . .] Frances is there looking at me already. I wonder how long she's been waiting for me. [. . .] His right hand hovers, barely touching the halo of yellow fuzz Frances gets from turning on her pillow, and his left hand is under and up her nightgown like a puppeteer's. He says something I can't hear, then breathes up hard through his nose, then 'my little girl', and the chewed-up word 'beautiful', then he shoves her down between his legs and pins one hand across her chest, the other one still operating underneath, they're both facing in the same direction now but Frances turns her face to keep our eyes together. His head snaps back and he jams her up between his legs once, again, three times and a half, until he trembles at the ceiling. That's when the fear goes out of him and he crumples around her and cries into her hair. Frances and I keep looking at each other until he falls asleep like that, then she crawls out from behind his arms and walks over to me. 'It doesn't hurt,' she says. [. . .] Sizzling comes from the kitchen across the hall. I don't like that smell of kidneys cooking. 'Me neither,' says Frances. (374–6)

In the re-representation of the event as painting, Mercedes watches and the two girls see each other. Mercedes not only recognizes familial violence in the painting, but she also allows herself to be pulled in by the subject/object of the painting, resulting in, what Marks would designate as, a 'visceral and emotional contemplation'.[75] The failure to respond to Frances's words reflects the impossibility of narrativization, but not a failure to witness. Mercedes uses embodied language to express disgust and Frances recognizes a similar feeling. The visceral reaction – the possibility of bearing witness – to the painting is distinct not because the words uttered are different but because Mercedes and Frances keep their 'eyes together'. They are drawn in by the look of the other, vulnerable to each other, and undone by what they witness *together*. However, Mercedes is only looking at a painting memory. Although this revised picture belatedly prompts Mercedes to respond – wrongly suspecting James is getting ready to kill Frances, she pushes him down the stairs to protect her – it is only a memory. That is, while the memory as painting gives us access to more detail about the night James started abusing Frances, the intersubjective relationship between Frances and Mercedes rarely occurs outside of Mercedes's pictorial memories. Although she sees the picture and smells its repulsion, she keeps these visceral sensations at bay by holding 'lemon oil' and a 'dust-rag' in her hand (374). The memories, thus, come forth in this visual

75 Marks, *The Skin of the Film*, p. 163.

medium to allow Mercedes a safe distance from their smell. While she looks back at Frances, who in searching for a witness looks at her, Mercedes will not translate this mode of witnessing into her everyday relationships. Recognition of familial violence takes place momentarily, for Mercedes, in the enclosed, safe space of the painting but does not bring about a questioning of her own responsibility in the reiteration of familial abuse. Indeed, Mercedes will go on to commit a further violence towards Frances by affirming her adherence to a racist structure of familial life. Mercedes may sense these material memories, but she will restore (embodied) order by refusing to feel the reverberations of these sensorial disturbances.

The materiality of memories portrays the politics, aesthetics and ethics of remembering as intimate processes that undo the self in relation to the other. The visuality of the painting creates an aesthetic where the viewer is drawn in as object and subject of the gaze. There is an impossibility of discerning a difference between viewer and viewed, and thus a sense of vulnerability in the face of memories is heightened. This mode of looking, an almost tactile viewing, destabilizes the colonial and patriarchal gaze of familial norms. It is an interrelational looking that calls for a response. However, it cannot be the single response of Mercedes, where one moment of violence may be stopped. It must be a much more indefinite questioning of the violence that is repeated through colonial and familial norms, and an infinite engagement that brings a cessation to intergenerational abuse.

Memories as storytelling

Witnessing is an incessant embodied engagement with historiography, and Frances bears witness to the unspoken and the unspeakable by simultaneously defying the familial strictures (as set down by James and Mercedes) and reaching to and perverting her heritage. She repeatedly tells Lily an ever-changing version of the events that surround the birth of Lily and Ambrose, and the death of Kathleen and Materia. Just as she rewrites and perversely performs canonical literary texts, Frances continually fictionalizes her life story and, in so doing, gives Lily (and the reader) access to an ever-growing dosage of truth. If James whitewashes the family history to conform to an Anglocentric Canadian image of national belonging, Frances does not simply add in a mixed-race heritage to the multicultural spectacle of Canada. Instead, she repeatedly returns to the site of trauma – the trauma of a familial sexual violence that is silenced by an idealized national narrative of heteronormative whiteness – to keep alive *and render public* the memories others would prefer to forget.[76]

Frances's storytelling is performative in its repetitive reiteration of the same tale. However, it is also performative in its search to both alter the existing national familial narrative and change the very structure of what counts as a viable familial existence.

[76] My reading of the novel in this section is significantly informed by Berlant and Warner's article 'Sex in Public'.

Most importantly, Frances reaches to embodied media, and not only to an unearthing of empirical facts, to bring about change. She queers the family – by defying its sexual morality – and creates less violent modes of belonging by testifying to the existence of Ambrose (of whom no one speaks). Proponents of false memory syndrome insist on both the accessibility of memory as a truthful event and the purported scientific veracity of narrative. Detailing how some historians denied the viability of an Auschwitz survivor's story because the facts of her narrative were incorrect (she wrongly described seeing four chimneys explode),[77] Laub tells how the woman was testifying 'not to the number of the chimneys blown up, but to something else, more radical, more crucial: the reality of an unimaginable occurrence'.[78] He asserts, 'She testified to the breakage of a framework. That was historical truth'.[79] Butler argues that trauma produces an 'epistemic violence'.[80] She adds, 'To insist, then, on verifying the truth is precisely to miss the effect of the violation in question, which is to put the knowability of truth into enduring crisis'.[81] Thus the search for an objective truth ignores the form taken by trauma, and is a refusal to respond to an address. However, the novel proves the veracity of Frances's testimony by engaging fiction to testify to trauma. In other words, it is through a creative, artistic process that Frances bears witness to what is outside of the familial frame of reference. Because there is no narrative space in the home to bear witness to the violence to which she has been subjected, Frances must find a way to break the sociopolitical authority of her father and the community.

The novel portrays Frances's intimate relationship with fiction and stresses her love of lies. When James and Mercedes comfort Frances at Materia's funeral because they believe she is crying (when in fact she is laughing), Frances has an epiphany:

> Frances learns something in this moment that will allow her to survive and function for the rest of her life. She finds out that one thing can look like another. That the facts of a situation don't necessarily indicate anything about the truth of a situation. In this moment, fact and truth become separated and commence to wander like twins in a fairy-tale, waiting to be reunited by that special someone who possesses the secret of telling them apart.
>
> Some would simply say that Frances learned how to lie.
>
> Of all her secrets, Ambrose was Frances's biggest. He was also her greatest gift to Lily. (142)

The idea of separating fact from truth pervades MacDonald's oeuvre and conveys how facts alone may be unreliable and misleading (e.g. the fact that James has four daughters does not convey the complexity or violence of their familial relations and that one of his daughters is also his granddaughter). By connecting the splitting of fact from truth to the idea of twins who have been separated, the passage evokes Lily's own separation from her (non-existent in the familial narrative) twin, Ambrose. The act of

[77] Felman and Laub, pp. 59–63.
[78] Ibid., p. 60.
[79] Ibid.
[80] Butler, *Undoing Gender*, p. 156.
[81] Butler, *Undoing Gender*, pp. 156–7.

lying is directly related to Frances's 'gift' to Lily and portrays how the uniting of one twin with the other will bring together fact and truth. According to the familial narrative, Lily has no twin (which is a fact insofar as he is dead). In response, Frances creates a fictionalized narrative where she gives life to Ambrose (which for the family is a lie) and reanimates a version of the truth. Fiction therefore serves as the medium through which fact and truth and Lily and Ambrose are reunited. Thus fiction becomes the only way to access truth in a situation where narratives are controlled by a patriarchal figure who seeks to reproduce a national myth of familial whiteness.

While I want to argue that fiction and the fictionalization of narrative are central to Frances's intersubjective mode of remembering with Lily, I also want to make clear that the novel portrays how lies, truth, fact and fiction circulate and intertwine more generally in social memory formation. Indeed, I would suggest that the novel does not create a hierarchy of truth over lies (as a moral mould for society). Rather, truth is a form of collective social consensus, and lies are knowledge formations that have gained little or no authority:

> Everyone knew that Kathleen was pregnant and that she died of the child. You'd have to be an idiot not to have figured that out, what with the girl's hasty home-coming and incarceration in the house. But the thing you do in a case like this is go along with the idea that the child is the offspring of its grandparents. Everyone agrees to this fiction, and the only people who'd breathe a word of the actual facts to the illegitimate child are those who are so malicious to begin with that they are easily dismissed as liars. As in truth they are. For the beneficent lie tells the truth about the child, which is 'you belong to this community', whereas the malicious truth-tellers use fact to convey a lie, which is 'you don't belong'. This is an imperfect system but it's the prevailing one. And as the years go by the facts get eroded and scattered by time, until there are more people who don't know than people who do. (165–6)

The fictionalization of Lily's history reinforces the truth of her place within the community, but also reveals how lies form histories and long-lasting community ties. Often lies are collectively mobilized to cover over incoherence, inconsistencies and/or violent aberrations. My point is not simply that truth is negotiable on a social level, but that fictional creativity may be necessary if other orientations are to be both imagined and enacted. Frances delves into chaotic and creative entertainment where she uses her body to experience worlds often unavailable in the religious spaces of nation, home and school. She takes her body into forbidden spaces – the speakeasy, her mother's parents' home and the French Mine – to touch, smell and taste unknown histories and to share what she does not know with Lily. Fiction for Frances is the chance to open up stories to other possibilities, not to control the narrative, but to explore the unknown.

Frances's turn to embodied media to express what she cannot quite remember correlates with Gilroy's exploration of the politics and ethics of what he terms 'Black Music'. Gilroy describes subcultural music as produced from 'the viscera of an alternative body of cultural and political expression that considers the world critically'.[82] Through artistic expression – that may appear incomprehensible, simple or spectacle-like to those who yield a biopolitical control – another mode of communicating with others becomes possible. Music – subcultural art – opens up the potential for politics, for enacting other ways of being communally. Frances is a musician, who follows her mother's musical love of ragtime and improvisation:

> Materia gets up and dances the *dabke*. Her mother taught her this dance, and Materia has taught Frances and Mercedes. [. . .] The trick is that the dancing and singing are unrepeatable. Once you know this you're ready to start learning.
>
> When the precious record wears out, Frances innovates with a comb and wax paper to approximate the reeds and strings. Far from thinking it a sacrilege, Materia considers it ingenious, and it is.
>
> Put the shell to your ear. You can hear the Mediterranean. Open the hope chest. You can smell the Old Country. (89–90)

Frances does not simply copy her mother, but improvises the music and the dance. Through their bodies they reach to a forgotten time and to an unlived memory of Lebanon. Like the '"riff" in jazz',[83] Frances's embodied art 'does not simply copy or imitate the manifest content of the text being read but actually makes something happen (or makes history in its own way) through associations and improvisations'.[84] Frances is making history by trying to remember not only the events wiped out in James's whitewashed histories, but also by forging narratives (through her bodily fictions) that destabilize the very ways in which histories are authorized and consolidated.

Speaking of her vague memories of the night Ambrose died, Frances tells Lily:

> On the day you were born a stray orange cat came in through the cellar door. [. . .] It climbed all the way up to the attic without a sound. It came in here where you were both sleeping and it leapt into your crib. It put its mouth over Ambrose's face and sucked the breath out of him. He turned blue and died. Then the orange cat put its paws on your chest and it was about to do the same thing to you but I came in and I saved you. Daddy took the orange cat and drowned it in the creek. Then he buried it in the garden. In the spot where the scarecrow used to be but now there's a stone. I helped. (205)

By incorporating a cat into the narrative, Frances takes on a skewed version of Mercedes's already incorrect interpretation of the night the latter saw Frances at the creek. In this version, no one is blamed for the loss of Ambrose, except the cat that has been punished for its wrongdoing. On the one hand, Frances's story does not tell Lily the truth about Frances's own involvement in the death of Ambrose. On the other hand, this fictionalized narrative tells Lily that she has a brother of whom no one speaks and

82 Gilroy, p. 39.
83 Dominick LaCapra, *History and Reading: Tocqueville, Foucault, French Studies* (Toronto, ON: Toronto University Press, 2000), p. 46.
84 Ibid., p. 45.

who died under tragic circumstances. Frances testifies 'to the breakage of a framework', and she also bears witness to the power of fiction to give life to the unspeakable.[85]

However, Frances is improvising and so she must endlessly repeat this tale. She also 'needs to say a story out loud to divine how much truth runs beneath its surface' (321):

> 'Okay. Well. Mumma went crazy from shame of what she did with the man from The Coke Ovens. Plus she was dying of a wound she got because Daddy had to cut you and Ambrose out of her stomach with his bayonet. [. . .] It was the middle of the night. Daddy left her sleeping and went to get the doctor. But she got up even though she was cut open.' Frances has slipped into the eerie voice of the stray-orange-cat story. It's the voice she uses when she is telling the truth. 'I was at my bedroom window wearing my tartan housecoat. I saw Mumma down in the creek. Ambrose was lying on the bottom. She was just about to do the same thing to you. But she looked up and she saw me watching her so she stopped. There was a bright bright moon and I just looked her in the eye like that till Daddy came and dragged her back to the house with you. Then she died.' (251)

The performative structure of testimony is the repeated undoing of existing parameters of knowledge in an intersubjective relationality with others. It is also an ethical response, a need to take responsibility for history by letting the riff rip the story apart and put it back together differently. Frances can talk creatively with Lily because Lily's green eyes are 'always prepared to take in a solemn truth' (181). Despite our knowledge of the inaccuracy of this description, the narrator insists that Frances 'has slipped into the eerie voice [. . .] she uses when she is telling the truth'. Frances makes a connection between the man who drove Kathleen to school (Leo Taylor) and Lily's birth mother. She conveys to Lily that her mother, whom she believes is Materia, died from the 'shame' of having had extra-marital sex with a black man. The reference to Leo demonstrates how Frances is getting closer to the truth about Lily's mother: she was the woman driven by Leo and she had an affair with a black woman. Frances feels – has an embodied awareness of – the shame surrounding Lily's birth and rightly connects it to issues of race and sexuality. She portrays herself as Lily's saviour and implicates herself in the events, as having the power to control the actions of others. The creation of an intersubjective relationship between mother and daughter, where each returns the look of the other, prevents the reiteration of familial violence. Thus, the suggestion that Frances is telling the 'truth' when we, as readers, already know what happened on this night (i.e. it was her at the creek and not Materia) portrays truth as that which bears witness to what broke out of the familial frame first time round. Truth is the impact of this narrative on both the teller and the listener as they reassess the facts of familial life. As they bear witness to unarticulated histories, they not only rewrite histories but they also feel these stories through, in and on their bodies.

As a result of Frances's repeated stories of Ambrose, Lily experiences nightmares that include 'Frances in the creek with the dark bundle' (226). When Lily first sees

[85] Felman and Laub, p. 60.

Ambrose in her dreams she 'does not yet recognize her twin' and so asks him, in a state between sleep and wakefulness, 'Who are you?' (226). Ambrose goes to respond:

> And as he does so, water gushes from his mouth and splashes to the floor. Now she screams. Now she is 'awake' – back in a state which is a definite place on a map. A place called Awake. On the other side of the country of Asleep. And you see this shaded area in between? Don't linger there. It's No Man's Land. (226)

Lily is not only beginning to visualize the drowning of her twin brother, but also to experience this nightmare as intimately tied to her own father's involvement in the war (where he spent much of his time in no man's land). Although Lily addresses Ambrose, she cannot hear his words. In response to her own and Lily's incomplete remembering, Frances takes Lily to the French mine where, she tells her, Ambrose lives:

> At night he dives down in this pool and swims in an underground river till it comes out at the surface and turns into our creek. He takes a breath and swims in the shallow water, long and white, all the way till he gets to our place. Then he climbs out over the top of the bank and slowly walks, dripping, across our yard and opens the kitchen door. He walks past the oven. He walks into the hall past the front room. He walks up the stairs without a sound, and past the attic door. He comes into the room where you're asleep. He stands at the foot of your bed and looks down at you. He has red hair.
>
> And then he leaves. But he can't swim back. He has to move the rock in the garden and go down a tunnel that's too small for him now, until he gets to the sad and lonely mine. He walks for miles in his bare feet past all the quiet soldiers and miners resting against the walls. And every time he makes the journey back to the pool, *his heart breaks*. So you see how much he loves you, Lily, to make such a trip night after night. (268–9, emphasis added)[86]

For Howells, the mine shows how 'the two girls are entering the topography of Frances's forgotten dreams'.[87] She adds, '[The] mine seems to be a kind of "black hole" or psychic space without limits in which unnameable desires and fears operate and where fantasies are played out'.[88] However, the description of it as an 'abandoned bootleg mine' (265) also explicitly connects the space they enter to the space from which Lily and Ambrose originally emerged: 'Kathleen is an abandoned mine. A bootleg mine, plundered, flooded' (136). I am not suggesting that Frances is taking Lily back to her mother's womb. Rather, I am arguing that she is taking her to a tangible and multisensorial space that is redolent of the maternal body within which Lily once coexisted with Ambrose. It is an embodied place that is familiar and disturbing to both her and Lily. While this interweaving of maternal space with the mine prompts an evident Freudian reading,

86 There are evident parallels between the story of Ambrose and the tale of the orange cat, especially the detail of how they reach the room where the unsuspecting people are sleeping. The 'red hair' of Ambrose further relates to the 'orange' of the cat, especially as his hair is described as 'angel orange' (273).

87 Howells, *Contemporary Canadian Women's Fiction*, p. 117.

88 Ibid., p. 118.

offered by many critics,[89] this trip is Frances's way of defying her father's orders: she was supposed to take Lily to Brownies and, instead, puts Lily in a scary and dangerous situation. The precariousness of the mine relates both to a physical danger of falling into its flooded waters and a psychic danger of learning too much. These concomitant dangers bring about Lily's capacity to take on (the story of) Ambrose; for Lily must be in a literal danger of becoming undone if she is to live with (knowledge of) Ambrose. More specifically, the mine, like the cave mind, is the space that contains fossilized layers of memory: Ambrose is buried in the garden, connected to the mine by the creek in which he drowned, and thus his remnants are to be found within this matter. The earth and the stone contain the memories that are absent in the Piper/Mahmoud histories. In order to bear witness to Ambrose's story, Lily and Frances must touch his literal traces stored in the remnants of the mine, and Lily must feel this material disturbance on the level of the soma if she is to hear Frances's body.

Although Howells describes Lily as Frances's 'innocent witness'[90] at the mine, I would suggest that their memorialization of Ambrose in a space that literally connects them to the earth within which he is buried comes closer to Oliver's description of witnessing as restoring subjectivity through the mutuality of response-ability:

> This is the moment Lily stops being afraid of anything Frances could ever say or do again. Stops being afraid of anything at all. She reaches out and takes Frances's hand. The white hand that always smells of small wildflowers, lily of the valley. The hand that has always done up Lily's buttons and laces, and produced wondrous objects. She holds Frances's hand and tells her, 'It's okay, Frances.'
>
> Frances's bruised face crumples and her forehead drops to her knees knocking her Girl Guide beret askew. Her stick arms encircle her legs and she cries. Lily strokes the sinewy back while Frances mumbles something over and over.
>
> Years later, Frances remembers that she was saying, 'I'm sorry, I'm sorry, Lily, I'm sorry.'
>
> But memory plays tricks. Memory is another word for story, and nothing is more unreliable. (270)

At the mine Frances gives (the story of) Ambrose to Lily, and Lily bears witness to Frances's testimony. Thus far, Lily has wanted to believe that Ambrose was a character in one of Frances's stories[91] but now she recognizes the truth in her words and in the earth:

> Frances doesn't need to tell Lily any more Ambrose stories after this because he has become Lily's story. Frances has finally succeeded in giving him to her. Lily is ok. For now. Frances can get on with other things. Her life. (278)

89 See, for example, Howells, *Contemporary Canadian Women's Fiction*, and Baetz.

90 Howells, *Contemporary Canadian Women's Fiction*, p. 118.

91 Lily and Frances bury Mercedes's meticulously drawn family tree (which Lily has coloured in and added detail to in order to make it look more like a real tree) at the site where Ambrose is buried. They move the stone and as they do the following conversation unfolds:

> 'Lily. Ambrose is just a story.'
> 'I know.' [. . .] 'Frances, you said Ambrose was just a story.'
> 'I changed my mind.'

Lily recognizes the truth in fiction, and thus renders human the non-existent Ambrose. Indeed, Ambrose had previously told Lily, 'I am No Man' (273). Butler suggests, 'The derealisation of the "Other" means that it is neither alive nor dead, but interminably spectral'.[92] When Lily sees her twin brother, he is shrouded in 'the decomposing bits of Frances's old white nightgown' (225). The nightgown, the earth and waters of the mine, and Frances's body touch Lily into remembering memories she never had and thus into recognizing the previously unreal as real.

Hearing Frances's story and recognizing its place within (the familial) reality is not simply to take in her words, but is to literally feel their embodied impact. After Lily visits the mine with Frances, she experiences a near-deadly fever:

> 'Who took my skin?'
>
> 'Soaked with fever.'
>
> Lily buries her face in her drenched pillow because the light is an eye operation.
>
> 'The light is off, Lily, see? There's no light on.'
>
> [. . .] They'll have to keep an eye on her for the rest of the night, if her temp goes up, if it goes up. . . . (274)

Lily is suffering the effects of gangrene, from the 'wound on her left heel [that] has reopened' (272). The original wound came from wearing her new shoes, which her father made for her to attend the Armistice Day Parade – a day to remember not only the end of the First World War but also when James raped Kathleen. This mark on the body of the effects of the new shoes is the literal impact of a day of global and familial remembrance. The impact of familial trauma – of the intimate effects of racialized ideals – is not publicly memorialized. The wound is reopened during the trip to the French mine, as if more memories are trying to get under her skin. The opening up of the body through pain, a literal cutting, shows that '"my body" does not "belong to me"' but is given over in a sociality with others that precedes it.[93] Lily's own question – 'Who took my skin?' – shows a loss of protective layers, a vulnerability to sensory overload that is further emphasized through her photosensitivity. The memories are cutting away at her skin, making it putrid and, through the ensuing fever, are coming close to killing her, as is expressed by the inability of the narrator to finish the sentence of what may happen should her temperature continue to rise. On one level, the skin, if understood simply as a protective layer, is failing to keep out that which may harm the body. On another level, the skin shows its vulnerability, its openness to the outside, and its connection to others, their histories and wider global events. The skin is susceptible to feeling memories, and her body thereby manifests the pain of remembering.

> 'Frances, don't!'
> 'Don't be a baby Lily, jeez, you're so easy to scare.'
> 'He was just a story, Frances.'
> 'All right Lily, he was just a story.' [. . .] Frances grins; 'No he wasn't.' (216–18)

92 Butler, *Precarious Life*, pp. 33–4.

93 Sara Ahmed and Jackie Stacey, 'Introduction: Dermographies', in *Thinking Through the Skin*, ed. by Sara Ahmed and Jackie Stacey (London and New York: Routledge, 2001), pp. 1–17 (p. 5).

After Lily's temperature breaks and her 'skin is no longer sore' (274), she responds to Ambrose's call to meet him at the creek. Connecting their untold story to that of their parents' elopement, Ambrose uses words reminiscent of those that described the night James and Materia were married: *'the spring in my garden pours down from Lebanon, come to me and I will give you rest'* (274). He then takes hold of Lily and immerses her in the creek along with himself. Similar to the events on the night they were born, he returns her to the edge of the water as he disappears:

> *I would take you to my mother's house, to the room of she who conceived me* – Lily has never got used to being alone. [. . .] He lays her gently on the bank and *her heart breaks*. Her tears begin to flow because he is leaving – *don't go!* He sinks into the water on his back – *take me with you!* (275, second emphasis added)

Just as happens to Ambrose every time he comes to see Lily, her 'heart breaks'. Repeating Frances's actions many years later, Ambrose covers Lily in the water of the creek in a symbolic act of 'rebirth'.[94] Through the refiguring of the death of Ambrose and of Frances's baptismal gesture, this magically real performative moment bears witness to the impossible. The memory comes forth through the body. The repetition of the same event many years later produces a different effect because Lily is able to bear witness to Frances's stories through her own bodily undoing. The performative structure of testimony is this bodily capacity to hear and feel histories and in so doing to open up the familial narrative and form to irrevocable change.

Frances has a sociopolitical response to Lily's willingness to take on (the story of) Ambrose. In other words, her responsibility is not over; she labours to remember. Frances's gift of (the story of) Ambrose to Lily allows Frances to focus on earning money – largely for Lily. She performs her multiple silenced heritages in public by 'playing Mumma's old vaudeville music from the hope chest', singing in 'pidgin Arabic' (292) and mimicking her mother's 'disturbing, unhealthy' (23) ability to play by ear. She is rummaging in the hope chest and bringing unspoken histories into the public arena by performing in her maternal uncle's speakeasy. Yet she improvises (293). Frances embodies both a critique and a spectacle of exotic and erotic difference. The melange of entertainment genres displays Frances's uncertain, playful and fictional knowledge of her heritage. She is repeating history, but it is not the same. This is a performative, musical repetition where what is unknown is about to change the present:

> Frances will bounce on your lap with your fly buttoned for as long as it takes for two bucks. Expensive, but consider the overhead in wardrobe alone. A hand job costs two-fifty – she has a special glove she wears, left over from her first communion. Another fifty cents buys you a patter, a song, any name you want to hear. Touch her little chest and cough up an extra buck; nothing below her belt.
>
> Frances starts to make money. Once she has acquired enough trinkets and trash to keep her gussied, she starts saving her money in a secret place. It's for Lily. Not for a 'cure' – Frances does not subscribe to Mercedes' devout yearnings. In fact,

94 Howells, *Contemporary Canadian Women's Fiction*, p. 119.

> Frances is unsure why she is sure the money is for Lily. She is putting it away 'just in case'. In case what? In case.
>
> Frances remains a technical virgin throughout. What is she saving herself for? She can't say. It's a feeling. There is something left for her to do. 'For Lily'. What, Frances? Something. (203)

Although the image of Frances bouncing on these men's laps recalls James's abuse of her, I would argue that this is not simply an unacknowledged traumatic repetition but the queer potentiality of repetition with a difference. It is an ethico-political turn to the body. In Gilroy's words, 'This politics exists on a lower frequency where it is played, danced, and acted, as well as sung and sung about, because words [. . .] will never be enough to communicate its unsayable claims to truth'.[95] Sex work is another way of communicating, of unlearning the restrictive family histories and of surviving. Frances does not fully understand why she must do this for Lily, but knows these reasons will become apparent: 'She is a commando in training for a mission so secret that even she does not know what it is. But she is ready' (307). Knowledge is not accessible or whole but is a trust in bodily sensations. Here, the body is not simply instinctive but is an affective register of what has failed to be recorded in the narratives of the national and religious family. Frances can trust her body because it has repeatedly bore witness to the events surrounding the night Lily was born. Indeed, this is why it is so important that Frances undertake work that centres on her body. Her sex work makes her father angry and upsets Mercedes because it defies the ordinance of the family where a woman's body is sacred and for the reproduction of children and ideals. And, her work is a visceral desire to remember.

The materiality of remembering is a shared responsibility felt between narrators and listeners, and experienced in-between the narrative. In bearing witness to the veracity of fiction, Lily takes on a significant role in Frances's performance: every night she helps Frances back into the house by letting down a sheet to Frances's call of 'Rapunzel, Rapunzel, let down your hair!' (294). They then speak to each other in their shared language:

> 'Frances. Al akbar inshallah?'
>
> 'In fallah inti itsy-bitsy spider.'
>
> 'Ya koosa gingerbread boy kibbeh?'
>
> 'Shalom bi' salami.'
>
> 'Aladdin bi' sesame.'
>
> 'Bezella ya aini Beirut.'
>
> 'Te' berini.'
>
> 'Te' berini.'
>
> 'Tipperary.' (295–6)

Salah infers that through this affective speech, fused 'with magic, music and dance', the girls transmit a discontinuous and dissonant linguistic and musical heritage, as well as

[95] Gilroy, p. 37.

memories of an historical shame and violence.[96] Both *L'Enfant* and *Fall* draw out the physicality of language, but where the visual shapes of the characters touch Ahmed, transporting him to another plane, here the texture of the words in the mouth and the sensation of language in the ears are emphasized. Frances and Lily use sounds rather than only the meaning of words to convey their attachment; it is an intimate language full of bodily memories. The move to the sounds of words, to a language formed of a collage of references without evident referents, conveys history as a concrete sensation and language as a material touch on the body. The words do not portray an external referential reality or an internal psychological state but the opaque musicality of communication. As MacDonald states,

> [Languages] are repositories. Emotional repositories. Repositories of history. [There] will be places in your heart and mind that are only accessed via the first language, the old language, the emotional language, the childhood language. [. . .] Language is a very intimate thing. It's like a loved one. [. . .] I mean, the little girls are closer to their mother as long as they're speaking Arabic. And if they don't have enough Arabic, they'll invent it. Invent a secret language that helps keep their bond alive, their connection to their mother.[97]

This non-representational linguistics shows not an absence of knowledge sharing, or communication, but one situated in a visceral improvisation where they come close to a sensorial relationship with Materia and her heritage. The affective embodied linguistic communication passes on what Frances knows of her mother to Lily while infusing it with knowledge of Kathleen's modernity and her own love of literature and film. The opacity of the language and its playfully fictional borrowings keep to the fore the impossibility of knowing (finally and definitively) their mother's histories. Affective language is an ethical mode of witnessing the untranslatability of unspoken – and yet shared – knowledge.

If the body can register unseeable and unspeakable memories, then Frances's act of conceiving a child with the man she believes is Lily's father, Kathleen's ex-driver Leo Taylor (322), is an attempt to give to Lily not only the sibling she lost but also embodied memories from both sides of her family. By leading the unsuspecting Leo to the French mine inhabited by Ambrose, to the space reminiscent of the cave mind, Frances brings Lily's uncertain and muddled histories together. I do not agree that this act is a simple transgression of 'the boundaries of sexual and racial codes' or a reflection of her 'longings for her lost dark mother'.[98] Instead, I would suggest that Frances uses the somatic register because it is the sole medium that remembers what has never been articulated (especially James's sexual abuse of Frances). She knows it stores memories and heritages, and she seeks to give these to Lily in embodied form. I would further argue that this is not a heteronormative conception: Frances and Lily insist that it was Teresa's bullet that inseminated Frances. Angry at Frances for potentially ruining her

96 Trish Salah, 'What Memory Wants: Broken Tongue, Stranger Fugue in *Fall on Your Knees*', *Canadian Review of American Studies* 35.2 (2005), 231–49 (pp. 242–3).

97 Lee Lockhart, pp. 141–2.

98 Howells, *Contemporary Canadian Women's Fiction*, p. 119.

brother's marriage and for having lost her own job, Teresa shoots Frances.[99] The latter is rushed to hospital losing an immense amount of blood and, as a result, the nurse tells Mercedes that it is impossible for the baby to have survived. Indeed, Frances's life is only saved by the blood Lily gives to her. This blood connection is not one of familial psychic identification (the ideology to which James adheres), but rather it is a practical medical saving device that nevertheless creates an interembodied connection between the two: Lily literally gives Frances a part of herself, of her body, so that Frances can go on living. Despite the nurse's affirmation, Frances blossoms into pregnancy and is able to unite herself with the woman she has desired since childhood.[100]

The violence of the act and the sensual calmness pregnancy brings to Frances convey how the most outlandish stories contain some truth. The story also displays Lily's complete acceptance and Mercedes's rejection of Frances's version (425). It is an embodied act which overcomes the Piper's racist relations with the Taylors and which connects them perversely together. This queer narrative of pregnancy situates the moment of conception not only in the encounter between Frances and Leo but also, more importantly, in that of Teresa and Frances. The latter brings the brother and sister together in her body (just as she is trying to bring together Lily and Ambrose and fact and truth), while giving the material object designed to kill the power to bring life. Violence, for Frances, is lived as the passionate expression of an attachment to histories that extend beyond the individual. Violence is figured as a means of remembering without being given access to memories. It decolonizes histories, and performatively opens the present to transformation. For Frances, the impossible is possible insofar as out of violence can grow memories embodied in another being who may begin to remember yet more. The sensuality of remembering, where Frances's pregnancy and cooking convey that it is 'as though Mumma were here' (430), allows James to speak to Frances. He accepts her 'coloured child' because he 'has simply forgotten how such a thing was ever able to call murder into his heart; the birth of an innocent child' (428). Insemination, as a violently queer act, is figured as taking 'hate away' (410).[101] Frances brings her queer sensuality home by cooking memories in the food her mother used to make. She opens her body out to others by decolonizing the home through her role as witness. Her storytelling continues as she shares what she knows of Materia through a sensorial register of food, music and dance, and as she silently absorbs James's narrative

99 Frances has been sneaking into the Mahmoud household, unbeknown to her grandfather, and stealing both valuable and sentimental objects for Lily. One of the most significant objects she steals is Materia's braid that was cut off as a form of punishment for marrying James. Wrongly, her grandfather accuses Teresa and reasons that one cannot trust a black worker, even though he was thinking about asking her to marry him.

100 Seeing Teresa in the distance about to shoot her, Frances is described as experiencing the following: 'The arrow is love, its pain spreads outward and the pain is faith, the source that launched the arrow was sorrow. "Teresa," thinks Frances [. . .]' (399). Frances has been in love with Teresa since the latter gave Frances a sweet at her mother's funeral. There is some suggestion that Frances confuses Teresa with her mother, particularly when Materia has been locked in the coal cellar by James and comes to see Frances covered in black soot.

101 Frances takes responsibility for the shooting after Teresa sings to her, saying to the police, in an English accent, that she shot herself 'for finding myself with child and without a husband' (411). Through this act 'Frances took Teresa's hate away' (411) and, thus, Teresa is able to restart an active sex life with her disabled husband.

of his rape of Kathleen and the birth of the twins. As Benjamin suggests, 'Thus traces of the storyteller cling to the story the way the handprints of the potter cling to the clay vessel'.[102] Frances bears witness to what has never been said, and lets the house and her ever-changing body remember what cannot be spoken. Sex work and music, as much as storytelling and dancing, are an ethical reaching out to others to share unarticulated and unspeakable histories through the body.

Intergenerational fossils

As an intergenerational fossil, the hope chest is the sensorial object through and around which Frances and Lily tell their stories. Every time they lift its lid the 'waft of cedar' (204) alters their physical and emotional state. Over the years they unwrap, replace and add to its often indecipherable contents. After reading Kathleen's diary, Frances places it (and Kathleen's green silk dress) in the hope chest. Along with these tangible memories, James gives to Frances his version of the Piper/Mahmoud histories. Yet the reader never hears his words. This absence of verbalization is not a lack of voice as such but is symbolic of James ceding his narrative authority. Having dictated the realms of the livable, his word-filled silence conveys how he no longer holds power over history. Furthermore, his silent testimony reflects Butler's own assertion that giving an account of oneself or addressing an other 'is not a feature of narrative, one of its many and variable attributes, but an interruption of narrative'.[103] This absence invites the reader to work with what cannot be communicated. Historiography, to use Ahmed's words, 'involves working with, "that which fails to get across", or that which is necessarily secret'.[104] It also emphasizes the reader's dependency on the witnesses' interpretations. Many years later Frances tells Mercedes, 'Daddy died in peace because he made his confession. [. . .] He confessed to me. And I forgave him' (557). Similar to Lily, who 'has already forgiven James for what she does not know' (449), Frances takes on the responsibility for Kathleen's story by keeping it alive and, in so doing, tries to lighten James's heavy burden. Although Mercedes insists Frances is 'not invested with the power to dispense the Sacrament of Penance –' (557), Frances, for the second time in her life, queerly performs a priestly role.[105] As a perversion of the religious order to which Mercedes so vehemently clings, Frances simply listens to what can only be articulated 'on the veranda' (433) and 'on the threshold' (434) of the house. James's words can only be heard just outside the earshot of the morally religious family (embodied by Mercedes who on catching a few of their words runs to her room and 'feels for her opal rosary' (434)). Frances bears witness to James's violent life by being present *and* by taking

[102] Walter Benjamin, 'The Storyteller: Reflections on the Works of Nikolai Leskov', in *Illuminations*, trans. by Harry Zorn, intro. by Hannah Arendt (London: Pimlico, [1955] 1999), pp. 83–107 (p. 92).

[103] Butler, *Giving an Account of Oneself*, p. 63.

[104] Ahmed, *Strange Encounters*, p. 155.

[105] Frances's role as priest, here, repeats her earlier act of baptizing the twins in order to save them from a violent, Catholic destiny.

responsibility for both the continued transmission of the narrative and for that which exceeds knowledge. Here, responsibility is not forged through a religious morality of right and wrong, although Frances does perform the sacrament of confession. Rather responsibility is a gift of another version of the family history that enables Frances to keep alive the fictionalized truthful tales of her childhood by passing them on to Lily (who then transmits them to Aloysius/Anthony and the reader).

As the 'cedar smell wafts up cloaking a second smell' (446), the reader's attention is drawn to a change in the sensorial experience of the hope chest. With the exception of Mercedes, who sees Frances's pregnancy as a shame on the family, Lily, James and local neighbours are happily anticipating the birth of Frances's baby. However, the occasion brings great sadness as Mercedes declares Frances's son died, like Other Lily, of sudden infant death syndrome. The simultaneity of her son's death with the discovery of Trixie, Frances's faithful three-legged limping cat, whose dead body is releasing a putrid odour in the hope chest, is an omen of the rancid events that Mercedes has contrived.[106] As Lily loyally and respectfully buries Trixie, she discovers her brother's remains. Lily finds the material evidence of Ambrose's existence and death, and thus the verifiable and tangible object that proves the truth in Frances's fictions. Unlike Lily who has listened endlessly to Frances's stories, Mercedes cannot bear to see or hear the truth of what the smells (and the skeleton) might mean. Where Mercedes has sought to make a saint out of Lily by constructing a disability narrative which mimics that of Saint Bernadette, she now decides that such an unearthing must be a sign that Lily is possessed by the Devil and that He must be exorcised from her.

Ever attentive to the sensorial and embodied changes around her, Frances recognizes the intensity and potential violence of Mercedes's reactions to Lily's unearthing. She therefore decides it is time for Lily to leave the family home with the money Frances has put aside for her:

> How can a person look into her own face and consent to be banished from it? For Lily, Frances is as first and familiar as the sky, as the palm of her own hand. The freckle on the nose, the green jewels in the eyes, the smart mouth, what does it mean to be banished from the face that first looked you into existence?
>
> 'I don't want to leave you.'
>
> Lily's forehead buckles but Frances insists, 'You have to go, little gingerbread boy, "run away and whatever you do, don't look back."'
>
> 'This isn't a story, Frances.' Anger ignites Lily's grief.
>
> 'Yes it is Lily. *Hayola kellu bas Helm.*'
>
> 'It is not!'
>
> '*Taa'i la hown, Habibti* – '
>
> 'No!'

106 'The cedar smell wafts up cloaking a second smell – in all likelihood another mouse entombed and decomposing. [. . .] A truly terrible smell now, the body having been disturbed. Lily takes the shallowest of breaths to avoid her gag reflex as she carries Trixie down the attic steps' (446).

'*Te'berini.*'

'Stop it!'

[. . .] 'Come here, Lily.'

[. . .] Frances opens her nightgown and guides Lily's mouth to drink. (450–1)

Frances does not try logical reasoning because Mercedes's belief that Lily is possessed by the Devil is as fantastical as the playfully truthful stories they share with each other. Frances therefore turns to their affective intimate language to portray the need for trust in her bodily understandings of events. The evocation of their musical, fairy-tale language draws Lily into her world through the concrete sounds of (often unlived) memories. It portrays how the truth is this outlandish fairy tale and not the reality Lily wants or perceives to be the case. Lily sees herself when she looks into Frances's face and there is a 'mutually constitutive exchange'.[107] Yet Lily misrecognizes the process of subjectivity as solely a physically intimate process and so Frances shares an intimate gift of recognition. She gives to Lily the milk destined for her own 'dead' child, and in a maternal gesture of nurturing life not so much takes the place of the mother as embodies their unique intimacy. Frances gives life to Lily in the same way that Lily gave life to her with her blood; she nourishes Lily with fluids of recognition of their mutual response-ability. The perversion of the mother/daughter relationship gestures to their queer familial relationship and to their embodied, fluid-sharing intimacy. This exchange is performative in its mimicking of a traditional practice and yet it seeks not only to give nourishment but to change history. Frances does not want Lily to be subjected to Mercedes's normalizing and curative religious acts and thus she ensures Lily leaves the familial space. Traces of embodied and unarticulated histories are passed on through this bodily gesture, and Lily knows that she must hear what is not said. The milk that oozes from Frances's body is a crossing of the skin boundary, of the surface that divides self from other, and, therefore, self flows into other without becoming other. There is a loss of individuality without a loss of self and, thus, a somatic registering of Frances's presence in Lily's body.[108]

Over the years Lily and Frances have repeated the same words and gestures when opening the hope chest and have sat together 'breathing in the soft cedar cloud' (439). Frances tells Lily to remove her mother's green silk dress and diary from the hope chest. The removal of fossilized memories from the repository of lost hope – which is Materia's olfactory connection to Lebanon and her family – is symbolic of the reverberations being felt. Lily is delving into multiple interconnected histories that have been hidden in the chest. Wearing the dress Kathleen wore to dance with Rose at the nightclub Mecca and the boots her father made for her, Lily heads on foot to New York to find her mother's lover. This section of the novel – 'Hejira' – traces not so much Lily's difficulty in getting to Rose as Kathleen's development as a singer

107 Marks, *The Skin of the Film*, p. 183.

108 Although she does not specifically address this issue, this reading of breast milk is situated in Imogen Tyler's work on pregnant bodies. See Imogen Tyler, 'Skin-tight: Celebrity, Pregnancy and Subjectivity', in *Thinking Through the Skin*, ed. by Sara Ahmed and Jackie Stacey (London and New York: Routledge, 2001), pp. 69–83.

in New York and her growing, eventual sexual, intimacy with her piano accompanist Rose.[109] Just as Rose's music is 'different every time' (482), the narrative loops back on itself like the '"riff" in jazz' that LaCapra describes.[110] This is repetition: it is as if the music demands to be replayed differently and thus the narrative requires constant repetition and revision. The act of Lily putting on her mother's dress ensures Rose will recognize Lily, and portrays Lily's desire to get close to her mother's past. Reminiscent of Otoh's donning of his father's clothes in *Cereus*, Lily is on a journey that will awaken, and cause others to relive, old memories. Lily is bringing out into public Kathleen's most private of artefacts and learning, through a disjointed but linear narrative, about her mother's time in New York. However, in order to hear this history she must also feel and smell her mother's history, through the dress, and let the sensory experience envelop her. There is no translation of Kathleen's words, as the reader, along with Lily, reads the narrative of Kathleen's diary. We are encouraged to understand a story and to witness our inadequacies insofar as we are unable to sense the indexical traces of the material objects (both the dress and the diary). The material, concrete nature of remembering shows that 'representation and knowledge are not to be explained exclusively on the level of language, but also participate in contact with the object represented'.[111] This personal – and public – text has historical valency and gives veracity to Frances's outlandish stories. Material objects are not only vessels for memories but are also physical connections between those who touch and who are touched by them.

The diary is Kathleen's act of writing herself into existence in ways that differ from her father's racist dreams and narratives. On the one hand, Kathleen is shaping her life and is a subject in control of her narrative. On the other hand, she describes feeling her parameters of reality come undone as she both falls in love with a black woman and begins to remember her mother through her multisensory experiences of New York. The music, the smells and the diversity of people remind her of a mother and a heritage that she does not quite know. When Rose sees 'the framed photograph of Daddy and Mumma on [Kathleen's] dresser' (503), a conversation about Materia's origins ensues, where Kathleen defends her whiteness:

> 'You look pure white.'
>
> 'I am pure white. My mother is white.'
>
> 'Not quite.'
>
> 'Well she's not coloured.' [. . .]

109 Howells defines 'Hejira' as 'the Arabic word for "escape" or "flight"' (Howells, *Contemporary Canadian Women's Fiction*, p. 120). Salah evokes its similarity to the idea of the fugue: 'In essence, fugue is flight. Fugue is dislocation and transport of body, spirit, psyche. It is a violent wrenching, an exile from self or home, hejira' (Salah, p. 234). Dina Georgis adds, 'The diary, entitled *Hejira* – which is Arabic for migration and is evocative of the Hindi word *Hijira* for transgendered/intersexed identity – chronicles Kathleen's coming of age in New York City as a young diva in training' (Dina Georgis, '*Falling* for Jazz: Desire, Dissonance and Racial Collaboration', *Canadian Review of American Studies* 35.2 (2005), 215–29 (p. 216)). In addition to these definitions, Hejira marks the beginning of the Muslim calendar but is also the title of a 1976 album by Canadian singer-songwriter Joni Mitchell, which chronicles her own trip across the US.

110 LaCapra, p. 46.

111 Marks, *The Skin of the Film*, p. 92.

'I'm sorry but you're not being honest with me. You are ashamed of your mother.' I got a sick feeling in my stomach. 'And I think that's a sorrowful thing,' she added.

The feeling was coming up through my skin. I was sure Rose could smell it. (504)

The photograph of Kathleen's parents, as the material trace of those pictured, brings into the open the possibility that Kathleen may not be 'pure white'. Rose's curt response, 'Not quite' captures the fear Bhabha describes as central to the colonizer's project of splitting the sense of self of the colonized: '*almost the same but not white*' and '*almost the same, but not quite*'.[112] However, Kathleen soon learns that Rose also harbours a similar shame of her mother who fails to fit into the black community of which Rose is a part: her mother, Jeanne, is white. The representations of skin as a failed referent lead many critics to read this relationship as revealing the ways in which all identity is performed. Stevenson argues that it is apparent that 'theirs is a *socially constructed* difference, rather than a biologically significant one'.[113] In Stevenson's formulation, the skin, including the skin of the photograph, shows that identitarian taxonomies are not related to the body but are determined by social norms and institutions. This fact, in turn, is said to lead to a re-evaluation of racial inequality. This argument is non-performative in that it claims to bring about what it names; it claims to undo sociopolitical hierarchies by revealing how the body is constructed. However, I would suggest that the novel repeatedly returns to the body through the sense of smell and shame to articulate the role of the skin in understanding one's sense of self as coming into being in relation to embodied others. The skin in the above passage demonstrates how the body is constrained through the flesh. In Elspeth Probyn's words: 'The feeling body has the consequence of summoning the past, which then closes down possibilities. A spectral past ensnares the future.'[114] Shame is the heightened embodied sense of one's skin failing to manifest only national and familial ideals.

Kathleen's sensation of shame of her mother's presence in and on her is felt as seeping from the inside out through the permeable epidermal surface. Just as when her mother touched her as a child,[115] Kathleen now fears that there is an odoriferous trace of her maternal heritage that could permeate forth. I agree with Stevenson that the nausea is 'symbolic of the resurgent knowledge of her past'.[116] It is also, more specifically, a bodily acknowledgement of an unknown past. The body is leaking histories that Kathleen has refused to feel in her desire to be the idolized daughter of her father. She cannot be said to remember in the sense of coherently recalling what her father has purposefully erased but she feels in her body the rising of something perturbingly uncanny. By arguing that

112 Bhabha, p. 128 and p. 122.

113 Stevenson, p. 50.

114 Elspeth Probyn, *Blush: Faces of Shame* (Minneapolis, MN: University of Minnesota Press, 2005), p. 55.

115 MacDonald describes the effects of Materia trying, but failing, to love Kathleen:

> Materia stroked the fire-gold hair and passed a warm brown hand across the staring green eyes. Kathleen tried not to breathe. Tried not to understand the [Arabic] song. She tried to think of Daddy and light things – fresh air, and green grass – she worried that Daddy would know. And be hurt. There was a smell. (39)

116 Stevenson, p. 50.

the body is only socially constructed what is lost is the skin's capacity to constrain how the self engages with others. Afraid that she may be read 'wrongly' (i.e. like her mother) back home, Kathleen makes a performance of her whiteness (71). Importantly, this performance is not simply an indication that identities are performative (something that we put on, usually in public), but shows the strength of performative identities in consolidating racialized hierarchies. To suggest performativity reveals solely how race is socially constructed ignores how the performativity of race reinforces social norms and how race is experienced through the body. Speaking on the subject of passing, Prosser states, 'What erupts in the trace is the encrypted transgression: family shame'.[117] Smell functions as a physical manifestation of the shame of her maternal heritage and portrays how Kathleen is learning anew to negotiate what she has ignored about her self and her mixed-race and imperialist histories.

The body is both a sociopolitical entity and matter that is shaped, but not determined, by norms. If, as Ahmed suggests, shame is about how the self relates to iself, then I agree that the '"apartness" of the subject is intensified in the return of the gaze; apartness is felt in the moment of exposure to others, an exposure that is wounding'.[118] This sense of optical distance, where embodied shame is *seen* by the other, is the gap where change does not or cannot always occur. Only a response that responds to this distance can bring about change. This distance cannot simply be surmounted, but it can be reconfigured and resensed. Indeed, Kathleen is now feeling a different sense of self emerge as she experiences New York and new sensorial sensations (food, sex, love, friendship, densely populated public transport). The skin becomes the very medium through which Kathleen communicates with Rose about these unarticulated histories.

Where the epidermal layers porously leak out untranslatable and unknown memories, the proximal fabrics that touch the body are fossilized histories that are slowly breaking through the existing parameters of reality (even while not necessarily yielding further information). Kathleen encourages Rose to go out in her dead father's suit, which she only ever wears at home alone. Frost asserts that 'one of them must adopt the role of the man if their relationship is to develop in the way they both subconsciously want it to' and that it 'does not matter too much to Kathleen which one of them plays which role'.[119] Similarly, Howells states that 'Rose is most truly herself when she is in disguise'.[120] Frost insists that this 'adoption of heterosexual roles' is an historical contextualization of lesbian desire in 1918 and that the significance of Rose's act is to '[underline] the arbitrariness, and contingency, of that assigned gender and

117 Jay Prosser, 'Skin Memories', in *Thinking Through the Skin*, ed. by Sara Ahmed and Jackie Stacey (London and New York: Routledge, 2001), pp. 52–68 (p. 59).

118 Ahmed, *The Cultural Politics of Emotion*, p. 105.

119 Frost, p. 206. Frost's reading is based on the fact that Kathleen tries to put on Rose's suit when Rose refuses to wear it, but I would argue that this is Kathleen provoking Rose in order to encourage her to don it.

120 Howells, *Contemporary Canadian Women's Fiction*, p. 121. Her suggestion that Rose is in disguise when dressed as a man is all the more surprising given that Kathleen states, 'It's clear which Rose is in disguise' (527).

that heterosexual framework'.[121] For these critics, whose work is exemplary of how performativity is used to read this novel, the relationship between these two women shows how the gender matrix, and its concomitant allies of sexuality and race, is arbitrary, as if the body plays no role in sex, race, gender, ability, sexuality, ethnicity, belonging and desires. The body becomes the means of showing the contingent power of any overarching system. It is my contention that it could only be Rose who could don her father's suit as she tries to touch his unknown history. This desire to come close to unspoken histories through clothes portrays that Rose is reaching out to a different present where she can have sex with a white woman. Furthermore, the heteronormativization of the relationship ignores the very ways in which their desires are queer in that they seek out paths that diverge from the unspeakability of non-normative genders and sexualities and mixed-race heritages and relationships.

When Otoh, in *Cereus*, puts on his father's suit, it is not to become a man; he has already been living as a man all his life. He takes his father's suit and hat so as to step into Mala's life. Two times come crashing together and result in the destruction of Mala's safe space but also in the possibility of Mala communicating with Tyler; the latter meeting Otoh; and Mala and Ambrose being reunited. For Rose and Kathleen, the act of putting on the clothes of someone from the previous generation also has the imperturbable effect of changing the present in unforeseeable ways. Kathleen describes the effects of Rose donning her father's suit:

> Dark and sweet, the elixir of love is in her mouth. The more I drink, the more I remember all the things we've never done. I was a ghost until I touched you. Never swallowed mortal food until I tasted you, never understood the spoken word until I found your tongue. I've been a sleep-walker, sad somnambula, hands outstretched to strike the solid thing that could awaken me to life at last. I have only ever stood here under this lamp, against your body, I've missed you all my life. (525)

As we saw in *Cereus*, the donning of the previous generation's clothes wakes up sleepwalkers (Ambrose and Kathleen) to the present. Putting on the fedora and suit brings to life a past that has been buried, forgotten or just put to one side. Both Otoh and Rose transition to live as men. While representations of gender transitions point to how gender identity is not determined by biological taxonomies, I would argue that it is not simply the transgressive nature of transitioning (its purported ability to undermine the normative nature of the gender dyad that a heterosexual matrix demands) that enables change. Rather, the desire to step into an other's clothes is an embodiment of other possibilities. Rose is taking an embodied risk that is not simply future-orientated (i.e. seeking out a new life for the self) but is also the possibility of living different pasts that are integral to the present (as much as to the future). Embodying the past through a gender transition further suggests a desire to take on the other's life, not to become other but to become other to one's self. It also simply shows the pleasure of living out one's desires.

121 Frost, pp. 206–7.

For Kathleen, Rose's transition awakens her senses and brings life where there has only been somnambulistic living. This is a performative intervention into history because Rose and Kathleen seek not only the pleasure of transgression (in many respects transgression could be dangerous for Kathleen and Rose). Rather, they seek to touch histories that cannot be known. They are unlearning the past and the present – largely through music, food and sex – and creating a different future (different from and yet attached to the violent one of their parents). This is queer postcolonial time where the past is crashing into the present in unthinkable ways and where bodies are sensing each other and thus starting to feel the unsayable and the unspoken.

The centrality of clothes to their relationship is confirmed when Kathleen literally binds them together by taking the sash from her own dress and winding it round Rose's father's fedora: 'I've given her the sash from my new green dress. I wound it round her charcoal hat to remind her' (528). The materiality of the sash, as if emotion or the body cannot suffice, contains the trace of Kathleen that connects her to Rose, while the hat connects Rose to the father she did not know. Clothes are not inert, inanimate objects but living materials full of the persons and histories they touched and touch. Unknown histories tingle on the skin, burst forth through fluids and are intensely sensed in queer intimacies. Interlaced with each other's bodies, they are less fearful of their bodies and how they might ooze out uncanny smells, feelings and histories: '"Look," I say. And I can feel the caress of her eyes. "Touch me." And it's the closest thing to having no skin. "Kiss me"' (531). The multisensory licking, touching, looking and smelling of the other's body is the beginning of the 'earthquake' to which Marks refers.[122] They begin to feel, smell and touch the past of which they know so little, and through this openness they try to forge a different present.

It is in this same green dress that Lily makes the journey from Cape Breton to New York, embodying the memories of the encounters between Rose and Kathleen while reading the diary in which Kathleen memorialized these events. The dress and the diary, like Rose's suit, are opaque, condensed sites of memories. Thus, when Rose sees Lily, she sees a memory of a lost time. While we, as readers, have just emerged from the diary time where Rose and Kathleen were together, Rose shifts out of the present time back to the events we just read:

> Rose takes a half-step towards her. Lily approaches. Rose puts forth her hands, slowly fingering the air as though searching for something in a dark wardrobe. Lily enters the embrace. When Rose shakes and shudders, Lily does not let her stumble.

[122] The importance of smell to their relationship is further emphasized when Rose tells Kathleen she can finally smell her:

> She said in a voice I'd never heard before, 'I didn't think you had a scent, but you do.' Which made me laugh because what a thing to say! But she explained, 'No. Everyone has a scent and you either like it or you don't or you're indifferent. And you had no scent. And I thought that was spooky.'
> 'You're easily spooked.'
> I love talking with our arms around each other.
> 'It made you seem not quite human,' she said. (525)

For Rose, the scent of the person is what makes them human rather than, as it is for Kathleen, something about which one should feel shame.

> While Rose grieves, Lily takes more and more weight [. . .]. 'Oh no, no, no,' because for Rose it has just happened. [. . .]
>
> 'I love you,' says Rose.
>
> 'I know.'
>
> 'Never leave you.'
>
> 'It's okay.'
>
> 'Kathleen.' (541–2)[123]

Just as Mala mistakes Otoh in his father's clothes for Ambrose, Rose mistakes Lily for Kathleen in the green dress. Lily embodies not only the memories lived by Rose and Kathleen, which are evoked through the dress and the 'searching for something in a dark wardrobe' (541), but also the memories of what she and Rose are yet to learn about the events that unfolded around Kathleen's death, including Lily's own birth. The past hurtles into the present as a gift from Frances and thus Rose is able to grieve the loss of Kathleen for the first time as if she has just lost her. Like Mala, Rose relives the past; its repetition, its re-appearance before her eyes, its physical presence in Lily is too much. Where Tyler intervenes as a multisensory listener and narrator, Lily takes the literal weight of Rose and through this intimate touch, which contains the memories of a previous contact with the woman who wore the dress, Rose can remember the violence of a past she has refused to acknowledge. Through the sartorial gesture of taking the 'charcoal fedora with an emerald band' (543) from where it is hanging and handing it to Rose, Lily seals the connection between her, Kathleen, Rose, Materia and Frances (who made their encounter possible).[124] With a gift of storytelling, Lily changes their bodies and histories. Rose remembers through her music, which 'defies discursive representation, [and] functions as an effective location for the unrepresentable character of traumatic history'.[125] Her music is a multisensory form of communication, which keeps alive the incessant retelling of histories that cannot be known and that cannot always be found in words.

Throughout the novel we witness multiple struggles to remember unspoken histories, and Mercedes undertakes her own form of remembering by making a traditional family tree for James, who never speaks of his family (207). This 'sober' and 'dispassionate' non-tree-like drawing renders invisible the queerness and mixed-race heritage of the Piper/Mahmoud histories (213). In Mercedes's eyes, Lily destroys this painstaking work when she redesigns it with a 'riot of golds and greens and ruby-

123 This passage recalls an earlier conversation between Rose and Kathleen where she promised never to leave her:

> 'I'm never going to leave you, Kathleen.'
> 'Don't ever leave me.'
> 'I never will.' (535)

124 When Materia plays the piano in public she wears a fedora. This hat ends up on the scarecrow, which becomes the site where Ambrose is buried. Sartorial objects are, as Marks describes, fossils containing sedimented layers of transnational histories, connected intimately. While Rose does not wear the same fedora, both women wear a fedora when playing their music.

125 Georgis, p. 215.

reds' (213) and names the absent family members. Although she names Other Lily and presents Trixie (the cat) as part of the family, Lily draws Ambrose in the earth as treasure inside a chest. Here, Ambrose can only be recognized through a pictorial representation that bears witness to his preciousness as he lies underground. Furthermore, because Mercedes is so upset, Frances and Lily inter the redesigned family tree (exactly where the unnamed Ambrose was buried many years earlier). When Lily later buries Trixie in this site, she uncovers not the family tree, which has now decayed, but the treasure that could not be audibly or visibly named in Mercedes's depiction of their family histories: Ambrose's skeleton. Histories are seeping out of the earth and leaking into the present. The material presence of histories is touching and perturbing familial life. Yet Mercedes will not listen to these unearthings, and thus Frances, just before she dies, has to use 'her last sprint of energy to pry the hands away [from Mercedes's ears], and to speak the words' (557). Mercedes's literal refusal to listen, by covering her ears, testifies to her function in this familial household as the one who silences others and preserves ideal narratives. However, when Aloysius/Anthony turns up on Lily and Rose's doorstep after Mercedes's death, he gives to the family an immeasurable gift of an image of familial life.

Aloysius/Anthony comes bearing the gift of a decolonized and queer family tree where we learn the extent of Mercedes's violence: she took Frances's baby from her, telling her he was dead, to avoid the shame of having a 'coloured' (428) baby in the house. Just as the green of Kathleen's dress is a remnant of the 'green jewels in [Frances's] eyes' (450) and a mirror of Lily's and Kathleen's green eyes, the 'green light in [Aloysius/Anthony's] hazel eyes' serves to trace him back to his mother and connect him to the rest of the Piper sisters and their unarticulated histories. As Lily begins to read the family tree, which joins her to her brother and shows Kathleen as her mother and James as her father, while connecting Kathleen to Rose and Aloysius/Anthony to Frances, Aloysius/Anthony begins to feel 'seasick' (565). Mercedes's gift to Lily is both a visual recognition of the violence of familial life and the restoration of the brother Frances so wanted to give to Lily to his place as her brother, nephew and cousin.[126] The markings that etch out these non-normative connections are traced in 'green ink' (565). The colour on the page is a remnant of the dress, the eyes and even the skin of Kathleen (534), Lily (181) and Ambrose (273); it brings life and disorder to a form that is normally teleological, constrained and verifiable; and it is a recognition that the living earth, in the form of the tree and the paper, remembers. The colour of the eye, rather than the eye itself, is the visual trace of unknown and yet to be articulated familial stories. When Otoh witnesses the children's violence towards Mala, the memory is not simply witnessed through the eyes that see but '[fixes] itself on his retina'.[127] The eye is a multisensory organ; it is literally touched by the violence and bears the marks of these unacknowledged histories. Aloysius/Anthony's embodied presence is testimony

[126] Because Lily is the daughter of James and Kathleen, she is both Frances's sister and her niece. He is therefore her nephew and cousin (i.e. the son of her aunt and sister, Frances). However, Frances also wanted to give Lily the brother she missed, and so he is an embodiment of these histories as a gift from Frances to Lily.

[127] Mootoo, *Cereus Blooms at Night*, p. 127.

to Mercedes's violence and to the truth contained within the colourful gift. Mercedes materially traces a family network that she could not bear to acknowledge while alive.

However, Aloysius/Anthony's sense of nausea portrays how histories are being disturbed within and around him. That he works as an ethnomusicologist serves to connect him to his family musical history of opera (Kathleen), ragtime (Materia), incessant improvisation (Frances) and jazz (Rose). Supposedly dead, he is out of time, just out of synchronicity and yet haunting the present as fully alive. Being in time and out of time, dead and alive, bearing gifts that reveal violence and that also unite him with his family, Frances's son is about to learn what we, as readers, already know. Or, perhaps this story will be different and perhaps he has his own story to tell. We are about to listen with and to Aloysius/Anthony, and thus the novel calls on the reader to start again by listening anew over and over again. Responsibility is this indefinite call to listen without end and to repeatedly respond. This is a response that necessities a listening that can hear more than words or narrative; this response must be in and of the body, and we must be prepared for the body to be perturbed. As listeners, we must be attentive not only to the unspoken, but also to what may be communicated through and on the body. These are histories that must be sensed and resensed, and thus the listeners might have to touch, smell and taste the unspoken, as well as see and hear the unspeakable. To slightly alter Baldwin's moving description of music: Multisensory epistemologies are 'our witness, and our ally.' Through these sensory engagements 'history becomes a garment we can wear and share'.[128] This sensory experience may not yield transparent knowledge, but it is an attempt to listen to the multisensory epistemologies that emerge when words cannot be spoken. Historiography is an embodied engagement that involves an endless creative narrativization of memories, which may require the fictionalization of truth as we bear witness to the unspeakable. It is an embodied commitment to infinitely listen, narrate and share histories through the materiality of familial life in all its queer postcolonial forms.

[128] James Baldwin, 'Of the Sorrow Songs: The Cross of Redemption', as cited in Paul Gilroy, *The Black Atlantic: Modernity and Double-Conciousness* (London: Verso Books, 1993), p. 203.

Conclusion: Embodying Other Stories

I tell a story about the relations I choose, only to expose, somewhere along the way, the way I am gripped and undone by these very relations. My narrative falters, as it must.[1]

Performative silence is [. . .] not simply political speech that might as well be spoken. It is also really silence, by which I mean noise: that circulating transpersonal, permeating, viscerally connective affective atmosphere that feels as though it has escaped 'the filter' to indicate, for good or for ill, a sensorium for a potential social world now lived as collective affect, or a revitalized political one.[2]

Silent bodies, or speaking with the body

Queer Postcolonial Narratives is an analysis of how we read literary texts, and it is a critical exploration of how we read bodies and objects. The book is concerned with the institutional apparatus of colonial rule, particularly the production and consolidation of racial, able-bodied, sexual and gender hierarchies and prejudices in and through the family home. I wanted to analyse everyday survival after unacknowledged trauma, and thus moments when words cannot be spoken, when violence and love are interrelated, and when memories are absent or unclear. Bodies that were abused and violated are central to this book, and yet how this flesh can be the medium through which unspoken or unspeakable memories are resensed and sometimes communicated is its focus. On the one hand, I wanted to ask: what can we hear when words cannot be spoken or when words do not quite convey what needs to be communicated? On the other hand, I wanted to suggest that communication is not just about words or body language. *Queer Postcolonial Narratives* argues that speaking with, through and on the body is possible, and that such embodied communication is a critical turn towards listeners and their responses. As Berlant suggests the flesh can speak and is thus the potential for a 'revitalized political' engagement.

1 Butler, *Precarious Life*, p. 23.
2 Lauren Berlant, *Cruel Optimism* (Durham, NC and London: Duke University Press, 2011), p. 230.

In much of her work, Butler critiques the exclusionary and violent structure of bodily taxonomies and categories of belonging, and argues that how we *read* bodies or how the failure of a body to be *readable* (according to bodily norms) has serious (i.e. real life) consequences.[3] Butler and Bhabha are both concerned with speech act theory, and how words act upon, shape, control and give life to the body and to the psychic sense of self. For Bhabha, literary texts open up a space where the cracks in time and in the master narrative change our understandings of history. In a much more philosophically grounded analysis, Butler plays and twists speech act theory – in a way that Felman insists was Austin's intention – to unravel how and why a gender dyadic structure and heteronormative familialism are appealing, dominant and often the only viable existence.[4] Both are attentive to the reiterative form of institutional norms through which bodies are contained, constrained and violated. Both are also hopeful of the potential for not only undermining narratives and institutional constraints, but also for imagining and creating the inconceivable and even the so-called impossible. *Queer Postcolonial Narratives* examined their intersecting theories to draw out the centrality of fleshy witnessing to the performative structure of power. It argued that this figure of the witness – who is often absent in current formulations of theories of performativity – is critical to the possibility of forging less violent modes of embodied being with others.

In 1959 Fanon's short collection of revolutionary essays was published under the title *L'An V de la révolution algérienne* [Year V of the Algerian Revolution].[5] Here, he describes the changing gender and familial relationships that emerge as the war for Algerian independence – from French colonial rule – intensifies. On the one hand, Fanon details the shift to European dress, which allows women to carry artillery unnoticed by colonial police who *see* only women adhering to colonial values.[6] On the other hand, he insists that the move *back* to the haïk enables the 'femme-arsenal'[7] [woman weapon] to strap explosions to her flesh, because the colonial forces *see* only poor, backward (i.e. apolitical) women.[8] Redolent of Mbembe's description of embodiment, suicide and the fight for independence, these women carry close to and on their bodies the resources (including weaponry) intended to secure independence from French colonial rule. Algeria's history of decolonization is narrated through the bodies of women; she literally 's'enfonce un peu plus dans la chair de la Révolution'[9]

3 For a more recent and in-depth critique of norms, see *Undoing Gender*.

4 See Felman, *The Scandal of the Speaking Body*.

5 The specificity of the French title, with its allusion to the adoption of the new calendar following the French Revolution (and thus the equating of the Algerian war of independence with the creation of the French Republic), is largely lost in the English translations. See Donna McCormack, 'Gender and Colonial Transitioning: Frantz Fanon's Algerian Freedom Fighters in Moroccan and Caribbean Novels?', *Journal of Transatlantic Studies* 7.3 (2009), 279–93.

6 Fanon describes how the colonial police forces learn, by torturing Algerian women in prison, that Europeanized women are carrying the weapons across the borders between the Algerian and the European parts of Algiers (Fanon, *L'An V*, pp. 41–4).

7 Ibid., p. 41.

8 Fanon describes how the women change their appearance and conform to the stereotypical image of 'une pauvre femme ou une insignifiante jeune fille' [a poor woman or an insignificant young girl] who wears the *haïk* (ibid., p. 45).

9 Ibid., p. 37.

[throws herself further into the flesh of the Revolution]. The flesh of women and the material that covers or reveals the body are signifiers of anti-colonial resistance, pro-French modernization and an expression of allegiance to a traditional image of Algerianness. The body cannot easily be read or interpreted, but Fanon makes it apparent that flesh and clothes are central to colonial resistance and post-independence identity formation.

Resistance to occupying and colonial forces often takes – and we may even say necessitates – bodily form. I have suggested that embodied resistance becomes particularly urgent or necessary when there is no possibility of recognition for the words articulated by the occupied, colonized or marginalized. By beginning this book with the figure of the suicide bomber, I wanted to draw immediate attention to how bodies communicate when words are unavailable, absent or unnecessary. It is my contention that violence to the self – possible destruction of the self – is sometimes a search for a different type of listener, for a witness who can listen when all institutions have failed to do so.[10] Embodied epistemologies are refusals to engage the occupiers on their terms and thus performative speech acts that try to instigate change. Hearing the unsaid – listening to others who may harm their selves (and possibly hurt others) – is the difficulty of bearing witness to national and familial trauma.

The suicide bomber embodies the visceral effects of colonization and the bloody fight for decolonization. Yet, s/he is not alone in turning to the body to fight a political cause. Gilroy analyses how resistance had to take multiple non-linguistic forms for the enslaved on plantations: 'There may, after all, be no reciprocity on the plantation outside of the possibilities of rebellion and suicide, flight and silent mourning, and there is certainly no grammatical unity of speech to mediate communicative reason'.[11] Gandhi protested peacefully against British colonial rule through hunger strikes, and more generally much of his political philosophy was intimately tied to the body (especially to the alimentary canal).[12] Berlant, in her recent book *Cruel Optimism*, states that in 1917 'ten thousand African Americans marched against lynching in silent protest in New York, an act of discipline so astonishing that the spectating crowds, too,

10 It should be clear that I am not suggesting either that the novels condone self-harm or that violence to the self is formulated as what some may call a 'cry for help'. I do not read the physical markings that the characters make as a cry for help, especially as in most cases there is no one there to witness these markings. Thus, I read this search for a witness as the search for an other who can hear when words cannot be spoken. This person or these people do not respond by making a normative intervention that would seek to make the person better or stop the person from harming him/herself. This listener is someone who must learn anew how to listen, and not assume knowledge of the act itself. Thus this is not about a cry for help, but a call for a reconfiguring of the ways in which communication takes place. This listener must listen over and over again to what may be incomprehensible, and work with their own undoing to respond to and be with this other person.

11 Gilroy, p. 57.

12 For an analysis of Ghandi's food politics, see Parama Roy, 'Meat-Eating, Masculinity and Renunciation in India: A Gandhian Grammar of Diet', *Gender and History* 14.1 (2002), 62–91. For an insightful exploration of the relationship between food, national and diasporic belonging, see Anita Mannur, 'Nostalgia: Authenticity, Nationalism and Diaspora', *Multi-Ethnic Literature of the United States* 32.4 (2007), 11–31. See also Mohandas K. Gandhi, *An Autobiography: The Story of My Experiments With Truth*, trans. by Mahadev H. Desai, foreword by Sissela Bok (Boston, MA Beacon Press, 1957).

organized to contribute absolute silence'.[13] Members of the IRA, who were imprisoned for their violence against the occupying British forces, resorted to hunger strike against the unjust conditions to which they were subjected.[14] When words could not be heard, the body became the only means of communication.[15] Hunger strikes, silent marches and destruction or harm to the self can be political actions that make manifest the extreme violence and inequality of the ruling system, and thus the impossibility of communication and justice under the existing institutional parameters.

I therefore concur with Brown that 'it is [. . .] possible to make a fetish of breaking silence'.[16] More importantly, I agree that the necessity of speech and the negation of silence as a political or viable response 'may feed the powers it meant to starve'.[17] I am concerned by the amount of literature produced on the imperative to speak and on the inherent negativity of silence. Gilroy, Brown, Gopinath, Berlant and Cvetkovich reassure me that while there is no reason to valorize silence as an idyllic state of being, it is a form of survival, resistance and communication. Thus, this book is, to a certain extent, a response to the repeated and dominant paradigm of speech in trauma studies. I agree with J. Edward Mallot that contemporary work on trauma tends to conclude 'not only that survivors experience some sense of relief in discussing the trauma, but that such disclosure is often a social responsibility as well; to remain silent risks prolonging an individual's suffering and the perpetuation of violence'.[18] From my readings of the literary texts, it should be clear that I am not underestimating the importance of narrative and words to surviving trauma. Indeed, I am not turning away from narrativization, rather I am theorizing how stories may emerge through communal, chaotic and embodied sharings. The formation of narrative need not be normative (in form, voice or matter) or dependent on institutional support or recognition.

13 Berlant, *Cruel Optimism*, p. 229.

14 For a detailed analysis of the hunger strikes, see F. Stuart Ross, *Smashing H Block: The Popular Campaign against Criminalization and the Irish Hunger Strikes 1976–1982* (Liverpool: Liverpool University Press, 2012). For a passionate view of the hunger strikes, see Jonathon O'Meara, 'Remembering the Past – Fran Stagg', 26 January 2006 <www.anphoblacht.com/contents/14729> [accessed 1 February 2012]. For a brief look at the struggles at governmental level to stop the IRA hunger strikers, see Owen Bowcott, 'Thatcher Cabinet "Wobbled" Over IRA Hunger Strikers', *The Guardian*, 30 December 2011 <www.guardian.co.uk/uk/2011/dec/30/thatcher-cabinet-hunger-strike-national-archives> [accessed 22 January 2012].

15 For those who fought for Irish republicanism, one could argue that the performative speech act, where they turned to the body to portray the impossibility of justice, fair treatment and unbiased trials, failed in that many of the men died.

16 Brown, *Edgework*, p. 84.

17 Ibid.

18 J. Edward Mallot, 'Body Politics and the Body Politic: Memory as Human Inscription in Shauna Singh Baldwin's *What the Body Remembers*', *Interventions: International Journal of Postcolonial Studies* 8.2 (2006), 165–77 (p. 168). Although Mallot does concede that 'it is not necessarily the case that every victim in the West wants to provide verbal testimony', he still suggests that it is through non-Western research and/or literature that another type of remembering can be theorized (ibid.). I would suggest that drawing such a distinction is too simple and does not allow for an expansion of the ways in which remembering may take place on particular, communal and global levels. Indeed, to make such a clear-cut distinction is to constitutively reinforce that those not in the West should remember differently and that all in the West have one specific way of recollecting, as if East and West were recognizable geographical, undebatable spaces. Despite this, I still find Mallot's critique of the imperative to speak of one's trauma very pertinent.

I am therefore in agreement with Kilby that 'we might do better to find ways of reading the silence left by the experience of violence'.[19] This will involve 'more creative and imaginative ways of reading, ways of reading freed from the conceits that determine what is normal, right and proper'.[20] Like Butler, I see political and ethical potential in how we respond to violence.[21] I also agree with Ahmed that to 'hear, or to give the other a hearing, is to be moved by the other, such that one ceases to inhabit the same place'.[22] This to me means that when Mala burns her tongue, Ahmed/Zahra cuts his/her body, and Frances turns to sex work, we may read these acts as effects of trauma. However, we might also have to listen to the viscera. The selected novels show that the flesh is testament to survival in the face of violence, particularly when institutions of care instigate and perpetuate the abuse. Becoming undone, unlearning the self and the self's relationality to others, and uninhabiting the familiar are all risky, scary and sometimes painful undertakings. To pathologize such bodily manifestations is always to see the same symptoms of trauma everywhere; it is to fail to bear witness to what else may be occurring in this turn to the flesh. It is a failure to hear something that may force us to rethink our own assumed (and sometimes correct) knowledge. It is the possibility of another type of listening and thus another response. Another hearing – a different response – may open up unknown paths of unpredictable survival with others.

Decolonizing normativity

In my encounter with the selected texts, I have never felt in control or as if at some point I might finally and definitively understand them. Where mastery of knowledge often appears as the goal of epistemological pursuits, I wanted to find a way to articulate how these texts create a vulnerability between reader and text and between the characters themselves. I wanted to draw out how queer theory intersects with postcolonial analyses in literature, but more importantly I wanted to explore how literary texts portray resistance to colonial structures through queer embodiments, desires and praxes. The bringing together of postcolonial studies and gender and sexuality studies has been driven by the selected texts, by their need for a theorization that critiques how colonialism is sustained through sexualized violence of racial and gender hierarchization and segregation. As Stoler explains, '[The] formalization of racial categories [was] contingent on the management of sex'.[23]

Bringing together disciplines is never an easy task, even when there are numerous examples of nuanced engagements with intersecting sites of power. Furthermore, part of the driving force to finish what has been an unwieldy project has been the multiple occasions on which I have been informed that queer and postcolonialism have little to do with real structures of power. When presenting work on queer postcolonial

19 Kilby, *Violence*, p. 39.
20 Ibid.
21 Butler theorizes responses to violence as ethical possibilities in *Precarious Life*.
22 Ahmed, *Strange Encounters*, pp. 155–6.
23 Stoler, *Race and the Education of Desire*, p. 44.

analyses at academic conferences I have often been told that such an approach is too particular or too specific, and is therefore not general enough to account for how society functions. This book contests the idea that theories of power can be gender or race neutral. Indeed, its central premise is that sex, race, desire, ability, gender and class are the very structures through which embodiment and power (biopolitics) emerge. For me, the assumed neutrality of power cannot drive a political project that aims to tackle the continued violence of colonialism and familial life.

If the bringing together of queer and postcolonialism was a response to the literary texts, it was also a response to what I see as an absence in cultural analysis where queer embodiment in postcolonial texts is not read as queer subjectivity but as metaphorical or allegorical figuration. I therefore wanted to draw out ways in which metaphors and allegories are also about embodiment, and thus to show how the body is a lived experience that may portray a sense of identity (especially for those on the margins, including queers and crips). The interdisciplinarity of the text was a desire to approach literature in ways that I could not always see in existing critical work.[24] Queer and disability can be symbolic, but for many they are everyday normalities, embodiments, desires and identities. To this extent, *Queer Postcolonial Narratives* is driven by questions that open up reading to queerer potentialities. I have not suggested that it is possible to create definitive answers, but rather I have sought to tease out how these questions may change our reading practices and thus our critical interpretations. I seek to rethink reading by addressing how knowledge becomes established. In order to achieve this goal, I have built on the work of both established theorists (particularly, Butler and Bhabha, but also Fanon and Felman and Laub) and the works of anti-racist, queer and postcolonial scholars, whose work is often on the margins or at the intersections of these disciplines (including Kyungwon Hong, Ahmed and Puar). It is through their work that I have formulated a theory of embodied reading that attempts to decolonize normativity. Thus, the questions that have driven this book are: what is the role of the body in memory formation; can we forge embodied epistemologies that testify to both colonial and familial violence; how can we hear when words fail; how can we transform and stay attached to traditional community formations (such as nation and family) and live non-violently; and are there methods of telling stories that decolonize language, bodies and modes of belonging?

Although disability is not visible in the title of this book, it is – as readers will notice – integral to my analysis of the selected novels. To this extent, disability is interwoven into the terms queer and postcoloniality. Undoubtedly, I take a risk in not making disability transparent from the start. Furthermore, I recognize that there is more work to be undertaken on disability in these particular novels and in relation to queer and postcolonialism. However, by weaving disability through the terms queer and postcolonialism, I hope to have shown how morphological diversity is integral to these epistemological traditions. Perhaps more importantly, in being orientated towards queer, I have given priority to a depathologizing of difference and have refused a medical model where a path to a 'better life' is proposed or enforced. There are clear

24 There are notable exceptions where critics go to great lengths to explore disability and/or queer as lived realities and metaphorical tools. See especially Gopinath, Cvetkovich and Barker.

benefits for some in changing their bodies or minds through medical interventions, and for many such investments will be essential, important and life changing. I want quite simply – and yet it seems quite difficult in a society that demands normativity and healthiness through particular sociopolitical (including medical) models – to show that getting better is not always a desirable goal, a necessary option or a viable possibility.

In particular, I resist the idea that politics only emerges once there is a move towards normative healthiness.[25] How we manage our queer, disabled, different, not so healthy, ill, morphologically diverse, intellectually varied bodies cannot be reduced to or even fitted into a normative narrative. There should not always be an imperative to tell the same story: from illness to health or from the closet to an openly gay identity. Creating space not just for other stories, but also for other ways of telling stories is central to the explorations in *Queer Postcolonial Narratives*. I wanted to show that narrative does not have to be an individual or institutional undertaking, and that we do not always have to speak to survive under violent circumstances. To decolonize normativity, we have to undo the normative impulse to make people better, as such aims often encourage or force people to conform to existing normative structures. The selected novels show that there are other ways of not only surviving but also of making life livable with others. Decolonizing normativity can be a creative and communal process that queers violent structures in order to live differently and to share through the body the unspeakable and the unspoken.

Visceral storytelling, or multisensory epistemologies

Queer Postcolonial Narratives is not only a story about telling stories, it is also about how we tell stories and why we might need to share our tales. Although we might generalize that most literature is concerned with storytelling, both queer and postcolonial fictions demonstrate a particular anxiety about how to narrate tales, how to deal with truths (or more precisely with the impossibility of final truths), and how to challenge narrative form in order to build a space for one's self and one's (queer) family. Similar to many postcolonial critics, Helen Gilbert and Joanne Tompkins argue, 'The storyteller, then, is a potential political agitator'.[26] They add, 'as Fatima Dike puts it, "we don't tell 'bedtime' stories to put people to sleep; we want to scare the shit out of them and wake them up"'.[27] Fanon also insists, 'The storyteller replies to the expectant people by successive approximations, and makes his way, apparently alone but in fact helped

25 See, for example, Puar's critique of the 'It Gets Better' campaign. Puar, 'The Cost of Getting Better'.

26 Helen Gilbert and Joanne Tompkins, *Postcolonial Drama: Theory, Practice, Politics* (London: Routledge, 1996), p. 137.

27 Fatima Dike, keynote address, *International Women Playwright's Conference*, Adelaide, Australia, 4 July 1994, as cited in Helen Gilbert and Joanne Tompkins, *Postcolonial Drama: Theory, Practice, Politics* (London: Routledge, 1996), p. 137.

on by his public, towards the seeking out of new patterns'.[28] Stories for those on the margins of society and who are subjected to institutional violence are often a primary source of survival. The histories we weave together with others can be the resources for creating modes of belonging, sensing the self and extending what was previously imagined as possible.

However, the selected literary texts show how marginalized peoples may be unable (out of fear, shame, self-protection or self-preservation) to articulate their histories. They may be restricted to a particular narrative form (e.g. the coming out story), or may be afraid of the possible consequences of speaking out loud (and this can include not being heard). If a person could not speak or could not be heard, then what methods of storytelling must be in place for stories to emerge? I wanted to address why the responsibility for narrative is often reduced to the survivor speaking, and is rarely a question of how we hear. Furthermore, I wanted to examine how we might respond when there are no words, or when words are expressed alongside others forms of communication. What I see in these novels is the search for another type of listening and for collectivities forged through storytelling. At stake in these collective embodied gatherings is the survival of all involved. All the texts portray how a sense of being with others, of belonging, is forged through the need to tell unspeakable and unspoken stories. Stories are communal, public and shared, and through the interweaving of each storyteller's tale a sense of collective trust emerges. Yet, as is apparent throughout this book, I have not described the communal gatherings that emerge in the novels as communities. These novels portray coming together with others as a tentative, often temporary and uncertain process. Responsibility for the stories keeps the trust and the ties alive. The sense of belonging that runs throughout this book is tied to traditional and recognizable structures of nation, community and family. However, because these supposedly safe spaces often fail to protect those subjected to abuse or are the means through which violence is enacted and enforced, the search for less violent lives is often a precarious and vulnerable process. As a consequence, there is a resistance to the normalizing violence of institutions, and there is a creative response that cannot simply be reincorporated into existing definitions of belonging. We might say that stories create a space for survival. However, the embodied nature of the stories and the sociopolitical dimension of the storytellers' tales suggest that stories alone will not stop or prevent violence.

The modes of storytelling analysed in this book all portray a crisis in knowledge. This simultaneous search for knowledge and yielding to the impossibility of complete knowledge are integral to the narratives of queer embodiments, desires and gatherings in postcolonial worlds. The impossibility of complete knowledge resists colonial epistemologies, which are based on the idea that all beings and objects can be categorized, catalogued and thus known. These texts narrate queer postcolonial histories, and yet paradoxically articulate the very impossibility of such a task. Literary criticism tends towards a need for more histories and many literary critics claim that

[28] Franz Fanon, 'Reciprocal Bases of National Culture and the Fight for Freedom', Congress of Black African Writers, 1959 <www.marxists.org/subject/africa/fanon/national-culture.htm> [accessed 22 January 2012].

in the plethora of narratives change will be achieved. In many ways, while I agree with the need for multiple stories from varying peoples, I remain unconvinced that the narrativization of more histories is enough. Queer postcolonial texts call for a response that exceeds history (as a series of events), that goes beyond the individual violence, and that can never end (as the extent of the violence remains unknown). Therefore queer postcolonial narratives do not offer histories that can simply be added to available national or familial narratives. Rather, they put into question existing narratives and their forms, destabilizing the emphasis in history making on narrative coherence and closure. They do not hierarchize a better narrative form, but instead turn to the body to weave words and flesh together. I would suggest that they undo the very ways in which knowledge is authorized, and thus forge embodied epistemologies as a resistance to the disembodiment of historiography.

These embodied expressions are not reducible to the body, but are as much about thinking with, through and on the body as they are about intellectual perceptions, interpretations and articulations. Although embodied memories are not necessarily translatable into words – and certainly there is an emphasis throughout this book on the histories that remain unspeakable – the process of narrativization of unknown or unspoken memories emerges through that body's sensorial engagement with others. Within a colonial framework where bodily functions and desires are debased, only some people are understood and defined as embodied. In such an economy, the body is negative and thus history is the reordering and recording of events through a disembodied, autonomous subjectivity that can access all knowledge. Mootoo, Ben Jelloun and MacDonald engage the debased senses to share some of the silenced and debunked histories of colonial life at home. It is a decolonizing of the imperial logic of knowledge that ties the senses to racialized, gendered and classed emotions, labour, sex and peoples. Characters dance their way into other characters' past and present lives, express bonds by sharing a loved one's clothes or objects, feel intimate with each other and to what is not spoken by eating together, and lick, kiss, smell and caress their way through relationships when there are no – or not the right – words. When you can taste the past, but do not understand what it means, smell a memory, but have no or few words for the emotion it brings, and when you touch an other and feel something beyond that moment, that is what I have sought to theorize in *Queer Postcolonial Narratives*.

This book is thus concerned with the impact of multisensory histories on bodies and modes of belonging; how sensorial communication may be translated into words; and how life may be rendered more livable through these sensory entanglements. I read these novels as questioning how we produce and reproduce knowledge, and as inviting us – out of necessity – to be attentive to the very viscera and sensorium through which we live in and experience the world. At stake in embodied epistemologies is not only a contestatory version of history, but also the very sources and forms that inform and shape how and what we remember. When we can be open to listening to the body – where openness signals not simply a willingness to hear (although this is necessary) but a repeated shifting of one's own sense of being (with others) and knowledge – then perhaps we can begin to *read* what was previously thought to be impossible. It is this responsibility for what we hear and *fail to hear* (or, more precisely, for what we sense or fail to sense), our responsibility for the untranslatability of history that requires a response to each other. It demands and invites another response.

I would describe the processes of reading queer postcolonial narratives as redolent of how Butler delineates passion, grief and rage as forging communal ties and yet as exceeding the parameters that delimit what it means to belong. Belonging and storytelling are an undoing of the self with others: '[They] tear us from ourselves, bind us to others, transport us, undo us, and implicate us in lives that are not are [*sic*] own, sometimes fatally, irreversibly'.[29] This undoing of the self through the acts of reading and storytelling – where plots may be difficult to follow, storylines are left unfinished, psychological explanations are absent, violent scenes are disturbing, the separation between textual space and real time is blurred, and the reader is repeatedly implicated in the actions of the story – creates a sense of responsibility. This is an ethics that is attentive to the call and yet that exceeds the individual response. An ethics of reading works with this infinite indebtedness to this call to recreate and reimagine knowledge *and* what counts as knowledge. An ethics of storytelling bears witness through the undoing of the embodied self in a multisensory communality.

Performative endings

I want to end where I began, and yet I will end differently. Ambrose insists, 'Endings are but beginnings that have taken to standing on their heads'.[30] And, the troubadour aveugle states, 'Peut-être que je finirai par savoir qui je suis. Mais cela est une autre histoire'[31] [perhaps, in the end, I shall know who I am. But that is another story]. Although the story must come to an end, it is only the beginning of another story. I chose to focus on a set of novels that endlessly repeat the same story for the ways in which they relate the performative structure of the nation to embodied performativity. Although there are some critics who address this intersection in the novels on which I focus, I see much of the work in this field as assuming the inherent transgressive and transformative nature of the performative.[32] By working with theorists of performativity, I have sought to tease out a central node in the performative structure of power: the endless repetitive process of witnessing. The figure of the witness is not new to performativity. Rather, I have sought to give life to a figure and give flesh to a process that is somehow forgotten, left out or ignored in current formulations of performative power. It is through Parker and Sedgwick's nuanced work on performativity that I first came to realize how central the witness is to structures of power. It was also through their work that I learned of the disempowerment of the queer witness. Where Parker and Sedgwick reiterate institutional power through a docile or passive body, I did not want to suggest that a way to challenge this disempowering situation was to be active.

29 Butler, *Undoing Gender*, p. 20.
30 Mootoo, *Cereus*, p. 184.
31 Ben Jelloun, *L'Enfant*, p. 185.
32 See previous chapters for more detailed analysis of this work.

Butler has shown us that challenges to norms require more than individual will. Rather, I wanted to ask what conditions are necessary for this body – these witnesses – to be heard? Reminded of Spivak's infamous question, 'Can the Subaltern Speak?', I built on Ahmed's interpretation of this question to think about how 'what Spivak emphasises [. . .] is that a testimonial ethics is not simply about speaking, but about *the conditions of possibility of hearing*'.[33] I see performativity – the repetitive structure of institutional norms – as a theory of how we hear these silent witnesses.

In order to give flesh to the witness, I have not so much invented its materiality, but instead repeatedly sought out places from existing theories of performativity where the body is the site through which change is achieved. In other words, performativity is not a disembodied theory, although it may be used in this way (just as any theory may be reinterpreted). Austin insists that body and language are entangled each in the other:

> There is indeed a vague and comforting idea in the background that, after all, doing an action must come down to the making of physical movements with parts of the body; but this is about as true as that saying something must, in the last analysis, come down to making movements of the tongue.[34]

Language is not only about how the viscera moves, but there is no language without these fleshy vibrations. Similarly, doing is not reducible to movements or acts, but doing something does involve moving and acting. Felman adds:

> The act, an enigmatic and problematic production of the *speaking body*, destroys from its inception the metaphysical dichotomy between the domain of the 'mental' and the domain of the 'physical', breaks down the opposition between body and spirit, between matter and language.[35]

Performativity is a concern with the physical; it is a theory where body and norms touch, clash, shape and violently control each other. It is about the materialization of matter through sociopolitical constraints, and it is a critical engagement with how the body emerges through its sensorial register. *Queer Postcolonial Narratives* has connected this silent queer witness to contemporary feminist theories of the senses to argue that multisensory witnessing opens up the possibility of hearing these embodied expressions.

The witness is not the guarantee of a successful transformation, but this figure is central to how change may be achieved. Indeed, its viscerality – the embodiment of witnessing – demonstrates how change must pass through the sense of fleshy self. In other words, *Queer Postcolonial Narratives* offers ways into thinking with the flesh and explores how the skin may constrain change. My aim was to capture how bodily sensations may foreclose the transformative potential of performativity. In turning to the senses, I analysed a register that is often elusive and difficult to describe. Yet the sensorial register is testament to how our bodies work to destabilize existing norms.

33 Ahmed, *Strange Encounters*, p. 157.

34 J. L. Austin, 'A Plea for Excuses: The Presidential Address', *Proceedings of the Aristotelean Society* 57 (1956–7), 1–30 (p. 4).

35 Felman, *The Scandal of the Speaking Body*, p. 65.

In all the selected novels, the body remembers, and embodiment is both epistemology and sensory disruption to normative demands. The senses open up the possibility of sharing stories that cannot be spoken, that are not remembered in coherent form, that have been silenced or that are too overwhelming for words. One could say that the senses might tell another story, or they might just call on an other to listen even when the story is not clear, refuses to be told or has been forgotten. In other words, the body repeatedly calls on the witness to listen again and again. Sensory storytelling may tell the same story, but there is always difference and always a need to listen differently. Performative endings are the demand for a response, a call to take on the responsibility for the telling of the story, to willingly repeat the tale even when narration is painful.

Embodied encounters

In this final section I want to conclude by beginning another story. In 2001 organ transplant surgeons in the United Kingdom agreed to remove Clint Hallam's transplanted hand. Although doctors claimed that the hand recipient had failed to adhere to his prescribed drug regime, Hallam insisted that the hand had been rejected by both his body and mind because 'enough is enough'.[36] Describing his own experience of heart transplantation, Jean-Luc Nancy places the 'je' [I] in inverted commas to portray the instability of the post-transplantation self.[37] For Nancy, the cadaveric organ undoes the self and 'l'incommunicable communique' [the unspeakable speaks].[38] Throughout the writing of this book, I began work on another project concerning embodiment, postcoloniality, social injustice, and care for self and others. In many ways the questions that drive this other project are similar to those that are foundational to the analyses throughout this book: what does it mean to be open to the other; how are ethical encounters possible after violence; how can we speak of this relationality between self and other; how are care and abuse intimately related; and how do we listen to histories?

I want to finish with a story of transplantation because what I have addressed in this book is what it means to survive on a daily basis when the self has been violated by institutions of care (namely the family and the colonial nation). Organ transplantation is a biotechnological intervention that enhances the lives of many, and patient and surgeon narratives testify to its life-prolonging qualities.[39] However, not only are there

36 'Surgeons Sever Transplant Hand', BBC News, 3 February 2001 <http://news.bbc.co.uk/1/hi/world/europe/1151553.stm> [accessed 22 January 2012].

37 Jean-Luc Nancy, *L'Intrus* (Paris: Éditions Galilée, 2000), p. 39. All translations are my own.

38 Ibid., p. 30.

39 For surgeon memoirs, see, for example, Thomas Starzl, *The Puzzle People: Memoirs of a Transplant Surgeon* (Pittsburgh, PA: University of Pittsburgh Press, 1992); and Roy Calne, *The Ultimate Gift: The Story of Britain's Premier Transplant Surgeon* (London: Headline Book Publishing, 1998). For organ recipient biographies, see, for example, Claire Sylvia, with William Novak, *A Change of Heart: The Extraordinary Story of a Man's Heart in a Woman's Body* (London: Little, Brown & Co., 1997); and Mary Gohlke, with Max Jennings, *I'll Take Tomorrow: the Story of a Courageous Woman Who Dared to Subject Herself to a Medical Experiment – the First Successful Heart-Lung Transplant* (New York: M. Evans & Co., 1985).

other stories emerging around the social injustice of organ allocation, but also there are other confirmed narratives of bodily violations by teams of doctors, sometimes carried out with national aid.[40] The anthropological research in this field is growing, and medical anthropologists are testifying to the rethinking of their own assumptions around collective storytelling in this difficult biotechnological care regime.[41]

I want to tell a much smaller story here, and yet one that is not any less significant or any less tied to the global structures that subject the ill or the dying to care and violence. When *some* transplant recipients articulate a connection to their donors, they narrate a story that exceeds the existing normative biotechnological narrative of organ transplantation.[42] Indeed, such attachments are pathologized and are often 'treated' with psychological interventions. While I am certain that *some* recipients find it necessary to undergo psychological intervention, I would question this normative drive to make people better by encouraging them to incorporate their own stories into an already existing form. What would it take to hear these stories? What would it mean to listen to what may sound incomprehensible? I would suggest that the act of listening could be the first step in realizing a mode of encountering others, of caring for and with others, that does not assume to know the experiences of health and illness. Indeed, the performative reiteration of transplant narratives as life saving and heroic may only render other post-transplant experiences more difficult to understand or live with. Again, we see that the performative structure of narrative and of biomedicine is normative. Despite multiple stories by recipients telling of their intimate connections to their donors, their narratives continue to exist on the margins where their experiences are largely ridiculed, pathologized and dismissed.[43] Indeed, many who do tell of their disruptive embodied experience, where self merges with an other without becoming other, often resort to a normative narrative structure where heteronormativity helps restore the order of the embodied self.[44]

I contend that the potential of performativity lies in the ethics of witnessing. If we are to hear something different from the ordinary, then we have to start listening to what may sound fictional or what may easily be discounted as impossible. These

40 See Mario Osava, 'BRAZIL: Poor Sell Organs to Trans-Atlantic Trafficking Ring', *IPS*, 24 February 2004 <www.ipsnews.net/2004/02/brazil-poor-sell-organs-to-trans-atlantic-trafficking-ring/> [accessed 28 February 2012]; Ami Cholia, 'Illegal Organ Trafficking Poses a Global Problem', *Huffington Post*, 24 August 2008 <www.huffingtonpost.com/2009/07/24/illegal-organ-trafficking_n_244686.html> [accessed 17 February 2011]; Ruth Richardson, *Death, Dissection and the Destitute: The Politics of the Corpse in Pre-Victorian Britain* (London: Routledge, 1988); and Linda F. Hogle, *Recovering the Nation's Body: Cultural Memory, Medicine and the Politics of Redemption* (New Brunswick, NJ: Rutgers University Press, 1999).

41 See Nancy Scheper-Hughes, 'The Last Commodity: Post-Human Ethics and the Global Traffic in "Fresh Organs"', in *Global Assemblages: Technology, Politics and Ethics as Anthropological Problems*, ed. by Aihwa Ong and Stephen J. Collier (Malden, MA: Wiley-Blackwell, 2005), pp. 145–67; and Lawrence Cohen, 'Operability, Bioavailability and Exception', in *Global Assemblages: Technology, Politics and Ethics as Anthropological Problems*, ed. by Aihwa Ong and Stephen J. Collier (Malden, MA: Wiley-Blackwell, 2005), pp. 79–90.

42 Sylvia makes explicit her connection to the donor.

43 See especially the texts by Sylvia and Gohlke.

44 Most transplant biographies speak of a heterosexual attraction or relationship and how it normalizes post-transplant life.

are not simple wilful acts, although we must begin with an openness to listening, to hearing that which moves us and undoes us. *Queer Postcolonial Narratives* asks that we live with this undoing of self, self with others, narrative (form and matter), and knowledge. When does a story become true? If enough autobiographies are published by recipients detailing embodiment as an intimate tie to a (usually cadaveric) other, will we then believe their stories? Our ethical responsibility is to listen to what we cannot understand, as well as to the familiar and the comprehensible. It is to bear witness to this intimate tie that is forged through self with others, that primary tie, that binds us together. In bearing witness to the unknown we open up knowledge to further questions and destabilize existing certainties and practices. In repeatedly listening and retelling these stories, we forge ties that extend beyond what we might understand as belonging. We form gatherings where we share such stories and question the stories we tell, but what we also do is forge alternative epistemological forms that can listen to what bodies may say.

The transplanted body has many untold histories that are inaccessible, that cannot be narrated and that may even feel inexplicable. What type of donor knowledge should be available; what does it mean to be indebted to others when the other's life depends on a donation of flesh; can we ensure a non-violent and equitable health care system; and what does it mean to be not just philosophically but also viscerally open to the other? Organ transplantation is taking openness of self and other on a new path, where histories of violation are often integral to the systems of care that offer a so-called new life. When recipients claim a tie to the donor, I would suggest that we listen to what is being said and that we listen to how this impossibility might communicate the intimacy of living with others. The recipient may not know the donor, but may certainly feel the other in the self. How to think through this intimate tie is one way of further opening up our understandings of embodied epistemologies and our ethical responsibility to each other. Indeed, as the selected novels suggest, our ethical responsibility is to keep listening and narrating with and through others, and in so doing to reimagine the possible. Bodies are coming undone and we must respond and let ourselves and our epistemologies become undone if we are to learn anew. It is through the intimacy of being with others that we may sense and resense impossible embodiments, desires and modes of belonging.

Bibliography

Primary texts

Ben Jelloun, Tahar, *The Sacred Night*, trans. by Alan Sheridan (Baltimore, MD: Johns Hopkins University Press, 2000).

— *The Sand Child*, trans. by Alan Sheridan (Baltimore, MD: Johns Hopkins University Press, 2000).

— *La Nuit sacrée* (Paris: Éditions du Seuil, 1987).

— *L'Enfant de sable* (Paris: Éditions du Seuil, 1985).

MacDonald, Ann-Marie, *The Way the Crow Flies* (Toronto, ON: Alfred A. Knopf, 2003).

— *Fall on Your Knees* (Toronto, ON: Vintage, 1997).

— *The Arab's Mouth* (Winnipeg, MB: Blizzard Publishing, 1995).

Mootoo, Shani, *Cereus Blooms at Night* (Toronto, ON: McClelland & Stewart, 1998).

— *Out on Main Street and Other Stories* (Vancouver, BC: Press Gang Publishers, 1993).

Secondary sources

Accad, Evelyn, *Sexuality and War: Literary Masks of the Middle East* (New York: New York University Press, 1990).

Achebe, Chinua, *Home and Exile* (New York and Oxford: Oxford University Press, 2000).

Agamben, Georgio, *Remnants of Auschwitz: The Witness and the Archive*, trans. by Daniel Heller-Roazen (New York: Zone Books, 2002).

— *Homo Sacer: Sovereign Power and Bare Life*, trans. by Daniel Heller-Rouzen (Stanford, CA: Stanford University Press, 1998).

— *The Coming Community*, trans. by Michael Hardt (Minneapolis, MN: University of Minnesota Press, 1993).

Ahmad, Aijaz, *In Theory: Classes, Nations, Literatures* (London and New York: Verso, 1992).

— 'Jameson's Rhetoric of Otherness and the "National Allegory"', *Social Text* 17 (1987), 3–25.

Ahmed, Sara, *Queer Phenomenology: Orientations, Objects, Others* (Durham, NC and London: Duke University Press, 2006).

— 'Declarations of Whiteness: The Non-Performativity of Anti-Racism', *borderlands e-journal* 5.3 (2005) <www.borderlands.net.au/vol5no3_2006/ahmed_nonperform.htm> [accessed 1 January 2012].

— *The Cultural Politics of Emotion* (Edinburgh: Edinburgh University Press, 2004).

— *Strange Encounters: Embodied Others in Postcoloniality* (London: Routledge, 2000).

— *Differences that Matter: Feminist Theory and Postmodernism* (Cambridge: Cambridge University Press, 1998).

Ahmed, Sara and Jackie Stacey, 'Introduction: Dermographies', in *Thinking Through the Skin*, ed. by Sara Ahmed and Jackie Stacey (London: Routledge, 2001), pp. 1–17.
Ahmed, Sara, Jane Kilby, Celia Lury, Maureen McNeil and Beverley Skeggs (eds), *Transformations: Thinking Through Feminism* (London: Routledge, 2000).
Alexander, Jacqui, 'Not Just (Any) *Body* Can be a Citizen: The Politics of Law, Sexuality and Postcoloniality in Trinidad, Tobago and the Bahamas', *Feminist Review* 48 (1994), 5–23.
— 'Redrafting Morality: The Postcolonial State and the Sexual Offences Bill of Trinidad and Tobago', in *Third World Women and the Politics of Feminism*, ed. by Chandra Talpade Mohanty, Ann Russo and Lourdes Torres (Bloomington, IN: Indiana University Press, 1991), pp. 133–52.
Alexander, Jacqui and Chandra Talpade Mohanty (eds), *Feminist Genealogies, Colonial Legacies, Democratic Futures* (New York: Routledge, 1997).
Ali, Suki, 'Troubling Times: A Comment on Judith Butler's "Sexual Politics, Torture and Secular Time"', *The British Journal of Sociology* 59.1 (2008), 35–9.
Amar, Ruth, *Tahar Ben Jelloun: Les Stratégies narratives* (Lewiston, NY and Wales: Edwin Mellen Press, 2005).
Anderson, Benedict, *Imagined Communities: Reflections on the Origin and Spread of Nationalism* (London: Verso Books, 1983).
Andrews, Jennifer, 'Rethinking the Relevance of Magic Realism for English-Canadian Literature: Reading Ann-Marie MacDonald's *Fall on Your Knees*', *Studies in Canadian Literature* 24.1 (1999), 1–19.
Angulo, María-Elena, *Magic Realism: Social Context and Discourse* (New York and London: Garland Publishing, Inc., 1995).
Anzieu, Didier, *The Skin Ego: A Psychoanalytic Approach to the Self*, trans. by Chris Turner (New Haven, CT: Yale University Press, 1989).
Appadurai, Arjun, 'Disjuncture and Difference in the Global Economy', *Public Culture* 2.2 (1990), 324–9.
Apter, Emily, *Continental Drift: From National Characters to Virtual Subjects* (Chicago, IL: Chicago University Press, 1999).
Apter, Emily and William Piets, *Fetishism as Cultural Discourse* (New York: Cornell University Press, 1990).
Armstrong, Isobel, *The Radical Aesthetic* (Oxford: Blackwell Publishers, 2000).
Armstrong, Louise, *Rocking the Cradle of Sexual Politics: What Happened When Women Said Incest* (Reading, MA: Addison–Wesley, 1994).
Ashcroft, Bill, *Caliban's Voice: The Transformation of English in Post-Colonial Literature* (London: Routledge, 2009).
— *On Postcolonial Futures: Transformations of Colonial Culture* (New York and London: Continuum, 2001).
— *Post-colonial Transformation* (London and New York: Routledge, 2001).
Ashcroft, Bill, Gareth Griffiths and Helen Tiffin (eds), *The Post-Colonial Studies Reader* (London and New York: Routledge, 2006).
— *The Empire Writes Back: Theory and Practice in Post-Colonial Literatures* (New York and London: Routledge, 1989).
Attridge, Derek, *The Singularity of Literature* (London and New York: Routledge, 2004).
— 'Trusting the Other: Ethics and Politics in J.M. Coetzee's *Age of Iron*', *The South Atlantic Quarterly* 93.1 (1994), 59–82.

Austin, J. L., *How to Do Things with Words*, Second Edition, ed. by J. O. Urmson and Marina Sbisà (Cambridge, MA: Harvard University Press, [1962] 1975).

— 'A Plea for Excuses: The Presidential Address', *Proceedings of the Aristotelean Society* 57 (1956–7), 1–30.

Baetz, Joel, 'Tales from the Canadian Crypt: Canadian Ghosts, the Cultural Uncanny and the Necessity of Haunting in Ann-Marie MacDonald's *Fall on Your Knees*', *Studies in Canadian Literature* 29.2 (2004), 62–83.

Baker, Alison, *Voices of Resistance: Oral Histories of Moroccan Women* (Albany, NY: State University of New York Press, 1998).

Balibar, Etienne and Emmanuel Wallenstein, *Race, Nation and Class: Ambiguous Identities*, trans. by Chris Turner (London: Verso, 1991).

Bannerji, Himani, *Thinking Through: Essays on Feminism, Marxism and Anti-racism* (Toronto, ON: Women's Press, 1995).

Barker, Clare, *Postcolonial Fiction and Disability: Exceptional Children, Metaphor and Materiality* (Hampshire: Palgrave Macmillan, 2011).

Barthes, Roland, *Camera Lucida: Reflections on Photography*, trans. by Richard Howard (New York: Hill and Wang, 1981).

Bataille, Georges, *Story of the Eye*, trans. by Joachim Neugroschal, with essays by Susan Sontag and Roland Barthes (London: Penguin Books, 1982).

— *Histoire de l'œil* (Paris: Société Nouvelle des Éditions Pauvert, 1967).

BBC, 'Surgeons Sever Transplant Hand', BBC News, 3 February 2001 <www.news.bbc.co.uk/1/hi/world/europe/1151553.stm> [accessed 22 January 2012].

Becker, Dana, *Myth of Empowerment: Women and the Therapeutic Culture in America* (New York: New York University Press, 2005).

Beckford, James A., 'Secularism and Coercive Freedoms', *The British Journal of Sociology* 59.1 (2008), 41–5.

Beddoes, Julie, 'From Post-age to New Age: *Fall on Your Knees* by Ann-Marie MacDonald', *Canadian Literature* 154 (1997), 132–4.

Bell, Vikki, 'Performativity and Belonging: An Introduction', *Theory, Culture and Society* 16.2 (1999), 1–10.

Benhabib, Selya, 'Subjectivity, Historiography and Politics', in *Feminist Contentions: A Philosophical Exchange*, ed. by Selya Benhabib, Judith Butler, Drucilla Cornell and Nancy Fraser (New York: Routledge, 1995), 107–26.

Benjamin, Walter, 'The Storyteller: Reflections on the Works of Nikolai Leskov', in *Illuminations*, trans. by Harry Zorn, intro. by Hannah Arendt (London: Pimlico, [1955] 1999), 83–107.

— 'The Task of the Translator: An Introduction to the Translation of Baudelaire's *Tableux parisiens*', in *Illuminations*, ed. by Walter Benjamin, trans. by Harry Zorn, intro. by Hannah Arendt (London: Pimlico, [1995] 1999), pp. 70–82.

Ben Mlih, Abdellah, *Structures politiques du Maroc colonial* (Paris: Éditions L'Harmattan, 1990).

Bennett, Donna, 'English Canada's Postcolonial Complexities', *Essays on Canadian Writing* 51 and 52 (1993/4), 1–14.

Ben Ouanes, Kamel, 'L'Itinéraire de la parole dans l'œuvre romanesque de Tahar Ben Jelloun', in *Tahar Ben Jelloun: Stratégies d'écriture*, ed. by Mansour M'Henni (Paris: Éditions L'Harmattan, 1993), 35–49.

Benthien, Claudia, *Skin: On the Cultural Border between Self and the World*, trans. by Thomas Dunlap (New York: Columbia University Press, 2002).

Berger, John, *Ways of Seeing* (London: BBC and Penguin, 1977).
Berlant, Lauren, *Cruel Optimism* (Durham, NC and London: Duke University Press, 2011).
— 'Intimacy: A Special Issue', in *Intimacy*, ed. by Lauren Berlant (Chicago, IL: University of Chicago Press, 2000), pp. 1–8.
— *The Queen of America Goes to Washington: Essays on Sex and Citizenship* (Durham, NC: Duke University Press, 1997).
Berlant, Lauren and Michael Warner, 'Sex in Public', in *Intimacy*, ed. by Lauren Berlant, (Chicago, IL: University of Chicago Press, 2000), pp. 311–30.
— 'Sex in Public', *Critical Inquiry* 24.2 (1998), 547–66.
Bersani, Leo and Adam Phillips, *Intimacies* (Chicago, IL and London: University of Chicago Press, 2008).
Bhabha, Homi, 'Homi Bhabha Talks with Noam Chomsky', *Critical Inquiry* 31.2 (2005), 419–24.
— *The Location of Culture* (London: Routledge, [1994] 2000).
— 'On Mimicry and Man: The Ambivalence of Colonial Discourse', *October* 28 (1984), 125–33.
Billingham, Susan, 'Migratory Subjects in Shani Mootoo's *Cereus Blooms at Night*', in *Identity, Community and Nation: Essays on Canadian Writing*, ed. by Danielle Schaub (Israel: Magnes, 2002), pp. 74–88.
Bloch, Ernst, *Aesthetics and Politics*, afterword by Fredric Jameson, trans. by Ronald Taylor (London: NLB, 1971).
Bogdan, Robert, 'The Social Constructions of Freaks', in *Freakery: Cultural Spectacles of the Extraordinary Body*, ed. by Rosemarie Garland-Thomson, foreword by Leslie A. Fiedler (New York: New York University Press, 1996), pp. 23–37.
Boujedra, Rachid, 'Pour le Bonheur du public français', *Le Monde* (15 décembre 1987), 4.
Bourdieu, Pierre, *Masculine Domination*, trans. by Richard Nice (Cambridge: Polity, 2001).
Bourget, Carine, 'L'Intertexte islamique de *L'Enfant de sable* et *La Nuit sacrée* de Tahar Ben Jelloun', *The French Review* 72.4 (1999), 730–41.
Bowcott, Owen, 'Thatcher Cabinet "Wobbled" Over IRA Hunger Strikers', *The Guardian*, 30 December 2011 <www.guardian.co.uk/uk/2011/dec/30/thatcher-cabinet-hunger-strike-national-archives> [accessed 22 January 2012].
Breen, Margaret Sönser and Warren J. Blumenfeld (eds), *Butler Matters: Judith Butler's Impact on Feminist and Queer Studies*, intro. by Margaret Sönser Breen (Aldershot: Ashgate, 2005).
Britton, Celia, *Edouard Glissant and Postcolonial Theory: Strategies of Language and Resistance* (Charlottesville, VA: University of Virginia Press, 1999).
Bronfen, Elizabeth, 'Femininity – Missing in Action', in *Jane Eyre: New Casebooks*, ed. by Heather Glen (Basingstoke: Macmillan, 1997), pp. 196–204.
Brooks, Peter, *Reading for the Plot: Design and Invention in Narrative* (Cambridge, MA: Harvard University Press, 1992).
Brown, Laura S., *Cultural Competence in Trauma Therapy: Beyond the Flashback* (Washington, DC: American Psychological Association, 2009).
— 'Feminist Therapy', in *Twenty-First Century Psychotherapies*, ed. by J. L. Lebow (Hoboken, NJ: John Wiley & Sons, 2008), pp. 277–306.
— 'Not Outside the Range: One Feminist Perspective on Psychic Trauma', in *Trauma: Explorations in Memory*, ed. by Cathy Caruth (Baltimore, MD: Johns Hopkins University Press, 1995), pp. 100–12.

Brown, Wendy, *Regulating Aversion: A Critique of Tolerance in the Age of Identity* (Princeton, NJ: Princeton University Press, 2008).
— *Edgework: Critical Essays on Knowledge and Politics* (Princeton, NJ: Princeton University Press, 2005).
— 'Wounded Attachments', in *State of Injury: Freedom and Power in Late Modernity*, ed. by Wendy Brown (Princeton, NJ: Princeton University Press, 1995), pp. 52–76.
Brüning, Angela, 'The Corporeal and the Sensual in Two Novels by Shani Mootoo and Julia Alvarez', in *The Society for Caribbean Studies Annual Conference Papers* 3 (2002), ed. by Sandra Courtman <www.caribbeanstudies.org.uk/papers/2002/olv3p17.PDF> [accessed 22 March 2008], pp. 1–19.
Bryce, Jane, '*Buxton Spice* and *Cereus Blooms at Night*', *WASAFARI* 30 (1999), 72–3.
Brydon, Diana, 'Canada and Postcolonialism: Questions, Inventories and Futures', in *Is Canada Postcolonial: Unsettling Canadian Literature*, ed. by Laura Moss (Waterloo, ON: Wilfred Laurier University Press, 2003), pp. 49–77.
Burke, Edmund, III, *Prelude to Protectorate in Morocco: Precolonial Protest and Resistance, 1860–1912* (Chicago, IL and London: University of Chicago Press, 1976).
Burns, Lorna, 'Politicising Paradise: Sites of Resistance in *Cereus Blooms at Night*', *Journal of West Indian Literature* 19.2 (2011), 52–67.
Burton, Antoinette, *Gender, Sexuality and Colonial Modernities* (New York: Routledge, 1999).
Butler, Judith, 'Sexual Politics, Torture and Secular Time', *The British Journal of Sociology* 59.1 (2008), 1–23.
— *Giving an Account of Oneself* (New York: Fordham University Press, 2005).
— *Precarious Life: The Powers of Mourning and Violence* (London: Verso, 2004).
— *Undoing Gender* (New York and London: Routledge, 2004).
— 'Afterword', in Shoshana Felman, *The Scandal of the Speaking Body: Don Juan with J. L. Austin, or Seduction in Two Languages*, trans. by Catherine Porter, foreword by Stanley Cavell and afterword by Judith Butler (Stanford, CA: Stanford University Press, 2003), pp. 113–24.
— 'Revisiting Bodies and Pleasures', *Theory, Culture and Society* 16.2 (1999), 11–20.
— *Excitable Speech: A Politics of the Performative* (New York and London: Routledge, 1997).
— *The Psychic Life of Power: Theories in Subjection* (Stanford, CA: Stanford University Press, 1997).
— 'Burning Acts – Injurious Speech', in *Performativity and Performance*, ed. by Andrew Parker and Eve Kosofsky Sedgwick (New York and London: Routledge, 1995), pp. 197–227.
— *Bodies That Matter: On the Discursive Limits of 'Sex'* (New York and London: Routledge, 1993).
— 'Critically Queer', *GLQ: A Journal of Lesbian and Gay Studies* 1.1 (1993), 17–32.
— *Gender Trouble: Feminism and the Subversion of Identity* (New York and London: Routledge, 1990).
Butler, Judith and Biddy Martin, 'Cross-Identifications', *Diacritics* 24.2 and 3 (1994), 3.
Butler, Judith and Gayatri Chakravorty Spivak, *Who Sings the Nation State?: Language, Politics and Belonging* (London: Seagull Books, 2007).
Calne, Roy, *The Ultimate Gift: The Story of Britain's Premier Transplant Surgeon* (London: Headline Book Publishing, 1998).
Campbell, Jan and Janet Harbord, 'Playing it Again: Citation, Reiteration or Circularity?', *Theory, Culture and Society* 16.2 (1999), 229–39.

Caplan, Karen Ann, *Trauma Culture: The Politics of Terror and Loss in Media and Literature* (New Brunswick, NJ: Rutgers University Press, 2005).
Caruth, Cathy, *Unclaimed Experience: Trauma, Narrative and History* (Baltimore, MD and London: Johns Hopkins University Press, 1996).
— 'Recapturing the Past: Introduction', in *Trauma: Explorations in Memory*, ed. by Cathy Caruth (Baltimore, MD: Johns Hopkins University Press, 1995), pp. 151–7.
— 'Trauma and Experience: Introduction', in *Trauma: Explorations in Memory*, ed. by Cathy Caruth (Baltimore, MD: Johns Hopkins University Press, 1995), pp. 3–12.
— 'Traumatic Awakenings', in *Performativity and Performance*, ed. by Andrew Parker and Eve Kosofsky Sedgwick (New York and London: Routledge, 1995), pp. 89–108.
Casid, Jill H., *Sowing Empire: Landscape and Colonization* (Minneapolis, MN: University of Minnesota Press, 2005).
Caverero, Adriana, *Relating Narratives: Storytelling and Selfhood*, trans. by P. Koftman (New York: Routledge, 2000).
Cazenave, Odile, 'Gender, Age and Narrative Transformations in *L'Enfant de sable* by Tahar Ben Jelloun', *The French Review* 64.3 (1991), 437–50.
Chakrabarty, Dipesh, *Provincializing Europe: Postcolonial Thought and Historical Difference* (Princeton, NJ: Princeton University Press, 2000).
Chatelier, Denis, *Je vis avec les mains d'un autre* (Paris: Robert Laffont, 2008).
Chatterjee, Partha, *The Nation and Its Fragments: Colonial and Postcolonial Histories* (Princeton, NJ: Princeton University Press, 1996).
Chin, Timothy S., 'Jamaican Popular Culture, Caribbean Culture and the Representation of Gay and Lesbian Sexuality in the Discourses of Race and Nation', *Small Axe* 3.5, 14–25.
Cholia, Ami, 'Illegal Organ Trafficking Poses a Global Problem', *Huffington Post*, 24 August 2008 <www.huffingtonpost.com/2009/07/24/illegal-organ-trafficking_n_244686.html> [accessed 28 February 2012].
Chossat, Michèle, *Ernaux, Redonnet, Bâ et Ben Jelloun: Le Personnage féminin à l'aube du XXIème siècle* (New York: Peter Lang, 2002).
Chow, Rey, 'Sacrifice, Mimesis and the Theorizing of Victimhood (A Speculative Essay)', *Representations* 94 (2006), 131–49.
Chrisman, Laura, *Postcolonial Contraventions: Cultural Readings of Race, Imperialism and Transnationalism* (Manchester: Manchester University Press, 2003).
Clarke, George E., *Odysseys Home: Mapping African-Canadian Literature* (Toronto, ON: University of Toronto Press, 2002).
Closson James, William, *Locations of the Sacred: Essays on Religion, Literature and Canadian Culture* (Waterloo, ON: Wilfred Laurier University Press, 1998).
Coetzee, J. M., *Age of Iron* (London: Secker and Warburg, 1990).
Cohen, Lawrence, 'Operability, Bioavailability and Exception', in *Global Assemblages: Technology, Politics and Ethics as Anthropological Problems*, ed. by Aihwa Ong and Stephen J. Collier (Malden, MA: Wiley-Blackwell, 2005), pp. 79–90.
Coleman, Daniel, *Masculine Migration: Reading the Postcolonial Male in 'New Canadian' Narratives* (Toronto, ON: University of Toronto Press, 1998).
Collins, David Norman, Roy Todd and Martin Thornton (eds), *Aboriginal People and Other Canadians: Shaping New Relationships* (Ottawa, ON: Ottawa University Press, 2001).
Condé, Mary, 'The Flight from Certainty in Shani Mootoo's *Cereus Blooms at Night*', in *Flight from Certainty: The Dilemma of Identity and Exile*, ed. by Anne Luyat and Francine Tolron (Amsterdam and Atlanta, GA: Rodopi, 2001), pp. 63–70.

Connor, Steven, *The Book of Skin* (London: Reaktion Books, 2004).
— 'Mortification', in *Thinking Through the Skin*, ed. by Sara Ahmed and Jackie Stacey (London: Routledge, 2001), pp. 36–51.
Conrad, Margaret and James K. Hiller, *Atlantic Canada: A Region in the Making* (Toronto, ON: Oxford University Press, 2001).
Cook, James W., Jr., 'Of Men, Missing Links and Nondescripts: The Strange Career of P. T. Barnum's "What is It?" Exhibition', in *Freakery: Cultural Spectacles of the Extraordinary Body*, ed. by Rosemarie Garland-Thomson, foreword by Leslie A. Fiedler (New York: New York University Press, 1996), pp. 139–57.
Cook, Vikki, 'Basking in a Cloudless Sky: Refiguring National Identity in Shani Mootoo's *Cereus Blooms at Night*', *Canadian Studies in Europe: The Making of Canada* 4 (2005), 41–51.
Crary, Jonathan, *Suspensions of Perception: Attention, Spectacle and Modern Culture* (London and Cambridge, MA: MIT Press, 1999).
— *Techniques of the Observer: On Vision and Modernity in the Nineteenth Century* (London and Cambridge, MA: MIT Press, 1999).
Crimp, Douglas, *Melancholia and Moralism: Essays on AIDS and Queer Politics* (London: MIT Press, 2002).
Critchley, Simon, 'Introduction', in *The Cambridge Companion to Levinas*, ed. by Simon Critchley and Robert Bernasconi (Cambridge: Cambridge University Press, 2002), pp. 1–32.
Currie, Sheldon, 'Review of *Fall on Your Knees* by Ann-Marie MacDonald', *The Antigonish Review* 113 (1998), 111–15.
Cvetkovich, Ann, *An Archive of Feeling: Trauma, Sexuality and Lesbian Public Cultures* (Durham, NC and London: Duke University Press, 2003).
Davis, Heather and Paige Sarlin, 'No One is Sovereign in Love: A Conversation between Lauren Berlant and Michael Hardt', *amour* 18 (2011) <www.nomorepotlucks.org/site/no-one-is-sovereign-in-love-a-conversation-between-lauren-berlant-and-michael-hardt> [accessed 29 November 2011].
Davis, Lennard J., 'Bodies of Difference: Politics, Disability and Representation', in *Disability Studies: Enabling the Humanities*, ed. by Sharon L. Snyder, Brenda Jo Brueggemann and Rosemarie Garland-Thomson (New York: The Modern Language Association of America, 2002), pp. 100–6.
Decaires Narain, Denise, *Contemporary Caribbean Women's Poetry: Making Style* (London: Routledge, 2001).
Déjeux, Jean, 'Réception de *La Nuit sacrée* de Tahar Ben Jelloun dans la presse européenne', *Sindbad* 67 (1988), 22–9.
Delanoë, Guy, *Lyautey, Juin, Mohammed V: fin d'un protectorat* (Paris: Éditions L'Harmattan, 1988).
Derrida, Jacques, *On Touching – Jean-Luc Nancy*, trans. by Christine Irizarry (Stanford, CA: Stanford University Press, 2005).
— *The Work of Mourning*, ed. by Pascale-Anne Brault and Michael Naas (Chicago, IL: Chicago University Press, 2001).
— *Writing and Difference*, trans., intro. and additional notes by Alan Bass (London: Routledge, 2001).
— *Memoirs of the Blind: The Self-Portrait and Other Ruins*, trans. by Pascale-Anne Brault and Michael Naas (Chicago, IL and London: University of Chicago Press, 1993).
— *Acts of Literature*, ed. by Derek Attridge (New York and London: Routledge, 1992).

— *The Truth in Painting*, trans. by Geoff Bennington and Ian McLeod (Chicago, IL and London: University of Chicago Press, 1987).
Descartes, René, *Discourse on Method, Optics, Geometry and Meterology*, trans. by Paul J. Olscamp (Indianapolis, IN: Bobbs-Merrill, [1637] 1965).
Dirlik, Arif, 'Bringing History Back In: Of Diasporas, Hybridities, Places and Histories', *The Review of Education/Pedagogy/Cultural Studies* 21.2 (1999), 95–131.
Donaldson, Laura E. and Kwok Pui-Lan, *Postcolonialism, Feminism and Religious Discourse* (New York: Routledge, 2002).
Dreyfus, Hubert L. and Paul Rabinow, *Michel Foucault: Beyond Structuralism and Hermeneutics*, afterword by and interview with Michel Foucault (Chicago, IL: University of Chicago Press, 1983).
Driedger, Leo, *Multi-ethnic Canada: Identities and Inequalities* (Toronto, ON and Oxford: Oxford University Press, 1996).
Dubey, Madhu, 'Postmodernism as Postnationalism? Racial Representation in U.S. Cultural Studies', *New Formations: A Journal of Cultural Theory/Politics* 45 (2001), 150–68.
Duggan, Lisa, 'Theory in Practice: The Theory Wars, or, Who's Afraid of Judith Butler?', *Journal of Women's History* 10.1 (1998), 9–19.
— 'Queering the State', in *Sex Wars: Sexual Dissent and Political Culture*, ed. by Lisa Duggan and Nan D. Hunter (New York: Routledge, 1995), pp. 179–93.
Dunn, Ross E., *Resistance in the Desert: Moroccan Responses to French Imperialism, 1881–1912* (London and Madison, WI: University of Wisconsin Press, 1977).
Durrant, Sam, *Postcolonial Narrative and the Work of Mourning* (Albany, NY: State University of New York Press, 2006).
Dvorak, Marta and Coral Ann Howells (eds), *The Literature of Atlantic Canada*, Special issue of *Canadian Literature* 189 (2006).
Edelman, Lee, *No Future: Queer Theory and the Death Drive* (Durham, NC and London: Duke University Press, 2004).
Edmondson, Belinda J. (ed.), *Caribbean Romances: The Politics of Regional Representation* (Charlottesville, VA and London: University Press of Virginia, 1999).
Elbaz, Robert, *Tahar Ben Jelloun ou l'inassouvissement du désir narratif* (Paris: Éditions L'Harmattan, 1996).
Erickson, John, *Islam and the Postcolonial Narrative* (Cambridge: Cambridge University Press, 1998).
— 'Veiled Woman and Veiled Narrative in Tahar ben Jelloun's *The Sandchild*', *boundary* 2.20.1 (1993), 47–64.
Fanon, Frantz, 'Reciprocal Bases of National Culture and the Fight for Freedom', Congress of Black African Writers, 1959 <www.marxists.org/subject/africa/fanon/national-culture.htm> [accessed 22 January 2012].
—*A Dying Colonialism*, trans. by Haakon Chevalier (London: Pelican Books, 1970).
— *The Wretched of the Earth*, trans. by Constance Farrington (New York: Grove Press, 1963).
— *L'An V de la révolution algérienne* (Paris: La Découverte, [1959] 2001).
— *Black Skin, White Masks*, trans. by Charles Lam Markmann, forewords by Ziauddin Sardar and Homi K. Bhabha (Sidmouth: Pluto Press, [1952] 1986).
Fausto-Sterling, Anne, *Sexing the Body: Gender Politics and the Construction of Sexuality* (New York: Basic Books, 2000).
— 'How to Build a Man', in *Science and Homosexualities*, ed. by Vernon A. Rosario (London: Routledge, 1997), pp. 219–25.

— *Myths of Gender: Biological Theories About Women and Men* (New York: Basic Books, 1985).

Fayad, Marie, 'Borges in Tahar Ben Jelloun's *L'Enfant de sable*: Beyond Intertextuality', *The French Review* 67.2 (1993), 291–9.

Felman, Shoshana, *The Scandal of the Speaking Body: Don Juan with J. L. Austin or Seduction in Two Languages*, trans. by Catherine Porter, foreword by Stanley Cavell and afterword by Judith Butler (Stanford, CA: Stanford University Press, 2003).

— *The Juridical Unconscious: Trials and Traumas in the Twentieth Century* (Cambridge, MA and London: Harvard University Press, 2002).

Felman, Shoshana and Dori Laub, *Testimony: Crises of Witnessing in Literature, Psychoanalysis and History* (New York and London: Routledge, 1992).

Ferguson, Moira, *Colonialism and Gender Relations from Mary Wollstonecraft to Jamaica Kincaid* (New York: Columbia University Press, 1993).

Firth, Kathleen, 'Resisting the Bible and the Whip: Trinidad's East Indians and the Canadian Presbyterian Missions', in *Colonies, Missions, Cultures in the English-Speaking World: General and Comparative Studies*, ed. by Gerhand Stilz (Tübingen: Stauffenburg Verlag, 2001), pp. 168–77.

Flaugh, Christian, 'On Normalities: Narratives of Bodies, Ability and Freaks of Culture in Twentieth-Century Francophone Literature', *Contemporary French and Francophone Studies* 10.2 (2006) 217–25 <http://dx.doi.org/10.1080/17409290600560344> [accessed 17 December 2007].

Fortier, Anne-Marie, 'Re-Membering Places and the Performance of Belonging(s)', *Theory, Culture and Society* 16.2 (1999), 41–64.

Foucault, Michel, *The History of Sexuality, Vol. 1: An Introduction,* trans. by Alan Sheridan (New York: Pantheon, [1976] 1978).

— *Discipline and Punish: The Birth of the Prison*, trans. by Alan Sheridan (New York: Random House, [1975] 1995).

— *The Birth of the Clinic*, trans. by Alan Sheridan (London: Routledge, [1963] 2004).

Fraser, Nancy, 'False Antitheses', in *Feminist Contentions: A Philosophical Exchange*, ed. by Selya Benhabib, Judith Butler, Drucilla Cornell and Nancy Fraser (New York: Routledge, 1995) pp. 59–74.

— 'Pragmatism, Feminism and the Linguistic Turn', in *Feminist Contentions: A Philosophical Exchange*, ed. by Selya Benhabib, Judith Butler, Drucilla Cornell and Nancy Fraser (New York: Routledge, 1995) pp. 157–72.

Freud, Sigmund, *The Ego and the Id*, trans. by Joan Rivière, ed. by James Strachey (New York: Norton, [1923] 1989).

— 'Mourning and Melacholia', *The Standard Edition of the Complete Psychological Works*, vol. 14, ed. by James Strachey (London: Hogarth, [1917] 1968).

— *Dora: An Analysis of a Case of Hysteria*, ed. and intro. by Phillip Rieff (New York: Simon & Schuster, [1905] 1997).

Frost, Corey, 'Intersections of Gender and Ethnic Performativity in Ann-Marie MacDonald's *Fall on Your Knees*', *Canadian Review of American Studies* 35.2 (2005), 195–213.

Fuller, Danielle, *Writing the Everyday: Women's Textual Communities in Atlantic Canada* (Montreal: McGill-Queen's University Press, 2004).

Fung, Richard, 'Bodies Out of Place: The Videotapes of Shani Mootoo', *Women in Performance: A Journal of Feminist Theory* 8.2 (1996), 161–73.

Furedi, Frank, *Therapy Culture: Cultivating Vulnerability in an Uncertain Age* (New York: Routledge, 2004).
Fusco, Coco, *The Bodies That Were Not Ours and Other Writings* (London: Routledge, 2001).
Fuss, Diana, *Identification Papers* (New York: Routledge, 1995).
— 'Interior Colonies: Frantz Fanon and the Politics of Identification', *Diacritics* 24.2 and 3 (1994), 19–42.
— *Essentially Speaking: Feminism, Nature and Difference* (London: Routledge, 1990).
Fuss, Diana (ed.), *Inside/Out: Lesbian Theories/Gay Theories* (London: Routledge, 1991).
Gallop, Jane, *Thinking Through the Body* (New York: Columbia University Press, 1988).
Gandelman, Claude, *Reading Pictures, Viewing Texts* (Bloomington and Indianapolis, IN: Indiana University Press, 1991).
Gandhi, Leela, *Postcolonial Theory: A Critical Introduction* (Edinburgh: Edinburgh University Press, 1998).
Gandhi, Mohandas K., *An Autobiography: The Story of My Experiments with Truth*, trans. by Mahadev H. Desai, foreword by Sissela Bok (Boston, MA: Beacon Press, 1957).
Garland-Thomson, Rosemarie, 'The Politics of Staring: Visual Rhetorics of Disability in Popular Photography', in *Disability Studies: Enabling the Humanities*, ed. by Sharon L. Snyder, Brenda Jo Brueggemann and Rosemarie Garland-Thomson (New York: The Modern Language Association of America, 2002), pp. 56–75.
— 'Introduction: From Wonder to Error – A Genealogy of Freak Discourse in Modernity', in *Freakery: Cultural Spectacles of the Extraordinary Body*, ed. by Rosemarie Garland-Thomson, foreword by Leslie A. Fiedler (New York: New York University Press, 1996), pp. 1–19.
Gauch, Suzanne, *Liberating Shahrazad: Feminism, Postcolonialism and Islam* (Minneapolis, MN: University of Minnesota Press, 2007).
— 'Telling the Tale of a Body Devoured by Narrative', *differences: A Journal of Feminist Cultural Studies* 11.1 (1999) 179–202 <http://muse.jhu.edu/journals/difference/v011/11.1gauch.html> [accessed 6 November 2004].
Georgis, Dina, '*Falling* for Jazz: Desire, Dissonance and Racial Collaboration', *Canadian Review of American Studies* 35.2 (2005), 215–29.
Gerber, David A., 'The "Careers" of People Exhibited in Freak Shows: The Problem of Volition and Valorization', in *Freakery: Cultural Spectacles of the Extraordinary Body*, ed. by Rosemarie Garland-Thomson, foreword by Leslie A. Fiedler (New York: New York University Press, 1996), pp. 38–54.
Gershovich, Moshe, 'Collaboration and "Pacification": French Conquest, Moroccan Combatants and the Transformation of the Middle Atlas', *Comparative Studies of South Asia, Africa and the Middle East* 24 (2004), 141–9.
Gilbert, Helen and Joanne Tompkins, *Postcolonial Drama: Theory, Practice, Politics* (London: Routledge, 1996).
Gillese, Virginia T., 'Isolation as Existence – *The Guest House and Other Stories* by Kristjanna Gunnars/ *Out on Main Street* by Shani Mootoo', *Canadian Literature* 145 (1995), 131–2.
Gilman, Sander, *Disease and Representation: Images of Illness from Madness to AIDS* (Ithaca, NY: Cornell University Press, 1998).
— *Freud, Race and Gender* (Princeton, NJ: Princeton University Press, 1993).
— *Inscribing the Other* (Lincoln, NE: University of Nebraska, 1991).

— *Difference and Pathology: Stereotypes of Sexuality, Race and Madness* (Ithaca, NY and London: Cornell University Press, 1985).

Gilmore, Leigh, 'Agency without Mastery: Chronic Pain and Posthuman Life Writing', *Biography* 35.1 (2012), 83–98.

Gilroy, Paul, *After Empire: Melancholia or Convivial Culture?* (Oxford: Routledge, 2004).

— *Against Race: Imagining Political Culture Beyond the Color Line* (Cambridge, MA: Harvard University Press, 2000).

— *The Black Atlantic: Modernity and Double-Conciousness* (London: Verso Books, 1993).

Glissant, Edouard, *Poetics of Relation*, trans. by Betsy Wing (Ann Arbor: University of Michigan Press, 1997).

Gohlke, Mary, with Max Jennings, *I'll Take Tomorrow: The Story of a Courageous Woman who Dared to Subject Herself to a Medical Experiment – the First Successful Heart-Lung Transplant* (New York: M. Evans & Co., 1985).

Goldie, Terry, 'Answering the Questions', in *Is Canada Postcolonial: Unsettling Canadian Literature*, ed. by Laura Moss (Waterloo, ON: Wilfred Laurier University Press, 2003), pp. 300–11.

— 'Introduction: Queerly Postcolonial', *ARIEL* 30.2 (1999), 9–26.

— 'Saint Fanon and "Homosexual Territory"', in *Frantz Fanon: Critical Perspectives*, ed. by Anthony C. Alessandrini (London: Routledge, 1999), pp. 75–86.

Gontard, Marc, 'Le Récit meta-narratif chez Tahar Ben Jelloun', in *Tahar Ben Jelloun: stratégies d'écriture*, ed. by Mansour M'Henni (Paris: Éditions L'Harmattan, 1993), pp. 99–118.

Gopinath, Gayatri, *Impossible Desires: Queer Diasporas and South Asian Public Cultures* (Durham, NC and London: Duke University Press, 2005).

Gordon, Neta, 'Twin Tales: Narrative Profusion and Genealogy in *Fall on Your Knees*', *Canadian Review of American Studies* 35.2 (2005), 159–76.

Gossai, Hemchand and Nathanial Samuel Murrell (eds), *Religion, Culture and Tradition in the Caribbean* (Hampshire: Macmillan Press, 2000).

Gould, Timothy, 'The Unhappy Performative', in *Performativity and Performance*, ed. by Andrew Parker and Eve Kosofsky Sedgwick (New York and London: Routledge, 1995), pp. 19–44.

Greenstein, G., 'Homi Bhabha and a Reply', *American Scholar* 61.4 (1992), 636.

Griffin, Tim, Beatriz Colomina and Homi Bhabha, 'Domesticity at War: Beatriz Colomina and Homi K. Bhabha in Conversation', *Artforum International* 45.10 (2007), 442–7.

Griffiths, Gareth, 'The Post-Colonial Project: Critical Approaches and Problems', in *New National and Post-Colonial Literatures*, ed. by Bruce King (Oxford: Clarendon, 1996), pp. 164–77.

Grosz, Elizabeth, 'Intolerable Ambiguity: Freaks as/at the Limit', in *Freakery: Cultural Spectacles of the Extraordinary Body*, ed. by Rosemarie Garland-Thomson, foreword by Leslie A. Fiedler (New York: New York University Press, 1996), pp. 55–66.

Habermas, Jürgen, *The Structural Transformation of the Public Sphere: An Inquiry into a Category of Bourgeois Society*, trans. by Thomas Burger (Cambridge: MIT Press, 1989).

Haddour, Azzedine (ed. and intro.), *The Fanon Reader* (London: Pluto, 2006).

Hage, Ghassan, *White Nation: Fantasies of White Supremacy in a Multicultural Society* (Annandale, NSW: Pluto Press, 1998).

Halberstam, Judith, *In a Queer Time and Place: Transgender Bodies, Subcultural Lives* (New York and London: New York University Press, 2005).

— '"A Writer of Misfits": "John" Radclyffe Hall and the Discourse of Inversion', in *Palatable Poison: Critical Perspectives on The Well of Loneliness*, ed. by Laura Doan and Jay Prosser (New York: Columbia University Press, 2001), pp. 145–61.
— *Female Masculinity* (Durham, NC: Duke University Press, 1998).
— 'Mackdaddy, Superfly, Rapper: Gender, Race and Masculinity in the Drag King Scene', in *Social Text: Queer Transexions of Race, Nation and Gender*, ed. by Philip Brian Harper, Anne McClintock, José Esteban Muñoz and Trish Rosen 15.3 and 4 (1997), 104–31.
Hall, Lynda, 'Shani Mootoo: An Interview with Lynda Hall', *Journal of Lesbian Studies* 4.4 (2000), 107–13.
Hall, Stuart, 'The Question of Cultural Identity', in *Modernity and Its Futures*, ed. by Stuart Hall, David Hold and Tony McGrew (Cambridge: Polity Press in association with the Open University, 1992), pp. 273–326.
Hamil, Mustapha, 'Exile and Its Discontents: Malika Mokaddem's *Forbidden Woman*', *Research in African Literatures* 35.1 (2004), 52–65.
— 'Rewriting Identity and History: The Sliding *Barre(s)* in Tahar Ben Jelloun's *The Sacred Night*', in *Maghrebian Mosaic: A Literature in Transition*, ed. by Mildred Mortimer (London: Lynne Rienner Publishers, 2001), pp. 61–80.
Hamilton, Roberta, *Gendering the Vertical Mosaic: Feminist Challenges to the Canadian State* (London: Canadian High Commission, 1998).
Haraway, Donna J., *Simians, Cyborgs and Women: The Reinvention of Nature* (London: Free Association Books, 1991).
— *Primate Visions: Gender, Race and Nature in the World of Modern Science* (London: Routledge, 1989).
Hardt, Michael, 'For Love or Money', *Cultural Anthropology*, 26.4 (2011), 676–82.
Harter, Deborah, *Bodies in Pieces: Fantastic Narrative and the Poetics of the Fragment* (Stanford, CA: Stanford University Press, 1996).
Hartman, Saidiya V., *Scenes of Subjection: Terror, Slavery and Self-Making in Nineteenth-Century America* (New York and Oxford: Oxford University Press, 1997).
Harvey, Robert, 'Purloined Letters: Intertextuality and Intersexuality in Tahar Ben Jelloun's *The Sand Child*', in *Articulations of Difference: Gender Studies and Writing in French*, ed. by Dominique D. Fisher and Lawrence R. Schehr (Stanford, CA: Stanford University Press, 1997), pp. 226–45.
Hawley, John C. (ed.), *Writing the Nation: Self and Country in the Post-Colonial Imagination* (Amsterdam and Atlanta, GA: Rodopi, 1996).
Hayes, Jarrod, *Queer Nations: Marginal Sexualities in the Maghreb* (Chicago, IL and London: University of Chicago Press, 2000).
Hegel, G. W. F., *Phenomenology of Spirit*, trans. by A. V. Miller (Oxford: Clarendon Press, 1977).
Hinchcliffe, Peter (ed.), *Family Fictions in Canadian Literature* (Waterloo, ON: University of Waterloo Press, 1988).
Hirsch, Marianne, 'Marked by Memory: Feminist Reflections on Trauma and Transmission', in *Extremities: Trauma, Testimony and Community*, ed. by Nancy Miller and Jason Tougaw (Urbana and Chicago, IL: University of Illinois Press, 2002), pp. 71–91.
— *Family Frames: Photography, Narrative and Postmemory* (Cambridge, MA: Harvard University Press, 1997).

Hogle, Linda F., *Recovering the Nation's Body: Cultural Memory, Medicine and the Politics of Redemption* (New Brunswick, NJ: Rutgers University Press, 1999).
Hoisington, William A., Jr., *Lyautey and the French Conquest of Morocco* (London: Macmillan Press, 1995).
hooks, bell, *The Will to Change: Men, Masculinity and Love* (New York: Simon & Schuster, 2004).
— *We Real Cool: Black Men and Masculinity* (New York and London: Routledge, 2004).
— *All About Love: New Visions* (New York: HarperCollins, 2001).
— *Art on My Mind: Visual Politics* (New York: New Press, 1995).
— *Black Looks: Race and Representation* (Boston, MA: South End Press, 1992).
House, Jim, 'L'Impossible contrôle d'une ville coloniale? Casablanca, décembre 1952', *Géneses* 86 (2012), 78–103.
Howells, Coral Ann, *Where Are the Voices Coming From? Canadian Culture and the Legacies of History* (New York and Amsterdam: Rodopi, 2004), pp. 53–60.
— *Contemporary Canadian Women's Fiction: Refiguring Identities* (New York: Palgrave Macmillan, 2003).
— *Private and Fictional Words: Canadian Women Novelists of the 1970s and 1980s* (London and New York: Methuen, 1987).
Howells, Coral Ann and Lynette Hunter (eds), *Narrative Strategies in Canadian Literature* (Milton Keynes: Open University Press, 1991).
Hunter, Lynette, *Literary Value/Cultural Power: Verbal Arts in the Twenty-First Century* (Manchester: Manchester University Press, 2001).
Hutcheon, Linda, *The Politics of Postmodernism* (London: Routledge, 2002).
— '"Circling the Downspout of Empire": Post-Colonialism and Postmodernism', *ARIEL* 20.4 (1989), 149–75.
— *A Poetics of Postmodernism: History, Theory, Fiction* (London: Routledge, 1988).
— *The Canadian Postmodern: A Study of Contemporary English-Canadian Fiction* (Toronto, ON and Oxford: Oxford University Press, 1988).
Ibnlfassi, Laïla, 'The Virgin, the Whore, the Witch and the Saint: Tahar Ben Jelloun's *La Nuit de l'erreur*', *Nottingham French Studies* 40.1 (2001), 13–19.
— 'The Ambiguity of Self-Structure: Tahar Ben Jelloun's *L'Enfant de sable* and *La Nuit sacrée*', in *Francophone Voices*, ed. by Kamal Salhi (Exeter: Elm Bank Publishers, 1999), pp. 157–69.
Irigaray, Luce, *Le Partage de la parole* (Oxford: European Humanities Research Centre, University of Oxford, 2001).
— *I Love to You: Sketch for a Felicity within History*, trans. by Alison Martin (New York: Routledge, 1996).
— *An Ethics of Sexual Difference*, trans. by Carolyn Burke and Gillian C. Gill (Ithaca, NY: Cornell University Press, 1993).
— *Elemental Passions*, trans. by J. Collie and J. Still (London: Athlone Press, 1992).
— *This Sex Which Is Not One*, trans. by Catherine Porter (New York: Cornell University Press, [1977] 1985).
Jacobs, Karen, 'Optic/Haptic/Abject: Revisioning Indigenous Media in Victor Masayesva, Jr. and Leslie Marmon Silko', *Journal of Visual Culture* 3.3 (2004), 291–316.
James, Louis, *Caribbean Literature in English* (London and New York: Longman, 1999).
Jameson, Frederic, 'Third-World Literature in the Era of Multinational Capitalism', *Social Text* 15 (1986), 66–88.

Jay, Martin, *Downcast Eyes: The Denigration of Vision in Twentieth-Century French Thought* (Berkeley, CA and London: University of California Press, 1994).
Kale, Madhavi, *Fragments of Empire: Capital, Slavery and Indian Indentured Labor Migration to the British Caribbean* (Philadelphia, PA: University of Pennsylvania Press, 1998).
Kamal-Trense, Nadia, *Tahar Ben Jelloun: L'Ecrivain des villes* (Paris: Éditions L'Harmattan, 1998).
Kamboureli, Smaro, *Scandalous Bodies: Diasporic Literature in English Canada* (Don Mills, ON and Oxford: Oxford University Press, 2000).
Kaye, Jacqueline and Abdelhamid Zoubir, *The Ambiguous Compromise: Language, Literature and National Identity in Algeria and Morocco* (New York: Routledge, 1990).
Kempadoo, Kamala, *Sexing the Caribbean: Gender, Race and Sexual Labor* (New York: Routledge, 2004).
Khanna, Ranjanna, *Dark Continents: Psychoanalysis and Colonialism* (Durham, NC: Duke University Press, 2003).
Kilby, Jane, *Violence and the Cultural Politics of Trauma* (Edinburgh: Edinburgh University Press, 2007).
— 'Carved in Skin: Bearing Witness to Self-Harm', in *Thinking Through the Skin*, ed. by Sara Ahmed and Jackie Stacey (London: Routledge, 2001), pp. 124–42.
Kincaid, Jamaica ,'In History', *Callaloo* 24.2 (2001), 620–6.
— *My Garden (Book)* (New York: Farrar, Straus & Giroux, 1999).
Kosofsky Sedgwick, Eve, *Touching Feeling: Affect, Pedagogy, Performativity* (Durham, NC and London: Duke University Press, 2003).
— *Tendencies* (London: Routledge, 1994).
— *Epistemology of the Closet* (Berkeley, CA: University of California Press, 1990).
— *The Coherence of Gothic Conventions* (New York and London: Methuen, 1986).
Kosofsky Sedgwick, Eve (ed.), *Novel Gazing: Queer Readings in Fiction* (Durham, NC and London: Duke University Press, 1997).
Kosofsky Sedgwick, Eve and Adam Frank, 'Shame in the Cybernetic Fold: Reading Silvan Tomkins', in *Shame and Its Sisters: A Silvan Tomkins Readers*, ed. by Eve Kosofsky Sedgwick and Adam Frank (Durham, NC and London: Duke University Press, 1995), pp. 1–28.
Koustas, June, 'Ann-Marie MacDonald in France: A Touch of Canada', *La Linguistique* 40.1 (2004), 97–107.
Kristeva, Julia, *Powers of Horror: An Essay on Abjection*, trans. by Leon S. Rondiez (New York and Guildford: Columbia University Press, 1982).
— *Pouvoirs de l'horreur: essai sur l'abjection* (Paris: Éditions du Seuil, 1980).
Kyong Chun, Wendy Hui, 'Unbearable Witness: Toward a Politics of Listening', in *Extremities: Trauma, Testimony and Community*, ed. by Nancy Miller and Jason Tougaw (Urbana and Chicago, IL: University of Illinois Press, 2002), pp. 143–65.
Kyungwon Hong, Grace, '"A Shared Queerness": Colonialism, Transnationalism and Sexuality in Shani Mootoo's *Cereus Blooms at Night*', *Meridians: Feminism, Race and Transnationalism* 7.1 (2006), 73–103.
Lacan, Jacques, *Ecrits: A Selection*, trans. by Alan Sheridan (London: Routledge, [1966] 1977).
LaCapra, Dominick, *History and Reading: Tocqueville, Foucault, French Studies* (Toronto, ON: Toronto University Press, 2000).

Lakoff, George, *Philosophy in the Flesh: The Embodied Mind and Its Challenge to Western Thought* (New York: Basic Books, 1999).
— *Women, Fire and Other Dangerous Things: What Categories Reveal About the Mind* (Chicago, IL: University of Chicago Press, 1987).
Laqueur, Thomas, *Solitary Sex: A Cultural History of Masturbation* (New York: Zone Books, 2003).
— 'Sex, Gender and Desire in the Industrial Revolution', in *The Industrial Revolution and British Society: Festschrift for R.M. Hartwell*, ed. by Patrick O'Brien and Roland Quinault (Cambridge: Cambridge University Press, 1993), pp. 100–23.
— *Making SEX: From the Greeks to Freud* (Cambridge, MA: Harvard University Press, 1990).
Laurence, K. O., *A Question of Labour: Indentured Immigration into Trinidad and British Guiana, 1875–1917* (Kingston, Jamaica: Ian Randle Publishers, 1994).
Lee Lockhart, Melanie, '"Taking Them to the Moon in a Station Wagon": An Interview with Ann-Marie MacDonald', *Canadian Review of American Studies* 35.2 (2005), 139–57.
Levinas, Emmanuel, 'Ethics as First Philosophy', in *The Levinas Reader*, ed. by Sean Hand (Oxford: Blackwell, 1989), pp. 75–89.
— *Totality and Infinity: An Essay on Exteriority*, trans. by Alphonso Lingis (Pittsburgh, PA: Duquesne Press, 1969).
Levinson, Brett, 'Sex Without Sex, Queering the Market, the Collapse of the Political, the Death of Difference and AIDS', *Diacritics* 29.3 (1999), 81–101.
Levy, Sophie, '"This Dark Echo Calls Him Home" – Writing Father-Daughter Incest in Canadian Immigrant Fiction', *University of Toronto Quarterly* 71.4 (2002), 864–80.
Lewis, Tanya, 'Eating Identity: Food and the Construction of Region in the *Cure of Death by Lightning* and *Fall on Your Knees*', *Essays on Canadian Writing* 78 (2003), 86–109.
Lindenlauf, Nelly, *Tahar Ben Jelloun: 'Les Yeux baissés'* (Brussels: Éditions Labor, 1996).
Lindfors, Bernth, 'Ethnological Show Business: Footlighting the Dark Continent', in *Freakery: Cultural Spectacles of the Extraordinary Body*, ed. by Rosemarie Garland-Thomson, foreword by Leslie A. Fiedler (New York: New York University Press, 1996), pp. 207–18.
Lionnet, Françoise, *Postcolonial Representations: Women, Literature, Identity* (Ithaca, NY: Cornell University Press, 1995).
— *Post/colonial Conditions: Exiles, Migrations and Nomadisms* (New Haven, NJ: Yale University Press, 1993).
— *Autobiographical Voices: Race, Gender, Self-Portraiture* (Ithaca, NY: Cornell University Press, 1989).
Lionnet, Françoise and Shu-mei Shih (eds), *Minor Transnationalism* (Durham, NC: Duke University Press, 2005).
Lloyd, Moya, 'Performativity, Parody, Politics', *Theory, Culture and Society* 16.2 (1999), 195–213.
Look Lai, Walton, *Indentured Labor, Caribbean Sugar: Chinese and Indian Immigrants to the British West Indies, 1838–1918*, intro. by Sidney W. Mintz (Baltimore, MD and London: Johns Hopkins University Press, 1993).
Lorde, Audre, 'Age, Race, Class and Sex: Women Redefining Difference', in *The Woman Question*, ed. by Mary Evans (London: Sage Publications, 1994), pp. 36–41.
— *Sister Outsider: Essays and Speeches* (Berkeley, CA: Crossing Press, 1984).

Lowe, Lisa, 'Literary Nomadics in Francophone Allegories of Postcolonialism: Pham Van Ky and Tahar Ben Jelloun', *Yale French Studies* 82.1 (1993), 43–61.

Maazaoui, Abbes, '*L'Enfant de sable* et *La Nuit sacrée* ou le corps tragique', *The French Review* 69.1 (1995), 68–77.

Mairs, Nancy, 'Sex and Death and the Crippled Body: A Meditation', in *Disability Studies: Enabling the Humanities*, ed. by Sharon L. Snyder, Brenda Jo Brueggemann and Rosemarie Garland-Thomson (New York: The Modern Language Association of America, 2002), pp. 156–70.

Mallot, J. Edward, 'Body Politics and the Body Politic: Memory as Human Inscription in Shauna Singh Baldwin's *What the Body Remembers*', *Interventions: International Journal of Postcolonial Studies* 8.2 (2006), 165–77.

Mannur, Anita, 'Nostalgia: Authenticity, Nationalism and Diaspora', *Multi-Ethnic Literature of the United States* 32.4 (2007), 11–31.

Maracle, Lee, 'The "Post-Colonial" Imagination', *Fuse* 16.1 (1992), 12–15.

Markotić, Nicole and Robert McRuer, 'Leading with Your Head: On the Borders of Disability, Sexuality and the Nation', in *Sex and Disability*, ed. by Robert McRuer and Anna Mollow (Durham, NC and London: Duke University Press, 2012) pp. 165–82.

Marks, Laura U., *Touch: Sensuous Theory and Multisensory Media* (Minneapolis, MN: University of Minnesota Press, 2002).

— *The Skin of the Film: Intercultural Cinema, Embodiment and the Senses* (Durham, NC and London: Duke University Press, 2000).

Marrouchi, Mustapha, 'My Aunt is a Man: Ce « je »-là multiple', *Comparative Literature* 54.4 (2002), 325–56.

— and Patricia Geesey, 'Breaking Up/Down/Out of the Boundaries: Tahar Ben Jelloun', *Research in African Literatures* 21.4 (1990), 71–83.

Martin, Biddy, 'Sexualities without Genders and Other Queer Utopias', *Diacritics* 24.2/3 (1994), 104–21.

Masmoudi, Ikram, 'Aventure et itinéraire d'un nom propre arabe dans *L'enfant de sable* de Tahar Ben Jelloun', *Arabica* 49.2 (2002), 235–44.

Masson, Jeffrey, *A Dark Science: Women, Sexuality and Psychiatry in the Nineteenth Century*, trans. by Jeffrey Masson and Marianne Loring (New York: Farrar, Strauss & Giroux, 1986).

Matthews, Sara, Trish Salah and Dina Georgis, 'Introductory Notes – Memory Foretelling the Story: Essays on *Fall on Your Knees*', *Canadian Review of American Studies* 35.2 (2005), 125–38.

Maugière, Bénédicte (ed.), *Cultural Identities in Canadian Literature* (New York: Peter Lang, 1998).

Mbembe, Achille, 'Necropolitics', trans. by Libby Meintjes, *Public Culture* 15.1 (2003), 11–40.

McClintock, Anne, '"No Longer in a Future Heaven": Gender, Race and Nationalism', in *Dangerous Liaisons: Gender, Nation and Postcolonial Perspectives*, ed. by Anne McClintock, Aamir Mufti and Ella Shohat (Minneapolis, MN: University of Minnesota, 1997), pp. 89–112.

— *Imperial Leather: Race, Gender and Sexuality in the Colonial Contest* (New York: Routledge, 1995).

— 'The Angel of Progress: Pitfalls of the Term "Post-colonialism"', in *Colonial Discourse and Postcolonial Theory: A Reader*, ed. by Patrick Williams and Laura Chrisman (London: Harvester Wheatshaft, 1994), pp. 291–304.

— 'Screwing the System: Sexwork, Race and the Law', *boundary* 11.19.2 (1992), 70–95.

McCormack, Donna, 'Illicit Intimacies, the *Rāmāyana* and Synaesthetic Remembering in Shani Mootoo's *Valmiki's Daughter*', in *Critical Perspectives on Indo-Caribbean Women's Literature* (Routledge Research in Postcolonial Literatures), ed. by Joy Mahabir and Mariam Pirbhai (New York: Routledge, 2012), pp. 203–28.

— 'Multisensory Poetics and Politics in Shani Mootoo's *The Wild Woman in the Woods* and *Valmiki's Daughter*', *The Journal of West Indian Literature* 19.2 (2011), 9–33.

— 'Gender and Colonial Transitioning: Frantz Fanon's Algerian Freedom Fighters in Moroccan and Caribbean Novels?', *Journal of Transatlantic Studies* 7.3 (2009), 279–93.

McNay, Lois, 'Subject, Psyche and Agency: The Work of Judith Butler', *Theory, Culture and Society* 16.2 (1999), 175–93.

McRuer, Robert, 'Cripping Queer Politics, or the Dangers of Neoliberalism', guest ed. by Joseph N. DeFilippis, Lisa Duggan, Kenyon Farrow and Richard Kim, 'A New Queer Agenda', *The Scholar & Feminist Online* 10.1–10.2 (2011/2012) <www.sfonline.barnard.edu/a-new-queer-agenda/cripping-queer-politics-or-the-dangers-of-neoliberalism/2/> [accessed 27 September 2011].

— *Crip Theory: Cultural Signs of Queerness and Disability*, foreword by Michael Bérubé (New York and London: New York University Press, 2006).

— 'Compulsory Able-Bodiedness and Queer/Disabled Existence', in *Disability Studies: Enabling the Humanities*, ed. by Sharon L. Snyder, Brenda Jo Brueggemann and Rosemarie Garland-Thomson (New York: The Modern Language Association of America, 2002), pp. 88–99.

McRuer, Robert and Anna Mollow, 'Introduction', in *Sex and Disability*, ed. by Robert McRuer and Anna Mollow (Durham, NC and London: Duke University Press, 2012), pp. 1–34.

McVeigh, Karen, 'Obama Tells Officials to Use Overseas Aid to Promote Gay Rights', *The Guardian*, 6 December 2011 <www.guardian.co.uk/world/2011/dec/06/us-overseas-aid-human-rights?INTCMP=SRCH> [accessed 6 December 2011].

Mehta, Brinda, *Diasporic (Dis)locations: Indo-Caribbean Women Writers Negotiate the Kala Pani* (Kingston, Jamaica: University of West Indies Press, 2004).

Mensah, Joseph, *Black Canadian: History, Experiences, Social Conditions* (Halifax, NS: Fernwood, 2002).

Mercer, Kobena, *Welcome to the Jungle: New Positions in Black Cultural Studies* (New York: Routledge, 1994).

Mernissi, Fatima, *Scheherazade Goes West: Different Cultures, Different Harems* (New York: Washington Square Press, 2001).

— *The Harem Within: Tales of a Moroccan Girlhood* (London: Doubleday, 1994).

— *The Forgotten Queens of Islam* (Cambridge: Polity, 1993).

— *The Veil and the Male Elite: A Feminist Interpretation of Women's Rights in Islam*, trans. by Mary Jo Lakeland (Reading, MA: Addison-Wesley, 1991).

— *Doing Daily Battle: Interviews with Moroccan Women*, trans. by Mary Jo Lakeland (New Brunswick, NJ: Rutgers University Press, 1989).

M'Henni, Mansour, 'Ecrivain (–) Public: Tahar Ben Jelloun', in *Tahar Ben Jelloun: stratégies d'écriture*, ed. by Mansour M'Henni (Paris: Éditions L'Harmattan, 1993), pp. 25–33.

Miller, Nancy and Jason Tougaw (eds), *Extremities: Trauma, Testimony and Community* (Urbana and Chicago, IL: University of Illinois Press, 2002).

Minh-ha, Trinh T., 'Not You/Like You: Postcolonial Women and the Interlocking Questions of Identity and Difference', in *Dangerous Liaisons: Gender, Nation and*

Postcolonial Perspectives, ed. by Anne McClintock, Aamir Mufti and Ella Shohat (Minneapolis, MN: University of Minnesota, 1997), pp. 415–19.
Mishra, Vijay, *The Literature of the Indian Diaspora: Theorizing the Diasporic Imaginary* (New York: Routledge, 2007).
Misrahi-Barak, Judith, '"Beginners" Luck among Caribbean-Canadian Writers: Nalo Hopkinson, André Alexis and Shani Mootoo', *Commonwealth Essays and Studies* 22.1 (1999), 89–96.
Mitchell, David T. and Sharon L. Snyder, 'Narrative Prosthesis and the Materiality of Metaphor', in *Disability Studies: Enabling the Humanities*, ed. by Sharon L. Snyder, Brenda Jo Brueggemann and Rosemarie Garland-Thomson (New York: The Modern Language Association of America, 2002), pp. 15–30.
Mitchell, W. J. T., *Picture Theory: Essays on Visual and Verbal Interpretation* (Chicago, IL: University of Chicago Press, 1994).
— *Iconology: Image, Text, Ideology* (Chicago, IL and London: University of Chicago Press, 1986).
Mohanty, Chandra T., 'Introduction: Cartographies of Struggle: Third World Women and the Politics of Feminism', in *Third World Women and The Politics of Feminism*, ed. by Chandra Talpade Mohanty, Ann Russo and Lourdes Torres (Bloomington and Indianapolis, IN: Indiana University Press, 1991), pp. 1–47.
Mootoo, Shani, *He Drown She in the Sea* (New York: Grove Press, 2005).
Morrison, Toni, *Beloved* (London: Vintage, 1997).
Moss, Laura, 'Is Canada Postcolonial? Introducing the Question', in *Is Canada Postcolonial: Unsettling Canadian Literature*, ed. by Laura Moss (Waterloo, ON: Wilfred Laurier University Press, 2003), pp. 1–23.
Moura, Jean-Marc, *Littératures francophones et théorie postcoloniale* (Vendôme: Presse Universitaire de France, 2001).
Mufti, Aamir and Ella Shohat, 'Introduction', in *Dangerous Liaisons: Gender, Nation and Postcolonial Perspectives*, ed. by Anne McClintock, Aamir Mufti and Ella Shohat (Minneapolis, MN: University of Minnesota, 1997), pp. 1–12.
Mukherjee, Arun Prabha, *Postcolonialism: My Living* (Toronto, ON: Tsar, 1998).
Nancy, Jean-Luc, *L'Intrus* (Paris: Éditions Galilée, 2000).
— *The Inoperative Community*, ed. by Peter Conner, foreword by Christopher Fynsk, trans. by Peter Connor, Lisa Garbus, Michael Holland and Simona Sawhney (London and Minneapolis, MN: University of Minnesota Press, 1991).
Nelson, William E., *Black Atlantic Politics: Dilemmas of Political Empowerment in Boston and Liverpool* (Albany, NY: State University of New York Press, 2000).
Niesen de Abruña, Laura, 'Homi Bhabha as Public Intellectual at the Turn of the Millennium', *Modern Language Studies* 33.1 (2003), 90–112.
Niranjana, Tejaswini, *Mobilizing India: Women, Music and Migration between India and Trinidad* (Durham, NC: Duke University Press, 2006).
— 'Left to the Imagination: Indian Nationalisms and Female Sexuality in Trinidad', in *A Question of Silence? The Sexual Economies of Modern India*, ed. by Mary John and Janaki Nair (New Delhi: Kali for Women, 1998), pp. 111–38.
— *Siting Translation: History, Post-Structuralism and the Colonial Context* (Berkeley, CA: University of California Press, 1992).
Nixon, Rob, *London Calling: V. S. Naipaul, Postcolonial Mandarin* (Oxford: Oxford University Press, 1992).

Noel, Peter and Robert Marriott, 'Batty Boys in Babylon: Can Gay West Indians Survive the "Boom Bye Bye" Possees?', *Village Voice* 12 (1992), 29–36.
Northrup, David, *Indentured Labor in the Age of Imperialism, 1834–1922* (Cambridge: Cambridge University Press, 1995).
Nussbaum, Felicity A., 'Toward Conceptualizing Diary', in *Studies in Autobiography*, ed. by James Olney (New York and Oxford: Oxford University Press, 1988), pp. 128–40.
Nussbaum, Martha, 'The Professor of Parody', *New Republic*, 22 February 1999 <www.tnr.com/archive/0299/022299/nussbaum022299.html> [accessed 18 January 2011].
O'Callaghan, Evelyn (ed.), *Women Writing the West Indies 1804–1939: 'A Hot Place, Belonging to Us'* (London: Routledge, 2004).
O'Meara, Jonathon, 'Remembering the Past – Fran Stagg', 26 January 2006 <www.anphoblacht.com/contents/14729> [accessed 1 February 2012].
Oliver, Kelly, *Witnessing: Beyond Recognition* (Minneapolis, MN: University of Minnesota Press, 2001).
Olson, Gary A., 'Staging the Politics of Difference: Homi Bhabha's Critical Literacy', in *Race, Rhetoric and the Postcolonial*, ed. by Gary A. Olson and Lynn Worsham (Albany, NY: State University of New York Press, 1999), pp. 3–39.
Ong, Aihwa, *Neoliberalism as Exception: Mutations in Citizenship and Sovereignty* (Durham, NC and London: Duke University Press, 2006).
— *Flexible Citizenship: The Cultural Logic of Transnationality* (Durham, NC: Duke University Press, 1998).
Oosterhuis, Harry, *Stepchildren of Nature: Krafft-Ebing, Psychiatry and the Making of Sexual Identity* (Chicago, IL: University of Chicago Press, 2000).
Orlando, Valérie, *Nomadic Voices of Exile: Feminine Identity in Francophone Literature of the Maghreb* (Athens, OH: Ohio University Press, 1999).
— 'Beyond Postcolonial Discourse: New Problematics of Feminine Identity in Contemporary Francophone Literature' (PhD diss., Brown University, Providence, 1996).
Osava, Mario, 'BRAZIL: Poor Sell Organs to Trans-Atlantic Trafficking Ring', *IPS*, 24 February 2004 <www.ipsnews.net/2004/02/brazil-poor-sell-organs-to-trans-atlantic-trafficking-ring/> [accessed 28 February 2012].
Ouzgane, Lahoucine, 'Masculinity as Virility in Tahar ben Jelloun's Work', *Contagion: Journal of Violence, Mimesis and Culture* 4 (1997), 1–13.
Pappenberg, Bettina and Marta Zarzycka, *Carnal Aesthetics: Transgressive Imagery and Feminist Politics* (London: Palgrave Macmillan, 2013).
Park, Sangkee, 'Homi Bhabha's Critique of Postmodernism', *Journal of English Language and Literature* 46.2 (2000), 549–73.
Parker, Andrew and Eve Kosofsky Sedgwick, 'Introduction: Performativity and Performance', in *Performativity and Performance*, ed. by Andrew Parker and Eve Kosofsky Sedgwick (New York and London: Routledge, 1995), pp. 1–18.
Parro, Gabriella, '"Who's Your Father, Dear?" Haunted Bloodlines and Miscegenation in Ann-Marie MacDonald's *Fall on Your Knees*', *Canadian Review of American Studies* 35.2 (2005), 177–93.
Parry, Benita, *Postcolonial Studies: A Materialist Critique* (London and New York: Routledge, 2004).
— 'Signs of Our Times: A Discussion of Homi Bhabha's *The Location of Culture*', in *Learning Places: The Afterlives of Area Studies*, ed. and intro. by Masao Miyoshi and H. D. Harootunian (Durham, NC: Duke University Press, 2002), pp. 119–49.

— *Delusions and Discoveries: India in the British Imagination, 1880–1930* (London: Verso, 1998).
Pathak, Zakia and Rajeswari Sunder Rajan, 'Shahbano', in *Feminists Theorize the Political*, ed. by Judith Butler and Joan Scott (New York: Routledge, 1992), pp. 257–79.
Patton, Cindy, 'Performativity and Spatial Distinction: The End of AIDS Epidemiology', in *Performativity and Performance*, ed. by Andrew Parker and Eve Kosofsky Sedgwick (New York and London: Routledge, 1995), pp. 173–96.
Pennell, C. R., *Morocco Since 1830: A History* (London: Hurst & Co., 2000).
— *A Country with a Government and a Flag: The Rif War in Morocco, 1921–1926* (Boulder, CO: Middle East and North African Studies Press, 1986).
Phillips Casteel, Sarah, 'New World Pastoral: The Caribbean and Emplacement in Gisèle Pineau and Shani Mootoo', *Interventions: International Journal of Postcolonial Studies* 5.1 (2003), pp. 12–28.
Pirbhai, Mariam, *Mythologies of Migration, Vocabularies of Indenture: The Novels of the South Asian Diaspora in Africa, the Caribbean and Asia-Pacific* (Toronto, ON: University of Toronto Press, 2009).
Probyn, Elspeth, *Blush: Faces of Shame* (Minneapolis, MN: University of Minnesota Press, 2005).
— 'Eating Skin', in *Thinking Through the Skin*, ed. by Sara Ahmed and Jackie Stacey (London: Routledge, 2001), pp. 87–104.
— *Carnal Appetites: FoodSexIdentities* (London and New York: Routledge, 2000).
— 'Beyond Food/Sex: Eating and an Ethics of Existence', *Theory, Culture and Society* 16.2 (1999), 215–28.
Prosser, Jay, *Light in the Dark Room: Photography and Loss* (Minneapolis, MA: University of Minnesota Press, 2005).
— 'A Palinode on Photography and the Transsexual Real', in *Extremities: Trauma, Testimony and Community*, ed. by Nancy Miller and Jason Tougaw (Urbana and Chicago, IL: University of Illinois Press, 2002), pp. 238–59.
— 'Skin Memories', in *Thinking Through the Skin*, ed. by Sara Ahmed and Jackie Stacey (London: Routledge, 2001), pp. 52–68.
— '"Some Primitive Thing Conceived in a Turbulent Age of Transition": The Transsexual Emerging from the Well', in *Palatable Poison: Critical Perspectives on 'The Well of Loneliness'*, ed. by Laura Doan and Jay Prosser (New York: Columbia University Press, 2001), pp. 129–44.
— *Second Skins: The Body Narrative of Transsexuality* (New York: Columbia University Press, 1998).
Puar, Jasbir, 'The Cost of Getting Better: Suicide, Sensation, Switchpoints', *GLQ* 18.1 (2011), 149–58.
— *Terrorist Assemblages: Homonationalism in Queer Times* (London and Durham, NC: Duke University Press, 2007).
Puiu, Dana, 'Face-to-face in an Afterword', in *Identity and Alterity in Canadian Literature*, ed. by Dana Puiu (Cluj-Napoca: Risoprint, 2003), pp. 279–80.
— 'Pre-face to Face: Canada, Chromatic Iceberg of Memory', in *Identity and Alterity in Canadian Literature*, ed. by Dana Puiu (Cluj-Napoca: Risoprint, 2003), pp. xxv–xxxvii.
Quayson, Ato, *Aesthetic Nervousness* (New York: Columbia University Press, 2007).
Rabinow, Paul (ed.), *The Essential Works of Michel Foucault, 1954–1984, vol. 1, Ethics: Subjectivity and Truth*, trans. by Robert Hurley (London: Penguin, 2000).
— *The Foucault Reader* (London: Penguin, 1991).

Rashid, Ian Iqbal, 'Introduction to the Videos of Shani Mootoo', *Wide Angle: A Film Quarterly of Theory, Criticism and Practice* 17.1–4 (1995), 341–2.
Renk, Kathleen J., *Caribbean Shadows and Victorian Ghosts: Women's Writing and Decolonization* (Charlottesville, VA: University Press of Virginia, 1999).
Richardson, Ruth, *Death, Dissection and the Destitute: The Politics of the Corpse in Pre-Victorian Britain* (London: Routledge, 1988).
Rifkind, Candida, 'Screening Modernity: Cinema and Sexuality in Ann-Marie MacDonald's *Fall on Your Knees*', *Studies in Canadian Literature* 27.1 (2002), 29–50.
Rivet, Daniel, *Le Maghreb à l'épreuve de la colonisation* (Paris: Hachette littératures, 2002).
— *Le Maroc de Lyautey à Mohammed V: le double visage du Protectorat* (Paris: Denoël, 1999).
Roberts, Gillian, *Prizing Literature: The Celebration and Circulation of National Culture* (Toronto, ON: Toronto University Press, 2011).
Robinson, Laura M., 'Remodelling an Old-Fashioned Girl: Troubling Girlhood in Ann-Marie MacDonald's *Fall on Your Knees*', *Canadian Literature* 186 (2005), 30–45.
— '"Crossing Nature's Divide": Miscegenation and Lesbianism in *Fall on Your Knees*', in *Identity and Alterity in Canadian Literature*, ed. by Dana Puiu (Cluj-Napoca: Risoprint, 2003), pp. 213–25.
Robolin, Stéphanie, 'Gendered Hauntings: *The Joys of Motherhood*, Interpretative Acts and Postcolonial Theory', *Research in African Literatures* 35.3 (2004), 76–92.
Rollin, André, '*La Nuit sacrée* au peigne fin', *Lire* 146 (1988), 147–59.
Rosario, Vernon A. (ed.), *Science and Homosexualities* (London: Routledge, 1997).
Rosello, Mireille, *France and the Maghreb: Performative Encounters* (Gainesville, FL: University of Florida Press, 2005).
— *Postcolonial Hospitality: The Immigrant as Guest* (Stanford, CA: Stanford University Press, 2001).
Rosen, Miriam, 'A Conversation with Tahar Ben Jelloun: Toward a World Literature?', *Middle East Report* 163 (1990), 30–3.
Ross, F. Stuart, *Smashing H Block: The Popular Campaign against Criminalization and the Irish Hunger Strikes 1976–1982* (Liverpool: Liverpool University Press, 2012).
Roy, Parama, 'Meat-Eating, Masculinity and Renunciation in India: A Gandhian Grammar of Diet', *Gender and History* 14.1 (2002), 62–91.
Rukszto, Katarzyna, 'Out of Bounds: Perverse Longings, Transgressive Desire and the Limits of Multiculturalism: A Reading of *Fall on Your Knees*', *International Journal of Canadian Studies* 2 (2000), 17–34.
Rye, Gill, 'Uncertain Readings and Meaningful Dialogues: Language and Sexual Identity in Anne Garréta's *Sphinx* and Tahar Ben Jelloun's *L'Enfant de sable* and *La Nuit sacrée*', *Neophilologus* 84 (2000), 531–40.
Saady, Fouzilla, 'Figure littéraire: écriture androgyne et discours subversif dans *L'Enfant de sable* et *La Nuit sacrée*', in *Traversée du français dans les signes littéraires Marocains*, ed. by Yvette Bénayoun-Szmidt, Hédi Bouraoui and Najib Redouane (Toronto, ON: Édition La Source, 1996), pp. 201–10.
Sacks, Oliver, *An Anthropologist on Mars* (London: Picador, 1995).
— *A Leg to Stand On* (London: Picador, 1991).
— *The Man Who Mistook His Wife for a Hat* (New York: Harper, 1990).
Said, Edward W., *Orientalism* (London: Penguin Group, 1991).
Saigh Bousta, Rachida, 'Béances du récit dans *La Nuit sacrée*', in *Tahar Ben Jelloun: stratégies d'écriture*, ed. by Mansour M'Henni (Paris: Éditions L'Harmattan, 1993), pp. 119–29.

— *Lecture des récits de Tahar Benjelloun: écriture, mémoire et imaginaire . . .* (Casablanca: Afrique Orient, 1992).
Salah, Trish, 'What Memory Wants: Broken Tongue, Stranger Fugue in *Fall on Your Knees*', *Canadian Review of American Studies* 35.2 (2005), 231–49.
Salhi, Kamal, 'Rethinking Francophone Culture: Africa and the Caribbean between History and Theory', *Research in African Literatures* 35.1 (2004), 9–29.
Samaroo, Brinsley, 'The Presbyterian Canadian Mission as an Agent of Integration in Trinidad during the Nineteenth and Early Twentieth Centuries', *Caribbean Studies* 14.4 (1975), 41–55.
Sarkar, Bhaskar, 'Tangled Legacies: The *Autos* of Biography', *Rethinking History* 7.2 (2003), 215–34.
Saunders, Kay (ed.), *Indentured Labour in the British Empire, 1834–1920* (London and Canberra: Croom Helm, 1984).
Saunders, Rebecca, 'Decolonizing the Body: Gender, Nation and Narration in Tahar Ben Jelloun's *L'enfant de sable*', *Research in African Literatures* 37.4 (2006), pp. 136–60.
Savory, Elaine, 'Towards a Caribbean Ecopoetics: Derek Walcott's Language of Plants', in *Postcolonial Ecologies: Literatures of the Environment*, ed. by Elizabeth DeLoughrey and George B. Handley (Oxford: Oxford University Press, 2011), pp. 80–98.
Scarry, Elaine, *On Beauty and Being Just* (London: Duckbacks, 2001).
— *The Body in Pain: The Making and Unmaking of the World* (New York and Oxford: Oxford University Press, 1985).
Scheper-Hughes, Nancy, 'The Last Commodity: Post-Human Ethics and the Global Traffic in "Fresh" Organs', in *Global Assemblages: Technology, Politics and Ethics as Anthropological Problems*, ed. by Aihwa Ong and Stephen J. Collier (Malden, MA: Wiley-Blackwell, 2005), pp. 145–67.
Schneewind, J. B., *The Invention of Autonomy: A History of Modern Moral Philosophy* (Cambridge: Cambridge University Press, 1998).
Serlin, David, 'Touching Histories: Personality, Disability and Sex in the 1930s', in *Sex and Disability*, ed. by Robert McRuer and Anna Mollow (Durham, NC and London: Duke University Press, 2012), pp. 145–62.
Sharpe, Jenny, 'Figures of Colonial Resistance', *Modern Fiction Studies* 35.1 (1989), 137–55.
Sharpley-Whiting, T. Denean, *Black Venus: Sexualized Savages, Primal Fears and Primitive Narratives in French* (Durham, NC: Duke University Press, 1999).
Shildrick, Margrit, 'Imagining the Heart: Incorporations, Intrusions and Identity', *Somatechnics*, 2.2 (2012), 233–49.
— 'Corporeal Cuts: Surgery and the Psycho-social', *Body & Society* 14.1 (2008), 56–75.
— *Embodying the Monster: Encounters with the Vulnerable Self* (London: Sage Publications, 2002).
Silverman, Kaja, *Male Subjectivities at the Margins* (London and New York: Routledge, 1992).
Sinfield, Alan, *Cultural Politics – Queer Reading* (London: Routledge, 1994).
Singh Baldwin, Shauna, *What the Body Remembers* (New York: Anchor Books, 1999).
Slemon, Stephen, 'Afterword', in *Is Canada Postcolonial: Unsettling Canadian Literature*, ed. by Laura Moss (Waterloo, ON: Wilfred Laurier University Press, 2003), pp. 318–24.
— 'Climbing Mount Everest: Postcolonialism in the Culture of Ascent', in *Postcolonizing the Commonwealth: Studies in Literature and Culture*, ed. by Rowland Smith (Waterloo, ON: Wilfred Laurier University Press, 2000), pp. 51–74.
— 'Post-colonial Critical Theories', in *New National and Post-Colonial Literatures: An Introduction*, ed. by Bruce King (Oxford: Clarendon Press, 1996), pp. 178–97.

— 'Magic Realism as Postcolonial Discourse', in *Magic Realism: Theory, History, Community*, ed. by Lois Parkinson Zamora and Wendy B. Faris (Durham, NC: Duke University Press, 1995), pp. 407–26.
— 'Post-Colonial Allegory and the Transformation of History', *The Journal of Commonwealth Literature* 23 (1988), pp. 157–68.
Smith, Tuhiwai, *Decolonizing Methodologies* (London: Zed Books, 1999).
Smyth, Heather, 'Sexual Citizenship and Caribbean-Canadian Fiction: Dionne Brand's *In Another Place, Not Here* and Shani Mootoo's *Cereus Blooms at Night*', *ARIEL* 30.2 (1999), 141–60.
Söderlind, Sylvia, *Margin/Alias: Language and Colonization in Canadian and Québécois Fiction* (Toronto, ON and London: University of Toronto Press, 1991).
Somacarrera, Pilar, 'A Madwoman in a Cape Breton Attic: "Jane Eyre" in Ann-Marie MacDonald's *Fall on Your Knees*', *Journal of Commonwealth Literature* 39.1 (2004), 55–75.
Sontag, Susan, *On Photography* (London: Penguin Books Ltd, 1978).
Spear, Thomas, 'Politics and Literature: An Interview with Tahar Ben Jelloun', *Yale French Studies* 82.2 (1993), 30–43.
Spivak, Gayatri Chakravorty, 'The New Subaltern: A Silent Interview', in *Mapping Subaltern Studies and the Postcolonial*, ed. by Vinayak Chaturvedi (London: Verso, 2000), pp. 324–40.
— *A Critique of Postcolonial Reason: Toward a History of the Vanishing Present* (Cambridge, MA: Harvard University Press, 1999).
— 'Can the Subaltern Speak?', in *Colonial Discourse and Post-Colonial Theory: A Reader*, ed. by Patrick Williams and Laura Chrisman (Hertfordshire: Harvester Wheatsheaf, 1994), pp. 66–112.
— *Outside in the Teaching Machine* (New York: Routledge, 1993).
— *In Other Worlds: Essays in Cultural Politics* (New York: Routledge, 1988).
Starzl, Thomas, *The Puzzle People: Memoirs of a Transplant Surgeon* (Pittsburgh, PA: University of Pittsburgh Press, 1992).
Stevenson, Melanie A., 'Othello, Darwin and Evolution of Race in Ann-Marie MacDonald's Work', *Canadian Literature* 168 (2001), 34–54.
Stilz, Gerhand (ed.), *Colonies, Missions, Cultures in the English-Speaking World: General and Comparative Studies* (Tübingen: Stauffenburg Verlag, 2001).
Stoler, Ann Laura, *Carnal Knowledge and Imperial Power: Race and the Intimate in Colonial Rule* (Berkeley, CA: University of California Press, 2002).
— 'Racial Histories and Their Regimes of Truth', *Political and Social Theory* 11 (1997), 183–255.
— 'Sexual Affronts and Racial Frontiers: European Identities and the Cultural Politics of Exclusion in Colonial Southeast Asia', in *Tensions of Empire: Colonial Cultures in a Bourgeois World*, ed. by Frederick Cooper and Ann Laura Stoler (Berkeley, CA: University of California Press, 1997), pp. 198–237.
— *Race and the Education of Desire: Foucault's 'History of Sexuality' and the Colonial Order of Things* (Durham, NC: Duke University Press, 1995).
— 'Making Race Respectable: The Politics of Race and Sexual Morality in Twentieth-Century Colonial Cultures', *American Ethnologist* 16.4 (1989), 634–60.
— *Capitalism and Confrontation in Sumatra's Plantation Belt, 1870–1979* (New Haven, CT: Yale University Press, 1985).
— 'Perceptions of Protest: Defining the Dangerous in Colonial Sumatra', *American Ethnologist* 16.4 (1985), 642–58.

Storm, Lise, *Democratization in Morocco: The Political Elite and Struggles for Power in the Post-independence State* (London and New York: Routledge, 2007).

Strong-Boag, Veronica et al. (eds), *Painting the Maple: Essays on Race, Gender and the Construction of Canada* (Vancouver, BC: University of British Columbia Press, 1998).

Sugars, Cynthia, *Unhomely States: Theorizing English-Canadian Postcolonialism* (Peterborough, ON: Broadview Press, 2004).

Sylvia, Claire, with William Novak, *A Change of Heart: The Extraordinary Story of a Man's Heart in a Woman's Body* (London: Little, Brown & Co., 1997).

Takemoto, Tina, 'Open Wounds', in *Thinking Through the Skin*, ed. by Sara Ahmed and Jackie Stacey (London and New York: Routledge, 2001), pp. 104–23.

Taylor, Laurel, 'Female Impersonation and Male Desire in Tahar Ben Jelloun's *L'enfant de sable*', *Women in French Studies* 7 (1999), 219–26.

Taylor-Guthrie, Danille (ed.), *Conversations with Toni Morrison* (Jackson, FL: University Press of Mississippi, 1994).

Tiffin, Helen, '"Replanted in this Arboreal Garden": Gardens and Flowers in Contemporary Caribbean Writing', in *English in International Contexts*, ed. by Heinz Antor and Klaus Stierstorfer (Heidelberg: C. Winter, 2000), pp. 149–64.

Titah, Rachida, *La Galerie des absentes: la femme algérienne dans l'imaginaire masculin* (Saint Etienne: Éditions L'Aube, 1996).

Torres-Saillant, Silvio, *Caribbean Poetics: Toward an Aesthetic of West Indian Literature* (Cambridge: Cambridge University Press, 1997).

Tougaw, Jason, 'Testimony and the Subjects of AIDS Memoirs', in *Extremities: Trauma, Testimony and Community*, ed. by Nancy Miller and Jason Tougaw (Urbana and Chicago, IL: University of Illinois Press, 2002), pp. 166–85.

Trumbach, Randolph, *Sex and the Gender Revolution* (Chicago, IL: University of Chicago Press, 1998).

Tyler, Imogen, 'Skin-tight: Celebrity, Pregnancy and Subjectivity', in *Thinking Through the Skin*, ed. by Sara Ahmed and Jackie Stacey (London: Routledge, 2001), pp. 69–83.

Vasseleu, Cathryn, *Textures of Light: Vision and Touch in Irigaray, Levinas and Merleau-Ponty* (London: Routledge, 1998).

Vergès, Françoise, *Abolir l'esclavage: une utopie coloniale, les ambiguïtés d'une politque humanitaire* (Paris: Albin Michel, 2001).

— *Monsters and Revolutionaries: Colonial Family Romance and Métissage* (Durham, NC: Duke University Press, 1999).

— *Outside the Fold: Conversion, Modernity and Belief* (Princeton, NJ: Princeton University Press, 1998).

— 'Raymond Williams and British Colonialism: The Limits of Metropolitan Cultural Theory', in *Views Beyond the Border Country: Raymond Williams and Cultural Politics*, ed. by Dennis L. Dworkin and Leslie G. Roman (New York: Routledge, 1993).

Viswanathan, Gauri, *Masks of Conquest: Literary Study and British Rule in India* (London: Faber & Faber, 1990).

Walker, Keith, L., *Countermodernism and Francophone Literary Culture: The Game of Slipknot* (Durham, NC and London: Duke University Press, 1999).

Walsh, Rebecca, 'Global Diasporas', *Interventions: International Journal of Postcolonial Studies* 5.1 (2003), 1–11.

Weigert, Laura, 'Autonomy as Deviance: Sixteenth Century Images of Witches and Prostitutes', in *Solitary Pleasures: The Historical, Literary and Artistic Discourses of*

Autoeroticism, ed. by Paula Bennett and Vernon A. Rosario (New York: Routledge, 1995), pp. 19–47.
Williams, Patricia J., *The Alchemy of Race and Rights: Diary of a Law Professor* (Cambridge, MA: Harvard University Press, 1992).
Woodhull, Winifred, *Transfigurations of the Maghreb: Feminism, Decolonization and Literatures* (Minneapolis, MN: University of Minnesota Press, 1993).
Wright, Katie, *The Rise of the Therapeutic Society: Psychological Knowledge and the Contradictions of Cultural Change* (Washington, DC: New Academia Publishing, 2011).
Wyile, Herb and Jeanette Lynes, 'Surf's Up!: The Rising Tide of Atlantic-Canadian Literature', *Studies in Canadian Literature* 33.2 (2008) <www.journals.hil.unb.ca/index.php/scl/article/view/11226/11978> [accessed 13 October 2011].
Xie, Shaobo, 'Writing on Boundaries: Homi Bhabha's Recent Essays', *ARIEL* 27.4 (1996), 155–66.
Yeğenoğlu, Meyda, *Colonial Fantasies: Towards a Feminist Reading of Orientalism* (Cambridge: Cambridge University Press, 1998).
Young, Iris Marion, *On Female Body Experience: 'Throwing Like a Girl' and Other Essays* (Oxford: Oxford University Press, 2005).
Zahiri, Mohammed and Rachid Ameziane-Hassani, 'The Father Figure in Tahar Ben Jelloun: *La Nuit sacrée, Jour de silence à Tanger* and *Les Yeux baissés*', *Callaloo* 15.4 (1992), 1105–9.
Zarka, Yves Charles, 'Michel Foucault: De la guerre des races au biopouvoir', *Cités: Philosophe, politique, histoire* (Paris: Presse Universitaire de France, 2000).

Index